TRANSITIONAL JUSTICE

NOMOS

LI

NOMOS

Harvard University Press

I   *Authority* 1958, reissued in 1982 by Greenwood Press

The Liberal Arts Press

II   *Community* 1959
III   *Responsibility* 1960

Atherton Press

IV   *Liberty* 1962
V   *The Public Interest* 1962
VI   *Justice* 1963, reissued in 1974
VII   *Rational Decision* 1964
VIII   *Revolution* 1966
IX   *Equality* 1967
X   *Representation* 1968
XI   *Voluntary Associations* 1969
XII   *Political and Legal Obligation* 1970
XIII   *Privacy* 1971

Aldine-Atherton Press

XIV   *Coercion* 1972

Lieber-Atherton Press

XV   *The Limits of Law* 1974
XVI   *Participation in Politics* 1975

New York University Press

XVII   *Human Nature in Politics* 1977
XVIII   *Due Process* 1977
XIX   *Anarchism* 1978
XX   *Constitutionalism* 1979
XXI   *Compromise in Ethics, Law, and Politics* 1979
XXII   *Property* 1980
XXIII   *Human Rights* 1981
XXIV   *Ethics, Economics, and the Law* 1982
XXVI   *Marxism* 1983
XXVII   *Criminal Justice* 1985

NOMOS LI
Yearbook of the American Society for Political and Legal Philosophy

TRANSITIONAL JUSTICE

Edited by

**Melissa S. Williams, Rosemary Nagy,
and Jon Elster**

NEW YORK UNIVERSITY PRESS • *New York and London*

NEW YORK UNIVERSITY PRESS
New York and London
www.nyupress.org

References to Internet websites (URLs) were accurate at the time of writing.
Neither the author nor New York University Press is responsible for URLs
that may have expired or changed since the manuscript was prepared.

Library of Congress Cataloging-in-Publication Data
Transitional justice / [edited by] Melissa Williams, Rosemary Nagy, Jon Elster.
p.   cm.
Includes bibliographical references and index.
ISBN 978-0-8147-9466-1 (hardback) — ISBN 978-0-8147-0497-4 (ebook) —
ISBN 978-0-8147-2527-6 (ebook)
1. Transitional justice. 2. Reparation (Criminal justice) 3. Criminal justice,
Administration of.   I. Williams, Melissa. II. Nagy, Rosemary. III. Elster,
Jon, 1940–
K5250.T725 2012
340'.115–dc23   2011051753

New York University Press books are printed on acid-free paper,
and their binding materials are chosen for strength and durability.
We strive to use environmentally responsible suppliers and materials
to the greatest extent possible in publishing our books.

Manufactured in the United States of America

10 9 8 7 6 5 4 3 2 1

CONTENTS

vii

PREFACE

This volume, the fifty-first in the NOMOS series, arose out of the papers and commentaries presented at the annual meeting of the American Society for Legal and Political Philosophy in conjunction with the American Political Science Association meetings in Washington, D.C., in September 2005. As with all NOMOS volumes, the theme was selected by the membership of the Society.

Because of his extraordinary expertise in the field of transitional justice, I invited Jon Elster to join me in co-convening those meetings and co-editing the volume. I am tremendously grateful that he agreed. His recommendations for participants in the conference contributed to its highly stimulating interdisciplinary discussion. Equally important, Professor Elster's knowledge of the current stage of empirical work on transitional justice led to a much deeper engagement between theoretical and empirical approaches in the present volume than would otherwise have been the case.

Elizabeth Kiss, David Dyzenhaus, and Debra Satz presented the three principal papers at the conference, stimulating excellent commentaries from Gopal Sreenivasan, Jeremy Webber, Bernard Boxill, Eric Posner, Gary Bass, and Adrian Vermeule. As the volume's contents reflect, several of these commentaries developed into substantial free-standing contributions to the scholarly literature. Others, while retaining their form as commentaries, introduce the key debates in the field into the conversation that runs throughout the volume. I extend my sincere thanks to all of the participants in the original conference for launching this conversation.

Warm thanks are also due to the contributors who joined the conversation a bit later, whom we recruited in order to cover territory that we felt needed more attention than had been achievable in the original conference. Pablo de Greiff, Monika Nalepa, David Cohen, and Leigh-Ashley Lipscomb have been tremendously generous in tailoring their work to the purposes of the volume. In addition, Jon Elster's contribution on the positive and negative relationships among the normative aspirations of transitional justice importantly shapes the discussion throughout the volume.

Rosemary Nagy has been an invaluable colleague in working closely with all the authors to engage them in conversation with one another and with wider themes in the literature. We have worked very closely in bringing this volume to completion and in crafting its Introduction. Her knowledge and insights, complemented by her efficacy as an editor, have been indispensable. I am deeply grateful for her steadfast commitment to seeing the volume through to successful completion, despite the many challenges we faced along the way.

The volume's managing editor, Erica Frederiksen, has also been tireless in her dedication to the volume's completion and meticulous in preparing the manuscript for publication. Erica is a doctoral candidate in the Department of Political Science at the University of Toronto, and her own work on restorative justice positioned her to make valuable substantive contributions to the formation of the individual chapters and to the Introduction. I am very much in her debt. Thanks are also due to Tobold Rollo for preparing the index.

On behalf of the entire editorial team, I also want to express our appreciation to Aiden Amos at New York University Press, both for her support of this volume and for her commitment to the series. The Press is notable for supporting the interdisciplinary approach of the NOMOS series long before interdisciplinarity took hold in the academy. Its leadership has been essential to our Society's ability to sustain a conversation among philosophers, legal scholars, and political scientists for more than half a century.

This volume proved more challenging to bring to completion than any previous NOMOS volume on which I have worked. Some of the reasons for the delays in its production arose from the process of recruiting new work; some arose from conflicts with other professional demands. Responsibility lies at my doorstep, however, and consequently I have even more reason to be grateful for the extraordinary patience of all of our contributors as they awaited the publication of their excellent work. I very much regret that they have had to wait so long.

Finally, and for the same reasons, I owe a debt of gratitude to the Executive of the American Society for Political and Legal Philosophy, past and present, for their support and encouragement through difficult times.

MELISSA S. WILLIAMS

CONTRIBUTORS

GARY J. BASS
Politics and International Affairs, Princeton University

DAVID COHEN
Rhetoric and Classics, University of California, Berkeley

DAVID DYZENHAUS
Law and Philosophy, University of Toronto

JON ELSTER
Rationalité et sciences sociales, Collège de France and Political Science, Columbia University

PABLO DE GREIFF
Director of Research, International Center for Transitional Justice

LEIGH-ASHLEY LIPSCOMB
Asian Studies, University of California, Berkeley

ROSEMARY NAGY
Gender Equality and Social Justice, Nipissing University

MONIKA NALEPA
Political Science, University of Notre Dame

ERIC A. POSNER
Law, University of Chicago

DEBRA SATZ
Political Science, Stanford University

GOPAL SREENIVASAN
Ethics and Philosophy, Duke University

ADRIAN VERMEULE
Law, Harvard Law School

JEREMY WEBBER
Law, University of Victoria

MELISSA S. WILLIAMS
Political Science, University of Toronto

INTRODUCTION

MELISSA S. WILLIAMS AND ROSEMARY NAGY

As we finalize this volume on transitional justice in April 2011, a historic transition is taking place across North Africa and the Middle East. In Egypt, a democratic uprising has brought an end to thirty years of dictatorship under President Hosni Mubarak. Senior officials in the Mubarak regime are already facing criminal prosecution, and there are visible steps toward the prosecution of Mubarak himself. Citizens are demanding the ouster of officials from leadership positions in the state bureaucracy and universities. A democratic referendum has approved a new interim constitution for the military caretaker regime, and free elections have been scheduled. The transition to democracy from Mubarak's dictatorship appears to be well under way, relying almost entirely on domestic institutions. Meanwhile, Libya's Muammar Qaddafi has refused to step down in response to protests and is using the full force of his military to suppress popular rebellion. The International Criminal Court has mounted an investigation into Qaddafi's role in possible crimes against humanity, and a United Nations–approved no-fly zone is being aggressively enforced by NATO forces. Should the rebels succeed in toppling Qaddafi, the work of transition will take shape swiftly and with the heavy involvement of international institutions.

As Egypt and Libya play out two starkly contrasting possible futures for dictatorships facing popular uprisings across the region, events in Ivory Coast remind us that there is no bright line between transitions from authoritarianism to democracy and transitions in the wake of civil conflict. There, former President Laurent Gbagbo refused to yield power after losing a democratic election

1

to Allassane Outtara. Instead of a peaceful change of government, the country descended into violent civil conflict, ending finally in Gbagbo's capture and arrest. Outtara has already promised that Gbagbo and his core military leaders will be tried in domestic courts for crimes against humanity and that he will establish a Truth and Reconciliation Commission to examine crimes on both sides of the conflict.

These signal events raise a range of questions that has become familiar from political transitions across the global stage over recent decades. What are the proper roles of criminal trials, commissions of inquiry, and evictions of state officials from positions of influence in securing a successful transition to democracy? Does the threat of prosecution for human rights violations cause dictators to use even greater repressive force to hold onto their power? Should transitional authorities focus on building new institutions for rights-respecting democratic order or on rectifying the wrongs of the dictatorship? What is the proper balance between the role of domestic institutions and that of international institutions in bringing about a successful transition?

It has never been clearer that the nature of a transition matters. The successful transformation of authoritarian or war-torn regimes into more-or-less democratic, rights-respecting ones depends on myriad factors, many of which appear beyond the control of any particular political actor. Yet, transitional periods call upon leaders to take responsibility for the history they will inescapably make through their actions in an uncertain present. Recent experience has generated a growing consensus that successful transitions require a societal effort to come to terms with the wrongs of the past. This experience has yielded a rich repertoire of institutional innovations upon which political actors can draw in crafting a more just society and increasingly refined normative criteria by which to judge their success or failure.

The dilemmas associated with regime change have been around at least since ancient Athenians sought to secure political order, restore legitimacy, and deal with the abuses of the prior regime when democratic orders twice overthrew oligarchic ones.[1] The term "transitional justice," however, is of quite recent vintage,[2] and it was not until the last decades of the twentieth century that it came to denote a distinct field of politico-legal practice and of scholarly inquiry. The stage was set in the late 1940s by the wave of criminal prosecutions for atrocities committed during the Second World War, most famously in the International Military Tribunal at Nuremburg. While war crimes tribunals were not an invention of this postwar period,[3] the Nuremburg trials played a critical role in establishing international human rights norms as standards for judging the wrongs of past regimes.[4] For a few decades, there was little theoretical or practical concern with transitional justice. In the 1980s, this began to change. The wave of democratization that swept through Latin America was punctuated by cries of "Nunca mas!"—"Never again!"—demanding accountability for human rights abuses under authoritarian regimes in Argentina, Chile, and elsewhere.[5] The post-1989 transformations of Central and Eastern Europe emphasized lustration (the vetting or purging of public officials who served in pro-Soviet regimes) and restitution as means of dealing with past abuses and easing transition to more rights-respecting forms of government.

Lessons from the Latin American experience spread to democratic transitions in other parts of the world. Following Chile's example, in particular, the use of truth commissions as substitutes for or complements to criminal prosecutions became widespread. Post-apartheid South Africa's Truth and Reconciliation Commission, created in 1995 under Nelson Mandela's leadership, built upon the Chilean experience by envisioning truth-telling as a method of societal reconciliation. The South African TRC set a new standard for the aspirations of transitional institutions as resources not only for redressing past injustices but also as laying the foundation for forward-looking or restorative justice in a renewed democratic community.

While deeply influential in encouraging the global proliferation of truth commissions, the South African model did not displace the central role of criminal prosecutions as a key instrument of transition. The International Criminal Tribunals for the former Yugoslavia and Rwanda (the ICTY and the ICTR), established in the 1990s to respond to ethnic cleansing and genocide, underscored the continuing importance of prosecuting criminal liability for gross human rights abuses. At the same time, they also revealed the limitations of an exclusive focus on prosecutions at the expense of more victim-centered forms of justice. Increasingly, a multipronged approach that includes international and/or domestic criminal trials, truth commissions, and reparations constitutes the transitional justice "toolkit." The role of international institutions in transitional justice has also evolved since the mid-1990s. Increasingly, as in the case of Rwandan *gacaca* courts, populations demand that justice be delivered in forms that are recognizable from the standpoint of local norms and practices.[6] Nonetheless, local forms of justice have not simply replaced international courts. To the contrary, the creation of the International Criminal Court (ICC) institutionalized an ongoing international role in transitional justice in lieu of ad hoc courts such as the Nuremberg Tribunal, the ICTY, and the ICTR. Viewing transitional justice through this narrative of recent historical experience enables us to identify a cluster of common challenges and common responses across transitions from authoritarianism to democracy, from civil war to peace, and from state-sponsored extralegal violence to a rights-respecting rule of law. Yet, the flow of ideas and of institutional patterns through time and across cases raises difficult normative and empirical questions.[7] What are the normative criteria that appropriately guide the design of transitional institutions? Do the various normative goals of transitional justice cohere, or do they conflict? Is it realistic to expect that political actors will cleave to the normative aspirations of transitional justice given the practical or prudential calculations they must make as they seek to establish order, manage the competing interests of powerful social and political actors, contain violence, and secure the economic resources necessary to sustain the new order? The challenges for our empirical understanding of transitional justice are no less complex. Given that each transitional context is unique, is it possible to make valid generalizations about the effectiveness of specific institutional devices in different conditions or about the most effective combinations of devices overall? Are there empirically sound measures by which we can judge the success or failure of specific transitions? What are the conditions under which transitional institutions succeed or fail? While the essays in this volume do not answer these questions univocally, they go a considerable distance toward clarifying the terms of debate over the theory and practice of transitional justice.

Dilemmas of Transitional Justice

Political actors in transitional periods often face stark trade-offs, even when their clear and dominant motivation is to do the morally right thing. Against the backdrop of a recent memory of violence and lawlessness, they must give special importance to securing peace and order. In doing so, they cannot avoid calculating the stakes that significant social groups or factions will have in supporting the new order—or in resisting it. At the same time, the brutality of the predecessor regime, which may have been stable for a considerable time, makes equally clear that order without justice is neither morally nor politically sustainable. A prudential modus vivendi among competing factions will not restore citizens' trust in government. To last, the new order must persuade its citizens that it will not repeat the wrongs of the past and that it has laid the foundations for more legitimate government in the future. This work of persuasion is a defining task of transitional orders and of the transitional justice mechanisms they employ.

The complex politics of transitional moments is mirrored in the complexity of the normative standards by which we judge them. Transitional institutions are expected to deliver justice to the perpetrators of past wrongs, recognition and reparation to their victims, a truthful and common public narrative of past wrongdoing, and the conditions for lawful order and societal peace. One of the core questions in the theory and practice of transitional justice is whether it is possible to achieve all these ends simultaneously or whether, instead, there are inescapable trade-offs among them. Thoughtful observers of South Africa's Truth and Reconciliation Commission, for example, expressed concern that in emphasizing the goals of truth, forgiveness, and reconciliation, it sacrificed the goods served by criminal justice.[8] These lines of argument suggest that political actors in transitional moments may have to make difficult, even potentially tragic choices among the goods at stake, trading off peace for justice or justice for truth.

Drawing on a wide range of cases of transitional justice, Pablo de Greiff argues that the dilemmas of transitional justice need not, in principle, result in such tragic choices. De Greiff's project here is guided by a reconstructive method by which he reads out of the interaction of different transitional mechanisms an account of the moral purposes they can serve *in tandem* that none, taken alone, can perfectly fulfill. Through this process, de Greiff distills four goals of transitional justice. Two of these are "mediate" in the sense that they are not direct causal outcomes of aims of particular institutions but are partially caused by them: *recognition* of the agency and suffering of victims of wrongdoing and *civic trust*, the capacity of citizens to rely on public institutions to act in accordance with shared values and norms, including the rule of law. Two other goals of transitional justice are "final" ends in the sense that their attainment depends on a great number of factors that are beyond the impact of particular mechanisms but that nonetheless can be served by them: *reconciliation*, understood as trust between citizens (as contrasted with the trust of citizens in the institutions of the state), and *democracy*.

In tracing out the ways in which different transitional mechanisms (e.g., truth-telling, criminal prosecutions, reparations, memorializations, vetting) serve these four goals, de Greiff makes the case for a holistic approach to the design of transitional institutions. No single mechanism can do all the work of transitional justice. Individual mechanisms are much more likely to meet with success if layered with complementary mechanisms carefully designed to work with each other to advance the immediate, mediate, and final goals of transitional justice. Even then, of course, there are numerous factors exogenous to transitional institutions that will intervene to condition their success or failure, and institutional designers need to attend to these as well. It is equally clear that a holistic approach to transitional justice does not mean that more institutions are necessarily better. As is painfully clear from the experience of East Timor, meticulously laid out in the chapter by David Cohen and Leigh-Ashley Lipscomb, the haphazard addition of under-resourced and multifarious transitional institutions can do more to undermine than to advance the larger goals of transitional justice. De Greiff's argument holds out the hope that, when well-designed, the institutions and purposes of transitional justice can work in harmony with one another.

On de Greiff's view, then, there is no deep incommensurability among the normative aspirations of transitional justice; there is no reason in principle why careful institutional design cannot create mutually reinforcing relationships among them. At their most robust, such virtuous circles can support the formation of strong, just, rights-respecting democratic societies. De Greiff's account of the moral principles for judging transitions sets high aspirational standards.

Jon Elster tells a more cautionary tale about the possibility of reconciling the plural ends and means of transitional justice into a unified scheme. Sometimes all good things do not and cannot go together, and such is regrettably the case with respect to the primary goals of transitional institutions: justice, truth, and peace. Each of these can be viewed through the lens of their instrumental or intrinsic value as goods. Justice (understood in both retributive and distributive terms) has intrinsic value derived from its demonstration of respect for the moral worth of citizens. But it also has instrumental value as a support for peace and stability. Certainly its denial can have destabilizing consequences. Of the three goods, only peace (Elster argues) is of purely intrinsic value, even if it is a condition of possibility for the other goods.

Elster enumerates both positive and negative relationships among these three goods in transitional contexts. On the positive side of the ledger—the terrain where he and de Greiff can agree with one another—both truth and justice can and often do serve civic peace. But we should not be overconfident that things will turn out well. Sometimes the anticipation of retributive justice forestalls peace, as wrongdoers try to delay the day of reckoning. Such was the case in Uganda, where the ICC's pursuit of justice in the midst of violence and negotiations became a stumbling block on the final road to peace.[9] Sometimes truth produces injustice, if vigilante vengeance unleashed against alleged perpetrators in truth commission testimony becomes a substitute for the due process of criminal trials. Although these conflicts between goods may not emerge in every transitional context, they might reasonably lead us to lower our expectations of transitional institutions. It may be that partial justice, partial truth, and relative peace are the best we can expect in many contexts. If that is right, we should not be content when transitional institutions fall below certain thresholds, but if we demand too much of them we may risk delegitimizing the modest achievements they are actually capable of delivering.

Justice may conflict with truth and peace, then, but different understandings of the *kind* of justice that should be served by transitional measures may also stand in some tension with one another. Scholars of transitional justice have often noted its Janus-faced quality. Moving a society from a rights-abusing to a rights-respecting legal-political order requires backward-looking justice that acknowledges the wrongfulness of past actions and seeks to correct wrongs through punishment, reparation, or both. Addressing the wrongs of the past, however, is not sufficient to create the conditions for a stable political society whose members have confidence that they will be treated fairly. Transitional orders need a forward-looking or prospective account of justice, as well as a backward-looking one.

As Jeremy Webber argues in his chapter, the difference between retrospective and prospective justice is a matter of focus and purpose, rather than of subject matter. Practices of forward-looking justice also reckon with the past, but in a manner different from that of retributive or corrective justice. Retrospective justice in both its retributive and its reparative forms seeks to approximate a reversal of the wrong, a restoration as far as possible of the status quo ex ante, as Debra Satz also points out in her chapter. It is an unattainable ideal, but we judge the success of retributive and reparative practices according to how closely they approximate it. In contrast, Webber notes, forward-looking justice reckons with the past "not primarily to correct a transaction but rather to adjust the parties' relations so that their interactions now take place on a sound foundation" (p. 104). This contrast between a transactional and a relational emphasis enables us to see that common techniques of transitional justice—reparations payments, official apologies, memorials—can be simultaneously backward-looking and forward-looking. In some cases, these practices may satisfy both understandings of justice; in others, serving prospective justice may entail a less rigorous pursuit of corrective justice.

Webber further deepens our understanding of the plurality of conceptions of justice by delineating a third conception that scholars of transitional justice have generally overlooked. This third form of justice concerns *whose* norms should govern in adjudicating disputes, in contexts where multiple cultural or religious normative orders are in play. Webber gives the example of Iraq, where consolidating transition has required structuring institutions for power-sharing among Shi'a, Sunni, and Kurdish populations and for reconciling these communities' differing understandings of the appropriate place of religion in public law. Bringing in examples from other transitions in vastly different contexts, Webber argues that fairness in reaching an adjustment between contending legal and political orders constitutes a distinct form of justice. Like retrospective and prospective justice, this third type is not unique to transitional settings but is often an important source of disagreements over what justice requires in transitional moments.

Webber's three conceptions of justice are not substitutes for one another. Each discloses a different angle of vision on what justice requires, and each accords a different significance to events of the past. Nor can they be subsumed under a more general or abstract account of justice. Although it may be possible and desirable to combine all three in a given context, they are not at root commensurable with one another. At the same time, Webber's account of justice is not minimalist or "thin." Each of the conceptions of justice offers an aspirational ideal that transitional institutions can seek to approximate, but in particular contexts they may prove to conflict with one another, quite apart from the constraints of realpolitik that condition transitional decision making.

The dilemmas of transitional justice do not disappear even if we narrow our focus to a single institutional device for realizing it. This becomes clear in Debra Satz's careful analysis of financial compensation as a measure for countering or repairing the wrongs of the past. Under what circumstances is it appropriate to use reparations payments to redress grave injustices of the past?

On a welfare economist's view, monetary compensation payments constitute a form of corrective justice to the extent that they leave a wronged person as well off as if the wrong had never occurred. This can work well enough in many individual cases. Money cannot replace nonmonetary losses or restore circumstances to what they were before the wrong was committed, but people are often willing to accept financial compensation as the best possible approximation of justice in such circumstances. Even in individual cases, however, money may not be an acceptable form of redress. Satz gives the example of the spouse who is unwilling to accept a cash payment as a means of repairing the damage caused by an extramarital affair.

The appropriateness of reparations for long-standing historical injustices on a societal scale is significantly more complex than in individual cases. Satz addresses four serious philosophical objections to compensation as a form of repair for past wrongs. First, the history of injustice affects not only how well people fare but what people exist. Second, when injustices are in the more distant past, it is difficult if not impossible to trace their harms to those who are living now. Descendants of victims may not themselves be victims. Third, the moral weight of claims for redress may fade over time, whether because the class of people harmed by an injustice eventually recovers or because more pressing claims of justice have since emerged. And, finally, even where a class of persons quite clearly suffers an ongoing systemic harm from past injustices, the passage of time makes it virtually impossible to arrive at a calculation of fair compensation that parties can agree upon. In some contexts, these arguments against compensation for historical injustice may have some force; in others, they can be met. In many cases, though, Satz argues that such objections are simply beside the point. Where historical injustice on a societal scale is at issue, the purpose of compensation is not to restore wronged groups to a position on an imagined indifference curve, as welfare economists would have it, but to express a shared public recognition that a serious wrong has occurred.

Like Webber, Satz emphasizes that, in moments of political transition or in cases of societal injustice such as slavery, apartheid, genocide, or the destruction of indigenous lifeworlds through colonization, monetary compensation has a forward-looking purpose and not only a corrective one. Compensation can be coupled with other measures to acknowledge and reaffirm the dignity of victims, repair social relationships, and promote trust among citizens. Monetary compensation, especially when added to other expressive practices such as public apologies, criminal prosecutions, and memorials, serves an important expressive function, conveying a society's willingness to bear real costs in order to repair the damage done by historical injustice. To be sure, a forward-looking rationale for compensation does not wholly invalidate the arguments against its use as a measure of corrective justice. Further, compensation can fail to meet its forward-looking purposes, as when the amounts are too paltry or the systems of distribution too arbitrary to convey the message that the society takes past injustices seriously. Economic redress is one part of a toolkit through which societies can lay the foundations for a more just future, but it is unlikely to do this work all by itself, and whether it succeeds will depend on how well it is designed and implemented and on what other measures are instituted alongside it. In this way, Satz's argument reinforces and adds depth to de Greiff's defense of a holistic approach to the design of institutions whose larger purpose is to enable a break with an unjust past and to create the conditions for a more just future. But as Elster, Webber, and Cohen and Lipscomb remind us, in various ways, the world in which transitional justice operates is at best complex and is often messy, uncoordinated, and under-resourced.

REALISM, IDEALISM AND NON-IDEAL THEORY

Contexts of transitional justice present stark examples of the gap between *is* and *ought*, between the facts on the ground and what we might wish for from a moral point of view. Frequently, the background of transition is a history of grave violations of the most basic moral principles of human dignity. The transitional moment is one when conscientious political actors are seeking to lessen the moral distance between what has been and what should be, at the level of broad social and political institutions.

In doing so, they confront a second set of challenges, different in kind from the dilemmatic choice among potentially conflicting moral goods: should their aspirations for transitional practices aim at the highest imaginable moral ends, or should moral aims be tempered by prudential attention to what is possible under the specific limitations of the circumstances they are in? What are the moral standards that the rest of us should use in judging their actions? Should we insist on the most demanding ideals of justice, based on the principles developed through high-level philosophical inquiry? After all, as Joseph Carens notes in a different context, "[w]e do not want to build the flaws and limitations of existing arrangements into our moral inquiry."[10] Alternatively, perhaps aiming too high is a recipe for failure, leading people to reject transitional measures because they do not live up to an idealized account of justice and, in so doing, to abandon imperfect but genuine gains.

In addressing these complex questions, the contributions to the present volume span a spectrum from realism to idealism on matters of ethics. Though none are unaware of the myriad constraints on transitional justice in practice, our authors offer a range of understandings about what it means for justice to be done. It might be tempting to frame their contrasting positions as mediating the tension between the poles of justice and expediency, a binary often reproduced as between "legalists" (who insist on full justice) and "pragmatists" (who prioritize democratic consolidation over justice.[11] But such a framing misses how justice comes in various forms, some of which (as Webber argues) tend to be lumped in with expediency. Or, as Sreenivasan's account of non-ideal theory shows, expediency itself might be understood as a part of justice. How we position justice in relation to real-life circumstances is, for all our authors, a matter of nuance, rather than a set of binary choices. Nonetheless, even our most "realist" contributors are clear that justice of some sort must be rescued from the grip of bare expediency. There is no such thing as an amoral view of transitional justice.

Returning to the example of compensation for past wrongs, we find that, in practice, schemes of reparation often fall egregiously short of what any theoretical account of justice would tell us is morally required. In an extended commentary on Satz's essay, Adrian Vermeule relates the actual performance of programs of compensation as they have played out in both transitional and non-transitional contexts. "Viewed in the concrete," he concludes, these programs and awards are often "disastrously unprincipled" (p. 163). Whereas any theory of corrective justice will tell us that compensation should come from the pocket of the wrongdoer and be paid into the pockets of those who were directly wronged, in practice compensation has often been paid by third parties to individuals who were only distantly related to the victim of injustice or to organizations established for the purpose of receiving the payments. Principles of proportionality dictate that those who were most responsible for the injustice should pay more than those who were less responsible, and those who were most harmed should receive more than those who were less harmed. In practice, the relationship between awards and harms inflicted or suffered is undeniably arbitrary. In principle, careful, fact-based judgments of liability and compensation should be the basis of awards. In practice, compensation is often the result of political compromise and backroom bargaining.

It is not difficult to explain the gap between the theoretical requirements of justice and the actual performance of compensation schemes. One reason, as Satz, Vermeule, and others note, is that the claims of justice are but one category among many of the demands on the public purse. Even if it were possible to arrive at a noncontroversial figure for a just scheme of compensation, the odds are that doing full justice to victims of past wrongs would come at the expense of other important public obligations. Another is the historical and political contingency of which claims of historic injustice gain a sufficient public following to pressure public officials to undertake measures of redress. As Vermeule notes, it is unjust that Japanese Americans who were interned during the Second World War received (very modest) compensation, while German American internees did not.

If reparations are such a flawed mechanism for redressing historical injustice on a societal scale, why are claims for reparations such a persistent political phenomenon? Vermeule's answer is that, even though these schemes are indefensible according to any principled theoretical account of what justice requires, they nonetheless constitute a form of *rough justice*, which is often better than no justice at all. There may be cases where attempting to approximate a first-best account of justice within prevailing constraints is morally worse than doing nothing at all. But there is no reason to suppose, in general, that a second-best attempt at justice is worse than doing nothing. The persistence of claims for historical redress is based on the sound intuition that it is better to do what justice we can, however imperfect, than to allow injustice to stand wholly unaddressed.

People accept rough justice when they have no real prospect of receiving justice properly so called. Perhaps true justice cannot be done because real-world conditions mean that too many sacrifices would have to be made to other public ends, including other claims of justice. For some wrongs, though, justice cannot be done because there simply is no human action that could even approximate a repair of the harm. Gary Bass focuses our gaze on the irreparability of genocide, mass atrocities, and war crimes. These demand punishment and retribution, but, even if every perpetrator in a genocide were punished (as never happens in history), it would not be enough. No conceivable punishment could balance the scales. Nor can reparations compensate for what was lost, even if they add expressive weight to public acknowledgments of the crimes' enormity. Justice cannot be done; it is unseemly to pretend otherwise. And yet we *do* pretend otherwise, Bass tells us, just insofar as we rely on reparations, punishments, memorials, or apologies to stand in for moral repair. Societies cannot stand still. Somehow, there must be a way to pick up the pieces and move beyond the atrocities. National political leaders bear a distinctive role in ensuring that this happens, and in playing it they cut ambiguous moral figures. Bass draws our attention, in particular, to the moral dilemmas in which leaders of democracies are caught when past atrocities obstruct their ability to address realpolitik concerns of security and economy. Such situations make for fascinating variations on the theme of dirty hands in politics, as emerges from Bass's comparison of two such moments in twentieth-century history.

Bass's core example is Israel's decision to normalize relations with West Germany in 1952. Israel needed this as a way of building alliances and establishing itself as a normal state. West Germany needed it in order to regain international legitimacy. Bass's story centers on the public distortions of truth that both David Ben-Gurion and Konrad Adenauer deployed in order to produce West Germany's public apology and reparations for the Holocaust. Without these acts, the Israeli public would never have accepted normalization. The reparations program functioned as a sort of "noble lie" through which these leaders succeeded in getting their publics to accept it as a measure of justice. It was a lie because of gross misrepresentations of truth, of the leaders' motivations surrounding the apology, and of the proximity of reparations to justice. But it was noble because it enabled both leaders to serve their nations' longer-term interests in security and, arguably, set them on a path toward a more-or-less decent politics.

Can it be morally praiseworthy for the leaders of a democracy to lie to their citizens? Bass's answer echoes Machiavelli's: history is the ultimate judge. In the Israeli case, it is plausible to argue that Ben-Gurion and Adenauer acted from an ethic of responsibility for their countries' well-being,[12] and their deceptions around the apology and reparations proved able, in the end, to get them past a critical impasse. It was better for both nations that relations between them were normalized, and the pretense of doing justice made that possible. Their actions look much more defensible than those of Japanese and Korean leaders, who also used public apology and reparations to try to normalize relations in the early 1960s. In that case, neither public was coaxed into thinking that even minimal justice was being done for the horrific cruelties inflicted by Imperial Japan on the Korean people. The apology may have served the United States' Cold War agenda, but the history of atrocities is still an unresolved strain on Japanese-Korean relations.

David Dyzenhaus's chapter also centers on the moral standards we should use to judge political leaders' efforts to overcome their nations' past wrongs and on the moral psychology through which we can make sense of their actions. His historical example is the actions of F. W. de Klerk and Nelson Mandela in bringing about the transition to democracy from apartheid in South Africa. What made transition possible, on Dyzenhaus's account, is that both leaders put aside a narrowly realpolitik focus on the course of action that would most advantage their respective factions in the short or medium term. Instead, both acted on the basis of a certain understanding of justice. De Klerk made the first move by unbanning the African National Congress and releasing Mandela and other ANC leaders from prison, effectively giving up his power. Mandela reciprocated by leading the ANC into negotiations to create a multiracial, rights-respecting democratic order instead of pressing the momentary advantage to seek the ANC's total political domination of white South Africans.

Dyzenhaus's analysis presses us toward the judgment that an uncompromising commitment to certain fundamental principles of justice is a condition of successful transition and away from the realist position that moral compromise is necessary. Counterintuitively, his theoretical account of the kind of justice that transition requires is drawn from Hobbes, a figure whom many regard as an arch-realist in matters of politics and morality. Dyzenhaus offers an avowedly "non-Hobbist" reading of *Leviathan* in order to bring out Hobbes's value as a theorist of transitional justice. On the standard reading of Hobbes, there is no pre-political standard of justice. It is the sovereign who determines what is just and unjust, permissible or impermissible. For Hobbists, in the pre-political state there are only interests vying for supremacy over one another. Against this view, Dyzenhaus reinterprets Hobbes's laws of nature to generate a moral psychology of the person who has a "relish of Justice," where Justice consists in the performance of promises made toward the end of establishing a stable civil order. Whoever first performs their part of an agreement aimed at peace and civil order generates a moral obligation in the other to respond in kind. The escape from a cycle of violence depends equally on the first performer's willingness to risk vulnerability and on the second party's willingness to forgo momentary advantage for the sake of longer-term peace. This, on Dyzenhaus's reading, is precisely what played out between de Klerk and Mandela, and this is what makes them exemplary political leaders.

What is innovative—and controversial—in this reading of Hobbes is that it puts forward a prepolitical account of morality as reciprocity and of justice as rule following. The lesson for political transitions is that there need not be a well-established civil order in order for justice to be done; what is required, instead, is that leaders follow the rule of reciprocity when others perform a peace-promoting action. The central task of transition, on this view, is to achieve legality, the stable following of recognized rules even where power-holders have the opportunity to sacrifice the rule of law for the sake of enhancing their power. This requires not only the actions of leaders but also the spread of a culture of legality through the general population—no mean feat in a society where a history of violence has sown deep-rooted mutual distrust. To bring it off requires a campaign of educating the public in an "ethos of justice"[13]—or, in Hobbesian terms, a "publique conscience of law." South Africa's Truth and Reconciliation Commission was a program of just this sort.

Transitional justice, for Dyzenhaus, is nothing other than the rule of law. This might appear deflationary to those, like de Greiff, whose aspirations for transition reach to the achievement of retributive justice, reconciliation, or democracy. But, on Dyzenhaus's view, it is "the kind of justice that has to be in place before order becomes something worth having and that also makes it possible for a society to decide other kinds of political issues in a civil fashion" (p. 202). This is a minimalist account of transitional justice,

but it is still an idealist one. The real-world constraints and conflicting interests that have to be negotiated in the process of transition may entail sacrifices to corrective justice, but, if they compromise on the goal of establishing a rule of law order, they are almost
certain to fail.

In his thoughtful commentary on Dyzenhaus, Eric Posner argues that moral theories and ideals, including those of legality, offer only limited guidance for transitional contexts. If retrospective
justice requires that human rights violations be punished but principles of legality prohibit the retroactive designation of actions
(which may have been sanctioned in positive law) as crimes, where
does that leave us? What will prove the most just outcome in a particular context cannot be read off from one or another theoretical
account of justice. Instead, the just outcome will consist in a compromise between conflicting understandings of justice, tempered
by a due regard for the practical constraints that political and legal
actors confront. The content of the most just outcome will vary
according to context, approximating one ideal of justice in one instance, a different ideal in another, and some sort of middle path
in most. "Local conditions, beliefs, and mores," Posner argues,
"determine what is just and practical in any given case" (p. 219).

Posner's account of transitional justice falls closer to the realist
end of the realist-idealist spectrum than does that of Dyzenhaus,
de Greiff, or Webber. Countering Dyzenhaus, he argues that there
is nothing in de Klerk's and Mandela's actions that requires us to
conclude that they acted from a sense of moral obligation, rather
than from a shrewd calculation of the rational self-interest of their
factions. De Klerk could see that the white minority could not sustain its power by force for much longer; Mandela calculated that
a violent revolution could not succeed. Both were exemplary leaders not because they sacrificed self-interest for moral principle but
because they were able to overcome the *ir*rational forces of racist
ideology and the thirst for vengeance that drove de Klerk's predecessor and many of Mandela's comrades, respectively. On this
reading, both were exemplary political leaders from a narrowly
"Hobbist" point of view, but the virtue they exhibited is prudence,
not justice: they are admirable for the psychological strength that
enabled them to see beyond their passions, rather than for their
willingness to sacrifice interest for principle. Their "transitional

prudence" led them, it is true, to support the emergence of a political system that the people could affirm as just and not merely ordered. This sort of prudence is one other transitional leaders would do well to emulate.

Posner is critical of Dyzenhaus's account of legality as a theoretical principle of justice, in part on the ground that it is too abstract to provide much guidance as to what steps should be taken and what institutions should be created in a particular transitional context. There is a parallel line of criticism against what we are here calling the "realist" approach. It calls for pragmatic compromise between alternative or conflicting ideal principles of justice, balanced by considerations of resource or other constraints on political actors. Yet, in arguing that some sort of balance must be struck, this method may not yield a determinate critical standard by which to assess the actual choices of decision makers. How are we to judge whether they have achieved the most just outcome available in the particular circumstances?

Gopal Sreenivasan, in his contribution, turns to the philosopher John Rawls's distinction between ideal and non-ideal theory as a resource for yielding more determinate moral judgments in circumstances where the demands of ideal justice cannot be met, of which the circumstances of regime change are a telling subset. Rawls's theory of distributive justice is advanced in the realm of ideal theory, that is, the specification of what justice would require under the best possible conditions. Rawls fully acknowledges the role of what he calls non-ideal theory for circumstances in which these conditions do not hold, and he distinguishes two branches —partial compliance theory, which adjusts ideal theory for circumstances in which individuals do not fully comply with justice (and so includes, for example, principles of criminal justice), and "transitional theory," which addresses circumstances in which a society's background (or historical) institutions are unjust—and asks how to transform institutions so as to bring them closer to the requirements of ideal justice. Each of these branches offers some determinate guidance on questions of moral obligation under less-than-ideal circumstances.

While the two branches of non-ideal theory are analytically distinct, thinking through what justice requires in real-world circumstances usually requires both. Giving an innovative twist to the

concept of "transitional justice," Sreenivasan argues that theorizing about the aftermath of regime change is an interesting and
useful site for the joint application of the two branches of non-
ideal theory. Sreenivasan complicates Rawls's view of non-ideal
theory in two ways. First, he argues that we should understand
partial compliance as a common feature not only of individuals
but also of institutions. This way of thinking of partial compliance theory helps us to make sense of, for example, war reparations as a performance between collective rather than individual
wrongdoers and victims. With respect to the second branch of
non-ideal theory, and like Webber and Satz, Sreenivasan distinguishes forward-looking and backward-looking moments in the
reform of previously unjust institutions. While Rawls's argument
highlights the forward-looking obligation to establish just institutions, Sreenivasan adds the notion that the successful implementation of forward-looking measures may require other measures that
express the wrongfulness of past actions and institutions.

What emerges from this analysis for theoretical accounts of
"transitional justice" understood as justice in the context of regime change? Most important for the present volume, Sreenivasan
clarifies our intuitions about the dilemmas of transitional justice
by showing that they may include trade-offs not only between justice and other goods (as in Elster's argument), or between alternative conceptions of justice (as in Webber's piece), or even between
ideal theory and real-world constraints, but also between the two
branches of non-ideal theory or even the subparts thereof.

To illustrate, Sreenivasan examines the choice between criminal
prosecutions and truth commissions that has been the mainstay of
so many debates in the transitional justice literature, showing that
partial compliance theory affords three different interpretations of
a choice in favor of truth commissions. On the first interpretation,
truth commissions are preferable because, in general, retributive
justice is not a morally defensible response to wrongdoing. On a
second interpretation, criminal punishment (retributive justice) is
the most desirable reading of partial compliance theory, but punishment happens to be unavailable within existing circumstances.
The first two justifications of truth commissions fall within partial
compliance theory alone. In contrast, a third interpretation of the
choice of truth commissions arises from a combination of partial

compliance theory and transitional theory. On this view, partial compliance theory taken alone would recommend criminal punishment. A forward-looking account of transitional theory, taken alone, would require simply that the society "move on" from its unjust past and establish a just constitutional order. A truth commission does not fit either bill but is nonetheless justifiable if we bring in the backward-looking component of transitional theory (i.e., the need to reckon with the past in order for the people to accept new institutions). On this account, the choice of a truth commission makes sense only if we understand victims' sacrifice (forgoing the punishment of wrongdoers) as a necessary condition for the creation of new, just institutions. Here, he writes, "the trade-off takes place specifically within non-ideal justice, either between its partial compliance branch and its transitional branch or, perhaps better, between the backward- and forward-looking moments of transitional theory" (p. 239).

Sreenivasan goes on to deepen his analysis of the much-neglected transitional branch of non-ideal theory, arguing that we do not need to reach agreement on an ideal theory of justice in order to arrive at a judgment of what justice requires in less-than-ideal circumstances. Developing what he calls "anticipatory theory" as a third branch of non-ideal theory, he argues that the gap between real-world circumstances and the requirements of justice is often so wide that there will be convergence across ideal theories on a minimum next step in the general direction of justice. While his own examples focus on questions of global distributive justice, we might read Dyzenhaus's account of transitional justice as the rule of law as an example of what Sreenivasan calls an "anticipatory" non-ideal theory of justice. We need not agree on an ideal theory of just constitutional order or of distributive justice to agree on the establishment of the rule of law as a duty of justice whose performance is a condition of possibility for the realization of any more ambitious ideal.

IS TRANSITIONAL JUSTICE SPECIAL?

A standard view of transitional justice is that it comprises extraordinary, special-purpose institutions applied on a time-limited basis to facilitate the shift from a now-defunct authoritarian or rights-abusing regime toward a rights-respecting liberal democratic constitutional order.[14] Within this view, the period of transition is understood as an interregnum period between the two regimes, in which neither the laws and standards internal to the old "bad" regime nor those internal to the new "good" regime apply in full. The time-limited character of transition has both pragmatic and normative significance. From a pragmatic point of view, transitional institutions should be time limited because they may place extraordinary demands on resources that are not sustainable over the longer run. From an ethical perspective, transitions should be time limited because they impose moral obligations and sacrifices that are inconsistent with the demands of justice in ordinary times. This supposition lies at the root of understandings of transitional justice as entailing moral compromise. If justice demands that all wrongdoers be punished or that all victims be compensated, the political constraints of a transitional context may require that justice be sacrificed for the sake of stable, relatively decent, political order—but it would be a moral mistake to "normalize" such compromises. Such is the logic of Gary Bass's account of political apologies. Sreenivasan's account of transitional theory as a branch of non-ideal theory gives the point a different twist: the work of bringing just institutions into being where they have not existed before may impose heavier duties of justice on actors than they would be asked to bear within the ideal theory of justice.

Taken as a whole, however, the contributions in this volume deeply challenge several of the assumptions that underlie the view that transitional justice is "special," fundamentally different from "just justice" or "justice in ordinary times." As Dyzenhaus makes explicit in his essay, three assumptions of this standard view are subject to doubt: first, that the problems of justice in transitional times are substantively different from the problems of justice in "ordinary" times; second, that transitions are radically discontinuous both with the prior bad regime and with the future good regime; and third, that the holy grail of transition is liberal constitutionalism such as we find in Western democracies.

All of our authors disagree with the first assumption, that the problems of justice in transitions are substantively different from those that we find in stable, "normal" times. Indeed, two contributors, Posner and Vermeule, jointly wrote a seminal piece some

years ago whose purpose was to debunk this view.[15] Their argument, which they reaffirm in their present contributions, is that,
while it is true that transitional justice sometimes requires moral
compromise or compromises between principles and expediency,
the same is true of justice in ordinary times. Plea bargaining, retroactive justice, opportunistic criminal prosecutions, and incomplete or unprincipled victim compensation schemes have all been
features of ordinary justice even in the most well-established liberal democracies. This is not to say that they are justified, but the
task of justifying these and other practices is not substantively different in transitional settings. Drawing an overly sharp contrast between transitional and non-transitional contexts obscures the fact
that *all* legal-political orders have to manage change, face hard
choices, and make compromises, including moral ones. And all of
them are subject to critical moral judgment as to whether the compromises they make are the right ones. As Dyzenhaus sums up the
point, "there is no problem that a transitional society presents that
is not found in stable liberal democracies" (p. 183).

Even though our authors agree that the moral standards for
evaluating institutions are not different in transitional and non-
transitional contexts, they do not claim that there is *no* difference
between transitions and "ordinary" times. The difference is one
of degree rather than of kind: the same dilemmas of justice arise
in greater number and with a greater intensity in transitional moments than stable political orders usually have to confront all at
once. De Greiff cautions that eliding this difference between transitional and non-transitional moments is risky because it obscures
the ways in which transitions establish new rules of the game for
"ordinary" institutions of justice and politics. As responses to the
utter failure of principles of justice to order law and politics, de
Greiff argues, transitions do not require distinctive principles of
justice, but they do address distinctive contexts: not just the imperfect world to which all accounts of justice must respond (e.g.,
through non-ideal theory) but "a very imperfect world" in which
noncompliance takes the form of egregious human rights violations and the effort to enforce compliance entails enormous costs.

For Webber, too, it is important to acknowledge that, while the
substantive content of justice does not differ across transitional and
non-transitional contexts, the relative weight of the three forms of

justice does. In transitional moments, Webber's second and third conceptions of justice—prospective justice and justice between contending normative orders—have a more pronounced salience. Whereas in ordinary times these forms of justice become obscured or marginalized, transitional periods throw them into sharp relief. Like de Greiff, Webber suggests that transitions are significant because the balance they strike among different forms of justice may become "hardwired" into the new institutional order (p. 102).

The second doubtful assumption of the "standard" view of transitional justice, that moments of transition are radically discontinuous with both the predecessor and the successor regimes, is also directly challenged by a number of our contributors. In highlighting the formative impact of transitions on the successor regime's political and legal order, Webber and de Greiff do want to insist that what happens during a transition constitutes a break with the past order and a moment of foundation-laying for the new one. Nonetheless, they could both agree with Dyzenhaus that the break between past and future is not a once-and-for-all affair, as the "standard" view represents it. The work of transforming an order from a rights-abusing to a rights-respecting state does not end once the new constitution is ratified, and it is dangerous to indulge the illusion that the work of reform is ever complete or, once achieved, irreversible. As Satz and Webber emphasize in their chapters, instances of historical injustice and egregious human rights violations occur in well-established liberal democracies, as well as in authoritarian regimes, and we need look only to the experience of indigenous peoples in settler democracies or of African Americans to remind ourselves of this fact.

The third assumption of the "standard" view, that Western-style liberal democracy is the appropriate aspiration for transitional orders, is rejected by some of our contributors and accepted by others. Dyzenhaus is most explicit in rejecting this standard by emphasizing the rule of law—nothing more and nothing less— as the substantive content of transitional justice. In this, he provides a ground for criticizing theorists of transitional justice for their chauvinism on behalf of Western liberal democracies on two points. The first is that they understate the universal and fundamental importance of the rule of law as the precondition of any more ambitious understanding of just legal-political order. The second line of criticism is that privileging the institutional forms of Western liberal democracy blinds us to just forms of political order that have emerged and that might be developed in other parts of the world. This position is most clearly staked out in Webber's piece, in which the third form of justice enables us to see that the institutional forms of Western democracies contain cultural and philosophical biases that can impede justice as it is understood in other ethical traditions or under political circumstances that diverge from the Western model.

The Impact of Transitional Justice Institutions

One point of agreement among all of our contributors is that no single institutional practice is likely to be able to realize all the normative ambitions of transitional justice. We may understand the moral goals of transitional justice holistically (as in de Greiff's argument), as a pragmatic trade-off between competing goods of justice, truth, and stability (as for Elster and arguably for Bass, Vermeule, and Posner), or as a balance across multiple readings of justice (as for Webber and Sreenivasan), but all of these views converge on the judgment that some combination of institutional mechanisms is necessary. Even Dyzenhaus, who alone among our authors propounds a unitary account of transitional justice, emphasizes the plurality of institutionalized practices needed to bring it about: a truth commission without accompanying programs of public education and judicial reform is unlikely to instill the "publique conscience" of law that undergirds rule-of-law orders. While Satz's focus is on a single institutional mechanism, she too argues that compensation schemes must be coupled with other means of countering past wrongs (e.g., truth seeking, memorials, prosecutions, apologies) in order to have their most beneficial impact.

Moreover, our authors agree that it is impossible to state in the abstract what combination of institutions will do most to advance the goals of transitional justice. Such judgments are inescapably contextual, and they vary according to diverse factors on the ground: the structure and intensity of political cleavages, state capacity, the motivations of the elite, the role of the military in past conflicts, the ethnic composition of the population, the severity and scale of past human rights abuses, and so on.

Advancing our knowledge about the capacity of transitional justice mechanisms to advance its moral goals, therefore, requires focused empirical analysis of the interplay between such variables and the actual performance of institutions. It is for this reason that the present volume includes two major empirical studies of transitional justice mechanisms as implemented in very different contexts: East Timor and the former Yugoslavia.

On the basis of extensive field work, David Cohen and Leigh-Ashley Lipscomb offer a thorough analysis of the East Timorese experience. Following the fall of Suharto's dictatorship in Indonesia, in 1999, Indonesian authorities occupying East Timor committed gross human rights violations to obstruct its independence. Over an eight-year period beginning in 2000, a dizzying array of transitional justice mechanisms were devised and implemented by the UN, the government of Timor-Leste, and post-Suharto Indonesia. These included independent public investigations of crimes against humanity, criminal prosecutions in regular and special courts, and Timorese and joint Indonesian-Timorese truth commissions.

Tragically, and despite the high caliber of early investigations of human rights violations, these institutions failed to achieve the core normative aspirations of transitional justice in East Timor. Using Elster's criteria of justice, truth, and peace, Cohen and Lipscomb argue that justice was ill served in that few cases were prosecuted and even fewer resulted in convictions. Despite the early efforts of the UN prosecutor, egregious sexual violence (including politically motivated rape) never resulted in criminal charges. Truth was better served by the reports of several commissions of inquiry and truth commissions, but these came at the heavy cost of the re-traumatization of witnesses, the failure to provide adequate support for victims, and the lack of an effective education campaign to disseminate findings among the general populace. Peace, which they here interpret as societal reconciliation, was frustrated by the opportunistic use of witness immunity programs by perpetrators.

While the case of East Timor does not tell against a holistic approach to the design of mechanisms, it does caution us against a lax interpretation of that approach in which simply adding more institutions is taken to represent commitment to transitional justice. The effective function of any single institution and of the coordination of different kinds of institutions (in particular, criminal prosecutions and truth commissions traversing national, transnational, and international spheres) requires factors that were notably absent in this case: the careful design of the full array of institutions at the outset, rather than "ad hoccery"; the commitment of adequate financial resources to carry out sound investigations, translate and disseminate reports, and provide meaningful victim support services; protections against the manipulation of either prosecutions or truth commissions by self-interested factions; and staffing the institutions with appropriately trained personnel. Cohen and Lipscomb sum up these factors in terms that resonate with the political psychology of transitional justice as highlighted in the contributions to this volume by Dyzenhaus and Posner. In the absence of elite actors' strong political will to achieve the ends of transitional justice, it matters little how many transitional mechanisms are put into place. Whether the motives of the elite are justice or self-interest, without their leadership and disciplining support of transitional justice institutions, those institutions are unlikely to attain their putative goals.

Monika Nalepa's study of transitional justice in the case of the former Yugoslavia focuses on just one institutional form, that of criminal justice. Like Cohen and Lipscomb, she raises the question whether the implementation of transitional justice achieves the goals of justice, truth, and peace as reconciliation. But, like other contributors, notably de Greiff and Elster, she resists the earlier tendencies in the literature to identify criminal trials with the good of justice. Recognizing that criminal trials can serve truth and peace as well as justice (just as truth commissions can serve some forms of justice and contribute toward the establishment of peace), she asks the focused question of how criminal prosecutions can contribute to what is arguably the highest moral end of transitional justice—peace understood as societal reconciliation.

One of the methodological challenges Nalepa confronts in her study is how to operationalize the normative aspirations of transitional justice so as to render them amenable to rigorous empirical analysis. What are the observable phenomena by which we judge whether reconciliation, in particular, has been advanced? In the case of the former Yugoslavia, she notes that, although the cities of Prijedor and Srebrenica suffered a comparable scale and extremity of human rights abuses during the war, generating large-scale population migrations away from these regions, the rate of return of refugees to Prijedor was significantly higher than that to Srebrenica. The return of refugees to a conflict zone, she argues, is a minimum condition for full-blown societal reconciliation understood as a restoration of social trust and a renewal of cooperation across group lines. Refugee returns, then, are a reasonable proxy for first-stage reconciliation.

Nalepa further notes that the prosecutorial strategy adopted by the International Criminal Tribunal for the Former Yugoslavia (ICTY) was somewhat different across different municipal zones. In some locales, the emphasis was on establishing a richer factual record of the chain of command through plea bargaining, whereas, in others, the strategy was to secure as many convictions as possible. Nalepa's empirical puzzle, then, is whether this difference between prosecutors' strategies is systematically related to differences in the rate of refugee returns and, hence, in the possibility of reconciliation. Using a combination of qualitative and quantitative methods, Nalepa arrives at the conclusion that, contrary to the inference we might draw from the cities of Prijedor and Srebrenica, in general a plea bargaining approach is associated with higher rates of refugee return than is an approach that maximizes the number of successful prosecutions. Plea bargaining, she argues, generates a more robust record of atrocities through the accumulation of testimony from a larger number of low-level perpetrators. In the process, it serves the goal of truth: establishing a common public narrative of the wrongs of the past. A higher number of convictions does represent the good of justice, for it is unjust for human rights violations to go unpunished. Yet, over all, Nalepa's evidence supports the conclusion that truth is more central than retributive justice to the possibility of reconciliation.

To this degree, the case of the former Yugoslavia reinforces the intuitions of political actors in contexts such as Chile and South Africa who favored truth commissions over criminal trials as the most salutary instrument of transitional justice. At the same time, Nalepa's argument undermines those variants of the "truth versus justice" debate which suppose that truth is best served by commissions and justice by criminal trials. Criminal trials, too, produce truth value, and it may turn out to be even more significant than the justice value they produce. Though Nalepa does not examine whether the truth produced by trials has greater efficacy with respect to reconciliation than that produced by truth commissions, her research opens up this question as one worthy of further empirical exploration.

A key strength of both of these empirical studies is that they explicitly engage propositions from the normative theory of transitional justice in seeking to assess the impact of different transitional justice mechanisms. Since the putative purpose of transitional justice institutions is to serve ends that are inescapably normative in their content, evaluating the actual performance of those mechanisms requires that scholars undertake the daunting task of translating abstract goods such as justice, truth, and reconciliation into terms that are susceptible of empirical analysis. This challenge does not distinguish transitional justice from any other field of inquiry that involves normatively laden concepts, but it is particularly daunting in a field where there is such deep contestation over the content of the moral purposes of political practices. One way in which Cohen and Lipscomb square up to this challenge is, for example, to understand the truth-producing value of commissions of inquiry in terms of the dissemination of reports in languages that are accessible to the mass of the population. Nalepa does so by interpreting quantifiable refugee returns as a partial measure of reconciliation. We are a long way indeed from being able to make strong claims about the causal mechanisms by which particular transitional justice institutions advance or fail to advance the goals they purportedly serve.[16] But works like these, which give specific content to abstract ideals, postulate causal relationships, and critically examine the evidence, are an indispensable step in that direction.

The normative aspirations of transitional justice, whether conceived in terms of peace, truth, or varying interpretations of justice, will always be "essentially contested concepts."[17] Although continued engagement between normative theorists and empirical social scientists will not resolve the conflict among alternative interpretations of these terms, a key task of such engagement is to clarify the categories of analysis by which we identify, interpret, and analyze political phenomena. As research on transitional justice continues, we hope that the engagement between normative theorists and empirical social scientists will be fully bidirectional, enriching the normative theory of transitional justice through novel operationalizations of its goals and enriching empirical study through the more precise articulation of the normative content of observable phenomena or institutionalized practices. We further hope the reader will agree that, taken as a whole, this volume contributes significantly to the deepening of this sort of engagement.

NOTES

1. See Jon Elster, *Closing the Books: Transitional Justice in Historical Perspective* (Cambridge: Cambridge University Press, 2004).

2. Early book-length treatments of the subject included Neil Kritz, ed., *Transitional Justice: How Emerging Democracies Reckon with Former Regimes* (Washington, DC: U.S. Institute of Peace Press, 1995), and Ruti Teitel, *Transitional Justice* (Oxford: Oxford University Press, 2000). Their publication encouraged the widespread scholarly use of the term.

3. Gary Bass, *Stay the Hand of Vengeance: The Politics of War Crimes Tribunals* (Princeton: Princeton University Press, 2000).

4. In "Transitional Justice Genealogy," *Harvard Human Rights Journal* 16 (2003): 72–94, Ruti Teitel characterizes the immediate postwar period as the first of three phases in the evolution of transitional justice.

5. Alexandra Barahona de Brito, *Human Rights and Democratization in Latin America: Uruguay and Chile* (New York: Oxford University Press, 1997); see also Paige Arthur, "How 'Transitions' Shaped Human Rights: A Conceptual History of Transitional Justice," *Human Rights Quarterly* 31 (2009): 321–67.

6. On the ways in which *gacaca* functions as a state-centered rather than community-based form of popular justice, see Susan Thomson and Rosemary Nagy, "Law, Power, and Justice: What Legalism Fails to Address in the Functioning of Rwanda's *Gacaca* Courts," *International Journal of Transitional Justice* 5, no. 1 (2011): 11–30.

7. See the recent special issue "Transitional Justice on Trial: Evaluating Its Impact," *International Journal of Transitional Justice* 4, no. 3 (2010); see also Hugo van der Merwe, Victoria Baxter, and Audrey Chapman, eds., *Assessing the Impact of Transitional Justice: Challenges for Empirical Research* (Washington, DC: U.S. Institute of Peace Press, 2009).

8. See, e.g., the essays by Amy Gutmann and Dennis Thompson, David A. Crocker, and Rajeev Bhargava in *Truth v. Justice: The Morality of Truth Commissions*, ed. Robert I. Rotberg and Dennis Thompson (Princeton: Princeton University Press, 2000).

9. See Adam Branch, "Uganda's Civil War and the Politics of ICC Intervention," *Ethics and International Affairs* 21, no. 2 (2007): 179–98. Though the indictments might have brought the Lord's Resistance Army to the negotiating table, they never signed the final peace agreement and have since migrated north, wreaking havoc and destruction in the Democratic Republic of Congo.

10. Joseph H. Carens, "Realistic and Idealistic Approaches to the Ethics of Migration," *International Migration Review* 30, no. 1 (1996): 166.

11. See Leslie Vinjamuri and Jack Snyder, "Advocacy and Scholarship in the Study of International War Crimes Tribunals and Transitional Justice," *Annual Review of Political Science* 7 (2004): 345–62. We leave aside their third category, the emotional-psychology approach.

12. Here, of course, the reference is to Max Weber's idea of an ethic of responsibility as set out in his famous essay, translated as "The Profession and Vocation of Politics" in *Weber: Political Writings*, ed. Peter Lassman, trans. Ronald Speirs (Cambridge: Cambridge University Press, 1994).

13. Dyzenhaus, this volume, p. 201, citing Jonathan Allen, "Balancing Justice and Social Unity: Political Theory and the Idea of a Truth and Reconciliation Commission," *University of Toronto Law Journal* 49 (1999): 315, 328–32, 335–38.

14. See esp. Teitel, *Transitional Justice*, chap.7.

15. "Transitional Justice as Ordinary Justice," *Harvard Law Review* 117, no. 3 (2004): 761–825.

16. For a survey of the empirical literature on the impact of transitional justice institutions and the limited conclusions we can draw from it, see Oskar N. T. Thoms, James Ron, and Roland Paris, "State-Level Effects of Transitional Justice: What Do We Know?," *International Journal of Transitional Justice* 4, no. 3 (2010): 329–54.

17. See William E. Connolly, "Essentially Contested Concepts in Politics," in his *The Terms of Political Discourse* (Princeton: Princeton University Press, 1993), 9–44.

1

THEORIZING TRANSITIONAL JUSTICE

PABLO DE GREIFF

Transitional justice has become the focus of intense interest by academics and practitioners alike. One revealing indicator of the notion's currency and of a growing common sense about its general character is the emergence of official and quasi-official international documents on transitional justice. Perhaps the most important example of such a document is the former UN Secretary General's Report, "The Rule of Law and Transitional Justice in Conflict and Post-Conflict Societies."[1] This report offers not only a definition of transitional justice but also a sophisticated understanding of the notion. It defines transitional justice as "the full range of processes and mechanisms associated with a society's attempts to come to terms with a legacy of large-scale past abuses, in order to ensure accountability, serve justice and achieve reconciliation,"[2] enumerates the main components of a transitional justice policy mentioning explicitly criminal justice, truth-telling, reparations, and vetting,[3] and, furthermore, stipulates that, far from being isolated pieces, these "mechanisms" should be thought of as parts of a whole: "Where transitional justice is required, strategies must be holistic, incorporating integrated attention to individual prosecutions, reparations, truth-seeking, institutional reform, vetting and dismissals, or an appropriately conceived combination thereof."[4]

The fact that a common sense is developing around transitional justice reflects that the field is no longer in its infancy. Independent of when the practice started, some of the seminal documents specifically on the topic are now more than twenty years old;[5] and yet, the field remains tremendously undertheorized. It is not just that the consensus around any given understanding of transitional justice and its components is far from complete; the consensus is, moreover, thin. Just to illustrate: the idea that transitional justice should be conceived of holistically, as stated in the Secretary General's Report, clashes, in practice, with the tendency of governments and others to think that the different measures can be traded off against one another.[6] The thinness of whatever agreement on a particular conception of transitional justice there might be can hardly be explained by saying that no single conceptualization has succeeded in gathering sufficient acceptance to become a sort of "paradigm"; the fact is that there have been very few attempts to articulate a conception of transitional justice systematically. Thus, to mention only some recent examples, Jon Elster explicitly disavows the intention to construct a theory of transitional justice;[7] David Crocker's "normative framework" for transitional justice,[8] as useful as it is in encouraging a broadening of the set of considerations that ought to be kept in mind in implementing measures to reckon with the past, still does not offer a comprehensive conception of transitional justice (it does not articulate the relationship that the different measures he examines have to one another, the relationship between these measures and the normative goals that he stipulates the measures should seek,[9] or, finally, the relationship among these different goals, some of which may clash). Finally, and most surprising, there is no fully worked-out conception of transitional justice even in the most influential works in the field.[10]

My aim in this chapter, therefore, is to present a normative conception of transitional justice.[11] While articulating a normative theoretical conception is not the same as articulating a *theory*, the two exercises are related. One of the main purposes of articulating a normative theoretical conception is to clarify the relationship among its constituent elements. In the case of transitional justice, this exercise pays rather large dividends; I shall argue that it yields a justification for the claim that transitional justice is a "holistic" notion. Success here would have the important practical implication that it would help us see why the selective application of transitional justice measures is misguided and why the frequently observed tendency to trade off one measure against others is inappropriate.

A second general reason to engage in normative theoretical work is that it can help guide action. The task of theory, according to my argument here, is not to develop formulae to which we can surrender the burden of exercising judgment; rather, theory can serve to clarify the nature and the full extent of our normative commitments. Fully articulating a conception of transitional justice can help us understand what we are committing ourselves to in adopting the notion. Normative theory, moreover, can guide action in a further way: in the normative domain, it is critical not just to understand *what* we are committed to but also *why* we are so committed. That understanding can make a crucial difference to *how* we act. A field that has been dominated by legal analysis stands to gain a lot if, in addition to giving to legal obligations the seriousness they deserve, the reasons why these obligations are accepted to begin with are clearly formulated. As an illustration, articulating a conception of transitional justice will guide action in a way that goes beyond what the discourse of legal rights on its own can do (despite the fact that, arguably, transitional justice as a field both rests upon and seeks to promote the entrenchment of legal rights). Understanding our commitments to particular rights (rights whose promotion is part of the transitional justice agenda) has consequences for the way one understands, for example, the role of victims in efforts to secure rights.

The chapter proceeds in four sections. In sections I to III, I present two arguments for understanding transitional justice holistically. These two arguments are analytically distinct but substantively convergent. The argument in section I concentrates on the conditions of the possibility of endowing weak and deficient measures with the *meaning* of justice measures. With this background, I then present in sections II and III a normative conception of transitional justice constructed around a set of ends that I argue are shared by the different transitional justice measures. To say that the ultimate aim of transitional justice is the promotion of justice (for example, in the sense of contributing to "giving everyone his or her due" or to strengthening the link between effort and success) is too abstract to be of real help. In a reconstructive spirit, I argue that attributing to transitional justice two mediate goals, namely recognition and civic trust (Section II) and two final goals, reconciliation and democracy (Section III), helps to make sense of the practices we associate with transitional justice, both in the sense of clarifying the relationship among those practices and in the sense of clarifying the relationship between transitional justice and other concepts and practices, including reconciliation and democracy. One of the virtues of this normative conception is that, rather than attributing to transitional justice the promotion of merely desirable goals, the two mediate and two final goals at issue can be understood as dimensions or, as I argue, as both preconditions and consequences of the effort to give concrete expression *through law-based systems* to the necessarily more abstract notion of justice.[12] Finally, Section IV provides a discussion of the nature of transitional justice. It argues against the view that transitional justice is "extraordinary" in the sense of a distinct type of justice on the one hand and that it is merely a compromise on the other. Making use of the distinction between justification and application, I argue instead that transitional justice articulates the requirements of a general understanding of justice when applied to the peculiar circumstances of a very imperfect world, that is, a world characterized by massive rule breakdown and great risks to the institutions that attempt to overcome such breakdowns.

I

Given the emerging consensus in the field, I do not take my main task to be to offer a novel definition of transitional justice. It is now commonly understood that the term refers to the set of measures implemented in various countries to deal with the legacies of massive human rights abuses. These measures usually include criminal prosecutions, truth-telling, reparations, and different forms of institutional reform (foremost among them vetting, particularly of security forces, which may include the judiciary). Although this is not a closed list—for instance, memorialization is an important element of most transitions and a natural complement to truth-seeking—the point now is to show that these are not elements of a random list. Rather, they are parts of a whole.

The first argument in favor of thinking about transitional justice holistically has a pragmatic beginning and a conceptual end.

Its point of departure is an effort to characterize the context in which transitional justice measures operate. The term "transitional justice" finds its natural place in what I have elsewhere characterized as "a very imperfect world."[13] An imperfect world, *simpliciter*, is one in which there is no spontaneous generalized compliance with even basic norms. Well-established legal regimes are parts of such worlds, for, while they are characterized by high levels of compliance, those levels never reach perfection, and, most important, this compliance is not spontaneous, as is shown precisely by the coercive nature of the legal regimes that impose both penalties and punishments for norm breaking. In contrast to such a world, a *very* imperfect world is one characterized not just by the massive and systematic violation of norms but also by the fact that there are huge and predictable costs associated with the very effort to enforce compliance. At the limit, in such a world, that effort puts at risk the very existence of the system that is trying to enforce its own norms. This, I think, is the primary domain of application of the term "transitional justice."[14]

We should acknowledge from the outset the limited reach of each of the measures that is part of a transitional justice policy. In fact, there is no transitional country that can legitimately claim great successes in this field. That is, there is no country that has undergone a transition that has prosecuted each and every perpetrator of human rights violations (let alone punished them in proportion to the gravity of the harms they caused); that has implemented a truth-seeking strategy that disclosed the fate of each and every victim or thoroughly identified the structures that made the violations possible; that has established a reparations program providing each and every victim with benefits proportional to the harm he or she suffered; or that, particularly in the short run, has reformed each and every institution that was implicated in the violations in question.

The weakness of each of these measures provides a powerful incentive to seek ways in which each can interact with the others in order to make up for their collective limitations. If one hews to the old understanding of justice in terms of giving to each his or her due[15] or of creating structures that make it more likely that there will be a close relationship between effort and success in people's lives, the great challenge faced by transitional justice measures becomes clear. That challenge, in the end, has a *semantic* dimension: how is it possible to give people reasons to *endow* these admittedly imperfect measures with the meaning of *justice* initiatives? The challenge is particularly serious given that most of these measures do nothing for most people directly. Those that do, mainly reparations, typically fall far short of any notion of proportionality.[16] In reality, what I, as a victim, see is that a handful of perpetrators (not necessarily those who abused me) get some form of punishment (surely not to the full extent they deserve and to the exclusion of complicit bystanders); that some report is compiled (which, even if it mentions my name, surely fails to do justice to the horrors I experienced or the overall ravages of massive violations); that I receive some money (what does money mean?) and services (most of which are of the basic sort that in other countries people receive simply in virtue of being citizens); and that some former official employees lose their jobs. Why should I regard such initiatives as *justice*-promoting? In summary, the challenge is to endow measures that could be seen as forms of scapegoating, mere words, "blood money," or inconsequential purges with the meaning that is required for them to be seen as instances of criminal justice, truth-telling, reparations, and institutional reform. Moreover, international experience suggests that if these measures are implemented haphazardly, piecemeal, and in isolation from one another, it is less likely that they will be interpreted as instances of justice and more likely that they will be seen as instances of expediency at best (this seems to be true even if some of the measures are aggressively implemented).

These remarks are not the result of mere speculation. Isolated and piecemeal prosecutorial initiatives have not quelled the claims for forms of justice other than more prosecution. This constitutes one of the greatest challenges faced by criminal trials that might be procedurally impeccable but that are structurally disconnected from other justice initiatives, as is often the case in international trials.[17] Truth-telling exercises, even such a thorough one as that in Guatemala (which indeed had two very good truth-seeking initiatives),[18] show that justice is not simply a call for insight but also a call to *act* on the truths disclosed. Convincing evidence about the difference it makes to link reparations programs to other justice initiatives comes from Morocco, a country that had a stand-alone reparations procedure with limited reach and, not long afterward, a more successful reparations effort linked with the work of a commission that, in addition to its truth-telling functions, also made far-reaching institutional reform proposals.[19]

Indeed, I think it is possible to go significantly further than the claim under consideration thus far. It is not just that individual transitional justice measures are less likely to be understood as justice measures if they are implemented in isolation from one another; the measures seem to be much more tightly related to one another than even this suggests. I want to argue that the relationships among the various measures form a thick web. Starting with reparations, to illustrate the point, it is clear that reparations in the absence of truth-telling are likely to be interpreted by victims as an effort to buy their acquiescence.[20] The point to notice, however, is that the relationship is bi-directional: just as reparations seem to call for truth-telling if the benefits are to be interpreted as a justice measure, truth-telling seems to call for reparations if words are to be seen, in the end, as more than inconsequential chatter. Similarly, beneficiaries of reparations programs are given stronger reasons to regard the sort of benefits usually conferred by these programs as reparations (as opposed to merely compensatory measures)[21] if they proceed in tandem with efforts to punish human rights violators. Conversely, since criminal prosecutions without reparations provide no direct benefit to victims other than a sense of vindication that otherwise does not change the circumstances of their lives, a policy based exclusively on prosecution is likely to be experienced by victims as an insufficient response to their own justice claims. Finally, vetting officeholders for past abuses is an important complement to prosecutions and reparations, for victims have little reason to trust institutions that continue to be populated by rights abusers. But vetting without substantive measures of corrective justice also rings hollow.

This pattern of bi-directional relations between reparations and the other transitional justice measures is replicated across the board. Criminal prosecutions, particularly considering their scarcity (even where there are some trials, the overwhelming majority of victims will not see *their* abusers prosecuted), can nevertheless be interpreted by victims as a justice measure, as something more than scapegoating, if they are accompanied by other truth-seeking

initiatives. Truth-telling initiatives also need to be "saved" from being interpreted as a form of whitewash in which the truth emerges
but no one pays any price. Similarly, it is easier for victims to see
criminal trials as more than scapegoating if they can regard them
as one of several accountability measures that the new regime is
implementing, measures that include the vetting of those responsible for human rights abuses. Again, what I want to emphasize
here is that this relationship holds in the opposite direction, as
well; we give reasons to save vetting from the charge that it is nothing more than a slap on the wrist (considering the abuses for
which those who are screened out of official position are allegedly
responsible), that is, we give reasons to take dismissals as a justice
measure if they are accompanied by the creation of robust prosecutorial mechanisms. The web of interrelationships that binds the
different transitional justice measures is thick, indeed.

Here my interest does not lie simply in pointing out the fact
that forging links among the different transitional justice measures
produces better results than having them operate in isolation from
one another—although, of course, I think that policymakers interested in "lessons learned" ought to heed this one. I am interested
in accounting for that fact. The underlying reason, in my opinion, has to do with what is at stake during a transition. In stating
it in this manner, I approach what I take to be a second argument
for thinking about transitional justice holistically, showing that, in
the end, the two arguments converge and are distinguishable only
at an analytic level. In the next section, I draw out this argument
more precisely. For the time being, I wish to underscore that the
various transitional justice measures are meant to show the currency of very basic norms. But, because the norms are so basic and
because they were so massively and systematically violated, showing
that they now hold sway requires a comprehensive effort. While restoring confidence in the force of more trivial norms might be easier, when norms that protect absolutely fundamental interests are
broken, this generates not only havoc but also a range of reactive
attitudes that can be overcome, if at all, only through coordinated
interventions that could in turn ground the reasonable belief that
the norms now play a meaningful role in guiding people's behavior, particularly that of power-holders.

In summary, it is reasonable to expect that measures that are
weak in relation to the immensity of the task that they face are

more likely to be interpreted as *justice* initiatives if they help to ground a reasonable perception that their coordinated implementation is a multipronged effort to restore or establish anew the force of fundamental norms.

This argument has two important practical consequences beyond improving the general effectiveness of transitional justice measures. The first is that the various transitional justice measures should be "externally coherent," that is, that they should be conceived of and implemented not as discrete and independent initiatives but rather as parts of an integrated policy.[22] The second practical consequence is that the argument cautions governments against trading measures off against one another. They must resist the tendency to expect victims to ignore lack of action in one of these areas because the government is doing something in one or more of the other areas. When a government says, for example, that it is all right to be weak in the prosecutorial domain because it will provide "generous" reparations, the argument helps to explain why benefits distributed under these circumstances are unlikely to be understood as justice measures. So, in addition to conflicting with international obligations that the government may have and with moral commitments, this sort of bargain is likely to undermine the possibility that whatever measures the government does implement will be interpreted as justice measures, rather than means of scapegoating, whitewashing, buying silence, or giving mere slaps on the wrist. It might overstate the case to say that this argument shows that isolated measures cannot be seen as justice initiatives and that they should not be tried, but the argument articulates a reason why there should be a *presumption* in favor of implementing them in relation to one another.

II

Each transitional justice measure can be said to pursue goals of its own and may serve more than one immediate aim at a time.[23] In the following, I would like to move beyond immediate goals to a higher level of abstraction and construct a conception that attributes to the various measures two mediate and two final goals.[24] Before proceeding, however, three initial remarks are in order.

The first concerns the nature of the position I am taking. In attributing to the measures the goals that I do, I am not saying that these are necessarily goals that they have been said explicitly to pursue. The strategy is reconstructive rather than descriptive: the different transitional justice measures *arguably* have as their mediate and final goals the ones I will mention presently. What grounds such a conception? The answer will not appeal to empirical observation first and foremost, although the evidence supports the claim that it is *possible* for transitional justice measures to contribute, even if modestly, to the attainment of these aims.[25] Rather, the aim of the chapter is to offer a conception of transitional justice as a theoretical construct. Like all theoretical constructs, this one aspires to account in a systematic fashion for a variety of phenomena whose interrelationship has caused puzzlement. In this case, the construct helps to account for the relationship among the different measures that are frequently said to be elements of transitional justice and does so in a way that shows they are part of a whole. It therefore grounds a presumption against their piecemeal implementation.[26] Further, the construct also clarifies the relationships among transitional justice, democracy, and reconciliation, which, in my view, is an abiding source of puzzlement and controversy.

Second, the conception on offer here is attractive not just because it provides us with a systematic account of complex phenomena by fixing on goals that these measures share. What is critical to notice is that these goals, as I show, are not simply desirable aims but that they are themselves systematically related to each other, and, more important, to the concept of justice.[27]

The conception, in a nutshell, is the following:

> Transitional justice refers to the set of measures that can be implemented to redress the legacies of massive human rights abuses, where "redressing the legacies" means, primarily, giving force to human rights norms that were systematically violated. A non-exhaustive list of these measures includes criminal prosecutions, truth-telling, reparations, and institutional reform. Far from being elements of a random list, these measures are a part of transitional justice in virtue of sharing two mediate goals (providing recognition to victims and fostering civic trust) and two final goals (contributing to reconciliation and to democratization).[28]

The third and final comment that needs to be made before proceeding is the following: the vocabulary of immediate, mediate, and final aims is not really adequate to the task I am proposing, particularly if these terms are primarily understood by their temporal connotations. I am using these terms to refer to proximity or distance not in time but in "causal" chains. The immediate goal of a particular measure is one that in theory can be brought about by that intervention (regardless of how much time this might take); thus, for example, those who think of deterrence as the immediate goal of criminal prosecutions think that prosecutions *can* bring about this effect (even if not in a short time). "Mediate" and "final," therefore, refer to degrees of separation from this position. The mediate aims of a measure are aims that it is reasonable to think the measure's implementation may further but whose accomplishment may also require a number of different measures. For example, reparations may contribute to making victims feel recognized but almost certainly cannot satisfy victims' claims for recognition on their own. That requires the implementation of a variety of measures, including those in the typical transitional justice portfolio. "Final ends" in the way I am using the term here are not the ends "for sake of which everything else is done," as Aristotle would have it in Book I of the *Nicomachean Ethics*, but ends whose attainment is causally even more distant and therefore whose realization really depends upon the contribution of an even larger number of factors, whose role, relatively speaking, increases in importance.

Thus, there are two axes along which I am classifying aims here: (1) the number of intervening factors, and (2) their relative importance in bringing about the desired results. While it is not unthinkable that transitional justice measures, if designed and implemented in what I have called an "externally coherent" fashion —that is, in a manner that attends to the many ways in which they interrelate both positively and negatively and tries to maximize the synergies—could make a contribution to the trust that citizens have in their institutions, it is obvious that strengthening democracy requires the intervention of a larger number of factors. In this mixture, the significance of transitional justice measures may end up being quite low relative to, for example, that of broader constitutional reforms and economic restructuring programs.

Having made these remarks, we can now build the conception stepwise.[29]

Recognition

First, it can be said that all transitional justice measures seek to provide recognition to victims.[30] The sort of recognition at issue is actually a complex one. To begin with, it refers to something akin to granting victims moral standing as individual human beings. Although for good reason a great deal of attention has been paid to the importance of recognizing the *agency* of individuals and the types of injustice that result from the failure to recognize their agency, there is a more basic form of injustice that stems from failing to recognize that, in addition to being the subjects of their own action, individuals are also the *objects* of the actions of others. At the limit, and at its most basic, this requires acknowledging that they can be harmed by certain actions. The sorts of precautions that are taken by those who intentionally harm—either to keep the harms secret, or to control those they harm, or to protect themselves from the psychological costs of voluntarily inflicting pain by means of various strategies of "dehumanization," plus the various strategies implemented to guarantee the effectiveness of humiliation[31]—all point toward assumptions made in practice about the agency of those being harmed and also about the effectiveness of our (harming) actions on them.[32] Almost without fail, one of the first demands of victims is precisely to obtain recognition of the fact that they have been harmed, and intentionally so.

But this is only one dimension of the sort of recognition that transitional justice measures arguably provide to victims. It is not primarily the victims' great capacity to endure *suffering* that needs to be acknowledged. Ultimately, what is critical for a transition, and what transitional justice measures arguably aim to do, is to provide to victims a sense of recognition not only as victims but as (equal) rights-bearers and, ultimately, as citizens. Particularly where marginalization has made it possible or easier to mistreat others (in various ways, including the failure to recognize individuals as anything other than parts of an undifferentiated mass), acknowledging the capacity to suffer is important but not enough. What is indispensable, and what arguably transitional justice measures have sought to accomplish, is to recognize that the other is the bearer of rights—and therefore to engage in modes of redress that can not only assuage suffering but also restore the rights that were so brutally violated and affirm victims' standing as full citizens.

This claim about the sort of recognition that transitional justice measures seek to provide to victims is neither descriptive nor predictive; whether transitional justice measures actually succeed in providing the relevant sort(s) of recognition is an empirical issue that depends upon many practical and contingent factors. But, in short, the argument is the following: from my standpoint, the various transitional justice measures can be interpreted as efforts to institutionalize the recognition of individuals as citizens with equal rights. Thus, criminal justice can be interpreted as an attempt to provide recognition to victims by denying the implicit claim of superiority made by the criminal's behavior through a sentence that is meant to reaffirm the importance of norms that grant equal rights to all.[33] Truth-telling provides recognition in ways that are still probably best articulated by the old difference proposed by Thomas Nagel between knowledge and acknowledgment, when he argued that, although truth commissions rarely disclose facts that were previously unknown, they still make an indispensable contribution in officially acknowledging these facts.[34] The acknowledgment is important precisely because it constitutes a form of recognizing the significance and value of persons as individuals, as citizens, and as victims. Reparations provide the material form of the recognition owed to fellow citizens whose fundamental rights have been violated. In light of the difficulties and deficiencies that normally accompany prosecutions and of the potential charge that truth-telling is "cheap talk," reparations buttress efforts aimed at recognition by demonstrating that the transitional government has made a sufficiently serious commitment to justice that it is willing to invest resources and, in well-crafted programs, by giving beneficiaries the sense that the state has taken their interests to heart. Finally, institutional reform, including vetting, is guided by the ideal of guaranteeing the conditions under which citizens can relate to one another and to the authorities as equals.

In summary, each transitional justice measure may be said to have an immediate aim or aims of its own. At a higher level of abstraction, however, all of them can be thought to pursue the goal of providing recognition to victims as individuals and as victims but also, and most fundamental, as bearers of rights. It is clear that this is a thoroughly normative-based conception of recognition, since recognizing victims as rights-bearers involves recognizing the norms that establish a regime of citizenship. Even recognizing victims as victims, however, involves acknowledging not so much sheer suffering as *harms*, which is a normatively thicker notion.[35] Indeed, transitional justice measures work—to the extent they do —only in virtue of their capacity for norm affirmation.

Civic Trust

The other aim that the various transitional justice measures seek to attain is the promotion of civic trust. Once again, this is not a description or a prediction. Whether or not the measures will succeed in inducing this effect is an empirical question that cannot be settled in advance, and certainly there are many ways for these measures to "go wrong."[36] But let me set that issue aside in order to concentrate on the theoretical claim. The first thing that needs to be done, of course, is to explain the sense of "trust" at issue here.

Let's start with a broad understanding of trust. Trust in general, as a disposition that mediates social interactions, "is an alternative to vigilance and reliance on the threat of sanctions, [and] trustworthiness . . . an alternative to constant watching to see what one can and cannot get away with, to recurrent recalculations of costs and benefits."[37] Trust, then, at a general level, contrasts with the sort of constant monitoring and appeals to sanctions that speak of suspicion.

Still by way of indirection, it can be said that while trusting someone involves relying on that person to do or refrain from doing certain things, trust is not the same as mere predictability or empirical regularity. If that were so, the paradigm of trust would obtain in our relationship with particularly reliable machines. That reliability is not the same as trustworthiness can be seen in our reluctance to say that we *trust* someone about whose behavior we feel a great deal of certainty but only because we both monitor and control it (e.g., through enforcing the terms of a contract), or because we take defensive or preemptive action.[38] Trust, far from resembling a sort of "mechanical reliability," involves an expectation of a shared *normative* commitment. I trust someone when I have reasons to expect a certain pattern of behavior from her, and those reasons include not just her consistent past behavior, but also, crucially, the expectation that among her reasons for action is the commitment to the norms and values we share. Trust develops out of a mutual sense of commitment to shared norms and values. This explains both the advantages of trust and the risks it always involves. In dispensing with the need to monitor and control, it facilitates cooperation immensely, and not only by lowering transaction costs; but as a wager (no matter how "safe") that at least in part for *normative reasons* those we trust will not take advantage of our vulnerabilities, we risk having our expectations defeated.

Now, the term "civic" in "civic trust" I understand basically as a limiting qualifier. Trust can be thought of as a scalar relationship, as one that allows for degrees. The sense of trust at issue here is not the thick form of trust characteristic of relations between intimates but rather "civic" trust, which I take to be the sort of disposition that can develop among citizens who are strangers to one another and who are members of the same community only in the sense in which they are fellow members of the same political community. True, the dimension of a wager is more salient in this case than in that of trust toward intimates, since we have much less information about others' reasons for actions. However, the principles or norms that we assume we share with others and the domain of application of these norms are much more general. To illustrate, the loyalty that binds me to a common political project and, therefore, to fellow citizens, is significantly thinner than the loyalty that binds me to intimates.

As compelling as this norm-based understanding of trust might be, however, it does raise a complication that needs to be addressed before we can proceed: it is not clear what, on this account, trust in institutions might mean. Strictly speaking, if trust is a relationship that cannot be reduced to mere empirical regularity but one that involves an awareness of mutual normative reciprocity, this is possible only among individuals, and then there is no such thing as trust in institutions. Nevertheless, we trust institutions and the people who inhabit them. How so? Claus Offe offers the following explanation:

> "trusting institutions" means something entirely different from "trusting my neighbor": it means *knowing* and recognizing as valid

the values and the form of life incorporated in an institution and deriving from this recognition the assumption that this idea makes sufficient sense to a sufficient number of people to motivate their ongoing active support for the institution and the compliance with its rules. Successful institutions generate a negative feedback loop: they make sense to actors so that actors will support them and comply with what the institutionally defined order prescribes.[39]

By way of contrast, people mistrust institutions because they suspect (correctly) that the values embodied by those institutions do not make "sufficient sense to a sufficient number of people to motivate their ongoing active support for these institutions and the compliance with [their] rules."[40] Trusting an institution amounts to knowing that its constitutive rules, values, and norms are shared by its members or participants and are regarded by them as binding.

So, how do transitional justice measures promote this sense of civic trust? In a nutshell, the argument is the following: prosecutions can be thought to promote civic trust by reaffirming the relevance of the norms that perpetrators violated, norms that turn natural persons into rights-bearers. Judicial institutions, particularly in contexts in which they have traditionally been essentially instruments of power, show their trustworthiness if they can establish that no one is above the law. Truth-telling can foster civic trust by responding to the anxieties of those whose confidence was shattered by experiences of violence and abuse, who are fearful that the past might repeat itself. Their specific fear might be that the political identity of (some) citizens has been shaped around values that made the abuses possible. An institutionalized effort to confront the past might be seen by those who were formerly on the receiving end of violence as a good-faith effort to come clean, to understand long-term patterns of socialization, and, in this sense, to initiate a new political project around norms and values that this time are truly shared.[41] Reparations can foster civic trust by demonstrating the seriousness with which institutions now take rights violations, a seriousness that is manifested, to put it bluntly, by the fact that "money talks." Civic trust is bolstered when, even under conditions of scarcity and competition for resources, the state responds to the obligation to fund programs that benefit those who were formerly not only marginalized but abused.[42] Finally, vetting can induce trust and not just by "re-peopling" institutions with new faces but by thereby demonstrating a commitment to systemic norms governing employee hiring and retention, disciplinary oversight, prevention of cronyism, and so on.[43]

Now, recall that part of the aim of developing a theoretical construct is to draw systematic links between apparently discrete phenomena. The conception of transitional justice I am articulating is tightly woven; it seeks to explain the relationship among the different elements of transitional justice by providing an account of the goals that these elements can be thought to pursue. But, before proceeding to the analysis of two further goals at the next level of abstraction, I want to make two remarks. First, there is a close relationship between the two goals that we have been examining, recognition and civic trust. To begin with, I have offered norm-based accounts of both recognition and of civic trust.[44] Indeed, the same basic norms are relevant for both recognition and trust. One way of articulating the relationship between recognition and trust is to say that recognition involves the acknowledgment of standing, of status, on the basis of which individuals can develop a particular set of attitudes in their mutual interactions and in their interactions with mediating institutions, namely the attitudes characteristic of trust.

Second, and much more important, it is a virtue of this conception of transitional justice that it is organized not around just any goals but around goals that are closely connected with justice. Both recognition and trust can be said to be preconditions as well as consequences of justice, at least of legally mediated efforts to achieve justice. Laws work on the basis of taking persons as legal subjects, that is, of recognizing the status of rights-bearers to individuals (and collectivities).[45] So, a precondition of legal action in pursuit of justice is the recognition of this status, which explains the importance of legal struggles for recognition, of "enfranchisement," and the tragedy of the various forms of failure of this most basic type of recognition as legal subjects and as rights-bearers. But, if it is right to say that recognition is a precondition of justice, it is not less so to say that recognition is a consequence of justice; over time, the operation of a legal system also facilitates the extension of recognition to those previously unrecognized.[46]

Similarly, trust is both a condition and a consequence of justice. On the one hand, the operation of legal systems relies upon complex forms of trust. Criminal legal systems must rely upon citizens' willingness to report both crimes that they witness and crimes that they suffer. And this willingness to report, of course, rests upon their trust that the system will reliably produce the expected outcomes. This is actually a complex sort of trust: in police investigations, in the efficiency of the court systems, in the honesty of judges, in the independence of the judiciary (and therefore in the executive's willingness to protect and promote that independence), in the at least minimal wisdom of the legislature, and in the strictness (but perhaps also the simultaneous humaneness) of the prison system, and so on. Needless to say, each of these objects of trust could be further analyzed.

On the other hand, a legal system does not simply rely upon the preexisting trust of citizens in one another and in the system itself. Legal systems, when they operate well, also catalyze trust in the system and among citizens; by stabilizing expectations, legal systems diminish the costs of trusting others, particularly strangers. By the same token, by accumulating a record of success in resolving conflicts between citizens, a legal system catalyzes trust in legal institutions, which will increasingly be appealed to for the resolution of differences.

In summary, a system of justice (a legal one, at least) is unimaginable without minimal levels of recognition and trust. Stable forms of recognition and trust, at least in a modern setting, are also unimaginable without the mediation of a legal system of justice. The two mediate aims pursued by transitional justice measures, then, are indeed closely related to justice, rather than just a pair of merely desirable ends.

III

Now, if providing recognition and fostering civic trust are, on this conception, two mediate aims of a comprehensive transitional justice policy, promoting reconciliation and democratization are two of its final aims.[47] Once again, I will build this part of the conception step by step.

Reconciliation

It makes sense now to return to a characterization of the contexts in which transitional justice primarily operates. But, whereas in the description of what I have called a "very imperfect world" I was focusing mainly on the risks or "costs" a legal regime has to endure in the very effort to enforce its own norms, here I focus on the quality of social relations in such a world. In order to clarify the meaning of the polysemic term "reconciliation"—which we must do if we are going to clarify its relationship with transitional justice —it helps to have a picture of what an *unreconciled* society might be. Obviously, neither the presence of disagreement, even of deep and passionate disagreements, nor the presence of unredeemed justice claims can be taken as the defining marker of an unreconciled society; disagreement is part and parcel of life in complex societies, and no society is completely free of justice claims yet to be redressed.

It turns out that a philosophical notion of resentment is useful for the characterization of an unreconciled society. Margaret Walker, in a series of splendid papers,[48] has developed a conception of resentment based on P. F. Strawson's notion of a reactive attitude.[49] On this account, resentment is not merely another name for generalized anger or other negative affective reactions but rather describes a specific type of anger, one that attributes responsibility for the defeat or the threat of defeat of *normative expectations.* To illustrate the two main elements in this account by means of contrast, the reaction to misfortunes, including accidents great and small, can very well be anger, even deep anger, and self-pity, but the reaction should not, properly speaking, be resentment, because what defeats my expectations is entirely fortuitous, and therefore no attribution of responsibility is plausible. Similarly, the reaction to the defeat of expectations that are based on preferences can be quite negative but cannot properly amount to resentment, for there is nothing to suggest that I have a right to have preference-based expectations met. Resentment, as Walker argues, "responds to perceived *threats to expectations based on norms* that are presumed shared in, or justly authoritative for, common life."[50]

An "unreconciled" society, then, would be one in which resentment characterizes the relations among citizens and between citizens and their institutions. It is one in which people experience anger because their norm-based expectations have been threatened or defeated. Expectations concerning basic physical security, for instance, are not whimsical; nor do they reflect mere preferences.

The idea that the state is the final guarantor of physical safety is part of the core of the notion of the modern state. Threatening or defeating those expectations not just usually but *properly* leads to feelings of resentment among victims and others. This anger is more than blind rage or deep frustration; it is ineluctably intertwined with a claim about the validity of the threatened or violated norm, a claim that, in turn, generates an attribution of responsibility for the threats or the violations and therefore for the accountability of those who so acted.

There is a further aspect of this norm-based articulation of the notion of resentment that contributes to making it particularly useful for our purposes. It provides an illuminating account of a dimension of massive abuse that has to be kept firmly in mind when thinking about the prospects of reconciliation. Victims of torture—among other forms of abuse—report a sense of loneliness and isolation.[51] Walker argues that resentment arises as a result of threats to and violations of not only norms but also one's standing to assert or insist upon the validity of those norms. To the extent that the norms in question are those that define social, moral, or interpersonal boundaries, massive abuse can lead to a form of "normative isolation," of "demoralization," that can be seen clearly when one considers that the "accusing anger" that resentment constitutes is one that invites others to come to one's defense, an invitation that in these cases ordinarily goes unheeded. Hence the solitude of the abused, a solitude that in aggregate terms deepens, *ex post*, the marginalization of groups that, *ex ante*, were often already socially marginalized.[52]

This seems to me to be a very good characterization of many transitional societies. But it is not merely a good description. It also connects easily with the normative conception I am articulating here, for another way of describing unreconciled societies is to say that they are characterized by massive and systematic failures of recognition, standing, and consideration that would entitle their citizens both to enjoy basic protections and to raise claims—and that these failures lead to a breakdown of social trust. By contrast, then, we can arrive at a conception of reconciliation:

> Reconciliation, minimally, is the condition under which citizens can
> trust one another *as citizens* again (or anew). That means that they

are sufficiently committed to the norms and values that motivate their ruling institutions, sufficiently confident that those who operate those institutions do so also on the basis of those norms and values, and sufficiently secure about their fellow citizens' commitment to abide by and uphold these basic norms and values.

There are many independent reasons to adopt this understanding of reconciliation.[53] In summary, this way of thinking about reconciliation abides by constraints that any defensible conception must respect. In addition to being compatible with religious accounts of reconciliation, this one is suitably detached from any particular tradition and thus adequate for pluralistic contexts. It does not take reconciliation to be "wiping the slate clean"; it does not constitute yet another way of transferring burdens to victims who, on many accounts, end up being made responsible for the achievement of reconciliation; and it acknowledges that reconciliation has an attitudinal dimension and yet does not reduce reconciliation to a psychological state.

An additional feature of this way of understanding reconciliation is that it does not take reconciliation to be a substitute for justice. Quite the contrary: this account of reconciliation dovetails with the conception of transitional justice I am offering. To the extent that transitional justice measures seek to provide recognition and to foster civic trust in the ways sketched earlier, they can be seen to make a contribution to reconciliation, given that reconciliation can be understood in terms of the currency of norms on which both recognition and trust rest.

However, it must be kept in mind that reconciliation has an attitudinal dimension. If reconciliation is to mean anything at all, it must refer to something individuals either experience or not. This means that the relationship between transitional justice and reconciliation is complex; there is a sort of unfillable gap between them: even if correctly and maximally implemented, the most that transitional justice measures can do is to give reasons to individuals to trust institutions. In other words, transitional justice measures, at their best, contribute to making institutions *trustworthy*. Whether or not they will in fact be trusted is a different issue. My sense is that the attitudinal change that is part of reconciliation also calls for initiatives that target a more personal and less

institutional dimension of a transition than the measures we have
been concerned with. Primary among these are official apologies
that go beyond generic acknowledgments of responsibility.[54]

Thus, to summarize, on the normative conception of transitional justice I am constructing here, transitional justice has as
one of its final ends the goal of contributing to reconciliation.
Implementing these measures, however, does not guarantee that
reconciliation will be achieved: reconciliation, on this conception,
describes a state in which social relations are characterized by a
civic and norm-based type of trust, and, while transitional justice
measures can contribute to making institutions trustworthy, actually trusting institutions is something that requires an attitudinal
transformation that the implementation of transitional justice
measures can only ground but not produce.

Democracy

As if it were not sufficiently controversial to argue that reconciliation is one of the final aims of transitional justice, I will now add
to this controversy by arguing that promoting or strengthening
democracy is another final end of transitional justice.[55] Because
the claim is controversial, it is important to reiterate the sense in
which it is meant: to say that promoting democracy is one of the
final goals of transitional justice does not mean that transitional
justice measures can bring about democracy on their own. This
claim is meant in the same sense in which I have spoken of the
other goals of transitional justice. In each case, I have argued that
the goal in question is one that, from a reconstructive perspective, helps to clarify the point of applying measures that in many
ways are demonstrably weak. The way the attribution of these goals
helps to clarify the point is not merely by linking those measures
with the possibility of achieving aims we might think to be desirable (like "recognition," or "civic trust," or "reconciliation") but by
the further step of showing that these aims can be understood as
dimensions or, as argued earlier, as both preconditions and consequences of the effort to give concrete expression through law-
based systems to the necessarily more abstract notion of justice.

Although the present argument is, strictly speaking, a particular instance of a more general argument establishing the relation-

ship(s) between democracy and justice,[56] here I will have to remain close to the concerns of transitional justice, taking as my starting point the now commonplace claim of scholars and practitioners alike that the implementation of transitional justice measures, singly and collectively, strengthens the rule of law. In the manner of normative theorizing, the fundamental argument for attributing to transitional justice the strengthening of democracy as one of its final goals is one that unpacks the implications of transitional justice's commitment to the rule of law.

Promoting the rule of law is one of the aims frequently attributed to transitional justice measures. Virtually all truth commissions to date have used the concept both in an explanatory role (lack of respect for the principles of the rule of law is one of the factors that leads to the rights violations under scrutiny) and as one of the objects of their work (their recommendations are intended to strengthen the rule of law).[57] Scholars largely agree both about the centrality of the concept and about the usefulness of transitional justice measures in efforts to reestablish the rule of law.[58]

The claim that transitional justice measures can contribute to the strengthening of the rule of law can be fleshed out in different ways, which include the following: criminal trials that offer sound procedural guarantees and that do not exempt from the reach of justice those who wield power demonstrate the generality of law; truth-telling exercises that contribute to understanding the many ways in which legal systems failed to protect the rights of citizens provide the basis on which, *a contrario*, legal systems can behave in the future; reparations programs that try to redress the violation of rights serve to exemplify, even if *ex post facto*, the commitment to the notion that legal norms matter; institutional reform measures, even basic reforms consisting merely in the screening and dismissing of those who abused their positions, increase the integrity of rule of law systems, at least prospectively.

All of these seem plausible accounts to me. Whether they obtain in fact is an empirical question, and therefore I will set it aside here[59] in order to return to the main task of the chapter, which involves, at least in part, clarifying the implications of undertaking certain normative commitments. When transitional justice promoters argue that transitional justice measures can make a contribution to the rule of law, they cannot have in mind merely a formalist conception of the latter, though the formal features of rule-of-law orders do matter. Requiring legislators to pass only general laws and insisting on their non-retroactive application and on their public nature—to mention only some of the requirements usually associated with the rule of law—are significant achievements, particularly in contexts where there are histories of unrestrained power. The requirement of generality in the law obviously prevents individuals from being singled out for discriminatory treatment; the constraint on retroactive laws protects individuals from some of the whims of power-holders; and the requirement of publicity allows individuals to form reasonable expectations about what is permitted and prohibited and introduces a requirement of rationality into law-making and of accountability into the exercise of power.[60] In these and other ways, the formalist ideal of the rule of law provides some protection to individuals from the arbitrary exercise of power.

And yet, a fully formalist understanding of the rule of law concept is not adequate to the task of transitional justice, as evidenced by the fact that many of the countries where transitional justice measures have been implemented are countries in which the rule of law, understood formally, *was* satisfied. Indeed, the reports of the truth and reconciliation commissions of both Chile and South Africa, for example, are critical of the formalist understanding of the rule of law the commissions found to be widespread in each country. "Justice as regularity," as John Rawls aptly described formalist understandings of the rule of law,[61] can, indeed, be satisfied independently of (other) criteria of justice. This is not news; as the legal philosopher Joseph Raz states, since the precepts of the rule of law "guarantee only the impartial and regular administration of rules, whatever these are, they are compatible with injustice."[62] This reminds us that, despite the analytical advantages that distinguishing the formal features of law may bring, those who are concerned with questions of justice and not only of institutional stability and order have reasons to adopt a thicker and more substantive conception of the rule of law than one that turns on impartiality and regularity. On the normative conception I am reconstructing here, transitional justice measures seek to make a contribution to justice in the world. The measures do so to a large extent in virtue of their ability to give force to certain basic norms. The point to notice now is that giving force to these norms is not a one-off affair, nor even a matter of making up for past breaches. Giving force to norms is a matter of showing their ongoing, continued relevance across time. This is one of the reasons why it makes sense to think that when transitional justice promoters say their measures promote the rule of law, they have in mind a conception of the rule of law that ultimately involves a commitment to a more substantive conception of justice, one that calls for political participation.

It helps to motivate the interest in clarifying the complex connection between transitional justice and democracy to examine why, for example, even a benign or "liberal" despot interested in redressing injustice is still a troublesome figure.[63] First, the benign despot's commitment to accountability measures should raise questions in the mind of transitional justice defenders. The closer the mantle of responsibility approaches the despot, the more likely it is that, in the absence of constraints, he will derail the accountability measures. Second, a preventive rationale typically underlies the work of transitional justice. Of course, it is not that democracies have a spotless human rights record, but on the whole they fare better on the protection of basic human rights than their alternatives, including, likely, our benign despot. While no type of regime offers iron-clad guarantees for the protection of human rights, democracies have a better record protecting the rights of their citizens than other kinds of regimes.[64] To the extent, then, that transitional justice promoters have an interest in prevention, the benign despot should give them some pause. Third, if transitional justice is going to mark a dividing line between an abusive past and a future rights-respecting regime, in addition to redress, there must be significant political transformation. Otherwise, the measures will be rendered ineffective, and there will be a great incentive to reapply them in the future to mark precisely this thick line. The despot's truth commission, for instance, will need to be followed, at some point, by another truth commission. Even under auspicious circumstances, transitional justice measures may not achieve their most immediate ends. In the absence of political transformation, it is not clear that even "successful" redress exhausts the justice agenda.

In the end, an understanding of how transitional justice measures achieve their aims should also motivate an interest in the
connections between transitional justice and democracy. Here I
would like to concentrate on just two mechanisms. First, the implementation of transitional justice measures plays a strong catalytic
role in the process of civil society organization.[65] The possibility of
securing a place for a truth commission or reparations program
on the political agenda almost invariably leads to the formation of
numerous and varied civil society organizations. Indeed, I would
argue that this is one of the ways in which the implementation of
transitional justice measures contributes to processes of democratization, but it is one of the characteristic marks of despotism and
authoritarianism everywhere that they impede the free operation
of civil society and the public sphere.[66] Second, to reiterate one of
my main points, transitional justice measures work, to the extent
they do, in virtue of their capacity to affirm norms. In the domain
of justice, however, as we know, what matters is not just what *type* of
norms we are expected to comply with but the ways in which those
norms are "produced." Understanding that transitional justice
measures work through these two mechanisms provides grounds
for questioning whether redress in the absence of political transformation should be taken to exhaust the agenda of transitional
justice promoters and, therefore, provides reasons why those advocates should be interested in the relationship between what they
seek to accomplish and democratic political practices.

One fruitful line of inquiry starts precisely with the commitment to the rule of law—not a formalist conception but a more
robust one that focuses on trying to secure due-process guarantees in the production as well as in the application of the law. And
this means that, ultimately, contrary to what many defenders of the
formalist conception hold, there is an internal relation between
constitutional democracy and the rule of law. Citizens can enjoy
as *rights*—and not merely as dispensations from those who hold
power—the protections that are meant to be provided by the traditional liberal civil rights enshrined in laws that satisfy the formal
conditions of the ideal of the rule of law only if, at the same time,
they can enjoy rights to political participation. Otherwise, their en-
joyment of the relevant guarantees depends upon the virtues of
rulers and judges, and citizens will not enjoy these protections as

rights. Conversely, citizens can exercise their rights to political participation fully and meaningfully only if their individual civil rights are guaranteed. In the absence of civil rights such as freedom of speech and even of privacy rights, which create space for the development of individual preferences, political participation turns citizens into instruments of those who hold political power.[67]

This, I think, is a sounder basis on which to think about the complicated relationship between transitional justice and democracy and helps systematize our reservations about letting redress in nondemocratic contexts become a paradigm of transitional justice work. Fundamentally, and at the deepest level, if transitional justice is concerned with contributing to giving force to a regime of equal rights, one that can instantiate a defensible conception of justice, strengthening a system of norms whose best characterization is that they are capable of guiding people's behavior—according to Raz, "the basic intuition from which the doctrine of the rule of law is derived"[68]—is, at best, a first step. Saying that one of the aims of transitional justice is the promotion of the rule of law helps to make sense of the practice only if the "rule of law" is understood in a way that coheres with an understanding of its ultimate aim (promoting a just social order), as well as with the more particular aims in terms of which the latter is specified (including recognition, civic trust, and reconciliation).

Ultimately, there are good reasons to think that the commitment of transitional justice promoters to the idea of the rule of law is really a commitment to the *democratic* rule of law: democracy is both a condition and a consequence of legally institutionalized efforts to establish justice. Thus, if it is true that transitional justice measures contribute to the establishment of law-based systems of justice both through catalyzing civil society organization and through the affirmation of norms that include the norms of full citizenship, transitional justice promoters do well to remember that transitional justice redress does not, in itself, *bring about* democratic transitions. Regime change typically precedes the implementation of transitional justice measures. Further, the measures work fully only if there is at least some tolerance for certain types of social participation. If transitional justice measures are to succeed in providing recognition to victims and promoting civic trust, for instance, this calls for the establishment of participatory procedures. A minimum level of respect for democratic, participatory rights is a precondition of the successful implementation of these measures. Both the struggles for recognition that are often required to establish a reparations program for victims (which involves the mobilization of significant public resources on behalf of groups that have traditionally been marginalized) and the attainment of the desired levels of civic trust (which involves establishing the currency of shared norms) require the institutionalization of forms of political contestation that secures the space for voices to emerge and have a chance of swaying others. In other words, this calls not just for the establishment and strengthening of the rule of law as formalists conceive of it but also for the strengthening of democratic forms of collective problem resolution.[69]

As justice measures, then, instruments of transitional justice should be understood as contributing to democratization. Democracy is valuable both inherently (as an expression of individual autonomy) and as a means for citizens to give concrete content to their understanding of justice by means of law. Of course, transitional justice cannot bring about democracy on its own, and its contribution, even under the best of circumstances, will be modest and one of many, many factors on which the fate of democracy will turn.[70]

IV

Having presented this normative conception of transitional justice in part around its mediate and final goals, I would like to conclude the chapter by showing how this conception not only helps to set some order to a discussion that has taken shape in a disorganized fashion within the field but also furthers the articulation of a compelling position in that debate. The discussion spins around a basic but fundamental question, namely, What type of justice is transitional justice? The question is sometimes raised by querying the sense of the qualifier "transitional" in the expression "transitional justice." Ultimately, the issue at stake, I think, is how to account for the fact that, in the wake of massive abuses, some of the "ordinary" expectations concerning what justice requires will not be satisfied. The discussion, such as there has been, can be organized into two different camps. One position accounts for the displacement of ordinary expectations by arguing that there is something distinctive called "transitional justice," which differs from ("ordinary") justice. Ruti Teitel's approach, which I discuss later, is a very influential example of this strategy but certainly not the only one.[71] Another tack is to say simply that transitional justice constitutes a compromise and then to discuss the nature of that compromise, either approvingly[72] or critically,[73] an approach to which I will return. Both of these positions (which end up sharing more than one may think at first) are problematic, for reasons I will explain. I therefore advance a third approach, according to which transitional justice is neither in itself a distinctive form of justice nor a mere compromise but rather a principled *application* of justice in distinct circumstances.

The "distinctive thesis," as one may call it, insists, to use Teitel's words, that "justice in periods of political change is extraordinary," that "the conception of justice that emerges [during periods of transition] is contextualized and partial," that "what is deemed just is contingent and informed by prior injustice."[74] Supporting this set of claims takes up the bulk of her book. Her strategy is to demonstrate that, at each of the levels of justice that she addresses, in transitional periods, legal mechanisms take on a more complex role than they have under "normal" circumstances.[75] The distinctiveness of transitional justice can be seen, then, Teitel argues, by fixing on its greater temporal complexity. She argues that whereas, under normal circumstances, legal mechanisms are *either* backward-looking (criminal, reparatory, and administrative justice) *or* forward-looking (rule of law measures and constitutionalism), the same legal mechanisms under conditions of transition become *both* retrospective *and* prospective. Thus, for instance, although criminal justice is "conventionally" conceived in backward-looking, retributivist terms, in periods of transition it also adopts a forward-looking, consequentialist character that can be seen, among other things, in the fact that transitional societies make efforts to use criminal justice, to the extent that they do, to draw a line between the new and the old regimes.

There is no question that the role of law in transitions is close to what Teitel suggests. It is questionable, however, whether this captures what makes transitional justice distinctive. It seems that the strategy forces her to mischaracterize the nature of law in non-transitional situations, for, after all, isn't law by its very essence always and inevitably as Janus-faced as Teitel suggests it is only in transitions? Law has a prospective, teleological dimension in that we pass laws in order to achieve certain goals. But, legitimate law is also always penetrated by ethical and moral concerns and constraints that give it another equally inevitable dimension, and this one includes a retrospective element.[76] Teitel's characterizations of law under normal circumstances are dubious: it is not that there is a great deal of consensus among either scholars or citizens about the fact that criminal, reparatory, and administrative justice ought to be conceived of as essentially retrospective or that the rule of law and constitutionalism ought to be thought of in essentially prospective terms. Posner and Vermeule provide plenty of examples of non-transitional judicial systems that have adopted the sort of dual complexity Teitel thinks of as the mark of the distinctive, "extraordinary" nature of transitional justice.[77]

One of the dangers of emphasizing the "distinctness" of transitional justice is that carving out different types of justice (and not just in terms of the familiar subject-based categories such as "distributive" justice or "corrective" justice but in terms of contexts such as "transitions," which in principle fall under the same general conception of justice) is that it defeats the very purpose of having overarching normative categories that are supposed to provide guidance across a variety of contexts. In the end, the move points in the direction of a type of casuistry in which no general principles are of use and normative guidance becomes subordinated to a type of contextualism that merges with common sense.

This problem, not surprisingly, afflicts Teitel's work; if one asks what her theory of *transitional* justice yields, the answer is disappointing. In one of the clearest statements of her position in the concluding chapter of her book, Teitel writes: "there is no single correct response to a state's repressive past. Which response is appropriate in any given regime's transition is contingent on a number of factors—the affected society's legacies of injustice, its legal culture, and political traditions—as well as on the exigencies of its transitional political circumstances."[78] This is uncontroversially correct. But surely one does not need sophisticated philosophical footwork to come to such a conclusion. Teitel is assuredly correct in thinking that transitional situations are particularly complex and that such complexity is fraught with perils, and she illustrates some of these hard choices effectively. However, while a descriptive account of transitions can acceptably stop at this point, a *theory* of transitional justice cannot afford such luxury. In addition to pointing out that politics and history are relevant, a theory is supposed to provide some guidance with respect to which of the compromises that politics and history seem to force upon us are legitimate and which are not.

The problem with carving up a general conception of justice in this way—like the problem with carving up a general conception of truth in analogous ways, as some authors in the field are also wont to do in talking about "historical" versus "forensic" versus other concepts of truth—is not merely that normative concepts lose their character (for they are stripped of their capacity to guide, to "norm" behavior) but also that, modifying the old fib that common sense is the least common of all senses to mean that it is the least *shared* of all senses, justice loses its capacity to provide shared solutions where they are needed the most, namely where societies are divided. Fragmentary conceptions of justice end up being of little use for societies in transition, not a small problem for a conception of "*transitional*" justice.

The second tack mentioned before for accounting for the fact that ordinary expectations of justice will not be satisfied by the implementation of transitional justice measures is to argue that transitional justice represents a compromise and, again, to react to this either approvingly or disapprovingly. This approach also generates difficulties of its own. In the first place, it seems to me to mischaracterize the reasons that have led various countries to adopt transitional justice measures; even if the implementation of such measures does not lead to the same results as would obtain under more ordinary circumstances, it is a bit glib to dismiss these reasons as simple compromises, as mere concessions to expedience. In the process, the stability and potential legitimacy of these choices are eroded.[79]

Second, and regardless of whether the compromise is regarded positively or negatively, this strategy depends upon emphasizing the continuities between transitional and ordinary justice to an extent that easily leads to a failure to acknowledge the significance of certain features of the transitional context, as well as of the function of transitional measures. This can be seen, for example, in Posner and Vermeule's effort to show the continuities between transitional justice and ordinary justice, which leads them to ignore the significance of transitional moments for the articulation and establishment of norms, values, and institutions, including those that both sustain and are sustained by legal systems of justice. This blind spot leads them to be indifferent to what I called the "semantic" dimension of transitional justice measures in section I of this chapter. To illustrate the point, when they argue that "restitution programs can be thought of as just another regulatory program—like the Endangered Species Act—or a transfer program that unsettles property rights in pursuit of some social goal[,]"[80] they seem to me to miss the crucial function that reparations programs are meant to play in helping draw a line between a past in which rights meant nothing or very little and a future in which rights do matter, a challenge and a function that the "ordinary regulatory program" normally does not face.

Finally, thinking about transitional justice as a compromise misunderstands the nature of the norms and principles that are allegedly compromised; as many have observed, international human rights law, particularly when it comes to remedies, has been formulated with the violation as a relatively isolated case in mind. That is, like most legal norms, these have been conceived for situations in which breaches are the exception rather than the norm. Insisting on a sort of mechanical application of these norms to situations of massive abuse (where what is critical is not simply a question of numbers but that the numbers manifest a breakdown of norms) ultimately risks rendering these norms irrelevant[81]—an ironic outcome, which converges with the indifference to norms that is a consequence of the first approach, as well.

In the end, as it should be obvious, these are instances of responses to the general question about the relationship between principle and context: one consists in prioritizing context and therefore either surrendering or modifying principles, and the other in leaving principles alone and not heeding context. As much as I object to arguments that characterize transitional justice as if it were a peculiar sort of justice, I take exception to those stances that fail to acknowledge that there is, indeed, something peculiar about the application of justice measures in transitional situations. But, then, is there a third alternative? Human rights defenders and transitional justice promoters should have an interest in preserving the relevance of general principles and norms such as those that establish obligations of justice, truth, and reparations as some of the relevant forms of redress for massive human rights violations. However, as the argumentative path I have taken reveals, for a conception that starts with accounts of what I have called a very imperfect world and of the nature of social relations in such a world (the description of "unreconciled" societies), context does matter. There is no question that temporal and other complexity is a characteristic both of the application and of the making of law in general and a fortiori both of transitional and non-transitional settings.[82] However, it is just as certain that the types of constraints and, indeed, the sorts of needs that law is expected to satisfy are distinctive in transitional contexts. The question, then, is how to establish the relationship between principle and context in such a way that principles stand, that they can offer guidance, without being blind to context. We need principles both to guide our choices and to account for and react to the abiding claims for justice during and even after transitional justice measures have been implemented.[83] But we need principles that will guide action in a way that is sensitive to context.

Here I think that the distinction between the justification and the application of norms becomes particularly useful.[84] This is not the place to attempt a justification of the general norms on which rest the obligations to provide remedies that include criminal justice, truth, and reparations for the violations of human rights—nor does the particular debate at issue require it, for the defenders of the two approaches I am considering do not call these into question, at least not directly. The question is how to understand that these general norms will be applied in one way when the case at issue is an isolated violation in an otherwise operative justice system and quite differently in a situation where massive violations have taken place. There is no question that there is a difference: in one case perpetrators will be prosecuted; that process will reveal the truth of what happened; the victim will be repaired in proportion to the harm suffered; and other administrative measures may also be taken. In the other case, it is highly unlikely that for each violation any of these things will take place. Part of my work in this field has consisted in the articulation of criteria of justice for different transitional justice measures, that is, criteria that justice measures can satisfy in the peculiar circumstances of a transition.[85] I do not think of these either as parts of a distinct conception of justice ("transitional justice" as if it were a separate conception apart from a general understanding of justice) or as mere compromises, concessions to expediency; rather, I see them as the articulation of what a general understanding of justice could mean when applied to the peculiar circumstances of a very imperfect world, that is, a world that satisfies two conditions: massive rule breakdown and great risks to the institutions that attempt to overcome such breakdowns. I take it that, in contexts characterized by these two conditions, legal remedies are instruments to make victims whole to the extent possible *but also* instruments for the constitution or reconstitution of a legally mediated system of justice as such.

From this standpoint, then, the "transitional" in "transitional justice" does not qualify justice, so the expression does not refer to a *distinctive* or peculiar type of justice. Strictly speaking, then, the expression is infelicitous, and it would be more appropriate to speak of "justice in times of transition" if one insists on using the expression "transitions" at all. The principles and norms of justice need not be changed in order to be applied in a way that is sensitive to context, and thereby their integrity and capacity to guide are preserved. But that does not mean that the principles and norms are "mechanically" applied either, that context does not matter, or that whatever is done in this area is a mere compromise. What changes is a matter of application, not only in the narrow sense of implementation but in the more fundamental sense of coming to an understanding of what it is reasonable to expect the principles in question to imply under specific circumstances. This is how the conception of transitional justice I have presented here emerged: as neither an alternative to the requirements of ordinary justice nor mere concessions to reality—as the normative nature of the conception reveals. Thinking that, strictly speaking, there is no such thing as "transitional justice" but only conceptions of what justice means when applied to transitional situations has two additional implications. First, the (successful) implementation of (thorough and legitimate) transitional justice measures *is* an

instance of justice.[86] Second, the implementation of these measures, even if successful, generates commitments that will likely remain unfulfilled in the immediate period of transition. Hence the
unfinished quest for justice in different dimensions (e.g., punitive,
compensatory) that has become a fixture in "post-transitional"
countries, which in my mind provides yet another incentive for
thinking about transitional justice as one stage in the search for
justice (and, indeed, one that enables later stages).

Concluding Remarks

In this chapter, I have presented a normative theoretical conception of transitional justice. The purpose of articulating such a
conception is the one that normally underlies the construction of
theoretical accounts, namely to draw systematic links between diverse phenomena and in this way to contribute to dispelling puzzlement. In this particular case, the "phenomena" that required
linking, are, first, the elements that are commonly understood to
be a part of a transitional justice policy, and second, the concept
of transitional justice and reconciliation on the one hand and democracy on the other. According to the conception I presented, in
addition to their own immediate aims, a first exercise in abstraction allows one to argue that the elements of transitional justice
share two "mediate" aims, namely providing a complex type of
recognition to victims and promoting civic trust. Abstracting yet
again allows one to argue that a comprehensive transitional justice
policy also has two "final" aims, namely promoting reconciliation
and strengthening democracy. This theoretical construct, then, is
supposed to ground the claim that transitional justice is a "holistic" concept.

   The philosophical strategy that I have used is to make this construct "normative" not just in the ordinary sense that contrasts with
"descriptive" (i.e., relating to how things *ought to be*) but in the
more specific sense of norm-based; the task, then, is to draw links
between norm-based accounts of recognition, civic trust, reconciliation, and democracy, something that I hope the chapter shows
to be both feasible and productive. Finally, the chapter shows how
such a normative conception contributes to clarifying the nature
of transitional justice, not as a distinct form of justice (the relevant

norms are familiar basic norms) or as a mere compromise but as
the articulation of the requirements of a general understanding
of justice when applied to the peculiar circumstances of a very imperfect world, that is, a world characterized by massive rule breakdown and great risks to the institutions that attempt to overcome
such breakdowns.

NOTES

I received useful comments on an earlier draft of this chapter from my colleagues at the International Center for Transitional Justice (ICTJ), Paige
Arthur, Louis Bickford, Roger Duthie, Mark Freeman, Michael Reed, Al-
exander Mayer-Rieckh, Debra Schultz, and Juan Méndez. Craig Calhoun
was generous in his reactions to the text, as were Anthony Duff, Sam Is-
sacharoff, Thomas McCarthy, Claus Offe, Max Pensky, Ruth Rubio, Pauls
Seils, Margaret Walker, Harvey Weinstein, Leif Wenar, and Pepe Zalaquett.
I presented earlier versions of the chapter at the Center for Ethics in
Public Life at Cornell University; to the members of the Human Rights/
Transitional Justice Network in Spain organized by FRIDE, ICTJ, and the
Human Rights Institute at Deusto; to audiences in Florence, Italy, both at
the European University Institute and at NYU's Conference Center at La
Pietra; and at the Political Theory Workshop at Yale. Melissa Williams and
Rosemary Nagy were both helpful and insightful in their comments on the
chapter. My gratitude to all. The views presented here are not necessarily
those of the ICTJ. Needless to say, remaining infelicities, grammatical and
substantive, are mine alone.

1. S/2004/616, August 23, 2004. Other important international documents on transitional justice and related topics include: UN Commission
on Human Rights, *Updated Set of Principles for the Protection and Promotion
of Human Rights Through Action to Combat Impunity*, E/CN.4/2005/102/
Add.1, February 8, 2005, and the accompanying reports by Diane Orentlicher, *Independent Study on Best Practices, Including Recommendations, to Assist
States in Strengthening Their Domestic Capacity to Combat All Aspects of Impunity*, E/CN.4/2004/88, February 27, 2004, and *Report of the Independent
Expert to Update the Set of Principles to Combat Impunity*, E/CN.4/2005/102,
February 18, 2005; UN General Assembly, *Basic Principles and Guidelines on
the Right to a Remedy and Reparation for Victims of Gross Violations of International Human Rights Law and Serious Violations of International Humanitar-
ian Law*, A/RES/60/147, March 21, 2006, and the UN Office of the High
Commissioner of Human Rights' entire series of "Rule of Law Tools for
Post-Conflict States" on various transitional justice measures. The binding

character of these documents is a separate question that I will not address here. It varies tremendously from case to case.

2. UN Secretary General, "The Rule of Law and Transitional Justice in Conflict and Post-Conflict Societies," 4.

3. Ibid., see, e.g., summary and 4.

4. Ibid., 9.

5. For (divergent) accounts of the history of transitional justice practices, see, e.g., Jon Elster, *Closing the Books* (Cambridge: Cambridge University Press, 2004), and Ruti Teitel, "Human Rights Genealogy," *Fordham Law Review* 66 (1997): 301–17, and "Transitional Justice Genealogy," *Harvard Human Rights Journal* 16 (2003): 69–94.

6. Editors' note: see the contribution by David Cohen and Leigh-Ashley Lipscomb in this volume for a critical account of the flaws in using multiple transitional justice mechanisms in East Timor.

7. See, e.g., Elster, *Closing the Books*, xi, 76–77, 137.

8. David A. Crocker, "Reckoning with Past Wrongs: A Normative Framework," *Ethics and International Affairs* 13, no. 1 (March 1999): 43–64, and "Transitional Justice and International Civil Society: Toward a Normative Framework," *Constellations* 5 (1998): 492–517.

9. These goals, according to Crocker, include truth-telling; creation of a platform for victims; accountability and punishment; the promotion of the rule of law; compensation; institutional reform and development; reconciliation; and the strengthening of public deliberation.

10. See e.g., Ruti Teitel, *Transitional Justice* (Oxford: Oxford University Press, 2000), which takes it for granted that the familiar legal responses to the violation of rights define the notion and concentrates, instead, on the question of whether these responses are "extraordinary" —that is, whether or not transitional justice is a distinctive conception of justice. The same can be said of Eric Posner and Adrian Vermeule, "Transitional Justice as Ordinary Justice," *Harvard Law Review* 117 (2004): 762–825.

11. On the difference between a general concept and a "conception," see, e.g., John Rawls, *A Theory of Justice* (Cambridge, MA: Harvard University Press, 1971), 5.

12. This theoretical construct can also have a salutary practical consequence in helping us articulate criteria of success in the implementation of transitional justice measures, a complex topic that I cannot address here. It goes without saying, however, that the ends that are attributed to particular policy interventions affect the way these measures are assessed. So, having an account of why it makes sense to attribute certain goals to particular measures is, in my opinion, a necessary step on the way to assessment. Here I can only add the following. The normative model I offer here would lead to the articulation of indices of success around recognition (for which participation can be taken as a proxy), of trust (for which

appeals to formal procedures of conflict resolution can stand), of reconciliation (trust in institutions plus attitudinal shifts), and of democratization ("formal" rule of law and political participation).

13. Pablo de Greiff, "Trials and Punishment: Pardon and Oblivion. On
Two Inadequate Policies for the Treatment of Former Human Rights Abusers," *Philosophy and Social Criticism* 22, no. 3 (May 1996): 93–112.

14. Obviously, describing the primary domain of application of the term
is not the same thing as describing an end-state; as will become clear in
what follows, the point of implementing transitional justice measures is to
make use of their "transformational" potential in order to make the world
not perfect but at least merely imperfect (as opposed to very imperfect).

15. See, e.g., David Miller, "Justice," in *Blackwell Encyclopedia of Political
Thought* (London: Wiley-Blackwell, 1991), 260–63.

16. See my "Addressing the Past: Reparations for Gross Human Rights
Violations," in *Civil War and the Rule of Law: Security, Development, Human
Rights*, ed. Agnés Hurwitz and Reyko Huang (Boulder, CO: Lynne Rienner,
2007), 163–92.

17. See, for example, the results of the research directed by Harvey
Weinstein and Eric Stover in *My Neighbor, My Enemy: Justice and Community in the Aftermath of Mass Atrocity* (New York: Cambridge University Press,
2004). In this book, an interdisciplinary group of experts explores both
the potential and the limitations of the ICTY and ICTR and persuasively
makes the case that international tribunals work best in conjunction with
a variety of other measures, including local initiatives more attentive to
social integration and reconstruction and to the needs and wishes of those
more directly affected by violence.

18. Comisión para el Esclarecimiento Histórico (CEH), Informe de la
Comisión para el Esclarecimiento Histórico. Guatemala, *Memoria del Si-
lencio* (Guatemala: UNOPS, 1999). See also Oficina de Derechos Huma-
nos del Arzobispado de Guatemala, Informe del Proyecto Interdiocesano
"Recuperación de la Memoria Histórica," Guatemala, *Nunca Más* (Guatemala, 1998).

19. From 1999 to 2001, the Independent Arbitration Instance (Instance
indépendante d'arbitrage [IIA]) operated in Morocco as a stand-alone
compensation procedure. It heard testimony from approximately 8,000
people and reached decisions in 5,488 cases, granting monetary awards
in 3,681 of those. In January 2006, after two years of operation, the Equity
and Reconciliation Commission (Instance Équité et Réconciliation [IER])
made its report public, including its decisions concerning reparations. In
this instance, reparations were part and parcel of a transitional justice policy (a transition without regime change in the standard sense, however)
that linked truth-telling and reparations closely. Furthermore, unlike the
IIA, which provided monetary compensation alone, the IER established

a program involving services, including health benefits, plus plans for a large collective reparations program targeting areas that had suffered in various ways during the reign of Hassan II.

20. Hebe Bonafini, leader of the Asociación Madres de la Plaza de Mayo in Argentina, long took the position that the only satisfactory response to their justice claims was the reappearance of their children and that therefore accepting other measures, including reparations, constituted a sell-out—a position that led to the breakdown of the Madres de la Plaza de Mayo into two different movements. The Moroccan experience with the Instance indépendante d'arbitrage referred to earlier illustrates how reparations measures delinked from other justice initiatives can prove to be unsatisfactory even if one does not hold Bonafini's hard-line position. See, e.g., Susan Slymovic, "No Buying Off the Past: Moroccan Indemnities and the Opposition," *Middle East Report* 229 (2003): 34–37.

21. The difference between mere compensation and reparation is that reparations, in order to be understood as such, must be accompanied by some sort of acknowledgment of responsibility (which need not be an acknowledgment of culpability).

22. See my "Justice and Reparations," in *The Handbook of Reparations*, ed. Pablo de Greiff (New York: Oxford University Press, 2006), 451–77, for an elaboration of the notions of internal and external coherence in transitional justice programming.

23. Thus, for instance, truth commissions serve victims by giving them a platform from which to voice their stories publicly for the first time and serve the interests of history by creating a credible record.

24. Since the argument moves at a higher level of abstraction and is not concerned with the immediate, specific goals of each of the transitional justice measures, presumably it is compatible with a range of accounts of what those immediate goals are. That range, however, is not infinite. There may well be accounts of the immediate goals of these measures that clash with the account of the mediate and final goals I offer here.

25. Given the explicitly normative nature of the conception, it of course cannot rest primarily upon observation, on pain of committing a naturalistic fallacy. The argument does not move from "is" to "ought." It is reassuring, however, that the goals the conception insists the measures should pursue can be observed to be attainable (at least to some degree) through their implementation. Though beyond my scope here, the implementation of transitional justice measures in Chile appear to have been modestly successful in this respect.

26. Of course, this is a defeasible presumption. The argument is not intended to show that isolated measures will never work.

27. In this sense, the argument militates against those who argue that prosecutions, truth-telling, reparations, and institutional reform are con-

tingent parts of a comprehensive transitional justice policy. If these measures are systematically related to justice, the presumption in favor of thinking them a part of transitional justice strengthens.

28. To the extent that presenting a conception is related to offering a "definition," the earlier statement has elements of a "descriptive definition," that is, one that captures how a term is used in fact (people do use the term to refer to measures implemented to deal with the legacies of massive human rights violations), and of both an "intensional" and an "ostensive" definition. The statement is "intensional" in the sense that it gestures in the direction of the threshold conditions that something has to satisfy in order to be a transitional justice measure, namely having as a point reestablishing the force of the human rights norms whose systematic violation characterized the predecessor regime. But it also has an ostensive element in the sense that it points to some of the measures that have been used in the past in order to achieve this end. In insightful comments on an earlier version of this chapter, Paige Arthur asked whether I am trying to define transitional justice in terms of constituent measures or in terms of its goals. In a sense, neither (for I do not take the fundamental task anymore to consist of offering a definition of transitional justice), and in a sense, both (for the measures and the goals are related in many ways—including the way in which intension and ostension are related: these measures are precisely such that they can be thought to be norm-affirming in the relevant sense). It is true, however, that my approach takes norm-affirmation as a goal to be fundamental for understanding transitional justice.

29. In attributing these four ends to transitional justice measures, in thinking about these ends as parts of causal chains and, as is inevitable, in having to order the presentation of the goals in some way, I am not suggesting that there are necessary causal relations between the different aims. In particular, I do not want to suggest that, say, providing recognition sets off a causal chain that leads to democratization, as will become obvious later on.

30. On the notion of recognition, see, among other things, Axel Honneth, *The Struggle for Recognition: The Moral Grammar of Social Conflicts* (Cambridge: MIT Press, 1995), his part of Axel Honneth and Nancy Fraser, *Redistribution or Recognition: A Political-Philosophical Exchange* (New York: Verso, 2003), and the papers by various authors, plus two thoughtful responses by Honneth, in *Recognition and Power*, ed. Bert Van Den Brink and David Owen (New York: Cambridge University Press, 2007). This section on recognition and the following one, on civic trust, track closely arguments I first made in "Justice and Reparations."

31. For examples and illuminating analyses of such strategies, see the issue on moral exclusion and injustice in *The Journal of Social Issues* 46, no. 1 (1990).

32. Onora O'Neill offers a compelling constructivist account of practical

reason. In her view, questions of moral standing—such as who deserves consideration—are better settled by focusing on the presuppositions of action. Most of our actions presuppose what she calls "plurality" and "connection"; when we act, we presuppose that there are others who can be affected by what we do and make further assumptions about their capability to respond (and to suffer). But these very abstract presuppositions generate certain commitments. As she puts it, "when agents commit themselves to the assumption that there are certain others, who are agents or subjects with these or those capacities, capabilities, and vulnerabilities, they cannot coherently deny these assumptions in working out the scope of ethical consideration to which they are committed." Onora O'Neill, *Towards Justice and Virtue* (Cambridge: Cambridge University Press, 1996), 100.

33. See Jean Hampton, "The Moral Education Theory of Punishment," *Philosophy and Public Affairs* (1981): 209–38, "A New Theory of Retribution," in *Liability and Responsibility*, ed. R. G. Frey and Christopher W. Morris (Cambridge: Cambridge University Press, 1991), 377–414, and her essays in Jeffrie Murphy and Jean Hampton, *Forgiveness and Mercy* (Cambridge: Cambridge University Press, 1988).

34. See Lawrence Weschler, "Afterword," in *State Crimes: Punishment or Pardon*, Aspen Institute Report (Washington, D.C., 1989).

35. Joel Feinberg, for example, argues that there are two different ways of understanding "harms": (1) harm as a setback to interests, and (2) harm as a wrong to another person. Only the latter is relevant to the law. See his *Harm to Others*, vol. 1 of *The Moral Limits of the Criminal Law* (Oxford: Oxford University Press, 1987), 31–36. Recognizing victims as rights-bearers obviously accentuates the normative dimension of recognition.

36. Failures, including through partiality and bias, lack of due process, or exclusion and inequitable treatment of groups of perpetrators or victims, can all be illustrated with real experiences.

37. Annette Baier, "Trust and Its Vulnerabilities," in her *Moral Prejudices* (Cambridge, MA: Harvard University Press, 1994), 133. I initially adopt Baier's characterization of trust but not the details of her conception.

38. See Laurence Mordekhai Thomas, "Power, Trust, and Evil," in *Overcoming Racism and Sexism*, ed. Linda Bell and David Blumenfeld (Lanham, MD: Rowman and Littlefield, 1995), 160.

39. Claus Offe, "How Can We Trust Our Fellow Citizens?" in *Democracy and Trust*, ed. Mark Warren (Cambridge: Cambridge University Press, 1999), 70–71.

40. Ibid.

41. See Pablo de Greiff, "Truth-Telling and the Rule of Law," in *Telling the Truths: Truth Telling and Peace Building in Post-Conflict Societies*, ed. Tristan Anne Borer (Notre Dame, IN: University of Notre Dame Press, 2006), 181–206.

42. See de Greiff, "Justice and Reparations."

43. See Pablo de Greiff, "Vetting and Transitional Justice," in *Justice as Prevention: Vetting Public Employees in Transitional Societies*, ed. Alexander Mayer-Rieckh and Pablo de Greiff (New York: Social Science Research Council, 2007), 522–45.

44. Insisting on the centrality of rights (as opposed to losses, for example) for transitional justice has practical consequences, including in the assignment of roles to each notion in reparations programs. For an argument that rights-centered programs can use the notion of losses but in an "external" role (i.e., to help craft benefits but not to justify or trigger them), see Ruth Rubio Marín and Pablo de Greiff, "Women and Reparations," *International Journal of Transitional Justice* 1, no. 3 (2007): 318–37.

45. As Jürgen Habermas puts the point, "The legal medium as such presupposes rights that define the status of legal persons as bearers of rights." *Between Facts and Norms*, trans. William Rehg (Cambridge, MA: MIT Press, 1996), 119. See also Habermas, "On Legitimation Through Human Rights," in *Global Justice and Transnational Politics*, ed. Ciaran Cronin and Pablo de Greiff (Cambridge: MIT Press, 2002), 197–214.

46. For an elaboration of this argument see my "Truth-Telling and the Rule of Law."

47. This is a good point to reiterate two sets of caveats. First, this is not a predictive claim; implementing transitional justice measures does not guarantee the achievement of either reconciliation or democracy. Second, to say that reconciliation and democratization are final ends of transitional justice does not mean that these are the sole reasons for the sake of which the measures ought to be implemented.

48. Margaret Urban Walker, chap. 4, "Resentment and Assurance" and chap. 3, "Damages to Trust," in her *Moral Repair: Reconstructing Moral Relations After Wrongdoing* (Cambridge: Cambridge University Press, 2006).

49. Cf. P. F. Strawson, "Freedom and Resentment," in his *Studies in the Philosophy of Thought and Action* (Oxford: Oxford University Press, 1968), chap. 1.

50. Walker, "Resentment and Assurance," 146.

51. See, e.g., Elaine Scarry, *The Body in Pain* (Oxford: Oxford University Press, 1987), and Lawrence Weschler, *A Miracle, A Universe* (Chicago: University of Chicago Press, 1998).

52. See Walker, "Damages to Trust."

53. See de Greiff, "The Role of Apologies in National Reconciliation Processes: On Making Trustworthy Institutions Trusted," in *The Age of Apologies*, ed. Mark Gibney, Rhoda Howard-Hassmann, Jean-Marc Coicaud, and Niklaus Steiner (Philadelphia: University of Pennsylvania Press, 2008), 120–36, which this section tracks, for further elaboration of the position and the relevant arguments.

54. Apologies may play an important role in aiding the required attitudinal transformation, as I argue in "The Role of Apologies."

55. I am particularly grateful to Craig Calhoun, Rosemary Nagy, Margaret Walker, Leif Wenar, and Melissa Williams for pushing me on the content of this section.

56. Sketching that broader argument would take us too far afield. For some of the relevant literature, however, see Habermas, *Between Facts and Norms*; Ian Shapiro, *Democratic Justice* (New Haven: Yale University Press, 2006).

57. See, for example, United Nations Security Council, *From Madness to Hope: The 12-Year War in El Salvador: Report of the Commission on the Truth for El Salvador*, S/25500 (1993), part V, "Recommendations"; Truth and Reconciliation Commission, "Institutional Hearing: The Legal Community," in *Truth and Reconciliation Commission of South Africa Report* (London: Macmillan Reference Limited, 1998), esp. vol. 4, chap. 4; Comisión de Verdad y Reconciliación, Perú, "Los factores que hicieron posible la violencia," tomo VIII, segunda parte, in *Informe Final* (Lima: Comisión de Verdad y Reconciliación, 2003), esp. chap. 1, part 4.

58. Even Ruti Teitel, who argues that during times of transition the notion of the rule of law becomes "extraordinary," makes the concept an important part of her work. See, for example, her "Transitional Jurisprudence: The Role of Law in Political Transformation," *Yale Law Journal* 106, no. 7 (1997): 2009–80.

59. In "Truth-Telling and the Rule of Law," however, I canvass some of the ways in which truth-telling, in particular, may be thought to promote the rule of law.

60. On the importance of the idea of publicity, see the beautiful essay by Onora O'Neill, "The Public Use of Reason," in her *Constructions of Reason* (New York: Cambridge University Press, 1992), 28–50.

61. Rawls, *A Theory of Justice*, 207.

62. Joseph Raz, "The Rule of Law and its Virtue," in his *The Authority of Law* (Oxford: Oxford University Press, 1979), 208.

63. Take, for example, the "liberal-minded despot" in Isaiah Berlin, "Two Concepts of Liberty," in *Four Essays on Liberty* (Oxford: Oxford University Press, 1969), 129. Berlin's despot is "unjust, . . . encourage[s] the wildest inequalities, care[s] little for order, or virtue, or knowledge" but leaves his subjects "a wide area of liberty . . . or at least curb[s] it less than other regimes."

64. See, e.g., Christian Davenport and David Armstrong, "Democracy and the Violation of Human Rights: A Statistical Analysis from 1976–1996," *American Journal of Political Science* 48, 3 (2004): 538–54. Just to reiterate the obvious, particular democracies have shown themselves to be capable of violating particular human rights as much as other kinds of regimes. This

discussion of the empirical relationship between democracy and human
rights would be further strengthened by a consideration of the distinctions
between different types of democratic regimes and of attempts to assess
the "quality" of democracy, but this would take us far afield. For an illuminating and sobering sample of this literature, see, however, Guillermo
O'Donnell, "Polyarchies and the (Un)rule of Law in Latin America: A Partial Conclusion," in *The (Un)Rule of Law and the Underprivileged in Latin
America*, ed. Juan Méndez, Guillermo O'Donnell, and Paulo Sergio Pin-
heiro (Notre Dame: University of Notre Dame Press, 1999), 303–38.

65. For the way in which this worked out in Peru, for example, see Lisa
Magarrell and Julie Guillerot, *Reparaciones en la Transición Peruana: Memo-
rias de un Proceso Inacabado* (Lima: APRODEH, ICTJ, OXFAM, 2006), esp.
chap. 6. In virtually every country in which a transitional justice measure
is proposed, civil society organizations and even coalitions of NGOs follow
shortly thereafter.

66. As Arendt put it, "[t]otalitarian government, like all tyrannies, certainly could not exist without destroying the public realm of life, that is,
without destroying, by isolating men, their political capacities." Hannah
Arendt, *The Origins of Totalitarianism*, 2nd ed. (New York: Meridian Books,
1958), 475.

67. The most convincing account of this relationship between democracy and the rule of law is offered by Jürgen Habermas in "On the Internal Relationship Between the Rule of Law and Democracy," in *The Inclusion of the Other*, ed. Ciaran Cronin and Pablo de Greiff (Cambridge: MIT
Press, 1998), 253–64, and in "On Legitimation Through Human Rights,"
in *Global Justice and Transnational Politics*, ed. Pablo de Greiff and Ciaran
Cronin (Cambridge, MA: MIT Press, 2002), 197–214. I track some of the
relevant arguments in my "Habermas on Nationalism and Cosmopolitan-
ism," *Ratio Juris* 15, no. 4 (2002): 418–38.

68. Raz, *The Authority of Law*, 102.

69. Some actors in the transitional justice field have, indeed, been
mindful of the connection between democracy and the rule of law; thus,
for example, the Truth Commission for El Salvador stated explicitly: "democracy loses ground when human rights are not fully respected; human
rights cannot be protected from arbitrariness without the rule of law which
is the expression of the democratic system of government." United Nations Security Council, From Madness to Hope, 174. Some international
organizations, such as the Council of Europe, the European Union, and
the Organization for Security and Cooperation in Europe, and the United
Nations Development Programme have also adopted expansive conceptions of the rule of law that explicitly draw a link between legality and
legitimacy and between legitimacy and democracy. It would not be bad for
transitional justice theorists to catch up.

70. It would be good for human rights activists to relinquish their Cold War–rooted reservations about articulating more clearly the relationship between human rights and democracy. During the Cold War, human rights activists made the (correct) choice to concentrate on denouncing abuses, rather than on promoting political change. To this positive reason a negative one was added, namely antipathy to what was (again correctly) perceived to be a U.S. government agenda. Some of the relevant conditions that made these judgments correct have changed, however, and therefore now is a good time to assert the relevance of the links between human rights and democracy. An additional rationale for doing so, moreover, is to take back the democracy-promotion agenda from the grips of security concerns and return it to the arena of justice imperatives.

71. André du Toit, for example, defends the South African approach to transitional justice by arguing that it formulated distinctive conceptions of justice and of truth. See "The Moral Foundations of the South African TRC: Truth as Acknowledgment and Justice as Recognition," in *Truth v. Justice: The Morality of Truth Commissions*, ed. Robert Rotberg and Dennis Thompson (Princeton: Princeton University Press, 2000), 122–40.

72. Jonathan Allen, in his "Balancing Justice and Social Unity: Political Theory and the Idea of a Truth and Reconciliation Commission," *University of Toronto Law Journal* 49 (1999): 315–54, presents a strong argument for thinking about the South African approach to transitional justice as a principled compromise.

73. See, especially, some of the earlier criticisms of transitional justice, which concededly, at the time, consisted mostly of the establishment of truth commissions; for example, Reed Brody, "Justice: The First Casualty of Truth?," *The Nation*, April 30, 2001, http://hrw.org/english/docs/2001/04/30/global12849.htm.

74. Teitel, *Transitional Justice*, 6.

75. There is a second strand of the argument that Teitel unfortunately does not develop, which is a shame, both because from my perspective it offered greater prospects of success but also because it would have constituted a truly important contribution. According to this tack, in transitional situations law per force has to broaden its attention from its usual focus on questions of individual responsibility to issues of collective responsibility. Regrettably, just as there is no sustained analysis of the notion of justice anywhere in the book, there is none of the notion of collective responsibility. But, whereas the familiarity of the former concept makes this omission less than fatal—although undesirable nevertheless—the absence of even well-settled intuitions about the latter concept deprives this second tack of the strategy of much of the plausibility it could have had.

76. In *Between Facts and Norms*, Habermas offers a systematic analysis of law of precisely this type, showing that complexity of the temporal sort

that Teitel attributes to transitional justice is a characteristic of both the application and the making of law. See esp. chaps. 3, 4, and 9.

77. Posner and Vermeule, "Transitional Justice as Ordinary Justice."

78. Teitel, Transitional Justice, 219.

79. Hence the efforts to meet this strategy half way by acknowledging that there is a compromise involved and yet arguing that this is a morally legitimate compromise. The most compelling version of this argument is still Allen, "Balancing Justice and Social Unity."

80. Posner and Vermeule, "Transitional Justice as Ordinary Justice," 786.

81. This can happen for many reasons, which include the following: the norms may be unsatisfiable under the specific circumstances of a transition; they may generate expectations that will condemn any viable alternative; or they may, given their nature, mischaracterize the task of justice initiatives in a transition, which, in contrast to the ordinary situation, in addition to making victims whole, must be the constitution or reconstitution of systems of justice.

82. The list of authors other than Habermas who could be cited in support of the complexity of law-making even in well-established societies is extensive. See, for example, Paul W. Kahn, *Legitimacy and History* (New Haven: Yale University Press, 1992), x. Kahn starts his book with the claim that "at the center of American constitutional discourse has been a focus on the problem of temporality within a system of self government" and that, as constitutional theory, his work is "an inquiry into the political problem of time."

83. Chile, in particular, constitutes an important example of the partiality of even arguably successful applications of transitional justice measures; the struggle for justice along different dimensions—criminal punishment, reparations, and even truth—did not cease with the TRC or even with the implementation of its recommendations.

84. As Klaus Günther puts it, it is important to distinguish "on the one hand, justifying a norm by showing that there are reasons, of whatever kind, to accept it, and on the other, relating a norm to a situation by inquiring whether and how it fits the situation, whether there are not other norms which ought to be preferred in this situation, or whether the proposed norm would not have to be changed in view of the situation." Günther, *The Sense of Appropriateness: Application Discourses in Morality and Law*, trans. John Farrell (Albany: State University of New York Press, 1993), and Jürgen Habermas, "Remarks on Discourse Ethics," in *Justification and Application*, trans. Ciaran Cronin (Cambridge, MA: MIT Press, 1993), esp. 35–39.

85. The main thrust of my work on reparations, for instance, consists of an articulation of a conception of justice fit for cases of massive abuse, as distinct from what I take to be the unimpeachable principle of *restitutio*

in integrum applied in the relatively isolated and judicially resolved case of a human rights violation in an otherwise operative legal system. See, e.g., "Justice and Reparations."

86. In this sense, for example, a responsible exercise of prosecutorial discretion that leads to fewer prosecutions than would have obtained in different circumstances, given not just the number of victims but the obviously systematic nature of the violations, is not, from this perspective, a "second best" outcome if evidence that would stand in court is simply unavailable, or if trying to get it would threaten the transition itself, or if breaches of justice of sufficient gravity would be a predictable part of the effort to put more perpetrators under trial, provided, of course, that these conditions really obtain and that other justice measures are also implemented. What is second (or third, or fourth, and so on) best is the context in which judicial action is expected to take place. There is no obvious failure in an outcome that fails to deliver "perfect" justice in a very imperfect world.

2

JUSTICE, TRUTH, PEACE

JON ELSTER

The mind seems to have a natural tendency to assume that all good things go together. This may be a result partly of what psychologists call "tradeoff aversion"[1] and partly of wishful thinking. Let me offer some examples.

Marx asserted that in the transition to Communism, one should try to "shorten and lessen the birth pangs."[2] For a given duration of the transition, less violence would obviously be desirable; for a given level of violence during the transition, the shorter it is, the better. But a more gradual transition might involve less violence.

The movement for "socially responsible investment" is based on the premise of "doing well by doing good."[3] In some cases, the profit motive and community benefits may indeed be maximized simultaneously, as when consumers refuse to buy goods produced with the use of child labor. Typically, however, mutual funds that refuse to buy alcohol and tobacco stocks do less well than others, because they cut themselves off from a valuable source of diversification.

Public policy is usually guided by concerns of distributive justice as well as efficiency. In practice, however, equity and efficiency may be at odds with each other, because of the problem of "the leaky bucket": when transferring wealth from a rich person to a poorer one, some wealth is usually destroyed (or not created).[4]

The French Revolution was based on the (mostly tacit) assumption that the values of equality, liberty, and fraternity supported and reinforced one another, so that more of one led to more of the others, not less. Although each of the three values is endlessly ambiguous, on many common understandings they are more likely to work against one another or limit one another than to favor one another. Radical thinkers claim that liberty is inconsistent with equality; libertarian thinkers that fraternity is inconsistent with liberty. Rawls claimed that strict equality was inconsistent with fraternity because it might make the worst-off worse off than they would be under a regime of moderate inequality.

In this chapter, I consider the relation among the aims of achieving *justice, truth,* and *peace* in *transitions from one political state to another.* I also address relations between *different forms of justice,* specifically between distributive and transitional justice. In part of the literature on these very diverse transitional issues there is an assumption, also usually tacit, that these values tend to support and promote one another. While this assumption may sometimes be justified, it can also lead us to neglect important tensions and to underestimate the need to make hard choices.

Although the bulk of the literature on transitions concerns transitions to *democracy* after an authoritarian or totalitarian regime,[5] there is an emergent understanding that questions of justice also arise in the transition to *peace.*[6] As I shall explain, these issues include but are not limited to transitional justice as traditionally conceived, notably punishment of wrongdoers and reparations to victims. In addition, transitions to peace involve stabilizing measures of various kinds to prevent the reemergence of conflict.

Whenever appropriate, I shall refer to current developments in Colombia, notably to the Justice and Peace Law (JPL).[7] As is well known, the Colombian situation is unique and highly complex. It involves not only the government and several insurgency groups but also paramilitary groups and drug lords. The highly opaque relations among these actors are determined by the interplay of money and violence, two currencies that in Colombia have been deployed in truly enormous quantities. Although these features may be unique, other aspects of the current situation in Colombia have much in common with what we observe in transitions elsewhere.

I shall proceed as follows. I first offer a few brief comments on, respectively, justice, truth, and peace, focusing both on the ideas themselves and on their value for individuals and for society. In doing so, my purpose is only to lay the necessary groundwork for later sections, not to undertake the impossibly ambitious task of providing a general analysis of these ideas and the reasons to value them. In the more substantive parts of the chapter, I address, first, the relation between *justice and truth*; second, that between *justice and peace*; third, that between *truth and peace*; and, finally, between *transitional and distributive justice*. I conclude by summarizing the main positive and negative relations among the three core concepts.

The idea of justice can be spelled out in many ways. For my purposes, the most important are distributive justice and various measures of transitional justice, notably retributive justice, restitutive justice, and compensatory justice. It is important to note that transitions to democracy or to peace may call not only for transitional justice but also for distributive justice. The need for distributive justice may come about in two ways. First, it may be as important to alleviate the suffering of non-targeted or "collateral" victims of conflict as to compensate targeted victims. Second, if distributive injustice, for instance in the form of unequal land holdings, was at the root of the conflict in the first place, redistribution may be necessary to prevent it from erupting again. Policies that only address the *effects of conflict* without also considering the *causes of conflict* may fail dismally. Colombia may be a case in point. I have argued elsewhere that transitional justice in Athens following the overthrow of the first oligarchic regime in 411 B.C. failed because of lack of attention to the elements of Athenian society and politics that had caused the oligarchic coup in the first place.[8] By contrast, the measures taken after the fall of the second oligarchic regime in 403 B.C. were durably successful because they addressed the main concerns of the oligarchs.

The value of justice can be either intrinsic or instrumental. Measures of transitional justice, notably punishment of wrongdoers and reparations to victims, are easily justified on intrinsic grounds. Instrumental arguments are more difficult to assess. According to an argument that is widely used in the human rights community, severe punishment of wrongdoers is needed as a "signal to the future" that will dissuade potential dictators or insurgents from trying to grab power. As I shall explain, I do not find that argument persuasive. According to another, instrumental argument, retribution and reparation are needed to stabilize the post-transitional society. I shall return to that issue, as well.

Let me now turn to *the idea of truth*. In the context of transitional justice, what we seek is not truth per se but *knowledge*—justified true belief. Hence, the idea of justification, or proof, is crucially important. The publication of the names of allegedly guilty individuals without documentary proof or an opportunity for the accused to refute the charges does not amount to knowledge. In addition, we may note that what matters is often *public knowledge*, rather than simply judicial knowledge that might be kept in camera.

The value of truth is twofold. On instrumental grounds, one is usually better able to realize one's aims if one has true beliefs about the world. Following a transition, for instance, it may be useful to be able to identify collaborators and agents of the previous regime to make sure they do not sabotage efforts to rebuild society. On intrinsic grounds, one may prefer to know the truth rather than live in a fool's paradise. A person may want to get access to his security file to learn whether certain individuals informed on him, even when the latter are no longer alive. Others, when faced with the same question, may decide that, for them, ignorance is bliss.

The idea of peace is understood in a large sense. It includes the absence of armed conflict between and within states, the absence of violent repression of the population by the government, and social or civic peace. The last idea is somewhat amorphous, but I take it to include (i) a low level of ordinary (criminal) violence, (ii) some form of psychological healing, and (iii) a cooperative attitude of public officials to the post-transitional regime. To put it the other way around, factors that undermine civic peace include high rates of crimes against persons, strong emotions of hatred and resentment, and sabotage of the new regime by agents and collaborators of the former regime.

The value of peace is mainly the intrinsic one of alleviating suffering and of allowing individuals to get on with their lives. Often we value peace in the ordinary sense—the sense in which it is the antonym of war—because it brings *peace of mind*. For this outcome to occur, the peace must obviously be perceived as *durable*. In my view, peace has no instrumental value in the sense of causing other desirable outcomes. Peace may be a condition for other good things—such as economic growth or even justice and truth—but it does not bring them about.

I remind the reader that these brief remarks about justice, truth, and peace are not intended to stand on their own as substantive arguments. Their function is only to provide a background for the analysis of pairwise tensions or synergies among these ideals.

I begin with *the relations between justice and truth.* Justice may *serve the goal of truth,* produced as a by-product of the ordinary workings of the justice system. Trials of wrongdoers make the wrongdoings known to the public, especially if the accused are tried on camera rather than in camera. The Nuremberg trials served this function, as did the trials of the Argentine military in the 1980s. In the latter country, when "the trial to the members of the military Juntas was initiated . . . the everyday media were flooded by the horrors of state terrorism."[9]

Truth may also *serve as a substitute for justice.* Truth commissions, in South Africa and elsewhere, are typically created in circumstances where the leaders of an autocratic regime retain enough power to block or severely limit the extent of penal proceedings after the transition. The creation of a truth commission can then serve as a compromise. The findings of these commissions vary in their extent. In many countries, the main task has been to document wrongdoings and to identify victims. In a few cases, notably South Africa and El Salvador, the task of identifying wrongdoers has also been part of the mandate of the commissions. In South Africa, the exposure of wrongdoers did not lead to their prosecution if the commission found that their crimes were motivated by political aims, rather than by malice or greed. The truth commission in El Salvador also named the wrongdoers, but Parliament granted them a full amnesty five days after the report was published.

Yet, even in the absence of mandate, truth-finding may reveal the identity of the perpetrators. In Argentina, on a parallel track to the trials of a small number of military personnel, the government created the National Commission of the Disappeared, which documented nine thousand persons who had "been disappeared." The commission itself did not name perpetrators, but someone inside it leaked 1,351 names to the press. Although Brazil never had an official truth commission, the Archdiocese of São Paulo secretly prepared a report on "Torture in Brazil" that received wide attention when it was published, in July 1985. Five months later, the Archdiocese published a list of 444 torturers. In Chile, the truth commission documented three thousand human rights violations and recommended extensive reparations. Although the report did not name perpetrators, the Communist party paper, *El Siglo*, published a list of the names of human rights violators.

In such cases, public knowledge of the identity of wrongdoers may, at least partially, serve the purposes of justice. According to Wechsler, the Brazilian torturers "had little more to suffer than the people's contempt."[10] This statement is somewhat misleading, however, since individuals publicly known to have committed wrongdoings may suffer social ostracism, which can be as painful as traditional forms of punishment. Thus, A. O. Lovejoy quotes Voltaire as saying that "To be an object of contempt to those with whom one lives is a thing that none has ever been, or ever will be, able to endure. It is perhaps the greatest check which nature has placed upon men's injustice,"[11] Adam Smith's observation that "Compared with the contempt of mankind, all other evils are easily supported,"[12] and John Adams's remark that "The desire of esteem is as real a want of nature as hunger; and the neglect and contempt of the world as severe a pain as gout and stone."[13] In addition to being targets of contempt and ostracism, known wrongdoers may also suffer physically. In Argentina, one navy captain who was well known for his brutal acts "suffered dozen of attacks . . . by strangers on the street or people who say he tortured them and their relatives."[14]

Shaming and revenge, even when based on accurate information, do not amount to justice, however. In a civilized society, justice should be left to the courts, not to observers of wrongdoings or to victims of wrongdoings. This statement is even more obviously true when names of wrongdoers are made public without proper verification of their guilt. In several post-Communist countries, lists of large numbers of alleged informers or collaborators have been posted on the Internet: seventy-five thousand in the Czech Republic and one hundred and sixty thousand in Poland. The security archives on which the lists were based are notoriously both *incomplete*, as full-time members of the security forces are usually not listed, and *inaccurate*, as some files are mere fabrications. In others words, the lists are likely to contain both false positives and false negatives.

Although one can easily imagine the reactions of the individuals who were named, there has not, to my knowledge, been any systematic study of the subject. In a small-scale precedent from 1998, an unknown organization in Lublin, Poland, published the names of 119 persons who had allegedly cooperated with the militia before 1989. Two of the individuals who were named killed themselves.[15] It seems plausible that the longer lists have had similar effects. Arguably, permitting this "rough justice" is worse than abstaining altogether from seeking justice. Note that in these cases, unlike the Latin American ones, there is not even the excuse that ordinary legal prosecution was unavailable.

Truth may also be an instrument for *providing justice to victims.* This idea comes in a modest and in a more ambitious version. In the modest version, fact-finding by truth commissions can lay the factual groundwork for reparations to victims. The South African and Chilean commissions, for instance, performed this task. The South African Commission also made the more ambitious claim that truth may contribute to "restorative justice." Knowledge of the facts is obviously a necessary condition for the victim-perpetrator interactions that are supposed to be at the core of restorative justice.

Whether—in the absence of retributive justice—these interactions are likely to do much good is another matter. First, some victims who testified before the South African Truth Commission found the process itself very traumatizing. *The process of recounting past sufferings may recreate them.* Second, knowledge about wrongdoings may be painful if one also knows that the wrongdoers will go free. Even though the ideal is *truth with justice,* truth *without* justice is not necessarily desirable. From the victim's point of view, knowing who the offender is *and* knowing that he will go free is likely to generate resentment and bitterness, rather than catharsis and healing. *Given* offender immunity, ignorance about offender identity might be better. According to one recent comprehensive survey, "we . . . lack clear evidence that truth telling produces psychological benefits for victims, or that healing at the individual level correlates with group-level reconciliation and other society-level outcomes."[16] Yet, independent of the feelings that may be created, I believe—as stated earlier—that the rule of law favors a clear separation of victim and offender, rather than their interaction.

There is also some evidence that, in the aftermath of a civil war, physical *separation rather than interaction* favors peace. The amnesty that the Athenian democrats granted to the oligarchs in 403 B.C.

went together with a demand that the oligarchs leave the city. The French wars of religion came to an end only when the Protestants were granted their own fortified cities, after the failure of earlier attempts to have Protestants and Catholics coexist on a local basis.[17] Referring to Bosnia, Monika Nalepa writes that "the strategy developed by the War Crimes Chamber staff is to begin prosecutions with those perpetrators who are most visible in public life. If administered consistently, this will gradually create an incentives mechanism for former perpetrators to shy away from public office. . . . This outcome also satisfies victims, who are not confronted by the glaring presence of their former perpetrators on a daily basis."[18] In the Colombian context, a relevant measure might be to ensure that demobilized paramilitaries and members of guerrilla forces do not resettle in areas where they inflicted harm on civilians. To cite another example, it may be impossible to settle the Israeli-Palestine conflict if Jerusalem is to be the Holy City of both religions.

Another truth-related measure is *judicial rehabilitation,* which occurs when an unjust conviction or condemnation from the previous regime is formally canceled under the new regime. To cite only one example among many, in Mongolia, since 1992, the Supreme Court has rehabilitated twenty-two thousand victims of Stalinist repressions. The process provides a certificate of rehabilitation to the families of the victims, with no compensation for economic loss, wrongful death, or other harms illegally inflicted by the Soviet state. In itself, rehabilitation can do no harm and may do some good. There is an obvious risk, however, that it may serve as a costless substitute for other measures that would have economic or political costs. Just as governments sometimes award tangible reparations because of the high *political* costs of punishment of wrongdoers, they may award intangible reparations because of the high *economic* cost of tangible ones.

Let me also consider official *apologies for wrongdoings.* Over the past fifty years, governments all over the world have expressed *regret, remorse,* and *apologies* and have asked for *forgiveness* for what their predecessors had done at various times in the past. Sometimes they have used more impersonal language, as when *deploring* these past actions or acknowledging that they were *wrong.* Among the acts that occurred prior to a regime transition and that have been the object of official apologies one may cite the Holocaust, the 1940 massacre of Polish prisoners in the Katyn forest, the decrees and laws enacted by the French Vichy government, the apartheid laws in South Africa, and the internment of Japanese prisoners of war in the Soviet Union after World War II.

Whatever their political or psychological efficacy may be, the moral status of these statements is highly ambiguous. Often, they are nothing short of meaningless. For a country to *deplore* what its government did in the past does not seem to differ from deploring what other governments are doing today. To *apologize* for what individuals who are no longer alive did to other individuals who are no longer alive is absurd on metaphysical grounds. Even when some of the victims are still alive, for someone other than the perpetrators to apologize is an equally empty gesture. At the same time, if the victims request and obtain some satisfaction from an apology, these metaphysical scruples may seem excessive. Yet, that is a matter of politics and psychology, not of morality.

As will be clear from these observations, I am somewhat skeptical about the value of intangible and symbolic reparations. Naming streets after victims or apologizing for events that took place several generations ago does not do much good for anyone. Unless governments are willing to put their money where their mouth is by adding tangible reparations to the intangible ones, such actions tend to fall in the category of "cheap talk."

I now turn to the *relations between justice and peace.* In 1944, Henry Morgenthau, Secretary of the Treasury in the Roosevelt administration, devised a plan for how to deal with Germany after it was defeated.[19] He wanted to set the clock back to 1810 and turn the country into a "pastoral economy." Morgenthau suggested that the coal mines in the Ruhr be flooded or dynamited and sealed for fifty years to make the Germans "impotent to wage future wars"[20] and urged that the Germans be prohibited from developing any kind of industry that could be converted into military production (ploughshares into swords): "If you have a bicycle, you can have an airplane. . . . If you have a baby carriage, you can have an airplane."[21] Although Morgenthau initially persuaded both Roosevelt and Churchill to go along with his plan, they backed off when it became clear that it might have negative effects on the conduct of the war and delay the peace. As General George Marshall, along with William Donovan, head of the Office of Strategic Services, and others, pointed out, knowledge of the extreme severity of their punishment would stiffen the German will to resistance. For this reason, and for several others, the plan was not implemented in its draconian form.

Justice and peace have been at odds in other cases, too. In Bosnia, France and Britain "saw the issue of war criminals as a potential impediment to making peace in ex-Yugoslavia, binding the hands of policymakers who might have to cut a deal with criminal leaders."[22] In another example, a "perverse scenario of inducing a dictator to fight for his survival may have happened recently when the prosecutor for Sierra Leone's International Criminal Tribunal indicted Charles Taylor in Nigeria. This action prevented diplomatic efforts from striking a deal with the former dictator, who arguably could have facilitated a smoother transition."[23]

We have to be careful, though, in characterizing these conflicts in terms of justice versus peace. Morgenthau's desire for a heavy punishment was based on a non-consequentialist desire for *vengeance*, rather than on a desire for justice. In recent discussions, the demand for severe punishment of dictators and autocrats has been based on the consequentialist argument that courts must set a clear precedent that would serve to dissuade would-be dictators in the future. As noted by Otto Kirchheimer, the precedent might "backfire . . . if it induced the leaders of a future war to fight to the bitter end rather than surrender and face the possible future of war criminals."[24] It is possible (although, in my opinion, psychologically implausible) that some aspiring dictators might refrain from grabbing power because of the consequences of losing it. It is certainly plausible, as we have seen, that the same fear may cause dictators to hang on to power longer than they would otherwise have done. I have yet to see a convincing argument why the first of these effects would dominate the second. Diane Orentlicher, a prominent scholar in the human rights community, merely asserts, with no argument (and one example), that "the prospect of facing prosecutions is rarely, if ever, the decisive factor in determining whether a transition will occur."[25] If that were so, why would the prospect of facing prosecution be a decisive dissuasive factor?

Even if an argument to that effect were forthcoming, the advocate of severe punishment would also have to show that the long-term net benefits dominate the short-term cost of prolonging or rekindling conflict. For the non-consequentialist, this cost is, of course, irrelevant. After the fall of the military dictatorship in Argentina, some human rights activists refused the pragmatic line of President Raúl Ricardo Alfonsín, who feared that extensive punishment of the military might trigger a new coup. Consequentialists cannot, however, ignore short-term costs or risks. To accept the prolongation of a given conflict for the sake of the non-beginning of future conflicts, they have to argue not only that the expected smaller number of future conflicts offsets their expected longer duration but also that the net effect in the future exceeds the costs in the present. If one believes—as I do—that neither of these arguments can successfully be made, the idea of "sacrificing peace for justice" by punishing dictators severely has no consequentialist foundation. In fact, if I am right in my belief that this policy would reduce the duration of current and future conflicts while having little impact on the number of conflicts, then a consequentialist argument could be made for treating all dictators leniently.

Yet, this policy could run into either of two related problems: unpopularity and lack of credibility. The population at large may require that those responsible for wrongdoing and atrocities be severely punished. If they are not, the government might fall and the peace process might come apart. The wrongdoers, however, may not be willing to step down if they face the prospect of spending the rest of their life in prison. The question, then, is whether there exists a degree of punishment that is severe enough to satisfy the population and mild enough to satisfy the wrongdoers. In Colombia, this window seems to exist because of the threat of extradition to the United States, which, as recent events show, is a highly credible one. At the same time, the Justice and Peace Law opened up the possibility that drugs lords could go free or receive reduced sentences and at any rate escape extradition to the United States by virtue of the clause that granted amnesty for crimes with an "indirect" political purpose, the drug trafficking being a "means" to finance political ends. This clause was later struck down by the Constitutional Court.

The law in its original form was negotiated between the government and the paramilitaries. The fact that this crucial clause was struck down by the court points to an intrinsic problem in the negotiated settlement of conflict in a democracy. When the government negotiates with insurgents or paramilitaries, the latter know—or should know—that the government is constrained by Parliament and the courts. It is in fact a defining characteristic of democracy based on the separation of powers that the government cannot force the legislative and judiciary branches to uphold its promises. This has been an acute issue in Latin American as well as in East European transitions.[26] In Colombia, *the threat of extradition was credible*, because the government had both the power and the motivation to carry it out if necessary, but it *could not make a credible promise of amnesty* for political crimes.

So far I have discussed tensions between peace and *transitional* justice. There is a need, however, also to address the relation between peace and *distributive* justice, a question that is especially important in the aftermath of civil wars. The general issue is the following: if a conflict settlement fails to address the root causes of the conflict and limits itself to the problems created by the conflict itself, the peace may very well fail to be a durable one. To be sure, the distinction between problems that caused the conflict and problems caused by the conflict is not always sharp, since the root causes may be exacerbated by the conflict. Yet, in many cases, it is clear enough. Root causes include distributive injustice, such as unequal distribution of land, but other causes such as religion and discrimination of minorities are also found. Here I limit myself to conflicts arising on distributive grounds, with the implication that a durable peace requires distributive and not only transitional justice.

The following anecdote provides an illustration. In one of the several conferences in Bogotá that I have co-organized with Antanas Mockus and then-Vice President Francisco Santos over the past years, James Fearon at Stanford University made the following perceptive remark: "If a conference on political conflicts in Colombia had taken place here forty years ago, the name most frequently cited would have been Marx. Today, it is Hobbes."[27] In Colombia today, *Hobbesian violence, rather than Marxian exploitation,* is perceived as the main social ill. To create a durable peace, however, it is not enough to address the issue of violence by measures of transitional justice. One also has to address the issues of exploitation, inequality, and poverty by measures of distributive justice.

Land reform is needed even more today than in the past, because of the vast landed properties concentrated in the hands of drug lords and paramilitary leaders. At the same time, it is more difficult than ever, because of the close links between land-owning members of Parliament and the drug lords. Note, however, that, for this group, confiscation and redistribution of land will be perceived as punishment.

Ideally, new regimes should aim at *both* transitional and distributive justice. In South Africa, the bulk of the black population received *neither*. Wrongdoers were not brought to justice, reparations to victims have been minimal, and there has been almost no land reform. The country today has among the highest rates of murder, armed robbery, and rape in the world. Although the causality is opaque, it is not unthinkable that this failure of civic peace can be traced back to the failures of justice. Although there is no *collective* violence that might be transformed into a civil war, the high level of individual violence shows that the conflict resolution is very far from perfect.

Given the need for both transitional and distributive justice, governments face the problem of allocating scarce resources. They must decide whether to give priority to compensating victims of the conflict itself or to improving the situation of the landless poor in general. In abstract terms, should compensation be made on the basis of *entitlement* or *need?*[28] The aim of a durable peace may favor the latter criterion and that of transitional justice the former. Whereas redistribution often encounters great resistance among entrenched elites, transitional justice may command greater agreement. In the current demobilization process in Colombia, scarce resources are also devoted to subsidizing the ex-paramilitaries to prevent them from taking up their arms again. Although this may be a necessary measure to ensure a durable peace, victims of the conflict may see this subsidy to perpetrators as deeply unjust.

I now turn to the relations *between truth and peace.* Earlier I distinguished between several components of peace. With regard to the impact of truth on peace, I shall focus on peace as the absence of violent repression and as civic peace.

The most important effect of truth commissions is perhaps to make it impossible to deny that massive wrongdoings took place prior to the transition. In South Africa, many members of the white elite might have refused—in more or less good faith—to believe claims about apartheid wrongdoings had they not been so fully documented in the hearings of the Truth and Reconciliation Commission. The work of the commissions in Argentina and Chile also made it impossible to sustain the myth that the dictatorships were justified by the task of weeding out criminal subversive elements. If the truth had not been publicly recognized, the new regimes might have been jeopardized and the previous repressive regime restored. The work of the truth commissions underwrote the enormously effective message "Never again."

The most important impact of truth on civic peace concerns the effort to stabilize the new regimes. If agents and collaborators of the old regime remain in high office after the transition, there is a risk that they may either work actively to undermine the new regime or be vulnerable to blackmail by members of the former security services who are aware of their past involvement. For both these reasons, it is important to find out the truth about their past. In Poland, Romania, Estonia, and Lithuania, security files have been used as an instrument of truth *revelation*, by creating an incentive for individuals to tell the truth about their involvement with the pre-transitional regime. In this procedure, known as "lustration," individuals seeking elective or high appointive office are asked whether they ever collaborated with the security services under Communism.[29] If they answer Yes, voters or administrators are free to elect or appoint them—or not. If they answer No and are later found out to have lied, they are blocked from office for a certain number of years. This solves the problem of retroactivity, since they are penalized not for "what they did then" but for "what they say now about what they did then." A similar procedure has been used in South Africa, where individuals who testify before the Truth and Reconciliation Commission may be denied amnesty if they do not tell the full truth about their involvement with apartheid crimes.

The *gacaca* courts in Rwanda offer sentence reduction in exchange for full disclosure. This idea is also applied in the Colombian peace process. The Justice and Peace Law has created the possibility of "gambling with the truth" by offering the incentive of reduced sentences in exchange for full confession and reparation to victims. If a serious wrongdoer gambles, that is, does not apply for the benefits provided by the law and loses, that is, is found out, he faces ordinary criminal law sentences, which are five or ten times more severe than those imposed by the Justice and Peace Law. If he wins, that is, if his crimes are not discovered, he remains free. The efficacy of this procedure obviously depends on the government's knowledge about serious crimes or, more accurately, on the belief of the wrongdoers about the government's knowledge and on its capacity to enforce prosecutions.

Before concluding, let me briefly discuss *the relations between transitional and distributive justice,* with the latter idea taken in a broad sense that also includes utilitarianism. In many transitional situations, the claims of the past have to compete with those of the present and the future. Entitlements have to be balanced both against the need to alleviate suffering and the needs of reconstruction. As resources tend to be especially scarce during times of transition, these tensions are likely to be acute.

Consider first alleviation of suffering versus entitlements. Although some *targeted victims* may have a stronger *legal* claim, *collateral victims* may have a compelling *moral* claim. In the debates in the French parliament during the Restoration, one speaker said that either the debt to the owners of confiscated property was *due in justice* and thus had to be fully repaid, which would perhaps absorb the whole territorial capital of France, or it was not, in which case it was only appropriate to allocate assistance to the needy.[30] In Colombia today, displaced individuals who were forced by guerrillas or paramilitaries to give up their property are entitled to get it back or to receive land of equivalent value. Other displaced individuals fled their land because they feared, perhaps on the basis of false rumors, that they would be forced to give up their properties. Although their need is just as great, they do not have the same legal entitlement. It is far from clear, however, that restitutive justice should take absolute precedence over distributive justice.

Consider next backward-looking entitlements versus future-looking reconstruction. After 1945, several German-occupied countries enacted legislation to compensate individuals for lost or destroyed property. These measures were, however, tempered by economic needs. The French law of October 28, 1946, did not indemnify the loss of "sumptuary" elements. The postwar years were a time of extreme penury in France. After four years of occupation and generalized looting, allied bombardments, and destructions caused by the struggles of the Liberation Movement, everything had to be rebuilt. The sumptuary was thus opposed to the necessary. For instance, neither jewelry nor works of art were indemnified. In Norway, too, the principle of *regressive compensation* for war damages was well established. The purpose of the postwar legislation was to assist survivors for purposes of reconstruction, not to re-create prewar fortunes. There was a general feeling that the whole country had suffered and a certain reluctance to compare sufferings. Similarly, in restitution after transition, one can impose an upper limit on the size of restituted plots. This policy was followed in Hungary in 1945 and in Romania in 1991.

Very generally, full reparation at a large scale may be economically unfeasible, especially if one calculates interest on confiscated property. According to some reports, the value of the assets confiscated from Hungary's Jews during the war, allowing for unpaid interest, was equivalent to the total national wealth of Hungary. Even without interest-payment, compensation to the three million Sudeten Germans expelled from Czechoslovakia after World War II would have bankrupted the Czech Republic. As I just noted, a similar observation was made about restoration of property during the French Restoration. It would be absurd to insist that reparative justice be done in full if, as a consequence, the heavens would fall. In this respect, reparation is similar to retribution. In many transitions, an unconditional effort to punish wrongdoers would have disastrous economic consequences. Countries that are undertaking a process of reconstruction need experts and administrators who may have been culpably involved with the previous regime. To punish them would at the same time be to punish their fellow citizens. Similarly, full reparation to victims might almost amount to a punishment of non-victims.

In summary, I have pointed to *six possible negative relations* among or within the three values:

N1. The anticipation of justice tomorrow may be an obstacle to peace today, if the anticipation of punishment or redistribution prolongs the conflict.

N2. Justice today maybe an obstacle to peace tomorrow. If severe punishment is intended to send a signal to future dictators and actually does so, the net effect may be to increase rather than decrease human rights violations.

N3. The pursuit of truth may be an obstacle to justice, if names of wrongdoers are published without due process.

N4. Truth may be an obstacle to justice, if symbolic measures of rehabilitation and apologies serve as substitutes for reparation.

N5. Truth may be an obstacle to peace, if truth-finding that reveals the identity of perpetrators is not accompanied by their punishment.

N6. Transitional justice may be an obstacle to distributive justice, if entitlement trumps needs in situations of extreme scarcity.

Note the difference between N1 and N2. The first is the question about *how to act in a given situation*. The second turns on a rule-consequentialist argument about the net long-term effect of a given *policy*.

In addition, I have pointed to *four possible positive relations*:

P1. Truth may be a condition for peace, by making it impossible to deny past injustices.

P2. Truth may be a condition for civic peace, by screening officials and politicians for possible collaboration with the pre-transitional regime.

P3. Transitional justice may be a condition for peace, by satisfying demands for retribution that, if unmet, might create unrest.

P4. Distributive justice may be a condition for a durable peace, by addressing the root causes of conflict.

There may be a tension between N1 and P3 or P4. In the worst case, the maximal punishment or redistribution that wrongdoers will accept may exceed the minimal measures that will satisfy the population. In other cases, as perhaps in Colombia, there may be a narrow window of consistency.

I have obviously been painting with very broad strokes. The purpose has been to sketch a conceptual framework, rather than offering a theory or a policy. I am too deeply aware of the ambiguities of actual conflicts and the inadequacy of formal analytical treatments to believe one can go very far in a discussion pitched at this level of generality. I hope, nevertheless, that the framework might suggest some hypotheses for the case studies that, ultimately, are the coin of the realm for social science.

NOTES

1. William Hedgcock and Akshay R. Rao, "Trade-off Aversion as an Explanation for the Attraction Effect: A Functional Magnetic Resonance Imaging Study," *Journal of Marketing Research* 46, no. 1 (2009): 1–13.

2. Karl Marx, "Capital, Volume 1, Preface to the First German Edition," in *The Marx-Engels Reader*, 2nd ed., ed. Robert C. Tucker (New York: Norton, 1978), 297.

3. Augustin Landier and Vinay B. Nair, *Investing for Change: Profit from Responsible Investment* (Oxford: Oxford University Press, 2009); Geoffrey Heal, *When Principles Pay: Corporate Social Responsibility and the Bottom Line* (New York: Columbia Business School, 2008).

4. Arthur M. Okun, *Equality and Efficiency: The Big Trade-Off* (New York: Brookings Institution, 1975).

5. Jon Elster, *Closing the Books: Transitional Justice in Historical Perspective* (Cambridge: Cambridge University Press, 2004).

6. See notably Tove Grete Lie, Helga Malmin Binningsbø, and Scott Gates, "Post-Conflict Justice and Sustainable Peace," World Bank Policy Research Working Paper No. 4191 (2007).

7. The law, which was adopted in July 2005 after extended negotiations between the paramilitary "United Self-Defense forces of Colombia" and the government, provides a framework for the demobilization and reinsertion of members of "illegal armed groups." Although it applies to guerrillas as well as to paramiliataries, so far only the latter have availed themselves of this option. Members of illegal armed groups who may choose to demobilize under the JPL are those who hope to avoid ordinary criminal prosecution, prosecution before the International Criminal Court, and extradition to the United States. In exchange for receiving shorter prison sentences than any of these options would involve, they must render full confessions, hand over illegal assets, cooperate in the dismantling of the armed group, and cease all illicit activities. Victims of crimes committed by the beneficiaries of the law can claim reparations funded by the assets that are handed over. For details, see Catalina Diaz, "Colombia's Bid for Justice and Peace," in *Building a Future on Peace and Justice: Studies on Transitional*

Justice, Peace and Development, ed. Kai Ambos, Judith Large, and Marieke Wierda (Berlin: Springer, 2009), 469–502, and Pablo Kalmanovitz, "Introduction: Law and Politics in the Colombian Negotiations with Paramilitary Groups," in *Law in Peace Negotiations,* 2nd ed., ed. Morten Bergsmo and Pablo Kalmanovitz (Oslo: Torkel Opsahl Academic EPublisher, 2010), http://www.fichl.org/fileadmin/fichl/documents/FICHL_5_Second_Edition_web.pdf, 1–25.

8. Elster, *Closing the Books,* chap.1.

9. Carlos H. Acuña, "Transitional Justice in Argentina and Chile: A Never-Ending Story?," in *Retribution and Reparation in the Transition to Democracy,* ed. Jon Elster (New York: Cambridge University Press, 2006), 211.

10. Lawrence Weschler, *A Miracle, a Universe: Settling Accounts with Torturers* (Chicago: University of Chicago Press, 1998), 76.

11. Arthur O. Lovejoy, *Reflections on Human Nature* (Baltimore: Johns Hopkins University Press, 1961), 181.

12. Ibid., 191.

13. Ibid., 199.

14. Calvin Sims, "Retired Torturer Now Lives a Tortured Existence," *New York Times,* August 12, 1997, A4.

15. Leszek Kuk, *La Pologne du post-communisme à l'anti-communisme* (Paris: Éditions L'Harmattan, 2001), 209.

16. Oskar N. T. Thoms, James Ron, and Roland Paris, "The Effects of Transitional Justice Mechanisms: A Summary of Empirical Research Findings and Implications for Analysts and Practitioners," working paper, Centre for International Policy Studies, University of Ottawa, Ottawa, April 2008, 21.

17. Olivier Christin, *La paix de religion: L'autonomisation de la raison politique au XVIe siècle* (Paris: Éditions du Seuil, Collection Liber, 1997).

18. Monika Nalepa, "Reconciliation, Refugee Returns, and the Impact of International Criminal Justice: The Case of Bosnia and Herzegovina," this volume.

19. See Elster, *Closing the Books,* chap. 7, for details and references.

20. U.S. Senate, *The Morgenthau Diaries* (*Germany*) (Washington, DC: U.S. Government Printing Office), 489.

21. Ibid., 876–77.

22. Gary Jonathan Bass, *Stay the Hand of Vengeance: The Politics of War Crimes Tribunals* (Princeton: Princeton University Press, 2000), 211.

23. Marek M. Kaminsky and Monika Nalepa, "Judging Transitional Justice: A New Criterion For Evaluating Truth Revelation Procedures," *Journal of Conflict Resolution* 50, no. 3 (2006): 396.

24. Otto Kirchheimer, *Political Justice: The Use of Legal Procedure for Political Ends* (Princeton: Princeton University Press, 1961), 325 n. 290.

25. Diane F. Orentlicher, "Settling Accounts: The Duty to Prosecute

Human Rights Violations of a Prior Regime," *Yale Law Journal* 100, no. 8 (1991): 2549.

26. Elster, *Closing the Books*, chap. 7; Monika Nalepa, *Skeletons in the Closet* (Cambridge: Cambridge University Press, 2010).

27. Editors' note: On Hobbes and transitional justice theory, please see Dyzenhaus in this volume.

28. Elster, *Closing the Books*, chap. 6; Pablo Kalmanovitz, "Justice in Post-War Reconstruction: Theories from Vitoria to Vattel" (Ph.D. diss., Columbia University, 2010).

29. Nalepa, *Skeletons in the Closet.*

30. André Gain, *La restauration et les biens des émigrés* (Nancy: Société d'Impressions Typographiques, 1928), vol. I, 371. For further discussion of these debates, see Elster, *Closing the Books*, 43.

3

FORMS OF TRANSITIONAL JUSTICE

JEREMY WEBBER

I. INTRODUCTION

Transitional justice is about situations in which a society is moving from a state of injustice to justice, from oppressive government to government that respects the rule of law, from authoritarianism to democracy. It is concerned with the administration of justice across such a change of regime. Hence its central questions: to what extent, and in accordance with what standards, is it appropriate to judge events that occurred under the former regime? What kinds of processes, what forms of recovery or punishment, are appropriate in such circumstances?

These questions are commonly approached as though they concerned departures from strict justice in the interest of achieving national reconciliation and ensuring the success of the transition or simply as a concession to the fact that those who benefited from the former regime retain considerable power and therefore have to be appeased. Posner and Vermeule, for example, in their survey of the area, say that standards of transitional justice "reflect liberal commitments leavened with prudential concern for good transition management. . . . Transitional justice requires a balance of liberal commitments and political precautions. It is achieved when liberal norms are respected to an extent necessary for, and consistent with, the consolidation of liberal democratic institutions."[1] Many transitions do involve the trading off of justice for political stability, but an exclusive concentration on this trade-off simplifies the issues. Often, the arguments among parties to transitions are over different conceptions of justice, not merely the balance between justice and expediency or even between justice and forgiveness. Not only is justice itself a complex and contested concept, but in many transitions there are, as I will argue, at least two substantially different forms of justice at issue and, indeed, often a third, which I will also describe. I call the first two forms "retrospective" (backward-looking) and "prospective" (forward-looking) justice and the third, "the adjustment of contending legal and political orders."[2] Many of the distinctive debates within the transitional justice literature concern the tensions among these three forms. Those tensions are often masked, however, by writers' tendency, if they do not overlook them entirely, to treat only retrospective justice as justice and to roll the other two forms into the capacious category of expediency.

In this chapter, I set out the three forms of justice, describe how they differ, suggest why they bear upon justice and not merely expediency, and indicate how their recognition would allow both observers and participants to make better sense of transitions. In particular, I describe how they address three problems that are central to many discussions of transitional justice:

1. The prescription of claims (the period after which new rights are obtained and original rights are lost through adverse possession, and the period after which claims are barred by statutes of limitations; I use the civil law term "prescription," which captures both the gain and the loss of rights);
2. The problem of inter-temporal judgment (what legal standards should be applied to events that occurred in a different time under a different regime); and
3. Issues of institutional competence and institutional innovation (for, as will become clear, different institutional structures are appropriate to the three forms of justice).

Many of these challenges also arise in a closely related context, that of compensation for historic injustice (for example, the wrongs of American slavery or the dispossession of indigenous peoples). Indeed, the forms of justice may be more apparent in those cases because they are less masked by the exigencies of a recent transition. The long passage of time also accentuates the issues of prescription and inter-temporal judgment. My argument is framed, then, in relation to those circumstances as well, not just the abrupt and recent changes in regime that are the focus of most of the transitional justice literature.[3]

Now, I should make clear the status of the three forms of justice. They are not tightly defined theoretical constructs that, once identified, solve by themselves the debates around transitional justice. As will become clear, there remains ample room for argument over the standards to be applied. They constitute general orientations, general ways of conceiving of the challenge of defining and pursuing the nature of justice. Their identification helps to clarify the questions at issue in transitional justice. The forms carry dispositions with respect to those questions, but one still needs to consider, in a particular case, how the content of the three forms should be defined and the appropriate balance among them. One of the great merits of identifying the forms of justice is that it allows one to address more effectively arguments over the standards to be applied and, in particular, what sorts of institutions are appropriate for settling those standards.

Nor are the forms utterly autonomous from one another. They are linked in at least two ways. First, they often draw upon similar phenomena in making their arguments, although those phenomena may serve substantially different roles in each form. Thus, as we will see, a concern for responding to past wrongs figures in both retrospective and prospective justice, although in different ways. Second, any adequate response to a particular transition may require that one pursue two or three of the forms of justice simultaneously; their interaction therefore becomes central. Prospective justice may, for example, limit the extent to which the full recovery dictated by retrospective justice is awarded. I am not, then, claiming any great purity for these forms either in concept or application. They are valuable because they help to clarify the complex of considerations raised in situations of transition, not because they represent airtight and independent categories.

Finally, in identifying these three relatively abstract forms, I do not mean to replace the thoroughgoing, context-rich grappling with specific cases so typical of the transitional justice literature. The great strength of that literature is its immersion in situations that combine a whole host of considerations, both principled and pragmatic, and its attempt to tease out of those situations insights that might otherwise be overlooked. This task is especially useful in that, for all their complexity and uniqueness, the cases discussed in the literature manifest recurring problems of importance to the extension of democracy and the rule of law and, indeed, more generally, to the maintenance of reasonably just institutions in the face of conflict over norms and procedures. The three forms of justice do not exhaust the insights to be gained from the study of justice in transition. I expect that we will find ourselves continually circling back to those situations, probing them for their lessons.

Indeed, one issue that remains to be fully explored is the inter-dependence of the definition of rights and obligations on the one hand and the presence of social solidarity on the other—or, to put it another way, the question of whether members recognize an ob-ligation to pursue justice in relation to other members and to ac-cept the overarching society's determinations of right.[4] Given that individuals argue strongly over the meaning and implications of justice, one of the great challenges facing any community is how to persuade people that they should acquiesce in the decisions made by a community's institutions even when they espouse a differing conception of right—as invariably occurs, to some extent, in all communities. That seems to be the challenge posed in particularly stark terms by transitional justice, which often concerns the rec-onciliation of partisans of the old and the new, as part of a new, reformed polity. Most of the transitional justice literature fails to grapple squarely with this as a problem of conflict over concep-tions of justice lodged in different segments of the population.[5] Instead, most writers tend to proceed as though there were one correct idea of justice (from which expediency may demand de-partures); the standards of the old regime in particular are treated as though they were entirely discredited. This is especially true given the tendency of transitional justice, in both theory and prac-tice, to focus on the most egregious acts committed under the old regime—crimes against humanity, and killings, injuries and other deprivations committed without any semblance of due process— actions where any justifications asserted by the participants seem (often rightly) groundless, spurious, even insincere.[6] But this focus on the extremes masks the genuine normative conflict that exists in many transitions. Conflicting conceptions of justice are almost always in play in the transitional period. A fundamental problem is how the new society should respond to this normative diversity. Should the norms of those leading the transition simply take precedence? Should a new, hybrid conception of justice be developed, one that retains some features of the old? Should the resolution be left to the new society's institutions, or should a particular outcome be hardwired into those institutions? Should segments of the society that espouse different norms enjoy institutional autonomy?

This chapter does not address these issues in anything like a comprehensive fashion. As will become clear, however, such questions are central to the third form of justice. The chapter, I hope, helps to inject them into the debate.

II. THREE FORMS OF JUSTICE

What, then, are the three forms of justice? I start by describing their principal characteristics, suggesting how they arise in transitional justice situations and how they are distinguished one from the other. In the following section, I indicate the contrasting ways in which they address the three problems identified earlier.

1. Retrospective Justice

Retrospective justice is the most familiar species of justice in liberal societies. It is the form that Aristotle called "corrective" or "rectificatory."[7] It is backward-looking in that it seeks to repair the consequences of a past instance of wrongful conduct. One party's wrongful action has caused another party to suffer a loss; the decision maker then intervenes to restore the balance, forcing the wrongdoer to make good the victim's loss. The ideal remedy is precisely calibrated to repair the loss caused by the wrongdoer's previous action. The measure of justice is therefore, as Aristotle says, "arithmetic."

A dominating feature of retrospective justice is the narrowness of its focus. The sole reason to intervene is the action on the part of the wrongdoer. That action limits the appropriate recovery. There is no examination of the general merit or need of either wrongdoer or victim. There is no attention to their future relationship. The original event is seen as a transaction between two parties, and the objective is to reverse that transaction so that the wrongdoer bears the consequences of his or her wrongful action. The general circumstances are irrelevant, except as they help to characterize and quantify that specific transaction.

The purest form of corrective justice is therefore the pursuit of a civil remedy to compensate the injured party for a wrong. Theories of the criminal law that focus on retribution (as opposed to deterrence or rehabilitation) also broadly conform to the retrospective model. They, too, focus entirely on the past event and seek to impose punishment that is carefully calibrated to the harm caused by and the social opprobrium attached to the wrongful conduct of the accused. To the extent that transitional justice responds to and seeks to repair specific wrongs of the past, as it often does, it adopts the form of retrospective justice.

2. Prospective Justice

But often in transitions, parties pursue a broader form of justice. They are concerned not simply with repairing past events but rather with changing their society for the future, reconstructing it on different—and, ideally, more just—foundations. Indeed, that tends to be the very essence of the transition. The parties seek to arrange relations within the society so that each party is treated appropriately from here on. When they do so, they are engaged in prospective—forward-looking—justice.

This form of justice conforms roughly to Aristotle's notion of distributive justice, in which each individual gets the honors and benefits that are his or her due.[8] Aristotle does not emphasize the temporal dimension as I do here. He focuses on the proportionate distribution of goods to citizens. But there are close similarities. Aristotle's distributive justice is not a function of a transaction between two parties. It is an all-things-considered adjustment of benefits that operates across the society so that each citizen enjoys benefits in due proportion. Its sphere is potentially much broader, then, than that of corrective justice, precisely because it is not delimited by a past transaction. The content of distributive justice depends on the specification of the relevant goods and the articulation of an appropriate theory of distribution. It is therefore more open-ended, subject to argument and contestation. But it still represents a genuine form of justice—an attempt to bring human beings into just relationship to one another.

Prospective justice also has many affinities to what has come to be called "restorative justice."[9] Both tend to be premised on the need to maintain community into the future; both shape their responses to past conduct with an eye toward future collaboration. I prefer the term "prospective justice," however, because it directs our attention toward the terms on which that future collaboration should take place, acknowledging that those terms may have to be transformed.[10] The language of "restorative justice" implies that a community has existed, has been broken, and now has to be reestablished. Its focus is overwhelmingly on restoration: of harmony, of peace. Its ambit may therefore be limited. Indeed, it is sometimes approached as though it were simply an alternative way of pursuing retrospective justice, one that attempts to meld compensation and personal reconciliation with punishment. In contrast, prospective justice demands attention to the terms upon which the future community should be structured.

Many of the approaches adopted within transitional justice are best conceived as examples of prospective justice. They may—indeed, they generally do—constitute a reckoning with the past, but that reckoning is pursued not primarily to correct a transaction but rather to adjust the parties' relations so that their interactions now take place on a sound foundation. The wrongs of the past —generally not just a discrete event but a whole course of conduct —have shaped the parties' relations in a way that is regrettable, damaging, unjust. The agents of justice intervene to confront that past so that the parties' relations might be placed on an appropriate footing.

This is most evident in the operation of truth commissions.[11] Those commissions generally do not seek to repair past events or punish past offenders (although they are sometimes used in parallel with such procedures). Rather, their distinctive role is to uncover the truth in the hope that the exposure of past wrongs will prevent their recurrence in the future; they allow victims to tell their stories so that, by cataloguing and denouncing instances of injustice, the values of the new society are affirmed; and they often seek to instill a commitment to those new values by acts of contrition on the part of agents of the old regime and, sometimes, by gestures of forgiveness and reconciliation on the part of the victims. The past is confronted, but with a predominant focus on how to go on from here.

Other remedies share this character. Official apologies are designed not to fix the past but rather to repudiate it, dissociating the current regime from that past and making clear that the new regime intends to base its actions on new principles. The same is generally true of purges of government officials: those purges are often justified less as a way of punishing specific officials for their past conduct (although punishment, too, may be present) than as a way of setting the state structure on a new path, removing officials who were closely involved in running the past regime and making room for people who had been systematically excluded.[12] Approaches to criminal prosecution that emphasize rehabilitation and deterrence—perhaps even forgiveness—also pertain to prospective justice.

Even the response that most resembles the remedies of retrospective justice—reparations—often has a strong dimension of prospective justice about it.[13] First, reparations often respond to the past precisely in order to place the descendants of the original victims in a better position today. The past events have impaired their ability to act in the present; past dispossessions, for example, may have consigned the victims' descendants to recurrent cycles of poverty. Establishing a just relationship for the future may require some restoration of land and other goods. Note, however, that to the extent that recovery depends upon prospective justice, it need not be determined by the amount of the original victims' loss. The measure is that necessary to establish an appropriate relationship today, not the losses of the past. Something less than full recovery may be sufficient. Second, in prospective justice, some payment may be needed to break with the actions of the past. Payment may be necessary as an earnest in order to emphasize the seriousness of an apology—to overcome the impression that words are cheap.[14] Again, however, such a payment need not amount to the full extent of the loss. Indeed, it may not even be paid to those who were wronged. In the settlement that the Government of Canada made with Japanese Canadians in 1988 for their forced relocation and the seizure of their property during World War II, a substantial

portion of the compensation was paid to a foundation for the promotion of human rights, not to survivors and their descendants.[15]
In fact, one suspects that the term "reparations" has come to be
applied to these payments precisely because it has broader connotations than the term "compensation."

Now, both reasons for compensation may operate simultaneously. In any transition, there may be good reason to compensate
specific individuals for specific losses (in the manner of retrospective justice) and to provide reparations to a broader class of people
in recognition of the general wrongs done to them (in the manner
of prospective justice). Criminal prosecutions generally combine a
concern for the past (retributive punishment) and a concern for
the future (denunciation of the previous acts, deterrence of future
crimes, rehabilitation of the offenders). Indeed, the two types of
response may work in tandem: in some cases, the pursuit of retrospective justice may appear to be essential to any attempt to establish a just society, especially if the wrongs at issue have been committed recently and all parties, victims and perpetrators, remain
on the scene. In those situations, retrospective justice may appear
to be a precondition to prospective justice.

But the two forms may also diverge. A good example is provided by the Constitutional Court of South Africa's decision in
Richtersveld.[16] The South African constitution deals with the legacy
of apartheid in a large variety of ways, providing, among other
things, for the restitution of parcels of land that had been taken
by the state on racially discriminatory grounds and for the redistribution of wealth to counter the general effects of apartheid.[17]
Restitution partakes more of retrospective justice, redistribution
of prospective justice. *Richtersveld* concerned a claim by a community, the core members of which were Khoi-San, to land that had
been taken from them in the 1920s in order to develop a diamond
mine. In its decision in *Richtersveld*, the court found that the Khoi-
San's land rights had been denied as a result of racially discriminatory law and awarded the land, including the diamond mine, to
the community. But note the tension between this decision and
the government's commitment to achieve a more just distribution
of resources across South Africa. The mine was worth about R10
billion and produced revenues for the government of about R84
million per year.[18] These resources would now be concentrated in

the hands of the local community and denied to the government, impairing the latter's ability to engage in redistributive policies. And, of course, the costs of that transfer would be borne by the post-apartheid government and its constituents, not by those originally responsible for the dispossession, who operated under a very different regime not at all accountable to the majority population and who were now long dead.

Now, in pointing to the tension between retrospective and prospective justice in this instance, I do not mean to suggest that the result was incompatible with prospective justice. Since European settlement began, the Khoi-San have suffered intensely from dislocation and dispossession. They remain a small and vulnerable minority in South Africa. It would be difficult to determine, without further inquiry, what resources would be necessary to place them in a position equivalent to that of other South Africans today. Moreover, the standard of distributive justice has to be assessed across the society as a whole: if substantial inequalities are tolerated elsewhere—if, for example, other natural resources remain concentrated in private hands—it would be unfair to subject the Richtersveld Khoi-San to a scrutiny that others, still in possession of their property, escape. Finally, note that it may be possible to structure the two types of claim so that both forms of justice are acknowledged and addressed. For example, restitution may be used to settle the underlying question of title, and a taxation regime, operating consistently across the entire society, may be used to accomplish redistributive ends. Indeed, something like this might be the best way to segregate the two forms of justice, analyze them on their own terms, and give each its due. Restitution in a case like *Richtersveld* might therefore be reconciled, to some degree, with prospective justice.

It is clear, however, that the two species of justice do operate by very different logics. If redistributive measures are taken after the fact, they will substantially qualify the effects of restitution. Note, too, that the *Richtersveld* situation poses challenges even for the achievement of retrospective justice, at least in its classical form, given that the government that accomplished the dispossession no longer exists in anything like the same form or with the same membership, and therefore cannot be made to bear the costs. Indeed, in the aftermath of *Richtersveld*, after difficult negotiations, the government and the community entered into an agreement that combined retrospective and prospective considerations, restoring property rights substantially to the community, providing some but not full compensation for diamonds extracted prior to the decision, converting the mining operation into a joint venture between the community and the state (in which the state retained a 51 percent share), and providing funds for reinvestment and community development.[19]

The tension between retrospective and prospective justice is not confined to a case like *Richtersveld.* The strategy of relying on truth commissions, rather than on criminal prosecutions, has been criticized by some commentators precisely because, in the interests of parties' future relations, it fails to do full retrospective justice.[20] Many arguments over the purging of officials of the old regime or over responses to past dispossession in societies other than South Africa are bedeviled by conflicts between retrospective and prospective standards: should responses focus upon the nature of past wrongs, or should they seek to manage parties' relations from here on?[21] Better solutions can be attained by teasing out the different forms of justice, inquiring into the standards appropriate to them, and deliberating over the relationships among them.

3. Adjustment of Contending Legal and Political Orders

The third form of justice concerns the adjustment of the juridical orders that should be deployed to achieve retrospective and prospective justice. Most discussions of transitional justice assume that the standards of justice are, in principle, unified. Often they argue as though those standards can be derived from universal principles of right or, as a surrogate for universal principles, from international law. At the very least, they tend to assume that the framework for determining the content of justice is unproblematic. If concessions are made to local variation, that again is treated as a matter of expediency.

But often there is great contestation over the framework within which justice is to be done. This is true in at least two ways. First, the very boundaries of the society may be in question. Every system of justice presupposes a society within which wrongs are corrected and benefits are distributed. But often, in transitions, the very dimensions of this society are challenged. The government may have used oppression not merely to maintain itself in office but also to incorporate and retain hold of disaffected cultural minorities. The dissolution of the old regime therefore raises the question of whether, in the reconstitution of the society, its boundaries should remain the same.[22] Second, every system of law, even if it does attempt to respect universal principles, pursues justice through a particular vernacular—a set of terms, concepts, exemplifications, and points of reference.[23] In transitions, there is often vigorous dispute over precisely whose language, whose tradition, should be used to achieve justice. Ignoring either of these dimensions can lead to a derailing of the transition. International and domestic actors can proceed as though their task were to achieve justice within a given framework, only to find that the framework implodes. Worse, actors can find themselves consolidating, sometimes inadvertently, conceptual or geographical boundaries that are themselves experienced as oppressive by a portion of the citizenry.

The transition in Iraq provides a good example.[24] There, the Coalition Provisional Authority under L. Paul Bremer approached its task as though it were simply one of eradicating a brutally oppressive and anti-American regime. Among other things, it instituted an especially thorough de-Ba'athification of the government and dissolved the armed forces. But, as soon became clear, these measures dramatically reduced Sunni participation in, and support for, the new regime.[25] Over time, U.S. policy in Iraq has evolved from a preoccupation with regime change to one of adjusting the relative relations of Shi'a, Sunni, and Kurd through power sharing in the central government, the elaboration of Iraq's federal structure, and the management of relations among the coalition forces, central government, and local militias. These challenges have implicated both aspects identified earlier. They have concerned the geographical dimensions of the society: can Iraq remain a unified country? Can its central government be made legitimate for all parties—Kurds, Sunni, and Shi'a? Might Iraq's federal structure be designed to finesse these issues? And they have also concerned the relations to be established among legal traditions: to what extent should Shi'a or Sunni religious law shape state policy? Is there a form of secularism that can accommodate Iraq's diversity?

How should the state relate to other dimensions of Iraqi political culture, such as the tribal structure of Sunni communities? How should Iraqi institutions respond to international norms or norms grounded in U.S. constitutional practice? I do not mean to suggest that, in Iraq, these issues have been addressed simply as matters of principle. As in all human affairs, baser motives have contributed to the outcome. But the relationship among competing legal and political orders has loomed large.

Examples might be multiplied. The transition from communism in central and eastern Europe cast into question the dimensions of many of those societies, resulting in the dissolution of the former Soviet Union, Yugoslavia, and Czechoslovakia and campaigns for the protection of minority rights—and sometimes further division—in many of the successor states. In South Africa, the desire to overcome the divisions of the past resulted in a concerted policy, especially on the part of the African National Congress, to assert the unity of the South African people against potential claims to cultural or group autonomy. That policy left its mark on the new South African constitution, especially its embrace of strong central institutions and its safeguards against the reemergence of apartheid in the private sphere.[26] There are also many cases in which controversy has arisen over the tradition of justice to be used in transitional situations. For example, the tensions between the Rwandan government and the International Criminal Tribunal for Rwanda over the trial of the *génocidaires* concerned not just the speed and volume of the prosecutions (although these certainly were at issue) but also, tied intrinsically to these concerns, the juridical philosophy that should direct the proceedings —whether the proceedings should be based on Rwandan traditions of community-based dispute settlement or on international (in fact predominantly Western) criminal-law norms.[27] Similar concerns have led to the creation of hybrid national/international tribunals in other situations.[28]

By drawing attention to these questions, I do not mean to prejudge the solutions. The justifications for secession, the creation of a federal structure, or the institution of regional autonomy are all profoundly complex, especially given the heterogeneity of human societies, the blurred boundaries of those societies, and the frequent coexistence of overlapping or competing definitions of community. To make headway on them, one needs to inquire into the nature of political and legal cultures, the manner in which communities might be structured in relation to those cultures, the factors that contribute to the viability of states, and the capacity —and institutional devices—for sustaining political community in culturally diverse societies.[29] To delve further into these questions would lead us far afield from the traditional territory of transitional justice.

One might be tempted, then, to hive them off, treating them as separate from transitional justice. That would be a mistake. Questions concerning this third form of justice are almost always present in transitional situations. Transitional justice is concerned, above all, with establishing a new political and legal order in place of one now seen to be illegitimate. Often, that illegitimacy is experienced differently in different segments of the population. The institutional dimensions of the society and the place accorded the traditions of minorities may well need to be addressed for all segments to be brought on board—and, if all segments cannot be brought on board, the consequences of separation or forcible incorporation need to be considered. Moreover, any attempt to address injustice inevitably adopts a particular language of justice and presumes particular dimensions to the society; any attempt to pursue transitional justice, then, takes a position on the normative character and structure of the society, whether consciously or not. That structure is rarely if ever given in transitional justice situations. There are generally many ways in which it might be defined and, often, there is more than one tradition of political and juridical inquiry on which such definitions might draw. It is better that the challenges of normative diversity be anticipated and addressed.

Finally, confining one's attention to retrospective and prospective justice and ignoring the third form may well lead one to mischaracterize the claims at issue. This is most evident in the case of indigenous peoples, who often find themselves subject to especially brutal treatment by oppressive regimes and who also form a central example in discussions of reparations for historic injustices.[30] Often, for example, indigenous claims are treated as though they were simply about rectificatory justice: they are about restitution *in integrum* of lands lost or compensation for government depredations. Indeed, retrospective claims are an element of many indigenous concerns. But indigenous peoples themselves frequently conceive of their claims in terms of prospective justice, either in addition to or instead of retrospective justice: they recognize that some form of sharing of their ancestral territories will be necessary, and they simply demand that the sharing occur on equitable terms. These prospective claims are not necessarily more tractable. Often the impact of nonindigenous activities upon the indigenous communities' livelihood has been extensive; any settlement will therefore involve real constraints on those activities. Moreover, the standard of what constitutes an equitable share is open to a wide range of definitions, with there often being a profound gulf between the definitions favored by the indigenous and those supported by nonindigenous parties. And, furthermore, even if a solution were found that satisfied retrospective and distributive justice, that would not exhaust indigenous concerns. Often, indigenous peoples seek, above all, to regulate significant dimensions of their lives according to norms rooted in their own traditions. Often, claims to land are as much about the capacity of indigenous peoples to sustain autonomous societies as they are about the restoration of indigenous property; they are intended to reestablish the territory of an indigenous society, not just to restore assets to indigenous individuals. All three forms of justice are therefore combined, with "dispossession" and "restoration" used to express all three. All the components of the claims need to be parsed, negotiated, and addressed.[31]

Indeed, some parties' commitment to their autonomy is so strong that they will forgo remedies based on retrospective and prospective justice if that is necessary to secure autonomy. Above all, they want to be free from the imposition of another community's language, laws, customs, and priorities. The Iraqi Kurds may provide a recent example. In fact, the parties' attitudes often have a federal character: the parties are firmly committed to autonomy, but, as long as sufficient autonomy is secured, they will be open to the pursuit of retrospective and prospective justice across cultural boundaries. And, even if they simply want to be free from involvement with another society, the societies may be so entangled that that may not be possible. They may be locked in a relationship whether they like it or not, and the only question therefore becomes how that relationship should be structured.

Frequently, then, situations of transitional justice involve this third form of justice, a form generally associated with the pursuit of self-determination. Its content is likely to be highly contested (as, indeed, is the content of self-determination). It is often best approached as a problem of fit—adjusting institutions to a very complex reality—rather than peremptory right. In those respects, however, it is not that different from prospective justice. My point in this section is not to prejudge the resolution of those challenges but merely to argue for the necessity of considering this as a third dimension of transitional justice—one that unsettles the common assumption that there is a single metric of justice at issue in transitional situations.

III. CONSEQUENCES OF THE FORMS OF JUSTICE

The three forms of justice help one to make better sense of controversies that figure prominently in the transitional justice literature. I have already discussed one such controversy when describing the forms of justice themselves: the extent to which, in transitional justice, the measure of damages (or punishment) diverges from what retrospective justice alone would require. Here I turn to three additional controversies: (1) the prescription of claims as a result of the passage of time; (2) the problem of judging claims relating to the past by the standards of today; and (3) the institutions appropriate to transitional justice. I will not canvass these questions exhaustively but merely show how the three forms of justice help to clarify the issues.

1. Prescription of Claims

Common law and civil law systems all provide that, after a certain time has elapsed, claims are lost. The prescription of claims is based on a number of considerations, including the desirability of having claims resolved quickly so that property rights are as dependable as possible (prescription periods encourage claimants to bring their claims expeditiously) and the challenge of establishing the facts after a long period of time has elapsed (evidence may no longer be available; memories may have faded). But the most important reason is one of substance—the idea that the sense of injustice, initially felt acutely, often wanes with time, that "time heals all wounds." This occurs for at least three reasons. First, the passage of time may have made it impossible to reverse the past injustice: parties may have died; the situation may now be so transformed that it is impossible to restore the original position. Second, as time passes, it becomes increasingly difficult to determine the effect of the original injustice on parties today because so many intervening events have occurred.[32] Third, over time, parties often adjust to the new state of affairs. People who have lost land pursue their lives elsewhere, form new attachments, and no longer depend upon the old land for self-fulfillment. At the same time, those who acquired the land develop their own connections to it; they build their lives around it. Indeed, the current owners may bear no responsibility for the original dispossession. It can make sense, then, for the law to adjust, at least to some degree, to the new situation.

Arguments based on prescription are raised in transitional justice and especially in claims made on the basis of historic injustice. Should parties be able to recover property seized by communist governments, or should one draw a line under the past, taking existing entitlements as one finds them?[33] Or consider the situation in *Richtersveld*. How far back should one go to reverse the consequences of a racially discriminatory dispossession? The South African constitution stipulates a precise date: June 19, 1913.[34]

We cannot answer all those questions here, but it is clear that the analysis will differ depending on the form of justice at issue. Arguments for prescription are most forceful in the case of retrospective justice. There, the entire purpose is to reverse an injustice that has taken place in the past. Retrospective justice is particularly vulnerable, then, to changes in circumstances that have occurred since that time. Once the situation has changed sufficiently, it may no longer be possible to reverse the loss in any real sense, even by substituting financial compensation. Moreover, because the injustice is emphatically grounded in the past, retrospective justice is especially vulnerable to the fact that parties will, with time, adjust to the loss.

The same is not true, however, if the claim is based on prospective justice. There, the injustice is not confined to the past. It is operating today in the very structure of the parties' relationship. As long as this is the case, it makes sense for the parties to address it today. But note that there the remedy will be determined not by the amount of the loss long in the past but by what is necessary to repair the parties' current relationship. The injustice exists today, and the remedy should be adapted to today. To put the argument another way, in prospective justice the factors that underlie prescription are taken into account by the very fact that it is today's relationship, not the original situation, that is the object of scrutiny. If the original injustice has been superseded, the supersession will be reflected in today's relations.

To see how an historic injustice can ground a prospective claim, consider the claim made by Japanese Canadians as a result of the seizure of their property and their removal in World War II.[35] The claimants argued not so much for the restoration of the specific losses incurred then but rather that, as long as the injustice was unacknowledged, those events continued to impair Japanese Canadians' relationship to Canada. They sought to repair that relationship, not simply to recover the loss they or their ancestors had suffered. In those circumstances, as long as the claim of continuing effect was right, prescription had no application. And, indeed, in the settlement concluded with the Canadian government in 1988, the outcome was adapted to the prospective nature of the claim, featuring an apology and the establishment of a foundation to commemorate the events and to work against racial prejudice.

With respect to the third form of justice, the effect of the passage of time is similar. Once again, the focus is overwhelmingly on the current situation. While past events may be relevant to the extent they have shaped current circumstances, the nature of the claim is grounded squarely in today's relations. The only kicker (and it is a large one) is that different normative traditions may be more than simply the object of parties' claims; the contending traditions may also furnish competing standards for the analysis and evaluation of those claims. They may, even in the case of retrospective justice, provide competing conceptions of the effect of the passage of time on injustice or, indeed, different conceptions of time itself.[36] The approach that one takes to achieving the third form of justice may therefore have an impact across transitional justice measures.

2. Inter-temporal Judgment

A second problem in transitional justice concerns the standards used to judge past events. Must those events be judged by the standards of the time, or should they be judged by our best understanding of justice today? To take the example from which all discussions derive: should the actions of Nazi officials be judged by Nazi standards, or are we entitled to judge them by our standards?

Once again, the considerations are quite different if one is dealing with retrospective rather than prospective justice. In retrospective justice, the injustice consists entirely in the fact that an illicit transaction has occurred and must now be reversed. It makes sense, then, to judge it by the standards of the time of the events —or to have exceptionally good reasons for overruling those standards, such as that the conduct violated considerations now judged to be so fundamental that they must be imposed retroactively. Even when today's standards are imposed, some concessions are likely to be made to the standards of the past—for example, that the standards imposed must have been accessible to the people concerned. In retrospective justice, the injustice is crystallized in the past. The appropriate standards tend strongly to be those of the past.

There are two important clarifications to this. First, any legal order consists of bundles of considerations that might be marshaled in different ways. When applying those considerations retrospectively, one is perfectly entitled to interpret the past order in a manner that now seems most sound.[37] For example, many vile regimes pay lip service to some standards of legality, especially the obligation to follow duly established laws. Otherwise, the regime would lose the ability to shape conduct through the promulgation of general norms. But, if this is so, then judges trying members of that regime are justified in holding them to those standards, even if there were extensive departures in practice and even if departures were condoned by the regime's leaders. That, after all, is what legal scholars and practitioners do when interpreting their own legal systems. Think, for example, of the assessment of the legality of interrogation techniques used by U.S. intelligence services under the Bush administration. Those actions are judged by one's best interpretation of the law at the time; the fact that breaches of the

law were condoned by the highest levels of the administration cannot make legal what is on one's best interpretation illegal. Indeed,
it is difficult to see how else one could reason with the standards
of the time. How else can one resolve conflicts among contending
interpretations of that law? Is one required to pick the most repre-
hensible alternative?

Second, the standards that one applies depend in part upon
the kind of judgment one is exercising. "Justice" is a capacious
term and includes decisions that can result in the punishment of
individuals and judgments limited to moral disapproval. I do not
mean to draw a hard and fast distinction between legal and moral
reasoning—my own preferred theory of legal interpretation sees
the first as a discursive subset of the second—but, to the extent
that one recognizes even a relative distinction between them, the
standards that one is entitled to draw upon differ as well. One is
entitled to invoke what would have been, at the time, more contentious considerations when engaging in moral judgment than
one would if one were reasoning within the law.

These clarifications are important; taken together, they suggest
that there is more potential for holding actors to account, even
within the standards of the past, than many discussions suggest.
The situation is substantially different, however, when one is engaged in prospective justice. Then, the focus is the injustice existing at the moment of judgment. The relevant standards are those
applicable now. If one is, for example, seeking to reconstruct the
administration of the state following the defeat of the Nazis, one
may have good reason to engage in more extensive de-Nazification
than would be justified by considerations of retrospective justice
alone. Of course, in this process, there will be important questions
about when and how de-Nazification should be visited upon individuals, and, in that process, some assessment of relative responsibility is likely to arise. But the fact remains that the predominant
focus is no longer the events of the past; the relevant standards of
justice are no longer confined to those of the time.

There might even be reasons for punishing individuals on the
basis of prospective justice, even when their conduct was in keeping with the standards of the time the events occurred. The need
to break with the past might be so compelling that those who most
exemplify the regime should be punished, even if it is difficult to

make the case that their conduct was unlawful at the time.[38] This may be a sufficient justification for punishing the leaders of the Nazis or an Eichmann. Given the manner in which normative argument proceeds through time, with norms consolidated through a process of assertion, counter-assertion, and judgment, the imposition of norms ex post facto might be more faithful to what was occurring in Nuremberg than the notion that those trials were based on a timeless, natural justice or on rules of international law operative when the Nazis were performing their atrocities. Even if the Nuremberg standards were, in 1930s Europe, norms of aspiration rather than accomplishment, there was good reason to insist upon them, to affirm them postwar.[39] Indeed, the selective nature of many attempts to try members of past regimes—focusing on the most egregious conduct or on a few exemplary offenders—suggests that often trials are used primarily to serve a prospective role.

Finally, note that the third form of justice injects yet another dimension into the assessment of the norms to ground judgment. If one is attempting to achieve justice across cultures, one has to consider not just how norms have changed through time but also how they differ across societies. If, in retrospective justice, actions should be judged by the norms governing the context in which they were performed, surely culture as well must be considered. The solution may involve a reading back of standards onto the context in much the same manner as just suggested in the case of prospective justice, but with the new standards informed by the interaction of cultures. This is not the place to discuss all the complexities of intercultural judgment, but the relevance of such an inquiry is clear.

3. Institutions

Institutional innovation has been prominent in transitional justice. Two institutions have received great attention in the literature, so much so that they are often treated as synonymous with transitional justice: war crime tribunals and truth commissions. But innovation extends well beyond these to include ad hoc structures for constitutional negotiation ("round tables," constitutional conventions, constituent assemblies); a host of special tribunals or commissions to restructure and purge the state administration;

and many others. And, of course, key roles have also been played by the ordinary institutions of public decision making: the courts, the legislature, and the administration (each of these often reformed in the course of transition).

Many considerations shape the choice of instrument, but the three forms of justice help to clarify the issues. Courts or court-like structures are especially appropriate for dealing with retrospective justice. There, the range of normative considerations is relatively confined, appropriate to resolution by a single decision maker or a panel chosen more for its professional expertise than for its representativeness. Moreover, in retrospective justice, one wants rigorous attention to be paid to the particular circumstances of the past event. Those facts are the gravamen of this form of justice. That attention is best secured by insulating the inquiry, at least to some extent, from today's political currents. That insulation is often best achieved by having an officer, one who enjoys judicial independence and acts within a highly rationalized procedure, apply an exigent standard of proof.

By contrast, courts are less suited to the pursuit of prospective justice. There, the considerations tend to be much more open-ended and contested. It is important that the mechanisms for addressing them be broadly participatory, less confined in their ambit, and less formal in their procedures, so that the choices have democratic legitimacy. Often, legislative decision makers or institutions that privilege negotiation are most appropriate. Moreover, in prospective justice, the demanding method of fact-finding typical of courts, focused on who did what on a specific occasion, is less essential. The facts relevant to prospective justice are more about the future consequences of present choices; they are often best resolved by institutions with a representative structure.[40]

Truth commissions are interesting because they are intermediate institutions. They are intended to expose the events of the past, and thus, by definition, they do pay careful attention to the past. Yet, their greater concern with questions of prospective justice supports their representative membership, their informal procedures, and the frequent inclusion of elements not found in courts, such as measures to support victims and to permit them to tell their stories fully, investigations into systemic abuses, the consideration of amnesty, and structured opportunities for confrontation, apology, and reconciliation.[41]

For its part, the third form of justice poses institutional demands associated with the need to create zones of autonomy and develop institutions to mediate among different normative traditions. Such solutions generally have to be developed through negotiations with strong minority participation; indeed, complex structures of negotiation have become typical of transitions. Once established, the new institutions frequently provide continued input from representatives of the different legal and political traditions. One sees this even in the organization of post-transitional courts, in which membership is often adjusted to reflect important divisions within the society. This is done for reasons of symbolism, to ensure that all parties can identify with the courts' decisions. But it also serves a substantive role by permitting the courts to incorporate a broader array of normative considerations into their decision making, the courts sometimes seeking to draw upon and reconcile different normative traditions. Some contemporary tribunals charged with deciding war crimes and crimes against humanity, for example, combine national and international judges and consider national as well as international law.[42] Indigenous representatives are sometimes included on judicial panels charged with deciding indigenous issues, sometimes as assessors, sometimes as full judges.[43]

Indeed, the identification of courts predominantly with retrospective justice and the use of other institutions to deal with the other forms of justice needs to be qualified in two important respects. First, it is a mistake to suppose that courts are concerned solely with retrospective justice, even if that is their principal area of expertise. In practice, they must also address other forms. For one thing, in any application of the law, the law must be interpreted, and, in that interpretation, judges necessarily draw upon prospective considerations.[44] In the criminal law, while some aspects of the proceedings are retrospective (the determination of guilt, the imposition of retributive punishment), others are manifestly prospective (the tempering of punishment by rehabilitation or deterrence). Now, judges' engagement with prospective justice tends to be limited; it is more ancillary, more interstitial, than primary. Judges nevertheless do make such judgments. They need to be constituted to enable them to do so—one good reason for the special attention to representation in the structure of posttransition courts.

Second, although courts are often poorly placed to decide questions within the other two forms of justice, their decisions can foreclose those questions, substituting the narrow optic of retrospective justice within a single legal tradition for what should be a broader set of considerations. This should be guarded against by policymakers and by judges themselves. A good example of judges' shaping their decisions in consequence is provided by the Canadian courts' approach to indigenous issues. Those courts have come to see that aspects of that relationship are much better handled by negotiations, precisely because they involve the reapportionment of resources and the restructuring of institutions in a manner responsive to indigenous traditions. They have tried to limit their decisions, then, to the recognition of the existence of an indigenous interest, specifying only its general outlines and exhorting the parties to negotiate. Judges have limited their involvement to the declaration of "framing norms," with the detail to be fleshed out through negotiations.[45]

IV. Conclusion

The three forms of justice help, then, to draw out the full array of normative considerations at issue in transitions. Transitional justice is about more than simply the tempering of justice by expediency. It is about judgment at a time of normative transformation, when a new order is being founded and institutions constructed through the decisions taken. In those decisions, transitional justice necessarily confronts the three forms of justice identified here: retrospective justice, prospective justice, and the adjustment of contending legal and political orders. Those three forms arise in ordinary times, as well, but in transitions the salience of the second and third forms of justice is especially pronounced because the whole purpose is to redefine the society.

Many of the characteristic debates of transitional justice are tripped up by the failure to perceive the different forms of justice. Measures of damages and rules of prescription appropriate to retrospective justice are presumed to apply to claims founded on prospective justice, creating a profound mismatch of claim and response.[46] Courts are left to provide remedies for prospective justice for which they are unsuited, while those institutions that could speak to the claims—such as legislatures—are tempted to hide behind the courts, treating their proceedings as definitive.[47] Or, worse, arguments founded on retrospective justice are taken to be exhaustive of all moral considerations, foreclosing other claims by default.[48] Finally, decision-making structures are established without attending to legal and political diversity, so that minorities find themselves subjected to norms and institutions to which they have little attachment.

The recognition of the forms of justice does not make such complex issues easy. There will be fierce debate over what prospective justice means, the arrangements appropriate to the co-existence of different normative traditions, the relationship to be established between prospective and retrospective justice, and so on, all in the context of the specific society and its particular history. But, at least, we, as commentators, will be addressing our arguments to the substance of the claims—and helping to clarify those claims—not blundering along under multiple misapprehensions. Moreover, we will be in a better position to address the all-important question of institutions. Often, in transitional justice, our task is not simply to stipulate the just solution. While we can serve an important role by clarifying options and assisting with normative judgment, in the last analysis the resolution has to be determined by the parties themselves, as they fashion their new social and political relations. Those decisions are made through institutions, structures that help to shape the possible outcomes. Clarifying the forms of justice can help us better match institutions to their role.

NOTES

My thanks to Marcia Barry and Kate Devlin for their excellent research assistance, and to Nathalie Des Rosiers, Avigail Eisenberg, Hadley Friedland, Matt James, Martin Krygier, Rosemary Nagy, Melissa Williams, and Zhang Qianfan for invaluable comments on earlier versions of this argument.

1. Eric A. Posner and Adrian Vermeule, "Transitional Justice as Ordinary Justice," *Harvard Law Review* 117 (2003–2004): 769. Pablo de Greiff, in his contribution to this volume, appears to reject this common tendency to trade off justice against political precaution. He wants to articulate an approach that rejects trade-offs among different transitional justice measures and that pursues those measures in the furtherance of a unified

conception of justice. But even his conception begins with a sense of limitation, of the inability to do full retrospective justice in "a very imperfect world" because of the "huge and predictable costs associated with the very effort to enforce compliance." The causes of this inability are not elaborated in his account, but they appear to involve judgments of political practicability that are often subsumed within expediency.

2. I am not the only one to use the terms "retrospective" and "prospective" justice. Posner and Vermeule adopt the terms "backward-looking" and "forward-looking," although they tend to give the concept of forward-looking justice a predominantly pragmatic cast: ibid., 766; Eric A. Posner and Adrian Vermeule, "Reparations for Slavery and Other Historical Injustices," *Columbia Law Review* 103 (2003): 692. See also Ruti G. Teitel, *Transitional Justice* (New York: Oxford University Press, 2000), e.g., 7, although she uses the terms to refer to retrospective and prospective considerations generally, not to different orientations toward justice.

3. I have addressed one such claim for historical redress in Jeremy Webber, "Rights and Wrongs, Institutions and Time: Species of Historic Injustice and Their Modes of Redress," in *Calling Power to Account: Law, Reparations, and the Chinese Canadian Head Tax Case*, ed. David Dyzenhaus and Mayo Moran (Toronto: University of Toronto Press, 2005), 165.

4. Charles Taylor, for example, has forcefully argued that perceptions of community and conceptions of right are interdependent. In order to care about establishing a relation of justice with others, one has to see oneself as bound to a certain solidarity with them: Charles Taylor, "Cross-Purposes: The Liberal-Communitarian Debate," in *Philosophical Arguments*, ed. Charles Taylor (Cambridge, MA: Harvard University Press, 1995), 181, especially at 187–89. In transitions, both the solidarity and the conception of justice are in issue simultaneously: one is often both seeking to establish a sense of solidarity and seeking to establish a potentially common, revised conception of justice. Establishing one often depends on making progress on the other.

5. Ruti Teitel's work is an exception, however, especially in the centrality she attaches to "normative shifts" in transitions: Teitel, *Transitional Justice*, esp. 5–7.

6. This is true, for example, of de Grieff's contribution to this volume, which defines transitional justice solely in relation to "massive human rights abuses." This makes it much easier for him to insist upon a unified conception of justice in relation to which all transitional justice measures are to be assessed. But transitional situations also raise issues that do not involve such a stark confrontation between good and evil, such as in debates over the restoration of property expropriated by the previous regime or the restaffing of government following a change in regime. There, as I will show, the different forms of justice clearly can come into conflict.

7. Aristotle, *Nicomachean Ethics*, trans. Christopher Rowe (Oxford: Oxford University Press, 2002), 1131b25ff.

8. Ibid., 1131a10ff.

9. See John Braithwaite, "Principles of Restorative Justice," in *Restorative Justice and Criminal Justice: Competing or Reconcilable Paradigms?*, ed. Andrew von Hirsch, Julian V. Roberts, and Anthony Bottoms (Oxford: Hart, 2003), 1–20; Gerry Johnstone, *Restorative Justice: Ideas, Values, Debates* (Cullompton, Devon: Willan, 2002); Howard Zehr, *Changing Lenses: A New Focus for Crime and Justice*, 3rd ed. (Scottdale, PA: Herald Press, 2005).

10. Compare Law Commission of Canada, *From Restorative Justice to Transformative Justice: Discussion Paper* (Ottawa: Law Commission of Canada, 1999).

11. For overviews, see Martha Minow, *Between Vengeance and Forgiveness: Facing History After Genocide and Mass Violence* (Boston: Beacon Press, 1998), 52–90; Priscilla B. Hayner, *Unspeakable Truths: Facing the Challenge of Truth Commissions* (New York: Routledge, 2002). The literature is especially large on the South African Truth and Reconciliation Commission. See, e.g., Martin Meredith, *Coming to Terms: South Africa's Search for Truth* (New York: Public Affairs, 1999); Alex Boraine, *A Country Unmasked: Inside South Africa's Truth and Reconciliation Commission* (Oxford: Oxford University Press, 2000); Charles Villa-Vicencio and Wilhelm Verwoerd, eds., *Looking Back, Reaching Forward: Reflections on the Truth and Reconciliation Commission of South Africa* (Cape Town: University of Cape Town Press, 2000).

12. See Teitel, *Transitional Justice*, 149–77 and 185–89; and Wojciech Sadurski, "'Decommunisation,' 'Lustration,' and Constitutional Continuity," in *Rights Before Courts: A Study of Constitutional Courts in Postcommunist States of Central and Eastern Europe*, ed. Wojciech Sadurski (Dordrecht: Springer, 2005), 223 (who notes the disjuncture between the public justifications given for decommunization and lustration—predominantly prospective —and those that he considers to have motivated many of the policies —retributive).

13. See Minow, *Between Vengeance and Forgiveness*, 91–117; Teitel, *Transitional Justice*, 119–47; Duncan Ivison, "Political Community and Historical Injustice," *Australasian Journal of Philosophy* 78 (2000): 360–73; David Lyons, "Corrective Justice, Equal Opportunity, and the Legacy of Slavery and Jim Crow," *Boston University Law Review* 84 (2004): 1375–1404.

14. Matt James, "Redress Politics and Canadian Citizenship," in *Canada: The State of Federation 1998/1999: How Canadians Connect*, ed. Harvey Lazar and Tom McIntosh (Montreal: Queen's University Press, 1999), 258–59; Minow, *Between Vengeance and Forgiveness*, 100 and 102–5.

15. Roy Miki and Cassandra Kobayashi, *Justice in Our Time: The Japanese Canadian Redress Settlement* (Vancouver: Talonbooks, 1991), 139; Audrey

Kobayashi, "The Japanese Canadian Redress Settlement and Its Implications for 'Race-Relations,'" *Canadian Ethnic Studies* 24 (1992): 1–19.

16. *Alexkor Ltd and the Government of the Republic of South Africa v. Richtersveld Community*, 12 Butterworths Constitutional Law Reports 1301 (2003). I am indebted to the discussion in Marcia Barry, "Now Another Thing Must Happen: *Richtersveld* and the Dilemmas of Land Reform in Post-Apartheid South Africa," *South African Journal on Human Rights* 20 (2004): 355–82.

17. Constitution of the Republic of South Africa (1996), sec. 25.

18. Barry, "Now Another Thing Must Happen," 356.

19. See the briefing of the South African Department of Public Enterprises to the National Council of Provinces Committee on Labour and Public Enterprises, June 24, 2008, reported on the website of the Parliamentary Monitoring Group, http://www.pmg.org.za/report/20080624-richtersveld-land-claim-settlement-alexander-bay-township-establishme.

20. See, e.g., the debate in Charles Villa-Vicencio and Erik Doxtader, eds., *The Provocations of Amnesty: Memory, Justice and Impunity* (Claremont, South Africa: David Philip Publishers, 2003).

21. See, e.g., regarding the restitution of property in the postcommunist context, "A Forum on Restitution," *East European Constitutional Review* 2, no. 3 (1993): 30–40, and, regarding the purging of officials, Sadurski, "'Decommunisation,' 'Lustration,' and Constitutional Continuity."

22. Indeed, in a celebrated article, Dankwart Rustow took national unity to be his only precondition to democratization: Dankwart A. Rustow, "Transitions to Democracy: Toward a Dynamic Model," *Comparative Politics* 2 (1970): 337–63 (I am grateful to Matt James for bringing this to my attention). He treated unity as an exogenously determined condition, already established and serving as a necessary (but not sufficient) foundation for the development of democracy. But in many transitions it is not simply given; the structure of the state is itself a matter for judgment, argument, and determination in the transition.

23. Jeremy Webber, "The Grammar of Customary Law," *McGill Law Journal* 54 (2009): 579–626.

24. My thanks to Peter Crawford for research on the evolution of the U.S.-led coalition's policy in Iraq, done under my supervision in fall 2007.

25. For accounts, see Eric Stover, Hanny Megally, and Hania Mufti, "Bremer's 'Gordian Knot': Transitional Justice and the U.S. Occupation of Iraq," *Human Rights Quarterly* 27 (2005): 830–57; David L. Phillips, *Losing Iraq: Inside the Postwar Reconstruction Fiasco* (Boulder, CO: Westview Press, 2005), 140ff.; Ali A. Allawi, *The Occupation of Iraq: Winning the War, Losing the Peace* (New Haven: Yale University Press, 2007), 147ff.

26. Kristin Henrard, *Minority Protection in Post-Apartheid South Africa: Human Rights, Minority Rights, and Self-Determination* (Westport, CT: Praeger, 2002).

27. See Mark A. Drumbl, *Atrocity, Punishment, and International Law* (Cambridge: Cambridge University Press, 2007). See also Phil Clark, "Hybridity, Holism, and Traditional Justice: The Case of the Gacaca Courts in Post-Genocide Rwanda," *George Washington International Law Review* 39 (2007): 765–838, who emphasizes the extent to which institutions grounded in tradition are adapted to address new challenges, often themselves becoming "hybrid."

28. See Cesare P. R. Romano, André Nollkaemper, and Jann K. Kleffner, eds., *Internationalized Criminal Courts: Sierra Leone, East Timor, Kosovo, and Cambodia* (Oxford: Oxford University Press, 2004); Sarah M. H. Nouwen, "'Hybrid Courts': The Hybrid Category of a New Type of International Crimes Courts," *Utrecht Law Review* 2, no. 2 (2006): 190–214.

29. I have addressed these questions in the Canadian context in, among other works, Jeremy Webber, *Reimagining Canada: Language, Culture, Community and the Canadian Constitution* (Montreal: McGill-Queen's University Press, 1994).

30. See especially Jeff Corntassel and Cindy Holder, "Who's Sorry Now? Government Apologies, Truth Commissions, and Indigenous Self-Determination in Australia, Canada, Guatemala, and Peru," *Human Rights Review* 9, no. 4 (2008): 465–89.

31. For an excellent example of this parsing, see the analysis of the debate over Maori rights in New Zealand/Aotearoa in Andrew Sharp, *Justice and the Maori: The Philosophy and Practice of Maori Claims in New Zealand Since the 1970s*, 2nd ed. (Auckland: Oxford University Press, 1997).

32. This is the principal foundation for Jeremy Waldron's argument regarding the supersession of historic injustice: Jeremy Waldron, "Superseding Historic Injustice," *Ethics* 103 (1992): 4–28; Jeremy Waldron, "Redressing Historic Injustice," *University of Toronto Law Journal* 52 (2002): 135–160. His argument is open to a number of objections, especially when applied to indigenous claims. Some relate to the questions canvassed in the text, especially Waldron's assumption that indigenous claims are simply about retrospective justice. Others relate to his assumption that indigenous dispossession occurred long in the past, when often the initial assertion of the government's title was purely theoretical, indigenous peoples were left in possession, and effective dispossession has occurred much more recently. For other criticisms, see Minow, *Between Vengeance and Forgiveness,* 107–10; Ivison, "Political Community and Historical Injustice"; Paul Patton, "Colonialisation, Historic Injustice: The Australian Experience," in *Justice in Time: Responding to Historical Injustice,* ed. Lukas H. Meyer (Baden-Baden: Nomos Verlagsgesellschaft, 2004), 159.

33. See "A Forum on Restitution," especially the contribution of George Sher, 37–38.

34. Constitution of the Republic of South Africa (1996), sec. 25, par. 7.

These cutoffs themselves pose serious problems. See Teitel, *Transitional Justice*, 134–38 and, more generally on questions of prescription, 138–41.

35. Miki and Kobayashi, *Justice in Our Time*; Kobayashi, "The Japanese Canadian Redress Settlement and Its Implications for 'Race-Relations.'"

36. See, for example, J. G. A. Pocock, "Law, Sovereignty and History in a Divided Culture: The Case of New Zealand and the Treaty of Waitangi," *McGill Law Journal* 43 (1998): 481–506.

37. This is an important dimension in David Dyzenhaus's discussion of these issues in, e.g., Dyzenhaus, "The Juristic Force of Injustice," in *Calling Power to Account*, ed. Dyzenhaus and Moran, 256, although Dyzenhaus goes further and argues that one can judge conduct on the basis of transhistorical requirements of legality.

38. Compare Teitel's emphasis on prospective reasons for punishment: Teitel, *Transitional Justice*, 28–67, esp. 66–67.

39. For a justification of the Nuremberg prosecutions that incorporates an argument along these lines, see Bernard D. Meltzer, "A Note on Some Aspects of the Nuremberg Debate," *University of Chicago Law Review* 14 (1946–47): 455–69. Meltzer's justification emphasizes that the standards were already part of the normative environment, especially internationally, before the war. As I note later, some ability of the actors to access the standards now imposed at the time the actions were being committed may be a precondition to the punishment of individuals. But the prior existence of those standards need not amount to their being the law of the time; on the contrary, they may have been at that time more a matter of aspiration than accomplishment. The prospective considerations justify their use in the later proceedings regardless. One might say that, as in many instances of transitional justice, the prosecution is hybrid, with its limitations as retrospective justice perfected by the strong considerations of prospective justice. Compare Robert D. Sloane, "The Expressive Capacity of International Punishment: The Limits of the National Law Analogy and the Potential of International Criminal Law," *Stanford Journal of International Law* 43 (2007): 39–94.

40. In Kenneth Culp Davis's famous distinction, one can therefore distinguish "legislative" from "adjudicative" facts: Kenneth Culp Davis, *Administrative Law Treatise* (St. Paul: West, 1958), vol. 2, s.15.03.

41. See note 12.

42. See note 29.

43. Most of these initiatives have occurred at the level of trial courts, generally in the context of criminal trials. There are increasing calls for the inclusion of indigenous representatives on the peak judicial institutions. Bolivia has adopted a new constitution creating a "plurinational" Constitutional Court with indigenous representation. See República del Bolivia, Constitución de 2009, arts. 196ff, available online at the Georgetown

University Political Database of the Americas, http://pdba.georgetown .edu/Constitutions/Bolivia/bolivia09.html; United Nations General Assembly, Eleventh Session, *Report of the Special Rapporteur on the Situation of Human Rights and Fundamental Freedoms of Indigenous People: Mission to Bolivia*, prepared by Rodolfo Stavenhagen, A/HRC/11/11, February 18, 2009, esp. par. 26, http://www2.ohchr.org/english/bodies/hrcouncil/ docs/11session/A.HRC.11.11.pdf.

44. For the combination of retrospective and prospective considerations at the heart of private-law adjudication in tort, see Peter Cane, "Corrective Justice and Correlativity in Private Law," *Oxford Journal of Legal Studies* 16 (1996): 471–88; Peter Cane, *Responsibility in Law and Morality* (Portland, OR: Hart, 2002), 181–90.

45. Jeremy Webber, "Beyond Regret: Mabo's Implications for Australian Constitutionalism," in *Political Theory and the Rights of Indigenous Peoples*, ed. Duncan Ivison, Paul Patton, and Will Sanders (Cambridge: Cambridge University Press, 2000), 75–76; Jeremy Webber, "Institutional Dialogue Between Courts and Legislatures in the Definition of Fundamental Rights: Lessons from Canada (and Elsewhere)," in *Constitutional Justice, East and West*, ed. Wojciech Sadurski (The Hague: Kluwer Law International, 2003), 78–80.

46. Jeremy Waldron has done just this in his arguments on prescription. See note 3.

47. See Webber, "Rights and Wrongs, Institutions and Time."

48. This is often the case in discussions of reparations, which frequently treat these as though retrospective justice were their only justification. See, e.g., Ellen Frankel Paul, "Set-Asides, Reparations, and Compensatory Justice," in *Nomos 33: Compensatory Justice*, ed. John W. Chapman (New York: New York University Press, 1991), 97; Posner and Vermeule, "Reparations for Slavery and Other Historical Injustices."

4

COUNTERING THE WRONGS
OF THE PAST: THE ROLE
OF COMPENSATION

DEBRA SATZ

1. Introduction

Demands for repair can sound in different registers. Think of a mundane case of harm, concerning harm to one person's property, occurring in the present. If A intentionally damages B's car, B can ask A to provide monetary compensation; to restore (if possible) her car to its undamaged state; to apologize or perhaps even to make a public acknowledgment of his responsibility. B can seek to have A prosecuted under law for his acts, seek mediation, or attempt to settle things on her own without third-party involvement. What B asks of A can reflect what B cares about, what she thinks she is likely to receive, or what she thinks she is owed. Different individuals in the same circumstances as B might ask for and accept different measures of repair. And different individuals in the same circumstances as A might respond to these demands in different ways.

This example involves a simple case of a single individual who suffers damage in the present to her property from a single individual who is directly (and intentionally) responsible. But, even here, demands for repair can vary, and responses that might be appropriate in one situation might not be appropriate in another.

Varying the relations between A and B, for example, might make apology seem especially important in one case and monetary compensation sufficient in another. If through negligence I break my son's favorite toy, it will seem heartless to offer him its cash equivalent while showing him absolutely no remorse or regret. In other cases, it can be difficult to know, when you have hurt someone, what response to his pain is appropriate and what, if anything, you can and should do if that response fails to repair.[1]

It is not easy to move from this simple example to the large-scale contexts in which demands for repair have recently been made: the contexts of Majdanek and Treblinka, the disappeared of Argentina and victims of Pinochet, the large-scale expropriations of Eastern Europe, the destruction of Aboriginal homelands, American slavery and Jim Crow. It is not only that these large-scale evils are difficult to contemplate and to understand and that they have caused losses that seem impossible to repair; it is also that they extend into the past and encompass many victims and perpetrators who are no longer alive. How can repair actually occur in these contexts?

Efforts to respond to and repair the wrongs of the past raise both practical and philosophical concerns. Such concerns include not only the questions related to identifying those who are the appropriate recipients of reparation and those who are obligated to bear the costs but also questions about the appropriate goal of programs aimed at countering wrongs (is it compensation, reconciliation, or punishment, for example?) and the best means for meeting that goal (is it money, apology, land redistribution, changes in law, or something else altogether?). Is there even a single best form, or should the form vary from case to case, and, if so, is there any basis for choosing between forms of remedy?

In this chapter, I explore the role of compensation in repairing historical wrongs. I focus on the standard welfare economist's view of compensation since this seems to be the one that is most often appealed to in philosophical and legal discussions of compensation. Furthermore, the default position in such discussions, as in American tort law, is that cash is the best form of compensation, a view that accords well with the economic conception of compensation. But, while cash compensation is a part of many claims of reparative justice, victims often focus on other demands. Are there good reasons for preferring other responses to historical wrongs, and, if so, what are those reasons? What role, if any, should compensation play in countering the wrongs of the past?

2. Countering Wrongs in Terms of Compensation

Victims of grave injustices or their descendants sometimes argue for compensation for the losses that they have suffered. Indeed, reparations in the form of financial compensation have been a part of many programs in which states are trying to remedy past harms.[2] In this section, I examine a common meaning of "compensation." However, I want to register two initial caveats to the idea of repair understood in terms of compensation. First, victims of large-scale injustices most often seek compensation as part of a larger set of goals. These include the goals of coming to terms with their pasts, receiving acknowledgment of the harms that were done to them, attempting to regain a way of life that was lost, and punishing the perpetrators. Second, the societies involved in reparative efforts also usually have larger goals than simply compensating losses. This is in part because projects of repair have a special place in societies undergoing transitions to democracy. Compensation, in this context, is the most tangible manifestation of the efforts of the new state to remedy the harms that these victims have suffered, and to re-instill a sense of trust and social solidarity. Compensation claims can also arise between states, as in the recent cases before the International Court of Justice. In these cases, states are also seeking compliance with international rules and a cessation of violations.[3] These caveats are meant to underscore the fact that compensation does not usually stand alone as a means of repair and that compensatory demands themselves may involve aims of retribution or deterrence.

How should we understand the term "compensation"? The term is familiarly seen as a form of payment for a loss or disadvantage. Judith Thomson develops the idea that compensation is a debt we owe someone when we have wronged him, a way of making up for what we have done.[4] This debt can be viewed in cash terms, or at least in terms of material goods, the provision of which is seen as making up for some loss of goods that has occurred by providing other goods in the same or another category.

It can also be understood in terms of less tangible goods such as apology and the public expression of responsibility.[5] Restitution is often defined as a subcategory of compensation where the good to be made up is precisely the good that was lost.[6]

Unfortunately, the idea of "making up for" a loss is imprecise, especially if we consider the cases in which restitution is impossible.

Welfare economists give us a more tractable interpretation of compensation: agent X compensates agent Y for his loss if and only if receiving this compensation leaves Y at least as high on an indifference curve as he would have been without receiving it but also without suffering the loss.[7] On this view, an agent is completely compensated for a loss when he is indifferent between his life as it was before the loss and his life as it is now after the loss but with additional goods. The agent has no reason to prefer his past situation before his losses to his current situation after the loss has occurred. More expansively, this idea of compensation can be applied to the agent's overall lifetime satisfaction: an agent is completely compensated when he receives the same lifetime sum of happiness that he could have expected to receive given his circumstances before experiencing the loss.

The goal of this view of compensation might be accomplished in any number of ways, although money is frequently the form such compensation takes, since money can be directed to the satisfaction of a wide range of an agent's preferences and satisfactions. Money is, or appears to be, an all-purpose means.[8]

This way of understanding compensation is only one of several possibilities: as I mentioned, understanding compensation in terms of restitution is another. Compensation as restitution is on the other end of the continuum from the economic idea of compensation as establishing an equal level of preference satisfaction because in the case of restitution there is no equivalent for the loss; only the restoration of the very thing lost will accomplish the work of repair. Between these polar points, we can also imagine views of compensation that restrict to some degree the scope of either the aim or means of compensation. For example, affirmative action has been defended as a means for making up for the educational opportunities (and not for other losses) that African Americans were previously denied.

While those who have different understandings of the appropriate goals of or means for compensation may converge on a specific policy proposal, they will have very different rationales. Someone who cares only about returning victims to a prior level of satisfaction might eschew money as a means of compensation in favor of an in-kind payment, but she will have only contingent reasons for preferring the in-kind payment. For example, Eric Posner and Adrian Vermeule argue that a payment of cash compensation to members of a Native American tribe who suffer from high rates of alcoholism, due largely to the original injustices suffered by the tribe, might serve only to exacerbate the effects of those injustices.[9]

There are three important points to note about what I am calling the economic view of compensation. First, it seems to presuppose a theory in which the only thing that matters (at least from the standpoint of public policy) is overall preference satisfaction: compensation aims to render an individual as satisfied after as before a loss. Second, it suggests that all such satisfactions can be put on a single scale and aggregated into an overall utility function. Third and finally, it suggests that the basis of a claim to compensation arises from the losses to a person's level of satisfaction and not the need to redress a particular wrong.

The goal of compensation understood in this sense appears reasonable in many contexts, and it is not my point to argue against it in all circumstances. Still, there are contexts in which people find compensation of this sort to be partly or wholly inappropriate. Before turning to the cases of historical injustices, I want to consider the three features of this view of compensation to see if we can understand why this is so.

2.1. Compensation as Equal Preference Satisfaction

Consider the following example, which I adapt from an article by Jo Wolff.[10] African American children in the United States receive, on average, an education inferior to whites. This inferior education effectively excludes many of them from even the possibility of attending a selective four-year college. It is a reasonable assumption that, under more just social circumstances, many of these children would have had a much better chance of attending a good university. Most of us would agree, further, that it is unfair that such children did not have such a chance. At the very least, such unequal chances violate the American dream. Suppose that we conclude that children who were effectively excluded from higher education, on the basis of their inferior education as children, now have a claim as adults to some form of redress. What form should this redress take?

Imagine a proposal to offer all African American children who have attended inferior schools a lump sum cash payment when they reach the age at which they would have graduated university. Imagine further that the African American adults to whom this payment was made would be satisfied with this payment and that society was willing to go on making such payments in compensation for its unequal schooling.

It is doubtful that many of us would feel that this payment really made up for the losses that these young adults suffered. Nor would we think that it was an appropriate response to the initial (and continuing) injustice. Why?

First, we might doubt that the uneducated adult really knows what he has missed by not attending college. Like John Stuart Mill, we might be tempted by the thought that the value of certain goods can be grasped only through experiencing those goods. People's preferences reflect their experiences. Further, using preferences as a basis of compensation in cases where people have little opportunity could lead to too little compensation, since many people adjust their desires to their opportunities (the problem of adaptive preferences).

Second, we might reflect on what it is a person loses when she receives an inferior education. On our list would undoubtedly be future earnings and the chance to pursue many high-paying and interesting career options that are only possible for someone with a good education. But we would likely also include the chance of a person to develop her capabilities.[11] The development of a person's capabilities can enrich the whole of her life. It changes the way she thinks about herself and perhaps even the way she thinks, enabling her to make her choices in a more informed way. This development of a person's capabilities may be valued for its income-earning dimensions, but such development is also valued by people on independent grounds.

A third and perhaps a deeper reason for rejecting this proposal is that we might think that, by focusing only on the losses to an individual's level of satisfaction, the proposal fails to counter the central wrong: society's objectionable norms and practices that led to so few African American children attending selective colleges. Improvements in a person's subjective preferences do not make up for disadvantages that have been publicly and unjustly imposed on him. If a person finds happiness in her life despite being oppressed by others, this hardly serves to justify (or undo or otherwise erase) the oppression.

In the case of cash compensation to African Americans who have been effectively excluded from higher education, the form of remedy in terms of financial compensation seems jarring because it does not match the type of harm it is being used to counter, the unjust foreshortening of their opportunities for development. This is also the reason why many people view cash compensation for past injustices to African Americans as misguided.[12] Nevertheless, as I discuss later, this lack of fit between wrong and remedy does not demolish the case for cash compensation, even in cases such as this one. In some circumstances, cash may be in fact the only reasonable option practically available. Perhaps it is too late, in the case of many of these adults, to return them to education and ultimately to college. In such cases, we need to ask whether a rough justice is better than no justice.[13]

2.2. Aggregation of Preferences into a Single Scale

A second assumption of full compensation is that we can aggregate all of an individual's satisfactions into a single scale, an overall utility function. But sometimes people view what they care about as incommensurable with other goods. In cases where restitution is being demanded, for example, an individual wants a particular good returned to her, such as a home, a homeland, or a particular family heirloom. In such cases, many people reject the idea that money can somehow compensate them for their loss. For example, eight Sioux tribes have refused to accept a US$122 million payment awarded to them in a 1980 U.S. Supreme Court case as compensation for the lands seized from them in the Black Hills.[14] They insist that the Black Hills belong to them and that no settlement is acceptable that does not include their return.

In other cases, people reject cash payment as insulting or demeaning; in their rejection, they say things like they do not want to be "bought off." When the Prime Minister of Japan offered a letter of apology and monetary compensation to some five hundred survivors among the two hundred thousand "comfort women" exploited as sexual slaves during World War II, only six women accepted the offer. Most of the women rejected the offer because the fund came from private sources rather than the government and was not accompanied by any official apology.[15]

Different forms of compensation send different and nonequivalent messages. If I cheat on my partner and then offer him money as compensation, he may surmise that I have not really understood the harm I have caused him. After all, I betrayed him; I did not merely cause him to suffer a tangible decline in his level of preference satisfaction. Repairing a betrayal takes a lot of emotional effort, time, and mutual understanding. In cases where past injustices have damaged not only people's possessions but also their self-esteem and trust, limited their options, and treated them with contempt, money can communicate that we think that these are just tangible losses that can be paid off.

The examples of some of the most emotionally powerful claims for repair, claims that emerge in the face of humanity's worst abuses—genocide, ethnic cleansing, torture, colonial domination, and enslavement—point to a similar problem with the assumption of commensurability. How can we possibly find an equivalent to compensate for these wrongs? When damages are offered as rectification for atrocities, no level of compensation seems sufficient —there is no payment that can wipe the slate clean. As one critic of the compensation paradigm for reparations puts it: "No market exists for the value of living an ordinary life, without nightmares or survivor guilt. Valuing the losses from torture and murder strains the imagination."[16]

While such difficulties with compensation do not rule out the possibility that cash payment may have an appropriate role (we do, after all, compensate accident victims or entertain wrongful-death suits), they suggest that not all payments are equivalent and that different losses may be incommensurable with one another, and that in some contexts money will be inappropriate.

2.3. The Obligation to Compensate Is Disconnected from the Wrong Done and from the Wrongdoer

The economic view of compensation does not specify the relationship between the compensator and the compensated. In theory, if an individual has suffered a loss, anyone can make up for the loss. But clearly this is not true of all kinds of losses. Suppose that my friend has lied to me. Her cousin cannot meaningfully apologize to me for her lie to me; only she (the liar) can do that. The Korean comfort women could accept reparation only from the government that had wronged them and not from anyone else. The very ability to compensate is in such cases a relational property.

Some philosophers writing about reparations, such as Bernard Boxill and Martha Minow, have argued that compensation cannot be the right paradigm for understanding what reparative justice means.[17] Reparative justice in the context of historical wrongs is by its nature concerned with repairing the moral relationships between victim and perpetrator: it is necessarily relational. By contrast, an agent may owe compensation even when he has done nothing wrong.

An example might help to draw out the distinction these critics of the compensation paradigm have in mind.[18] Suppose that your father steals my bicycle and gives it to you. You are unaware that the bicycle was stolen. I die, but my son eventually finds out about the theft. Even though you are an innocent third party, you arguably still have a compensatory duty to return the bicycle. But you have no duty to restore a relationship with my son, for you have done nothing to damage it.

Reparatory duties thus differ from compensatory duties. But we have to be careful about the conclusion we draw from this. Compensation might itself be a way of repairing relationships, and, even if is not a sufficient means for doing so, it might sometimes be a necessary one. People often say that "talk is cheap" and that you should "put your money where your mouth is." President Clinton's exploration of an apology to slaves' descendants, unaccompanied by compensation, met with a great lack of enthusiasm. Moreover, sometimes victims are not interested in healing their moral relationships with the perpetrators. Even if compensation cannot be the whole of repairing the past, it can be (and often has been) a significant part. Indeed, until quite recently, most demands for repair following historical injustice were primarily financial.

However, the critics are correct in pointing out that the idea of countering a *wrong* is central to the case of reparations for historical injustices. In some cases, wrongs do not show up as losses in satisfaction. If our obligation to act is in response to the fact that

we are in some way complicit in a wrong, then focusing on preference satisfaction is misleading. For even if there were no effects on
an agent's preferences, an obligation to counter wrong can persist,
especially to the extent that the wrong continues to have effects
through society's norms and practices.

In sum, I have argued that there are three considerations relevant to determining the kind of compensation that is appropriate
in response to a wrong:

- Compensation should be targeted (where possible) to the
  wrong it is meant to redress;
- Compensation should respect the varied harms that victims
  have suffered and not try to reduce these harms to a common currency;
- Compensation should be understood relationally and should
  make sense in light of the basis of our obligation to repair.

These considerations do not show that the economic view of compensation is always inappropriate, but I believe that they do help
explain why we have strong intuitions that it is inappropriate in
certain cases. In particular, it seems partly or wholly inappropriate in cases in which we think that the specific injustice centrally
involves something other than a loss to welfare, in cases where the
lost objects are irreplaceable, in cases where problematic social
practices and norms serve to perpetuate the original injustice, and
in cases in which we think that the losses can be "made up" only
in very specific ways. The examples of the Korean comfort women
and the demands of the Sioux tribes suggest the need for a more
case-specific view of the appropriate metric of compensation, a
view that ties compensation more closely to the particular harm
that is being compensated for.[19]

3. COUNTERING THE WRONGS OF THE PAST IN TERMS OF COMPENSATION

In some ways, compensation claims for past injustices resemble ordinary claims of corrective justice. But they differ in three important respects. First, in ordinary cases, the perpetrator has harmed
the victim and is now obligated to do something to make up for

the harm (or at least benefit the victim). But, in compensation for historical injustices, the class of victims and the class of those held responsible for compensation can include people who were not direct victims, as well as people who were not directly responsible for the wrongs done. Many philosophers have argued that the descendants of original victims were not harmed by those injustices, given a plausible conception of harm.

Second, and related, claims based on past wrongs can range over multiple generations and across very different circumstances. In the case of a piece of property unjustly expropriated in the past, for example, there are likely to have been intervening owners, some of whom have built their lives around this property.

Third, the harms of slavery and other historical injustices were systematic, rather than discrete. This makes their causal effects on current disadvantages almost impossible to determine precisely.

Even if the economic conception of compensation is appropriate in theory, it seems to face four serious philosophical worries in the context of repairing the wrongs of the past that stretch back in time and have multiple dimensions.

First, some theorists argue that injustices affect not only how people fare but also what people there are. Present claimants have no basis on which to make their claims of harm since, but for the injustice, they would not have been born.

Second, even if this problem can somehow be addressed, it has been argued that the descendants of injustice were not themselves victims of that injustice. In the case of slavery, contemporary descendants were not enslaved.

Third, critics argue that the original claims that people have to property or possession fade with time. In particular, these claims can be superseded by changing circumstances, as well as by the claims of intermediary owners. Jeremy Waldron, in making this argument, questions whether some aboriginal claims to land— which originated in contexts when land was plentiful—are still valid when land is scarce.[20]

Fourth, there are significant problems of calculation, even if we exclude the complex (and perhaps unanswerable) questions of how to put value on those losses due to torture, the expropriation of slave labor, the destruction of families and cultures, and genocide. Even ascertaining the valuation of more ordinary property losses may be impossible when those losses occurred in the distant past. What would the value of land or other property seized more than two hundred years ago be to current beneficiaries? If we think of the problem primarily in terms of the economic valuation of the original asset, we are likely to be plagued with counterfactual problems (would the original owners have been good stewards of the resource, or would they or subsequent generations have gambled it away?),[21] as well as calculation problems (what rate of compounding should we use to calculate the assets' net worth?).[22] While over a relatively short time period such questions might be given straightforward (if not altogether uncontroversial) answers, it is nearly impossible to provide clear answers over longer time periods. It is not simply that moving away from the parties directly harmed to consider descendants complicates the evaluation problems. Rather, it is that there is simply no clear fact of the matter about what full compensation for wrongs committed far in the past requires.

Some of these worries can be addressed in specific reparative contexts: for example, the worry about nonexistent beneficiaries seems less compelling in cases where claims are being put forward on behalf of a tribe or ethnic/cultural group that has retained its identity over time. It might also be noted that the original victims themselves sometimes bring forth claims of compensation. Finally, some of these concerns can be answered to the extent that less individualistic views of responsibility for wrongdoing are persuasive.[23]

In the end, however, these objections seem to many to be beside the point. For these objections can be acknowledged without entailing that the case for compensation is completely demolished. For the case for compensation for historical injustices primarily rests on the mutual recognition of a wrong, and even those who disagree about the quantitative extent of the wrong might nevertheless agree that there needs to be some response to the commission of a wrong. Even if we cannot determine the exact level of compensation that descendants are owed, we might be able to show that, if not for the wrong, they (or any other descendants who happened to have been born) would plausibly be better off than they are now.[24] So understood, compensation would take on a different goal from that of literally making up for historical violations. I believe that, indeed, this is the significant underlying purpose of compensation in intergenerational contexts: its role is to help reestablish relations of trust and mutual respect in the context of a torn past.

4. A Response: Compensation Remade

A plausible strategy for countering some of the objections to using compensation in cases of historical injustice would be to attempt to shift the focus away from the ties between people and possessions to the ties between people and their descendants. The tie between people and their children is stronger than the tie they have to many other things and might explain why intergenerational compensation makes sense even when the original victims are dead. In her *Taking Responsibility for the Past,* Janna Thompson develops a theory of reparative compensation in terms of a theory of intergenerational ties and obligations.[25] Since I believe that this theory is quite promising, I want to spend some time discussing its strengths and weaknesses.

On Thompson's view, at least when the original victims are dead and the wrongs are in the past, the loss to be compensated is not best conceived of as a loss of external goods to be measured in terms of financial compensation. Rather, the loss is to be conceived of in terms of intergenerational relationships. Insofar as societies are intergenerational communities, she argues, they depend for their moral and political integrity on their members "accepting transgenerational obligations and honoring historical entitlements."[26] Historical obligations belong in the first instance to members of structured intergenerational communities, and it is also such communities whose members can bring claims of repair. Thompson's primary example is that of Australian aboriginal communities and their claims for the restitution of ancient homelands. The dependence of a community on the economic and cultural resources of their national territory gives immediate descendants a right of repossession. Their ancestors were engaged in transgenerational projects and activities associated with their way of life, and it was their way of life that they hoped to pass on to their children. She writes,

> when a nation is dispossessed, this is not only a great evil to existing members; it harms their successors, robbing them of the

inheritance to which they are entitled, and by so doing disrupts
their ability to carry on their common life. Nothing but the return
of their national territory counts as appropriate reparation for
this wrong.[27]

In the case of individuals who are not members of communities,
the basis for their claims for compensation rests with the fact that
they stand in specific relations to the victims of past injustice (that
is, they are their descendants).[28]

Recognizing the value of family relations and national communities makes it reasonable for the state to support a presumption
of inheritance, even when we do not know in fact that given individuals would have passed assets to their children. If we think that
parents express their love and ties to their children by passing certain assets to them and that such expression is valuable and legitimate, then we have reason to uphold a presumption of intergenerational transmission of assets, especially with respect to goods that
have special meaning to the family members.[29]

For Thompson, the wrong of many past injustices is not loss of
property (although it can also be that) so much as the loss of an inheritance from one generation to the other. A society owes it to its
past generations to honor their wishes and to respect the ties that
they had to their descendants, as much as it owes its descendants
compensation for having unjustly interfered with those ties.

Thompson's theory thus conceives of a legitimate claim for
compensation as stemming from the moral duty a society has to
respect the interests of its members in passing on an inheritance
to their children. The theory derives its force from the fact that
claims of compensation do seem stronger when the good to be
compensated has a special meaning in the life of a family or community. To see this, it is helpful to consult your intuitions about
the strength of the claims stemming from two different cases of
expropriation: the loss of a piece of real estate and the loss of a
farm that has been in the family for generations. Insofar as the
family farm is tied to an ongoing way of life, invested with identity and memory, the case for restoring it seems stronger than the
case of restoring a capital investment. Family farms can have an
ongoing connection to the lives of people in a multigenerational
family that a piece of commercial real estate does not. Thompson

is therefore right to emphasize that within the life of a family, or more expansively, a people, some goods play a special role in sustaining the identity of that family and peoples over time. They are rightly conceived of as parts of an intergenerational project. This then allows a partial answer to Waldron's superseding worry: it is harder to supersede claims that play an important role in a community's or family's life. The ties between people and their children are stronger than the ties they have with their property. If we assume that most people strongly desire to see their descendants participate in carrying on the family line, then it is not unreasonable to suppose that they would have passed on their assets to them. Honoring the relationships that people have with their children entails that certain property rights not be so easily superseded.

But we must be careful not to exaggerate the implications of Thompson's idea: the ties between generations are thickest in the cases of direct descendants, and we may suspect that those ties weaken with time. In the case of historical title to land, less immediate successors grow up in new places and adjust their expectations and adapt to new environments. More generally, in the case of individuals far removed from the victims of injustice, the claims for inheritance are weakened, since we assume that people pass on their assets to those that they love and know. However, there may be some heirlooms that have been in a family for so many generations that even remote descendants might plausibly have a claim to them.

Thompson's theory focuses on the central problem of time and its effects on compensation claims but shifts the discussion away from what happens to property over time to what happens to the descendants of victims of injustice. To the extent that the goods of inheritance are specific—land, home, family heirlooms—it lies closer to the restitution view of compensation than to the economist's view of compensation as equal preference satisfaction.

Can Thompson's view of reparative compensation replace the economist's view of compensation and other alternatives in illuminating the basis of the claims for countering the wrongs of the past across generations? While her view is illuminating in some specific contexts (and probably the contexts in which people think the case for intergenerational compensation is most plausible), I do not think it makes sense of all such cases. It cannot therefore replace the economic view, although it can supplement it in particular instances.

Consider the example of reparations paid to victims of the Holocaust and their descendants. Jews who were sent to concentration camps were robbed of many goods, but this is hardly the worst of the injustices they suffered. The outright denial of their most basic human rights, the fact that they were treated worse than animals, the cruelty and humiliation they suffered, the rapes, beatings, and forced labor—these were more serious than the theft of material goods. And it was these harms—as well as the ultimate harm of extermination—that formed the basis for claims by descendants, and not the loss of an "inheritance," unless we understand that term so capaciously that it includes a world that was lost. An analogous argument can be made with respect to the case for reparations for slavery.

These examples suggest that, while Thompson's theory provides a plausible basis for compensatory reparations and is perhaps the most compelling theory of intergenerational compensation we have, it is limited in its applications. There is more than one true justification for compensation across generations. In practice, we recognize many different kinds of claims as relevant considerations for intergenerational compensation: theft, assaults on dignity and humiliation, the infliction of severe mental and physical injury, violations of reciprocity, loss of inheritance, destruction of property, and unjust killing.

To the extent that we find demands for compensation for past injustices, like the Holocaust, slavery, apartheid, and genocidal killings, plausible, I suspect that this is because we understand such claims fundamentally as means to reestablish relationships of mutual respect among persons and groups whose relationships have been severely damaged by past denials of that respect. The relevant relationship here is not between individuals and their descendants but between each of us now as inheritors of the legacies of an unjust past. The question that gives compensation for these past wrongs its point in this case is: what can we do now, in light of our past wrongs, to appropriately express the social value of mutual respect and trust that we want to characterize our society? As Tom Hill writes in defense of affirmative action, "We cannot change our racist and sexist past, but we can also not express full respect for those present individuals who live in its aftermaths if we ignore it."[30]

Hill argues that affirmative action is best understood as a means to convey a message, sincerely and effectively. In the absence of concrete action, talk of repair can seem empty. The message of affirmative action for Hill is that we as a society are willing to bear some costs to win back the trust of African Americans who regard their society with suspicion and resentment. Even if we cannot precisely quantify the degree of harm done to blacks, we cannot ignore the past and its role in shaping opportunities and relations. We may not be able to achieve full justice for victims and descendants, but doing nothing is usually worse than doing something imperfect.[31] In some cases of intergenerational compensation repair, then, the message sent by compensation can be more important than its tangible effects.

5. Practical Objections to Compensation

Even if compensation is an appropriate response to historical injustice in some contexts, and even if it can sometimes be an important component of repair, there are serious limitations to its usefulness in practice. Most countries simply lack the financial resources to offer full compensation to victims in cases in which the victims number in the thousands or even millions.[32] It is a challenge in many cases even to respond to the massive number of victims and large range of violations, as well as to overcome the disparities that are evident in isolated judicial remedies. In such contexts, the very idea of compensation in proportion to harm raises challenges. Being fair to all the victims may mean that full compensation for their losses, even if it could be calculated, is impossible. In addition, there are competing and sometimes more urgent needs in many of the contexts in which demands for reparatory compensation are made.

Given the total funds available and the presence of competing contemporary aims, governments have typically chosen an allocation to victims that involves less than full compensation. But less than full compensation raises problems of its own.[33] As a compromise, it seems less attractive and on less sure conceptual foundations than the case for full compensation. And it runs the risk that as a partial payment it will not heal but only open wounds.

This means that, practically speaking, financial compensation programs will need to be coupled with other forms of countering past wrongs that serve to reinforce the dignity of victims, repair the broken relationships and promote civic trust. Many reparations programs have emphasized not monetary compensation but truth-seeking, prosecutions, memorials of victims and resisters to injustices in monuments, national museums dedicated to public education about past injustices, and apologies.[34]

6. CONCLUSION

Successor governments sometimes undertake obligations to redress the victims of their predecessor regime, and such obligations are often assumed under the passage of time. Different forms of redress seem more appropriate in different circumstances, and in this chapter I have been concerned to understand why. Is compensation a plausible form of reparation? While some worries about the usefulness of compensation in the context of historical injustice are well founded, they yield no persuasive general challenge to compensation. Indeed, many of those who ask for compensation are under no illusion that there is any payment that can bring back what they have lost. As Jon Elster observes, life has no "undo button."[35] Instead, victims are seeking a second best and rough form of justice. For this reason, economic compensation remains a form of redress that belongs in the toolbox of those seeking to counter the crimes of the past. While it is imperfect and unlikely to admit of precision, it can be the best alternative available to victims. However, I have argued that the applicability of that form of compensation is limited by principle and by practice. In principle, it is inappropriate in contexts in which claimants seek to repossess a particular good that has been wrongfully taken from them. This has especially been the case with land, ancestral remains, works of art, and other property claims.[36] In other cases, what is needed is primarily to reestablish relations of respect, among both groups and individuals, that have been badly frayed by injustice. Compensation serves, in this case, less as the dutiful payment of a debt incurred in the past than as a means of expressing sincerity and respect and reestablishing relationships based on mutual respect. Compensation in this case may take the form of apology, reform of institutions, and measures aimed to restore trust. Still, in other cases, the type of harm that was done may call for a specific form of response. In practice, economic compensation must compete with other aims and needs.

There is no single best form of compensation and no single justification for offering it. Instead, philosophers writing on compensation should pay close attention to the specific circumstances in which such demands arise, as well as the way particular programs are implemented. Given how difficult it can sometimes be, even in simple cases, to repair a hurt, we should not be surprised that sometimes those who offer compensation sometimes get it wrong.

NOTES

"Countering the Wrongs of the Past: The Role of Compensation" reprinted by permission of Oxford University Press from *Reparations: Interdisciplinary Inquiries*, ed. Jon Miller and Rahul Kumar (Oxford: Oxford University Press, 2007), 176–92. Thanks to Gary Bass and Adrian Vermeule, who provided helpful comments on this chapter for a panel organized by two of the editors of this volume, Melissa Williams and Jon Elster. Thanks also to Rahul Kumar for his comments on an earlier draft and to Rahul and Jon Miller for helpful prodding and inordinate patience.

1. Avishai Margalit discusses some of the dilemmas of forgiving and asking for forgiveness in *The Ethics of Memory* (Cambridge: Harvard University Press, 2002).

2. Examples include U.S. payments to Japanese Americans interned in World War II, U.S. payments to victims of the Tuskegee syphilis experiments, German payments to Holocaust survivors, Czech payments to those whose property was confiscated by the Communist government, and Canadian payments to Aboriginals for the forced assimilation of their children.

3. Some recent cases involving requests for reparations include Armed Activities on the Territory of the Congo (*Congo v. Uganda*; *Congo v. Rwanda*; *Congo v. Burundi*); Aerial Incident of August 10, 1999 (*Pakistan v. India*); Convention on the Prevention and Punishment of the Crime of Genocide (*Bosn&Herz. v. Yugo.*).

4. Judith Jarvis Thomson, "Preferential Hiring," in *Equality and Preferential Treatment*, ed. Marshall Cohen, Thomas Nagel, and Thomas Scanlon (Princeton: Princeton University Press, 1977), 19–39.

5. Note that the Greek verb for forgiveness (*afinmai*) means the cancelling of a debt.

6. See Janna Thompson, *Taking Responsibility for the Past: Reparation and Historical Injustice* (Cambridge: Polity Press, 2002).

7. See, e.g., Robert Nozick's formulation in his *Anarchy, State and Utopia* (New York: Basic Books, 1974), 57.

8. Rawls refers to income and wealth as primary goods, all-purpose means to an agent's ends.

9. See Eric Posner and Adrian Vermeule, "Reparations for Slavery and Other Historical Injustices," *Columbia Law Review* 103 (2003): 689–747.

10. Jonathan Wolff, "Addressing Disadvantage and the Human Good," *Journal of Applied Philosophy* 19, no. 3 (2002): 207–218.

11. Ibid., 207–8.

12. In Randall Robinson's reparations-for-slavery proposal, payments would go for educational scholarships to black children and youth, aiming to redress directly the effects of past injustice on educational opportunity.

13. The phrase "rough justice" comes from Adrian Vermeule's comments on my paper at the 2005 annual meeting of the American Society for Political and Legal Philosophy, on which the present chapter is based. Editors' note: A revised version of Vermeule's comment appears as chapter 5 of this volume.

14. *U.S. v. Sioux Nation of Indians*, 448 U.S. 371 (1980). This is discussed in detail in Rebecca Tsosie, "Acknowledging the Past to Heal the Future: The Role of Reparations for Native Nations," in *Reparations: Interdisciplinary Inquiries*, ed. Jon Miller and Rahul Kumar (Oxford: Oxford University Press, 2007), 43–68.

15. Cited in Martha Minow, *Between Vengeance and Forgiveness* (Boston: Beacon Press, 1998), 105.

16. Ibid., 104.

17. Bernard Boxill, "The Morality of Reparation," *Social Theory and Practice* 2, no. 1 (1972): 113–23. Minow writes that "social and religious meaning rather than economic values lies at the heart of reparations." Minow, *Between Vengeance and Forgiveness*, 110.

18. I adapt this example from Boxill.

19. Notwithstanding these objections, compensation in the form of cash could be defended in many cases as a second best, where other, more attractive alternatives are not feasible. So, even if these objections are right in theory, their implications depend on the array of viable alternative options.

20. Jeremy Waldron, "Superseding Historic Injustice," *Ethics* 103, no. 1 (1992): 4–28. See also Waldron, "Why Is Indigeneity Important?," in *Reparations: Interdisciplinary Inquiries*, ed. Jon Miller and Rahul Kumar (Oxford: Oxford University Press, 2007), 23–42.

21. See Waldron, "Superseding Historic Injustice."

22. Tyler Cowen points out the extreme importance of compounding decisions to economic valuation. If we are trying to decide on compensation for a US\$1 billion loss suffered five hundred years ago, if we choose to compound at 1 percent per year, the assets will be valued at US\$2.7 billion; if we compound at 3 percent per year, the assets will be worth US\$19.2 billion; if we compound at 5 percent, the assets will be worth US\$131.5 billion. See Cowen, "Discounting and Restitution," *Philosophy and Public Affairs* 26, no. 2 (1997): 168–85.

23. See Christopher Kutz, *Complicity: Ethics and Law for a Collective Age* (Cambridge: Cambridge University Press, 2000).

24. Glenn Loury argues for an "interpretive" justification for targeted compensation for African Americans. He claims that, given the overlapping nature of generations, parents inevitably influence the lives of their children, in part through the transmission of social capital and wealth. Thus, it is plausible to assume that African Americans today still suffer from disadvantages associated with slavery, even if we cannot say precisely how much. See Glenn C. Loury, *The Anatomy of Racial Inequality* (Cambridge, MA: Harvard University Press, 2002) and Loury, "Transgenerational Justice: Compensatory versus Interpretative Approaches," in *Reparations: Interdisciplinary Inquiries*, ed. Jon Miller and Rahul Kumar (Oxford: Oxford University Press, 2007), 87–113.

25. She also develops a theory of how current generations can bear responsibility for past injustices done by their predecessors. See also Thompson, "Coming to Terms with the Past in Australia," in *Reparations: Interdisciplinary Inquiries*, ed. Jon Miller and Rahul Kumar (Oxford: Oxford University Press, 2007), 69–84.

26. Thompson, *Taking Responsibility for the Past*, xviii.

27. Ibid., 61.

28. However, she notes that they can bring such claims forward only if there is an institutional structure that bears responsibility for honoring their ancestors' wishes to see their children flourish.

29. Thompson, *Taking Responsibility for the Past*, esp. 123–32.

30. Thomas E. Hill, "The Message of Affirmative Action," *Social Philosophy and Policy* 8, no. 2 (1991): 108–29.

31. Note that I write "usually" and not "always."

32. E.g., in Brazil, the Black Consciousness Center at the University of São Paulo has presented a demand for compensation for US\$6 trillion, the equivalent of twelve years of Brazil's GNP.

33. There are also complicated questions related to determining the full compensation value of seized property.

34. Examples include Peru, South Africa, Sierra Leone, and Congo. Some of these are discussed in Pablo de Greiff, "Justice and Reparations,"

in *The Handbook of Reparations*, ed. Pablo de Greiff (Oxford: Oxford University Press, 2006), 451–77.

35. Jon Elster, *Closing the Books: Transitional Justice in Historical Perspective* (Cambridge: Cambridge University Press, 2004), 167.

36. It may sometimes be a second best when there are reasons why such goods cannot be recovered or current title transferred.

5

REPARATIONS AS ROUGH JUSTICE

ADRIAN VERMEULE

I agree with much of Debra Satz's nuanced overview of compensation for historical injustices.[1] On both principled and pragmatic grounds, such compensation is exposed to many familiar objections and misfires in a familiar set of hard cases. Indeed, there is a marked disconnect between the arguments and the policies in this area. Philosophers and others have thoroughly demolished the compensatory rationale for reparations,[2] yet governments, including the U.S. government, keep enacting programs of this sort, and such programs overwhelmingly tend to include compensatory cash payments along with in-kind compensation, in-kind restitution, apologies, and other noncash components. It seems that there is some persistent social demand for cash reparations accompanied by compensatory rhetoric, a demand that survives each new intellectual demolition.

Why is this? In a spirit of interpretive charity or sympathy, I want to suggest that there is a widely shared intuition or complex of intuitions underpinning the persistent demand for compensatory reparations programs.[3] This intuition has been called *rough justice*.[4] It would be self-defeating to attempt a precise definition of rough justice, but here is a working approximation: rough justice is the intuition that sometimes it is permissible, even mandatory, to enact a scheme of compensatory reparations that is indefensible according to *any* first-best criterion of justice. Rough justice is indefensible; it seems attractive only when compared to no justice—when

151

it is recognized that the status quo of inaction is also a proposal, one that may fare even worse, according to the same criteria that would condemn the relevant reparations proposals.

If the internal logic of the many programs of compensatory cash reparations one actually observes is that of rough justice, first-best critiques of reparatory compensation are beside the point, although pragmatic considerations remain relevant. There are well-known arguments to the effect that doing something imperfect can, perversely, be inferior to doing nothing, but I do not believe that such arguments work in the settings we shall be discussing. I also suggest that it will not do to worry too much about the conceptual foundations of compensation, because some or most of the relevant worries are radically overbroad. They would condemn not only proposals for compensatory reparations but also the ordinary mechanisms of compensation in non-transitional legal systems. This is a corollary of the main point: reparations proposals are no more than roughly just, but that is chronically true of the ordinary legal system, as well.

OBJECTIONS TO COMPENSATORY CASH REPARATIONS

Satz reviews some problems of both reparatory compensation in general, and of cash compensation as opposed to in-kind varieties. I focus on cash reparations justified in compensatory terms, as this is the hardest case for a sympathetic reconstruction of the implicit goals of reparations programs. It is not difficult to see the point of apologies, memorials, and so on, but when the government gives the Issei and Nisei interned in the Second World War a cash payment of $20,000 each,[5] the puzzles are apparent on the face of things. How could such a payment possibly make sense? There is a kind of intellectual asymmetry about programs like this: it seems much easier to poke conceptual holes in schemes of cash reparations than to make any sense of the political and social demand for them.

Satz crisply summarizes the standard objections to justifying such payments in compensatory terms. First, the welfarist idea that cash can provide the payee with the same level of preference satisfaction that she would have enjoyed had the wrong never occurred is problematic here, because of the problems of experience goods[6] and adaptive preferences.[7] Although the former problem applies only in cases of denied opportunities relative to a counterfactual baseline, such as exclusion from education, the latter problem could also apply in cases of loss from a preexisting baseline, such as physical liberty.[8] Moreover, it is not enough to raise the payee to the welfare level that she would *now* occupy had the wrong never occurred; the interim welfare loss during the period of deprivation must also be taken into account. This problem could be solved with a higher payment, but the point is that it makes the payments one actually observes seem patently inadequate. I return to this point later.

The second large problem Satz identifies is that money may be incommensurable with the goods, material or intangible, lost as a result of the injustice. When injustices are inflicted—and I will stipulate that they were in the internment case—cash payments seem to miss the point. As Satz puts it in another connection, "financial compensation seems jarring because it does not match the type of harm it is being used to counter."[9] The third problem is that reparations programs are often not well tailored to their compensatory rationales, even where they have such rationales. There is often a mismatch between the wrongdoer and the payor (usually taxpayers); a mismatch between the victim (who may be dead) and the payee; or a mismatch between the cash form of compensation and the character of the harm done (the incommensurability problem again). In some programs, more than one of these mismatches can be found.

COMPENSATION, ROUGH JUSTICE, AND THE LEGAL SYSTEM

Satz's points are clear-minded and, on their own terms, incontestable. The harder question is what to do with them. Many of these points would sweep in or over many ordinary cases in nontransitional legal systems.[10] One or another of the conceptual problems with compensation pop up in most civil cases, and in some cases all of them pop up simultaneously.

In a footnote, Satz observes that "compensation in the form of cash could be defended in many cases as a second best, where other, more attractive alternatives are not feasible."[11] But this is the normal state of the whole legal system. When a protected minority is denied equal access to employment or educational opportunities, the twin problems of experience goods and adaptive preferences arise. When a worker loses an arm or a life in an industrial accident and sues the firm, perhaps posthumously, it is not news to judges or legal scholars that cash compensation is difficult to defend in principle. A damages award is incommensurable with the plaintiff's arm or life. Preference satisfaction is not the yardstick by which ordinary people would judge the award; nor do lawyers, judges, and jurors really think they are placing the plaintiff (or the plaintiff's family) "at least as high on an indifference curve as he would have been without receiving [compensation] but also without suffering the loss."[12] And, as we shall see, often it is the case either that the payor is not the wrongdoer, the payee is not the one who suffered harm, or both.

In such cases, the argument for the cash payment is twofold. One argument prominent in law and economics is that money should be extracted from the wrongdoer in order to create specific and general deterrence of future wrongdoing. On this view, the money is paid to the plaintiff only because, absent the payment, plaintiffs would lack sufficient incentives to litigate and would incur socially inefficient precautions to prevent harm.[13] I bracket this view here—just as, in discussing reparations, I will bracket the (remote) possibility that reparations might deter the future commission of injustices by the payor group or others.

The argument on which I focus is different; I believe that it is widely assumed by lawyers, judges, and legal scholars not yet converted to law-and-economics. The implicit argument is that cash payments in cases of this sort are rough justice: they are not really defensible according to any first-best normative criterion, but they are what Satz rightly calls a second-best expedient. What makes the expedient attractive is that, even though it is morally indefensible from a strictly first-best perspective, the status quo is even less morally defensible, assuming that one can coherently speak of comparisons and matters of degree in such things.

In most ordinary civil cases, the alternative to a cash payment is usually no remedy at all. In some cases in-kind remedies are available—in an employment case one might instate or reinstate the worker, perhaps with back pay—but in standard accident or injury or wrongful-death cases it is dollars or nothing. As between the wrongdoer and the party who suffered wrong (or his descendants), a rough version of corrective justice suggests that the former should pay something, more than zero, to the latter, even if there are intractable objections to any particular account of how much and why.

In this system, valuation and measurement problems, incommensurability problems, and many of the other issues that Satz discusses are papered over by the institutional expedient of entrusting damage awards to juries, with loose judicial oversight. The advantage of juries is that they (1) need not give any rationale for their decisions and (2) as collective actors, need not hold any unanimous rationale for their decisions but can proceed on the basis of compromise or incompletely theorized agreements.[14] There is no principled defense of this institutional practice. The only defense is that no award would be even worse and that no principled arguments for any *particular* award would be tenable. Satz observes that "[the objections to compensation] can be acknowledged without entailing that the case for compensation is completely demolished. . . . Even if we cannot determine the exact level of compensation that descendants [of victims] are owed, we might be able to show that if not for the wrong, they . . . would plausibly be better off than they are now."[15] Replace the reference to descendants with a more general term like "plaintiffs," and one has the basic intuition of rough justice that animates much of the non-transitional legal system.

So far we have assumed that the defendant/payor is the party who inflicted the wrong and the plaintiff/payee is the party who suffered the wrong. In both reparations programs and ordinary civil cases, however, either or both of these constraints can be relaxed. In the legal system, one commonly observes payments to injured parties from corporations, successor corporations, municipalities, provincial and national governments, and other entities that are not obviously the "same" party as the wrongdoer, especially if a great deal of time has elapsed. There are well-known theoretical problems here about ethical individualism, legal identity, group membership, and individual responsibility for institutional action,[16] which I propose to leave firmly alone. Suffice it to say that, from the standpoint of the legal system, it is hardly unusual that the German government and German firms paid money to victims of Nazism or that the U.S. government paid money to victims of the Japanese internment policy. One would need a very strong theory of complicity to think that (a majority of?) individuals alive today are responsible for the wrongs addressed in these programs. Yet, to the lawyer's sensibility, these cases are not importantly different from cases in which the government committed a tort or breached a contract many years ago, under circumstances that tolled the statute of limitations. In both settings, it seems better to do very rough corrective justice than to offer no corrective justice at all, even if the consequence is that the costs of taxation to fund the awards will fall on living individuals with only attenuated responsibility for the original harms.

As for the constraint that the plaintiff/payee should be the wronged party, it, too, is sometimes relaxed both in reparations programs and in the ordinary legal system. In civil cases brought by individuals, although there is a nominal bar on the sale or assignment of tort claims by the victim, insurance companies routinely step into the victim's shoes and litigate the claim by subrogation. It is routine that damages are paid to descendants in wrongful-death cases. It is also routine that the plaintiff is a government or organization litigating either in its "own" right, whatever that may mean, or as a representative of victims.

So, too, in reparations programs that are actually implemented, one often observes payments to descendants of wrongdoers. In 1994, the State of Florida paid cash compensation to both survivors and descendants of survivors of the racist Rosewood massacres in 1923. In 1992, the Chilean government awarded a monthly pension in perpetuity to certain descendants of Pinochet's victims.[17] In such cases, the argument for compensation is not really based on the idea that the descendants were wronged in their own right, by occupying a worse position or lower level of welfare than they would have occupied in some counterfactual world without the wrong. Rather, the rough intuition is that, in strictly comparative terms, there is no better stand-in for the deceased payees—a view that seems vague and difficult to defend but that strikes many as superior to the alternative of awarding no money at all.

Even more common than payments to descendants are cases in which payments are made to organizations or institutions—again taken, in some very rough sense, to represent or stand in for the victims. The German payments for Nazism went to individual survivors in some cases, but other payments went to Jewish organizations and to the State of Israel. This poses an issue of group entitlement that is the mirror image of the group responsibility issue on the payor side. Here, too, one would need a very robust theory of group identity or membership to deny that the payee and the victim have diverged. Here, too, however, there does not seem to be any qualitative difference between reparations programs and the legal system or even a marked difference in degree. Even absent some robust theory of group identity, there is a common intuition that steering compensation payments to the Jewish organizations and to Israel is in some rough sense better than throwing up one's hands, and there is no party who is obviously a better stand-in for the deceased victims.

Cash Reparations as Rough Justice

I have emphasized the continuities between the ordinary legal system and reparations. If compensation in ordinary civil cases rests on a rough intuition that payments indefensible on first-best grounds are nonetheless superior to the status quo of no payment, it is unsurprising that there is a similar rough-justice argument for cash payments in programs like the Japanese internment reparations statute. Chris Kutz describes cash payments of this sort as "symbolic financial compensation."[18] This is exactly right, even or especially if we understand Kutz to use "symbolic" pejoratively, as a synonym for "partial" or "inadequate," rather than as a synonym for "expressive."

In this pejorative sense of the term, the intuition behind a scheme of symbolic cash payments to victims is just that some compensation, even partial or inadequate compensation, is superior to a program containing no cash compensation at all. Full compensation, even if we could overcome the conceptual and epistemic problems with specifying what the measure of full compensation would be, is ruled out by political constraints, and, even if it were not, no first-best theory of corrective justice would justify a facially inadequate payment of the sort embodied in the internment reparations program. Such programs are compromises with political and budgetary constraints, between or among various conceptions of the relevant harm and between or among various measures of the harm somehow defined. The defense of such programs, if it is one, must be that ruling out full compensation does not entail no compensation at all. That is just a non sequitur. Whatever argument we use to poke holes in such programs will also condemn the status quo even more strongly.

This helps to explain or justify the striking institutional fact that reparations programs are almost never ordered by courts in the name of legal principle. Rather, they are the product of bargaining and compromise, usually within legislatures or at least with the participation of legislatures and other political bodies. The institutional parallel between reparations and jury awards of compensation is that legislatures, like juries, are better suited than judges to devise unprincipled schemes of rough justice. Judges are uncomfortable with arbitrary compensatory awards and with politically textured compromises. And, of course, judges face a further constraint, which is that a judicial order mandating compensatory cash reparations might be ignored or evaded by the legislative institutions that control the government's purse.

Sometimes it is suggested that the cash component of reparations programs should not be understood as compensatory at all. Rather, the point of including "symbolic" cash is just to put backbone in the really symbolic elements of the program, namely apologies, memorials, or other public gestures of atonement for wrongdoing. Absent the cash, the symbols of atonement would be cheap talk. This view is in some tension with the incommensurability concern; perhaps adding money sullies the apology rather than making it sincere. Offering an apology for some wrong one has committed would usually become a more offensive gesture, rather than a more credible expression of remorse, were a $100 bill to be thrown in—although this may be a strictly interpersonal point that does not hold for government payments. In any event, the credibility-enhancing view solves only part of the problem. It explains why the payor should surrender money, but it cannot explain why the cash should be transferred to the program's beneficiaries. If a costly signal is all that is needed, the money might just as well be burned or sent into outer space. What makes these programs compensatory, in some recognizable sense, is the rough-justice intuition that at least some money not only should be extracted from wrongdoers or stand-ins for wrongdoers but should actually go to the victims of wrongdoing.

SOME OBJECTIONS TO ROUGH JUSTICE

Let me finish by considering some objections to the philosophically relaxed view I have sketched so far. Satz and others point out that compensatory programs must compete with other programs, given an overall governmental budget constraint.[19] This is true of all programs, however, including strictly forward-looking social investments justified on cost-benefit grounds. The point gets no unique purchase against reparations programs, whether fully compensatory or partially compensatory. In another version of the argument, Kutz says that "[a] compensation scheme, even if not maximalist, is a significant draw on the state treasury, and so competes against other urgent claims. To compete favorably as a matter of right, the compensation scheme requires a principled argument that partial payment (as opposed to cheaper symbolism) really is required as a matter of justice."[20] But justice need not be equated with principle. The argument for such programs is not that they are principled in any first-best sense but that they are nonetheless just in a rough sense, compared to no payment at all.

Kutz also objects to roughly just programs of cash reparations on another ground: "[p]artial payment might just as well irritate as salve old wounds in a way that a nonmonetized gesture will not. Of course money is nice, and some is better than none. But it seems likely that anything short of the maximalist program [of full compensation] will leave claimants dissatisfied that justice has been done at all, much less fully."[21] Disputing someone else's casual empiricism is boring for bystanders, but this seems implausible. Almost all extant programs of cash reparation have been partial, and, of these, the great majority have been straightforward successes in some rough sense—at least in the sense that they do not leave widespread dissatisfaction in their wake.

Kutz's argument for the perversity of partial payment is an application of the general theory of second best: where some distortion or constraint blocks complete implementation of the first-best policy, attempting to approximate the first-best as closely as possible (given the constraint) might make things worse, not better.[22]

If Kutz's argument works in fact, then it works in fact, but the general theory of second best does not guarantee that it will work. All the theory says is that it cannot be shown, a priori, that approximating an unattainable first-best as closely as possible is necessarily the best strategy.[23] It remains possible, in any particular case, that the approximation strategy is best in fact. In this case, there is little evidence that partial payment indeed has perverse effects.

At a minimum, whether partial payment is better than nothing depends on the political process by which the payment is accomplished, on the perceived alternatives, and on the accompanying symbolism.[24] The framing of the alternatives is probably important: if the perceived alternative to rough justice and partial payment is no justice at all, rather than full compensation, we may expect partial payment to produce a surprising level of satisfaction. Accompanying symbolism, including apologies, can help political leaders to depict partial payment as consequential redress. This inverts the usual idea about the relationship between apologies and cash. Rather than cash being necessary to make an apology credible, an apology might be necessary to make the cash satisfying.

Of course, commitment problems are important, both for cash and for noncash forms of reparation. As there is no legal mechanism that could bar multiple reparations for the same historical injustice, in principle there is nothing to bar advocates for redress from claiming, after partial payment has occurred, that the payment was inadequate. Furthermore, payment for one injustice may set a social precedent for new reparations claims. On the supply side, the worry about commitment problems, precedent-setting, and slippery slopes dampens support for slavery reparations to African Americans. Once partial reparations for slavery have been granted (and the reparations will necessarily be partial, in light of political and budgetary constraints), what bars new claims for further compensation? What about reparations for Jim Crow and other post-slavery injustices? In contrast, reparations programs that are enacted tend to be targeted to beneficiary classes that will soon die off. In such cases, the commitment problems are reduced because there will soon be no extant group to press a new claim; the beneficiary class is typically small, which reduces the cost of the program, and the imminent demise of the beneficiaries means that it is now or never.[25] It is hardly clear that any first-best principle could justify a pattern so shot through with political compromises, but the status quo of no payment is shot through with political compromises that are even less appealing.

EQUALITY AND ROUGH JUSTICE

Finally, there is the problem of equal treatment. A program of partial cash compensation might raise equality concerns on two counts: equality between the compensated and the uncompensated, and equality within the compensated class. As to the first concern: on equality grounds, Jon Elster argues against the idea of "doing what one can" in transitional justice in post-Communist societies. If full compensation for all is unattainable, the second choice should be compensation for no one, rather than compensation for some.[26] The argument depends crucially on the fact that "essentially everybody suffered under Communism,"[27] either through affirmative deprivations or denial of opportunities. Thus, compensation to all victims would amount to nothing more than shifting money from all to all, an incoherent enterprise. Elster's argument does not apply in a society where not everybody has a plausible claim to have suffered historical injustice. In that case, the reparations program shifts money from all to some or from some to some, which is perfectly coherent (whether or not desirable). Furthermore, the compensated and the uncompensated are not similarly situated, and there is no equality objection.

To be sure, we might worry that the compensated are only a subset of those who have suffered historical injustice in the relevant society. Why should Japanese American internees receive compensation while German Americans who were also interned in the Second World War do not?[28] If German Americans are included, why not go beyond war internments to compensate African Americans or their descendants, Chinese Americans or their descendants, and so on? But a familiar point to constitutional lawyers is that government has legitimate interests in proceeding "one step at a time."[29] The benchmark for assessing government performance is not any particular statute or program but an aggregate of statutes and programs over time.

Suppose, however, that the succeeding steps are never taken.

This would mean that political constraints will have produced an arbitrary underinclusiveness in reparations policy: some groups that deserve compensation will obtain it (in the rough-justice sense of partial cash compensation plus symbolism), while others never will. This is indeed one of the rougher features of reparations programs, but that feature is shared by a large number of programs in non-transitional legislation and adjudication. For any number of legal, political, and economic reasons, including the limited capacity of the judicial system, the set of groups or individuals with plausible claims to compensation is far larger than the set of those compensated in fact. Any theory of equal treatment that would entail condemning large chunks of the legal system is well out of bounds.

The second equality concern is that, in programs such as the Civil Liberties Act, compensation is not individuated, despite relevant differences in suffering or rights-violations across subgroups of the beneficiary class.[30] This is not an argument against partial compensation; it is an argument for individuated partial compensation. Here, too, however, any theory of equal treatment strong enough to condemn nonindividuated reparations would necessarily overshoot, condemning quotidian non-transitional programs. Consider workers' compensation, which awards damages on a set schedule for the loss of limbs despite obvious variation across persons, and agency cost-benefit analysis, which uses a nonindividuated value of a statistical life despite obvious variation across persons.[31] One point in favor of standardization is that it conserves on administrative costs, perhaps so much that there will be a larger pot of money to be distributed. Another point is that the standardization of benefits may create or enhance a sense of solidarity among the beneficiary class, whereas individuation would produce invidious comparisons and intragroup jealousies. We may even speculate that avoiding such jealousies and promoting intragroup solidarity help to produce the sense that justice has been done, even by a scheme of partial compensation.

THE LIMITS OF ROUGH JUSTICE

Let me briefly emphasize the limits of the rough-justice intuition. The intuition is underspecified, in the sense that it does not arbitrate between or among proposals that are all (1) roughly superior to the status quo and (2) not ruled out by political or institutional constraints. The force of the intuition is negative: it rebuts an explicit or implicit claim that compensatory reparations should be dismissed as "unprincipled" or "incoherent" from a first-best perspective. Satz and others raise several thoroughly pragmatic worries about compensatory reparations programs, and I have no general quarrel with such points. The only issue about them is whether they are true in fact. In some cases, as with Kutz's argument that symbolic cash compensation or partial payment is generally perverse, I have gone on to suggest that the concern is not empirically warranted, but there is no larger claim to be made about such arguments.

Conclusion

Insofar as reparations programs, especially cash reparations programs, are justified on compensatory grounds, they are indeed subject to all the conceptual problems that Satz and others have identified. In response, I have offered two points, which I believe are related. The first point is that many of the problems with compensation exist in ordinary, non-transitional legal systems as well; if taken seriously, the conceptual worries prove far too much. The second point is that reparations programs of the sort we actually observe are typically indefensible on any plausible first-best criterion of justice. What animates them is the sense of rough justice: the sense that no compensation would be, in some sense, even less tolerable than a spasmodic lurch in the general direction of justice. It is not so much that "we should do what we can"; it is, rather, that we can at least do better than we have. So the intuition runs, and it is not defeated or even engaged by pointing out that doing better than we have will require arbitrary and indefensible compromises with political and economic constraints.

The relationship between these two points is that compensatory reparations programs, by and large, do not seem systematically more objectionable than other compensatory projects that emerge from the legal system. Viewed in the concrete, both transitional and non-transitional programs or awards of compensation are often disastrously unprincipled. We must step back a mile or three, to reflect that in many cases the only other option not ruled out by political constraints—doing nothing at all—would be even worse.

NOTES

Thanks to Don Herzog, Jacob Levy and Eric Posner for helpful comments and conversations. Sean Heikkila provided helpful research assistance.

1. Debra Satz, "Countering the Wrongs of the Past: The Role of Compensation," in this volume.

2. For an overview of the critical problems, see Tyler Cowen, "How Far Back Should We Go? Why Restitution Should Be Small," in *Retribution and Reparation in the Transition to Democracy*, ed. Jon Elster (New York: Cambridge University Press, 2006), 17–31.

3. A different route would be to develop a strictly positive account of the political supply of such programs on rational self-interest grounds. I believe such an enterprise is a nonstarter; whatever version of interest-group theory one assumes, it is impossible to explain reparations programs without positing impartial or altruistic preferences on the part of (some decisive subset of) the payors. For a positive account of reparations that assumes "sympathy" for beneficiaries on the part of taxpayers, see Saul Levmore, "Changes, Anticipations, and Reparations," *Columbia Law Review* 99 (1999): 1657–1700.

4. See Aviezer Tucker, "Rough Justice: Rectification in Post-Authoritarian and Post-Totalitarian Regimes," in Elster, *Retribution and Reparation in the Transition to Democracy*, 276. Although I use the term in the same spirit as Tucker, I define it somewhat differently and do not mean to attribute my claims to him.

5. Civil Liberties Act of 1988, 50 U.S.C. app. 1989b.

6. See Philip Nelson, "Information and Consumer Behavior," *Journal of Political Economy* 78 (1970): 311, 312.

7. See Jon Elster, *Sour Grapes: Studies in the Subversion of Rationality* (New York: Cambridge University Press, 1983).

8. See Jon Elster, *Closing the Books: Transitional Justice in Historical Perspective* (New York: Cambridge University Press, 2004), 181.

9. Satz, "Countering the Wrongs of the Past," 135.

10. A similar claim is made, with respect to other varieties of transitional justice, in Eric A. Posner and Adrian Vermeule, "Transitional Justice as Ordinary Justice," *Harvard Law Review* 117 (2004): 761.

11. Satz, "Countering the Wrongs of the Past," 148 at n. 19.

12. Ibid., 132.

13. Richard A. Posner, *Economic Analysis of Law*, 6th ed. (New York: Aspen, 2003), 206.

14. Cass R. Sunstein, "Incompletely Theorized Agreements," *Harvard Law Review* 108 (1995): 1733.

15. Satz, "Countering the Wrongs of the Past," 140.

16. For a discussion of these problems, see Christopher Kutz, *Complicity: Ethics and Law for a Collective Age* (New York: Cambridge University Press, 2000).

17. These and other reparations programs are summarized in Eric A. Posner and Adrian Vermeule, "Reparations for Slavery and Other Historical Injustices," *Columbia Law Review* 103 (2003): 689.

18. Christopher Kutz, "Justice in Reparations: The Cost of Memory and the Value of Talk," *Philosophy and Public Affairs* 32 (2004): 277, 279.

19. Satz, "Countering the Wrongs of the Past," 147.

20. Kutz, *Complicity*, 304.

21. Ibid., 303–4.

22. See Lipsey and Lancaster, "The General Theory of Second Best," *Review of Economic Studies* 24 (1957): 11.

23. See Avishai Margalit, "Ideals and Second Bests," in *Philosophy for Education*, ed. Seymour Fox (Jerusalem: Van Leer Jerusalem Foundation, 1983), 77.

24. I am indebted to Jacob Levy for this point, which has doubtless lost force in transmission.

25. Levmore, "Changes, Anticipations, and Reparations."

26. Jon Elster, "On Doing What One Can," *East European Constitutional Review* 1, no. 2 (1992): 15.

27. Ibid., 16.

28. See *Jacobs v. Barr*, 959 F.2d 313 (D.C. Cir. 1992), cert. denied, 506 U.S. 831 (1992).

29. *Williamson v. Lee Optical*, 348 U.S. 483, 489 (1955).

30. The Civil Liberties Act is cartoonish in this regard, offering an identical $20,000 payment to each sufferer. *Civil Liberties Act of 1988*.

31. See Cass R. Sunstein, "Valuing Life: A Plea for Disaggregation," *Duke Law Journal* 54 (2004): 385; Eric A. Posner and Cass R. Sunstein, "Dollars and Death," *University of Chicago Law Review* 72 (2005): 537.

6

REPARATIONS AS A NOBLE LIE

GARY J. BASS

It is easy enough to imagine reparation for little harms. But what is to be done after a death—since the life can never be brought back—or after major atrocities or wars? Is there any such thing as repair after such awful wrongs?[1]

Jonathan Randal forthrightly entitled a book on the Kurds *After Such Knowledge, What Forgiveness?*[2] In the Jewish tradition, one is not forgiven by God on Yom Kippur until one has made reparation to the wronged human. In a murder case, that can never really be done. There is no repair after Srebrenica, let alone the welfare economist's ideal of equal preference satisfaction. The people are dead; the little eastern Bosnian industrial town is divided; the community will not be the same in the lifetimes of anyone who lives there now. The proper mood is painfully captured by the Polish poet Wislawa Szymborska:

> After every war
> someone has to clean up.
> Things won't
> straighten themselves up, after all.
>
> Someone has to push the rubble
> to the side of the road,
> so the corpse-filled wagons
> can pass.

166

Someone has to get mired
in scum and ashes,
sofa springs,
splintered glass,
and bloody rags.

Someone has to drag in a girder
to prop up a wall,
Someone has to glaze a window,
rehang a door.

Photogenic it's not,
and takes years.
All the cameras have left
for another war.[3]

Of course, we must try to rebuild, however inadequately, since there is no alternative. But we should avoid language that implies a kind of Whig vision of history, where it all somehow turns out for the best.[4]

Instead, it might help to search for another metaphor: the noble lie. "Could we," Socrates asks, "somehow contrive one of those lies that come into being in case of need . . . some one noble lie to persuade, in the best case, even the rulers, but if not them, the rest of the city?"[5] The Platonic noble lie is about the fitness of the guardians to rule, but the basic idea of a noble lie can travel much further.

In the aftermath of a genocide, there is no such thing as adequate repair or reparation. Genocide and mass atrocity cannot be undone. But, while that may be literally true, the people of Bosnia, Rwanda, and Sierra Leone need to live their lives. In order to do so, it is politically necessary to provide some tokenistic measure of justice or reparation in order to mollify the victims enough that they will participate in the normal political life of their country and their region. At best, the noble lie could convince the rulers as well as the rest of the country. It will not really be justice, but that is what we will call it.

So this chapter proceeds as follows. After a theoretical discussion, this chapter presents an empirical example of relatively successful reparations that can be seen as a noble lie: West German reparations to Israel.

Victims often simply want retribution. They see it as justice that the people who made them suffer should be made to suffer themselves. In a survey of mostly Shi'a Iraqis in southern Iraq in June and July 2003, there was virtual unanimity that those responsible for war crimes and crimes against humanity should be punished —fully 98 percent so said. Among the varieties of punishment, a solid 22 percent went for what could be called extralegal methods of punishment: execution, torture, hanging, revenge killing, or "eye for an eye" principles. Many of the respondents suggested punishments: "execution as a severe punishment, but in the city for all to see," "I myself want to punish them," "execute them," and "torture them just as they tortured me then kill them."[6] But this kind of alarmingly harsh retribution is feasible only in small and symbolic ways. The low estimate is that one hundred thousand people died in Bosnia from 1992 to 1995, but it is impossible to kill Radovan Karadzic one hundred thousand times. (The United Nations war crimes tribunal won't even kill him once.)

Perhaps the most dramatic international act of compensation was the partition resolution passed by the United Nations in 1947, creating the state of Israel—alongside a Palestinian Arab state, which unfortunately still has not arrived—in large part due to sympathy for the Jews after the Holocaust, as well as perhaps some bad conscience about how little the Allies had done to rescue the European Jews during the genocide. But even this grand act of compensation hardly makes up for the losses. There is no plausible Whig reading of twentieth-century Jewish history.

At the domestic level, we use fine-grained distinctions to mete out justice, and we insist that the precision of those distinctions is a crucial part of the justice of our criminal system. For instance, mandatory minimum sentences for crack cocaine have been a scandal when they have resulted in harsher punishment for crack cocaine than for powdered cocaine (the preferred form for more affluent drug users). We have rigorous definitions of the degrees of assault: assault with intent, assault with a deadly weapon, aggravated assault, and so on. But what can we make of the systematic murder of seven thousand Muslims at Srebrenica?

As Hannah Arendt wrote, "For these crimes, no punishment is severe enough. It may well be essential to hang Göring, but it is totally inadequate. That is, this guilt, in contrast to all criminal guilt, oversteps and shatters any and all legal systems. That is the reason why the Nazis in Nuremberg are so smug."[7] Martha Minow rightly noted, "Mass violence is different. Torture, kidnappings, and murders—regimes of rape and terror—call for more severe responses than would any ordinary criminal conduct, even the murder of an individual. And yet, there is no punishment that could express the proper scale of outrage." So, Minow argues, war crimes trials "depend for the most part upon symbolism rather than effectuation of the rule of law."[8]

Reparations are the civil accompaniment to war crimes trials: in other words, war tort trials.[9] War crimes tribunals are called a form of justice, and properly so, but they are invariably too small-scale to do what they are advertised as doing: dealing fairly with the killers. That would be both impractical and politically problematic, simply because there are so many killers. There were, by one estimate, more than one hundred thousand perpetrators of the Holocaust, and perhaps as many as five hundred thousand.[10] But, by 1948, only 3,500 Germans had been tried (not just for murdering Jews but for other war crimes too).[11] At most, a war crimes tribunal offers the symbolism of wider justice, but only for a handful of the perpetrators does it provide the reality of accountability. By putting some of the top leadership on trial, the world creates a "noble lie" that justice has been done, and now the perpetrators and victims can get on with their lives.

In normal tort law, the size of the wrong is, at least in some rough way, matched with the size of the measure of redress. But that cannot be done in war torts. When true equity is impossible, then the best one can hope for is to make a symbol of redress so attractive that it gains widespread popular acceptance. For instance, during the struggle against apartheid, the African National Congress (ANC) had originally hoped to put guilty Afrikaners on trial. But they lacked the military power to do so when F. W. de Klerk was offering a negotiated transition. As Archbishop Desmond Tutu later frankly wrote, "Neither side could impose victor's justice because neither side won the decisive victory that would have enabled it to do so, since we had a military stalemate."[12] With that blunt reality, the ANC and its allies used the Truth and Reconciliation Commission to make the resulting amnesties as dignified as possible, bolstered by the moral charisma of the great Nelson Mandela and by appeals to Catholic beliefs in forgiveness and the traditional African concept of *ubuntu*.[13] The expedient rediscovery

of concepts of forgiveness and *ubuntu* was a form of noble lie—
and was, in the event, probably the best that South Africa could
have done.[14]

People will surely disagree about how much emphasis to put on
the adjective or the noun in "noble lie." Afrikaners complicit with
white supremacism can use the Truth and Reconciliation Commission as an opportunity to pretend that they have just suddenly become aware of the evil that was being committed by the apartheid
regime. This is surely something that makes one queasy, but it is a
politically expeditious fiction. It would not be good history or morally proper for Chinese to forget the rape of Nanjing, but it would
make it easier for Japan, South Korea, and China to manage their
international diplomacy.[15] (It would help if Japanese politicians
would stop making provocative visits to the Yasukuni war shrine for
so long as it honors Class A war criminals.) More optimistically, the
use of a "noble lie" can take the wind out of the sails of nationalist
grievance. When Willy Brandt dropped to his knee at the Warsaw
ghetto monument, it made it easier for West Germany to be reinte-
grated into Europe.

THE INADEQUACY OF REPARATIONS

As Debra Satz argues in this volume, victims cannot really be made
to forget grave harms by compensation. She uses the powerful example of disadvantaged children deprived of a college education,
who may never fully develop their capabilities and may not fully
grasp what it would be like to have gone to college. In cases of
mass atrocity, the cruelty and indignity cannot be offset by money.
As Martha Minow wrote, "money can never bring back what was
lost. Even the suggestion that it can may seem offensive."[16]

Worse, Satz points out, people are not the best judges of
whether they have been adequately compensated for a loss. A
Kosovar nationalist mother whose son joined the Kosovo Liberation Army and was killed in the name of the liberation of Kosovo
may not actually have been properly compensated by Kosovo's autonomy (and probable eventual statehood), even if she thinks the
sacrifice was for a worthy cause. Generally, we trust victims and survivors as judges of what constitutes minimal compensation because
they are the best judges of their own misery and when it ends. Of
course, when a victim says that compensation is inadequate, we are

under a particular duty to pay attention. But Satz reminds us that victims can be unreliable.

Some of what victims want is an apology: an admission that wrong was done. In reparations cases, it sometimes seems that victims want that demonstration of remorse as much as the actual monetary compensation. Of course, for refugees or people from impoverished countries, money can be crucial. But Armenian Americans, rather than extracting pork from local governments in New York and California, are remarkably fixed on extracting formal resolutions acknowledging the genocide of 1915. They are in it for the remorse, not the money.

This isn't to say that money doesn't matter, of course. Wars and atrocities leave bitter destitution in their wake, and they often happen in countries that were sunk deep in poverty to begin with. The Marshall Plan helped Europe get back on its feet. This could not, of course, fully make up for the losses and deaths of World War II. Nor could it qualify as adequate reparations, since it came from the Americans, rather than from the Germans. But the Marshall Plan radically altered the future lives of millions of Europeans. Political scientists have reached consensus that there is a sturdy link between per capita gross national product and the stability of democracy: when GNP is above $5,500, democracy tends to endure.[17] Surely an economic aid plan that kept Bosnia over that target range would be a real achievement.

But the bottom line is that reparations can never be adequate if measured against the depth of the wounds. There is a simple disconnect between the imagination of those bent on destruction and those hoping for reconstruction. Pol Pot killed on a terrifyingly massive scale; those who hope to rebuild Cambodia lack the political and economic resources to make amends on a similar scale. Leaving aside the question of how to assign value to lost lives, even the scale of economic devastation and social dislocation is beyond the ability of most postwar governments to match—especially in fragile and poor countries.

ISRAEL AND WEST GERMANY

As an example, take Israel's decision to normalize its relationship with West Germany in 1952. Much of what the Israeli and West German governments said in justification of their actions was, to

a varying degree, false. Both Israel and West Germany were motivated more by national security than by a proper reckoning with
the past, but politicians were forced to make disingenuous claims
about their high motivations. International security compelled
both Israel and West Germany to move forward. This would later
be dressed up by both sides with rhetoric about justice and repair.

Principle might have dictated Israeli isolation from a West Germany that, for all its remarkable postwar progress, was, just seven
years after the end of World War II, only partially denazified in
1952.[18] This was not yet today's thoroughly democratic and liberal
Germany, where the Nazis are dead or very old and where national
culture is as anti-Nazi as could be imagined. After independence,
Israel boycotted Germany, in a popular expression of national outrage over the Holocaust. All Israeli passports came stamped as in-
valid in Germany.

But, in 1952, West Germany and Israel agreed on a reparations package. David Ben-Gurion, Israel's prime minister, was
mostly driven by security and economic interests. Israel desper-
ately needed allies. As Shimon Peres said, "We may curse it [Ger-
many] in the Knesset, but I never saw curses create armoured divisions."[19] Israel was badly isolated in its first years, without a reliable
superpower patron. Peres was the prime architect of Israel's first
major alliance, with France, as the two countries made common
cause against Arab nationalism.[20] But Peres, according to his biog-
rapher, thought that "in order to make progress with one [Euro-
pean] country, it was necessary to have the understanding of the
others. This mutuality was especially true of the Franco-German
axis, around which European co-operation had coalesced."[21] A
better relationship with West Germany would also help Israel with
the United States, moving Israel into the NATO camp at the same
time that Egypt was moving into the Soviet camp. As America was
attempting to build up a democratic West Germany as a bulwark
against the Soviet Union, it was not helpful for Israel to be under-
mining the Federal Republic.[22]

West Germany, for its part, was glad to have the added legitimacy of formal approval by the Jewish state. Abba Eban noted
"that the motives that prompted Dr. Adenauer to offer reparations
were far from lofty."[23] Tom Segev, an Israeli historian and journal-
ist, describes Ben-Gurion as "[c]old, pragmatic, and powerful" in

his drive to open relations between Bonn and Jerusalem. Segev writes, "Most Israelis, including policymakers, felt a sense of obligation to emotion and conscience, to morals and history. Yet, when forced to decide, most gave priority to state, economic, and personal interests."[24]

Many Israelis were horrified by the prospect of normalizing ties with Germany. *Yediot Ahronot* and *Ma'ariv*, moderate independent dailies, raged against Ben-Gurion's decision. Azriel Karlebach, *Ma'ariv*'s editor-in-chief, bitterly hoped that progressive forces would "ensure peace in Europe by eradicating Germany from the face of the earth."[25] Fearing dissent in the ranks, the left-wing Mapai party quashed a suggestion to let its Knesset members vote their consciences.[26] Both the left (the Communists of Mapam) and the right (the Revisionist Zionists of Herut) held rallies against the deal, with Menachem Begin at the fiery forefront. "We will be killed rather than let this come about," he told a rally. "This will be a war for life or death. A Jewish government that negotiates with Germany can no longer be a Jewish government." He wildly continued: "There is no German who did not kill our fathers. Every German is a Nazi. Every German is a murderer. Adenauer is a murderer."[27]

Thus, Adenauer had to make a public apology before West Germany could enter into serious negotiations over money with Israel. A West German apology was both a moral stand and a political necessity for Ben-Gurion. So, in front of the Bundestag, Adenauer made his own lie:

> The overwhelming majority of the German people abominated the crimes committed against the Jews and did not participate in them. During the National Socialist time, there were many among the German people who showed their readiness to help their Jewish fellow citizens at their own peril—for religious reasons, from distress of conscience, out of shame at the disgrace of the German name. But unspeakable crimes have been committed in the name of the German people, calling for moral and material indemnity, both with regard to the individual harm done to the Jews and with regard to the Jewish property for which no legitimate individual claimants still exist.[28]

This is, at best, a stretch. Adenauer, in his attempt to create a "usable past" for the Federal Republic, substantially overstated the extent of German opposition to the extermination of the Jews. Israel had tried to dictate much of the text, but not successfully. The awkward phrase about how Germans "abominated" the Holocaust was an Israeli suggestion, to replace Adenauer's "had not wanted any part" of the Holocaust. Ben-Gurion had wanted Adenauer to acknowledge Germany's guilt, but the most Adenauer would do was accept responsibility for "crimes committed in the name of the German people." Germany refused to accept the principle of reparations for a general harm to the Jewish people and instead insisted on specific individuals and lost property. Adenauer's government, for its part, struck out a passage that mentioned the German army, which the Israelis saw as a sign of an attempt to whitewash the army's complicity in the Holocaust.[29]

Ben-Gurion, too, had to lie. He publicly justified his decision in very different terms from the realpolitik that actually underlay it. As the director-general of the Israeli foreign ministry wrote, instructing his staff on how to reply to Adenauer's speech: "Add a few moral arguments."[30] Facing the Knesset, Ben-Gurion had to make an argument about the necessity of reparation. He could not reach Begin's nationalist heights, but he tried: "However, even after the defeat of the Hitler regime, the German people . . . continues to enjoy the fruits of that massacre and pillage, of the plunder and robbery of the Jews who were murdered. The government of Israel considers itself bound to demand of the German people restitution for this stolen Jewish property. Let not the murderers of our people also be the beneficiaries of its property!"[31] Although Ben-Gurion privately believed that West Germany was "the different Germany,"[32] he did not dare say so in the Knesset in 1952. He could not tell the blunt truth about the strategic imperative of a better relationship with West Germany.

Ben-Gurion said that reparations would make it possible to face West Germany on decent terms. Ben-Gurion could not argue that he was getting reparations for blood, which is priceless, but only that he was recovering the stolen property of the dead. (This was not the Israeli tack in the bargaining over Adenauer's statement about the deal. To the contrary, Israel unsuccessfully pressed the West German chancellor to declare that he was reimbursing the Jews not simply for stolen property but also for "general injury done to the Jewish people.")[33] Ben-Gurion himself saw reconciliation with Germany as part of the overall normalization of the Jewish people, but he could not use that argument in broader public debate. Having pushed Adenauer into making that Bundestag declaration, Ben-Gurion had just enough cover to do what realpolitik dictated.

It should be noted that Ben-Gurion was not always such a stickler for the principle of the return of property to its original owners, let alone the principle of apology. Without suggesting the two are equivalent, the Palestinian refugees who fled or were expelled from Mandatory Palestine during the 1947–49 War of Independence, in addition to enduring suffering and dispossession, left behind substantial amounts of property and land, totaling 120 million Israeli pounds, according to the UN's postwar Palestine Conciliation Commission.[34] Almost all of the property left behind, especially housing for the use of new immigrants, was seized by the Israelis. "The Israelis," writes the historian Howard Sachar, "regarded this émigré property as a windfall of the first magnitude."[35] All of this went on under the Mapai government of Ben-Gurion.

Israel's normalization with West Germany paid noticeable dividends. In 1956, Adenauer refused to join John Foster Dulles in trying to force Israeli troops out of the Sinai. Peres widened the relationship to include clandestine arms sales.[36] With Israel eager to build its own international recognition, opposing West Germany's could only have been counterproductive. In other words, normalization and reparations were the best strategic move for Israel—regardless of what many Israelis might say about it morally.

CONCLUSION

It is perhaps not surprising that Adenauer lied in front of the Bundestag and Ben-Gurion lied in front of the Knesset. That is, after all, what heads of state often do in front of their parliaments. In this case, the rulers knew that the truth was something very different from what they were saying to the city. But it suggests that the politics of apology are potentially very different from the philosophy. How do we judge Ben-Gurion and Adenauer? Did they act well?

It is uncomfortable to say that democratic politicians behaved properly by ignoring public opinion. The best leadership would be that which persuaded its public—and especially the survivors of atrocity—to accept reparations not as real justice but as the best that can be achieved. In other words, Ben-Gurion would have been most praiseworthy if he could have successfully explained to the Israeli public the realpolitik necessities of their situation. Thus, the reparations would have taken on democratic legitimacy.

But, since reparations are always inadequate to past horrors, democratic politicians often fail to make their case to their angry publics. If these leaders go forward anyway, since they are putting their political judgment above that of the populace, we must expect their judgment to be very good—ideally, to be vindicated by history. There are plenty of other cases where that did not happen. In the early 1960s, to take another example where the Cold War's exigencies forced a reckoning with the legacy of World War II, the Kennedy administration hoped to get Japan and South Korea to normalize relations. For liberal Japanese, the prospect of normalization with Park Chung Hee's military dictatorship was disturbing; for Koreans, the nightmare memories of Imperial Japan's cruelty were unresolved. But South Korea needed economic aid from Japan, not just the United States. And, most important, the United States was digging in deeper in Vietnam and needed South Korean help there. So, in February 1965, Shiina Etsusaburo, Japan's foreign minister, arrived in Seoul and delivered a rather murky apology: "We feel great regret and deep remorse over the unhappy phase in the long history of relations between the two countries." In June 1965, Japan and South Korea signed a Basic Treaty, with Japan paying out US$300 million in grants, US$200 million in low-interest loans, and US$300 million in private commercial credits. There were angry demonstrations against the treaty in South Korea's big cities. In the end, some historians have claimed, Japanese aid made it possible for Park to send some three hundred thousand South Korean troops to fight alongside the Americans in Vietnam. But the "history issue" still simmers between South Koreans and Japanese.[37]

Here is a case where there is almost nothing to like. First, the Japanese government's attitude was a far cry from, say, that of Willy Brandt in Warsaw. The Liberal Democratic Party said as much as was necessary to get a deal and even then put the words in the mouth of the foreign minister. But this was hardly a forceful

Japanese drive for reconciliation. Second, on the Korean side, Park could not be plausibly seen as representing the South Korean people, since he had seized power in a coup. Indeed, Japan offered to pay compensation directly to individual South Koreans, but Park instead took the grants himself and used them not to pay war victims but for building infrastructure. Park's regime paid out only about 10 percent of the US$300 million grant, in 1975. These meager handouts were denied to injured veterans, forced laborers, and so-called comfort women—Korean women forced into sexual slavery by Imperial Japan.[38] Third, internationally, the whole normalization project was in aid of an unjust American war effort in Vietnam, which undermined national and international security across Asia. There were plenty of lies, but they were not noble.

In comparison to the South Korean example, the Israeli case looks substantially better. Ben-Gurion might have gone against the will of some sizable portion of his electorate, but he had at least been elected. And his political judgment was, in this hard case, correct. As for Adenauer, even if he did not go far enough, he was far more forthcoming than his Japanese counterparts. One can praise Adenauer and Ben-Gurion as diplomats and politicians, and ultimately they probably helped build a more progressive future for both states. They certainly helped the national security of both states. Still, the only judgment that cannot be made is that a reparations package of about US$820 million constitutes fair compensation for the Holocaust.[39]

NOTES

1. See Elazar Barkan, *The Guilt of Nations: Restitution and Negotiating Historical Injustices* (New York: Norton, 2000), 317–22.
2. Jonathan Randal, *After Such Knowledge, What Forgiveness?: My Encounters with Kurdistan* (Boulder, CO: Westview, 1999).
3. Wislawa Szymborska, "The End and the Beginning," in *Miracle Fair: Selected Poems of Wislawa Szymborska,* trans. Joanna Trzeciak (New York: Norton, 2001), 48.
4. Herbert Butterfield, *The Whig Interpretation of History* (New York: Norton, 1965), 5–8.
5. Plato, *Republic,* trans. Alan Bloom (New York: Basic Books, 1968), book III, 414c, 93.

6. Lynn Arnowitz, Vincent Iacopino, Susannah Sirkin, and Holly Burk-halter, "Southern Iraq: Reports of Human Rights Abuses and Views on Justice, Reconstruction and Government," Physicians for Human Rights briefing paper, September 18, 2003, 6–7.

7. Hannah Arendt to Karl Jaspers, August 17, 1946, in their *Correspondence 1926–1969*, ed. Lotte Kohler and Hans Saner (New York: Harcourt Brace, 1992), 54.

8. Martha Minow, *Between Vengeance and Forgiveness: Facing History After Genocide and Mass Violence* (Boston: Beacon Press, 1998), 121–22.

9. Barkan, *The Guilt of Nations*, 317–22; Marc Trachtenberg, *Reparation in World Politics: France and European Economic Diplomacy, 1916–1923* (New York: Columbia University Press, 1980); Leslie T. Hatamiya, *Righting a Wrong: Japanese Americans and the Passage of the Civil Liberties Act of 1988* (Stanford: Stanford University Press, 1993); Gary J. Bass, "Jus Post Bellum," *Philosophy & Public Affairs* 32, no. 3 (Fall 2004): 384–412.

10. Daniel Jonah Goldhagen, *Hitler's Willing Executioners: Ordinary Germans and the Holocaust* (New York: Random House, 1997), 167.

11. Telford Taylor, *Nuremberg and Vietnam: An American Tragedy* (Chicago: Quadrangle Books, 1970), 28. I once wrote: "There is no such thing as *appropriate* punishment for the massacres at Srebrenica or Djakovica; only the depth of our legalist ideology makes it seem so." Gary J. Bass, *Stay the Hand of Vengeance: The Politics of War Crimes Tribunals* (Princeton: Princeton University Press, 2000), 13.

12. Desmond Mpilo Tutu, *No Future Without Forgiveness* (New York: Doubleday, 1999), 20.

13. Tina Rosenberg, "Recovering from Apartheid," *The New Yorker*, November 18, 1996, 86–95.

14. See also Kader Asmal, Louise Asmal, and Ronald Suresh Roberts, *Reconciliation Through Truth: A Reckoning of Apartheid's Criminal Governance* (New York: St. Martin's Press, 1997); Anthony Sampson, *Mandela: The Authorized Biography* (New York: Knopf, 1999), 520–33; R. W. Johnson, *South Africa's Brave New World: The Beloved Country Since the End of Apartheid* (London: Allen Lane, 2009), 272–305; and Martha Minow, "The Hope for Healing: What Can Truth Commissions Do?," in *Truth v. Justice: The Morality of Truth Commissions*, ed. Robert Rotberg and Dennis Thompson (Princeton: Princeton University Press, 2000), 235–60.

15. See Joshua A. Fogel, ed., *The Nanjing Massacre in History and Historiography* (Berkeley: University of California Press, 2000).

16. Minow, *Between Vengeance and Forgiveness*, 93.

17. Adam Przeworski, Michael Alvarez, Jose Cheibub, and Fernando Limongi, *Democracy and Development* (New York: Cambridge University Press, 2000), 98.

18. See Thomas Alan Schwartz, *America's Germany: John J. McCloy and*

the Federal Republic of Germany (Cambridge, MA: Harvard University Press, 1991).

19. Matti Golan, *Shimon Peres: A Biography*, trans. Ina Friedman (London: Weidenfeld and Nicolson, 1982), 70.

20. Alistair Horne, *A Savage War of Peace: Algeria 1954–1962* (London: Macmillan, 1977), 157–58.

21. Golan, *Shimon Peres*, 69.

22. Tom Segev, *The Seventh Million: The Israelis and the Holocaust*, trans. Haim Watzman (New York: Hill and Wang, 1994), 191–92.

23. Nicholas Balabkins, *West German Reparations to Israel* (New Brunswick, NJ: Rutgers University Press, 1971), 93.

24. Segev, *The Seventh Million*, 191.

25. Ibid., 206–7.

26. Ibid., 209.

27. Eitan Haber, Ze'ev Schiff, and Ehud Ya'ari, *The Year of the Dove* (New York: Bantam Books, 1979), 234.

28. Segev, *The Seventh Million*, 202.

29. Ibid., 202–4. On the Wehrmacht's role in the Holocaust, see Omer Bartov, *Hitler's Army: Soldiers, Nazis, and War in the Third Reich* (New York: Oxford University Press, 1992).

30. Segev, *The Seventh Million*, 205.

31. Michael Bar-Zohar, *Ben-Gurion*, trans. Peretz Kidron (London: Weidenfeld and Nicolson, 1978), 196.

32. Segev, *The Seventh Million*, 191.

33. Ibid., 204.

34. Benny Morris, *The Birth of the Palestinian Refugee Problem 1947–1949* (Cambridge: Cambridge University Press, 1987).

35. Howard M. Sachar, *A History of Israel: From the Rise of Zionism to Our Time* (New York: Knopf, 1989), vol. 1, 437.

36. Golan, *Shimon Peres*, 70–71.

37. Franziska Seraphim, *War Memory and Social Politics in Japan, 1945–2005* (Cambridge, MA: Harvard University Press, 2006), 202–5.

38. Ibid., 204–5. See George L. Hicks, *The Comfort Women: Japan's Brutal Regime of Enforced Prostitution in the Second World War* (New York: Norton, 1997).

39. Segev, *The Seventh Million*, 233.

7

LEVIATHAN AS A THEORY OF TRANSITIONAL JUSTICE

DAVID DYZENHAUS

[M]en . . . cannot without the help of a very able Architect, be compiled, into any other than a crasie building, such as hardly lasting out of their own time, must assuredly fall upon the heads of their posterity.

—Thomas Hobbes, *Leviathan*

INTRODUCTION

Thomas Hobbes's *Leviathan* is a theory of transitional justice. While Hobbes starts his account of the process by which civil society is achieved in the state of nature, as a matter of fact his audience was not composed of individuals who were at war with each other. Rather, they were people, divided into political factions, who had just emerged from a civil war and who faced the task of reconstructing a society torn apart—though not totally destroyed by—the war. *Leviathan*, in my view, contains both significant instruction about how to achieve civic peace in the face of deep ideological division and an account of how to construct political and legal institutions in order to maintain that peace.

Still, it might seem odd to claim that *Leviathan* is about transitional justice. After all, Hobbes said that the notion of justice has "no place" in the state of nature.[1] His chain of reasoning is: what defines a state of nature is that there is no "common Power"; one needs a common power to have law, so there is no law; and, since justice is simply the justice of the positive law (the commands of the sovereign),[2] claims about justice and injustice make no sense

180

in a state of nature.[3] Within a state of nature, such claims, like claims about right and wrong, simply represent the desires and aversions of the individuals engaged in the perpetual power struggle that characterizes that state. Until the condition of civil society is established, marked by the existence of a sovereign with power to enforce his commands, talk of morality and justice has no place.

Now, transitional justice might not seem strictly speaking to be about a state of nature. Rather, it is about a state somewhere in between a state of nature and civil society. In other words, a society in transition is more like the society that was Hobbes's actual audience in *Leviathan*—a society that has more resources than its bootstraps and in which there is a political entity with a hold, albeit rather tenuous, on power. The problem for that political entity is how to consolidate power to the point where there is a well-established sovereign at the same time that it manages the difficult tensions and dilemmas that tend to face transitional societies.

Because that is the problem of a transitional society, it is not, on Hobbes's understanding, a civil society. He did not think it any easier to get to civil society from any point on a continuum between the state of nature and civil society than it is from the state of nature itself. More accurately, he can and has been interpreted as denying that there is such a continuum. One has either civil society or a state of nature—there is no intermediate stage. A political entity that is not a well-established sovereign is a mere faction, contending with others in a state of nature. Moreover, Hobbes seems deliberately to set up the problem of transition from the state of nature to civil society so that it is impossible to effect a transition. In order for a sovereign—the representative of the common power—to come into being, all the individuals who will be subject to his power must enter into a contract with one another whereby they consent to obey him. In fact, he comes into existence through the contract.[4] But contracts are worthless without a common power to guarantee them, so no such contract—nor any other contract—can be made before the sovereign comes into existence. It follows that individuals in a state of nature who both attempt to contract with others and make the first performance of their alleged contracts simply betray themselves to those others. It thus seems that the process Hobbes describes as sovereignty

by institution[5]—in which individuals covenant with one another to
obey a sovereign—is impossible.

In sum, whatever the makeup of Hobbes's audience, his theory
of justice looks like not a theory of transitional justice but a theory
of justice for those who are living in a civil society, one that successfully has made the transition from the state of nature. Further, that
theory looks unacceptably authoritarian to liberal democrats. Justice for Hobbes is nothing more than what the law commands and
injustice what it forbids. His point is that we should always obey the
sovereign, whatever he commands, since we have no other public
standard of justice. The only exception Hobbes appears to make
is that we are under no duty to obey when the law threatens our
death. So why bother in the context of a discussion of transitional
justice with a theory that seems to have no application to transitions and that is in any case unacceptably authoritarian?

I will argue that there is a match between Hobbes's audience
and his theory of justice. It is a theory that works well for transitions even though it makes no special allowance for them, and that
is because there is reason to doubt all but one of the main assumptions made by many theorists of transitional justice. If correct, that
doubt leads to doubt about whether there is such a distinct field of
inquiry.[6] I will also argue that the resources that make it so also, at
the least, blunt its apparent authoritarian edge.

The first of the doubtful assumptions made by many theorists
of transitional justice is that transitions present problems of justice
that are different in kind from those presented by stable societies.
The second is that transitions are radically discontinuous both
with the bad past from which the transitional regime had to escape
and with the liberal democratic future into which it is hoped the
society will emerge. These two assumptions require that we think
of transitional regimes as exceptions to our ordinary theory of
justice, the one appropriate for stable liberal democracies. That
requirement brings to light a further doubtful assumption: that
the societies in which most theorists of transitional justice live are
the societies that transitional regimes should aim to emulate in
most respects, because these societies are by and large both stable
and just.

In other words, I take theories of transitional justice to be of the
following type. They assume that the problem is to escape from

the legacy of T_1 (the bad regime) by addressing it in T_2 (the transitional regime) in order to get to T_3 (stable, liberal democracy). Since in T_2 one is dealing with the legacy of antidemocratic illiberalism, the theory of justice appropriate for T_3 does not suffice. For example, retroactive laws might be required in order to bring wrongdoers to justice for acts that were either not considered crimes under the positive law of T_1 or for which the positive law of T_1 indemnified them. But, in liberal democratic regimes, retroactive justice, especially in criminal matters, is generally prohibited. Conversely, even when officials according to the positive law of T_1 clearly were guilty of crimes but enjoyed impunity for political reasons, it might be that the circumstances of T_2 make it imprudent to punish them. For it is a characteristic of many transitional regimes that those who held power during T_1 decided that their growing weakness required entering T_2 but retain enough power to bring the transition to a crashing halt if they feel too threatened. In addition, it is also often a feature of transitions that the expertise of those who occupied official positions during T_1 is required during T_2 until people are trained to replace them. Thus, it might be rational to find strategies to avoid punishing criminal officials and politicians even if their crimes were so heinous that they would require severe punishment were they committed during T_3. Indeed, as anyone familiar with the transitional justice debate knows, the issue with this example is often said to go well beyond prudence. A significant part of the attraction to the idea that transitions require a special theory of justice came from the fact that the work of the South African Truth and Reconciliation Commission could be understood in accordance with a model of restorative justice, which seemed to hold out the promise of being a new paradigm of justice.[7]

While I have doubts about whether this model is appropriate for transitions,[8] I want to note only that the debate about the merits of restorative justice has just as much purchase in stable liberal democratic regimes as it does in transitional regimes. I am confident, with others,[9] that there is no problem that a transitional society presents that is not found in stable liberal democracies. I also think one should be wary of the thought that one of the features of T_3 is that it is non-transitional. That is, I do not think one should equate stability with "non-transitionality" or stasis. Finally, I think one should be wary of the thought that the success of a transition, the arrival of a society in T$_3$, is necessarily to be marked by that society's adoption of a particular theory of political and social justice, an ideology (used here in the non-pejorative sense).

Even if I am right that there is no problem that a transitional society presents that is not found in stable liberal democracies, it is the case that transitions are more dramatic in that they usually present many of these problems at the same time. But the particular make up of each might be no different from analogues in the stable liberal democracies, and all that might differ is the institutional incapacity of the transitional regime to address the problem, especially given the sheer number of problems that confronts the regime. Of course, the fact of institutional incapacity combined with the issue of number might require that we come up with a different theory of justice, but that has to be demonstrated, not assumed. It might be, that is, that the kinds of moral dilemma presented to transitional regimes are to be resolved using whatever theory of justice seems most appropriate for our own societies. There is also reason to be wary of claims about institutional incapacity, in whatever context they are made.[10]

Notice that, once these assumptions come into view, transitional justice theories begin to look not all that different from Hobbes's theory, or at least the account of Hobbes I sketched earlier. Transitions are to a definite stable destination, one that is qualitatively different from the immediate past. In addition, what impels a society to take up the transitional journey is something that Hobbes might have thought very closely approximated the thought experiment of the war of one against all he describes in chapter 13 of *Leviathan*. The decision to go on that journey by both the beneficiaries and the losers under the old bad regime is usually prompted by the realization that, unless they undertake the journey, the probability that political struggle will become something like Hobbes's state of nature is very high.

There might then seem to be only two differences between theories of transitional justice and Hobbes. Transitional justice theorists do not agree with Hobbes that justice is simply the content of the sovereign's commands or positive law, made in accordance with whatever institutional structure a political order happens to have. Rather, theories of justice provide us with standards that are transcendent in the sense that they are standards against which one can evaluate both the institutional order and the laws it makes. In addition, the theorists think that there is such a theory appropriate to the transition that gets us to the civic peace of stable liberal democracies. Following from the first difference, that theory is not merely about how best to maintain order during a transition, which brings me to the last and perhaps only correct assumption that characterizes theories of transitional justice.

This assumption is so obvious that it might seem superfluous to state it. It is that peace and order without justice are not worth having, not only from the standpoint of morality but because such a peace will not work in the interests of society. I agree with this assumption and thus also with the thought that theories of justice provide us with transcendent standards of evaluation. However, I want to keep in mind that it is not irrational to dispute this assumption. It is not irrational to say with Hobbes that anyone who has properly contemplated what it would be like to live in a state of nature will, as long as he is sufficiently farsighted, conclude that life in a stable political order is to be preferred, even if that order appears to him to be unjust or to be the wrong sort of order, for example, a monarchy rather than a democracy. Anyone, that is, will have this stance who meets two conditions. First, he has understood the "miseries, and horrible calamities, that accompany a Civill Warre; or that dissolute condition of masterless men, without subjection to Lawes, and a coërcive Power to tye their hands from rapine, and revenge." Second, he knows that "all men are by nature provided of notable multiplying glasses, (that is their Passions and Selfe-love,) through which, every little payment appeareth a great grievance; but who are destitute of those prospective glasses, (namely Morall and Civill Science,) to see farre off the miseries that hang over them, and cannot without such payments be avoided."[11]

But, while this argument is both an important resource for Hobbes and by no means irrational, it is not in fact all he has to say about how civic peace is to be achieved. To suppose that this is all he has to say is to accept that the Hobbist (or standard) interpretation of Hobbes is the correct one—the interpretation that has it that claims of justice have no place in the state of nature and that the content of justice is simply what a particular sovereign happens to decree, so that there are no transcendent standards of justice. Even those who think that the Hobbist interpretation of Hobbes is correct have to admit that Hobbes himself does not think that the obligation to obey the law of one's sovereign comes from the mere fact that he has superior power. For example, Quentin Skinner depicts Hobbes as a defender of "*de facto* sovereignty," that is, as a Hobbist.[12] But he recognizes that his account trivializes the emphasis Hobbes wants to put on consent as the legitimating basis of power. Put differently, Hobbism—which infers absolute authority from absolute power—does not take into account the fact that Hobbes finds himself compelled to show what might make power legitimate, that is, what makes a sovereign into an authority, someone who wields what Hobbes calls in the Introduction to *Leviathan* "just Power."[13]

As I will show, order is not achievable for Hobbes unless it is based on both justice and morality, resources that, contrary to the Hobbist or standard interpretation of Hobbes, exist in the state of nature. Those who wish to bring about civic peace must orient themselves to all these resources, the very same resources that the sovereign of a stable order must draw on in maintaining that order. Again, contrary to his general reputation, Hobbes seems to think that all societies, no matter how stable, are not for that reason non-transitional when it comes to justice, if only for the reason that the society's standards of justice, in the sense of its ideologies, will change with any important reform of positive law. Hobbes gives us no reason to suppose that any particular stage should be taken as that society's destination, and so the sovereign's task must include ensuring that a society remains stable despite the fact that it is likely in perpetual transition. In fact, the epigraph to this chapter should be interpreted as articulating Hobbes's concern that civil society is unlikely ever to reach the stage of being a "firme and lasting edifice."[14] Sovereigns always have to take the role of architects, though they do not have the freedom to design society from scratch. Rather, with their subjects, they have to inhabit the crazy building in which they happen to find themselves, even as they try to reconstruct it.

In other words, Hobbes has no special theory of justice for transitions because his universal theory of justice is one of transitional justice. Moreover, partly because of this last feature, Hobbes's theory of justice has the advantage that it applies across the board, so that we do not have to conclude with critics of liberal theories of justice that the theories apply only when they are not needed, that is, when societies already exhibit their main characteristics. In part, Hobbes's theory can manage this task because while it is universal, it is relatively modest. But it is not so modest as to have no bite.

In order to support my claims I will now turn to a discussion of some discrete themes in *Leviathan*. I will start in what might seem like an odd place—Hobbes's theory of international relations. I will then show how insights from that theory apply with even greater force to transitions, at least to transitions of a particular type. That will lay the basis for my argument that a theory of transitional justice is an account of the importance of a civic education in legality or the rule of law. But that theory is a universal one, applicable to all societies.

HOBBES'S THEORY OF INTERNATIONAL RELATIONS

As Noel Malcolm has pointed out, examples of an actual state of nature in which all individuals are at war with each other are not that easy to come by.[15] Indeed, a too little noticed feature of Hobbes's state of nature is that he does not define it as actual fighting but more in the nature of "Foule weather," that is, in the "known disposition thereto, during all the time there is no assurance to the contrary."[16]

Hobbes, Malcolm says, finds the most realistic example of such a potential state of war in international relations—which *Leviathan* depicts as a stand-off between jealous, well-armed, sovereigns.[17] But, despite the fact that Hobbes says of the state of nature that the "notions of Right and Wrong, Justice and Injustice have there no place,"[18] later in *Leviathan* he says that sovereigns are governed by the same law that governs men who have "no Civil Government." Both sovereigns and such masterless men are still subject to natural law, the laws of nature, but subject only in the sense that they are bound "in the Conscience onely," there "being no Court of Naturall Justice."[19] This sense of being bound is elaborated in a famous passage in one of the two chapters in which Hobbes sets out the laws of nature, where he distinguishes between being bound only by one's conscience, bound in the internal court, and being bound to act, or bound in external court.

> The Lawes of Nature oblige *in foro interno*, that is to say, they bind to a desire they should take place; but *in foro externo*, that is, to the putting them in act, not alwayes. For he that should be modest, and tractable, and perform all he promises, in such time, and place, where no man els should do so, should but make himselfe a prey to others, and procure his own certain ruine, contrary to the ground of all Lawes of Nature, which tend to Natures preservation.[20]

Hobbes follows this passage with one in which he says that in the state of nature one can break the laws of nature either by an act that in fact violates one of the laws or by doing something with the "purpose" of breaking one of the laws, even if as a matter of fact one does not break the law.[21]

Now, it might seem that this sense of obligation is empty since, while the individual in the state of nature or any sovereign are bound by the laws of nature, they must do whatever they think necessary to ensure their survival. This impression is reinforced by the passage in which Hobbes says that "The Law of Nature, and the Civill Law, contain each other and are of equall extent" and then seems to go on to make it clear that it is from the commands of the sovereign that individuals should take their public standards of equity, justice and "morall Vertue."[22] It seems to follow that the sovereign's interpretation of what the laws of nature require is definitive, as is the individual's interpretation in the state of nature.

In Malcolm's view, however, Hobbes's theory has to be understood at three different levels: the level of psychology, where evaluative terms such as "pleasant" and "unpleasant" are indeed subjective; the level of morality, where pride, humility, equity, and other terms for actions are of universal application and thus "neither subjective nor arbitrary"; and the level that Malcolm calls "jural," where terms such as "right" and "wrong," "just" and "unjust," have meanings that are "both universal and analytic"—"'unjust,' for example, means 'in breach of covenant,' the covenant being a transfer of rights."[23]

Malcolm then observes that "Hobbes carefully manages the transition in his argument from the psychological level to the moral, and again from the moral to the jural." Whatever the differences between desires at the psychological level, peace is required for their fulfillment, and so the laws of nature, which are the rules of morality that conduce to peace, have to be observed. As Hobbes put it, "The Lawes of Nature are Immutable and Eternall; for Injustice, Ingratitude, Arrogance, Pride, Iniquity, Acception of persons and the rest, can never be made lawfull. For it can never be that Warre shall preserve life, and Peace destroy it." Hobbes concludes that the science of these laws is the "true and onely Moral Philosophy. For Morall Philosophy is nothing else but the Science of what is *Good*, and *Evill*, in the conversation, and Society of man-kind."[24]

The transition to the jural comes about because the laws of nature require that people covenant with one another to obey a sovereign, a covenant that gives to the sovereign wide authorization to legislate for what is now a jural community. But, as Malcolm recognizes, the authorization is not without limit. Hobbes is adamant that the sovereign's laws cannot be unjust since there is no standard of justice other than that decreed by the positive law. Indeed, it is necessary that the sovereign have a monopoly on legislative power and that his subjects be under an obligation to obey his laws in order for peace and stability to prevail. Nonetheless, Hobbes also emphasized that the sovereign could "commit Iniquity,"[25] which, as Malcolm observes, means that morality remains an "objective standard" in civil society. As Malcolm also points out, Hobbes does not confine the situation where the laws of nature bind *in foro externo* to that of civil society. Hobbes states that one is bound *in foro externo* as long as one has assurance of performance from the other party to a contract, which means that, if the other party performs his part of the contract in the state of nature, one is bound to reciprocate.[26] In other words, *in foro externo* obligation is not confined to the situation in which state coercion follows failure to perform; it also arises where failure to perform is immoral because one is under an obligation to respond to another's first performance.

Now, for Malcolm the important lessons to be learnt are for Hobbes's theory of international relations. Moral laws do exist both in the state of nature and in international society. But generally one has the right, the right of nature that Malcolm regards as a moral right, to act in ways that violate those laws unless there are special circumstances, notably a contract with first performance by the other party completed.[27] Malcolm shows that Hobbes not only saw how treaties and agreements could stabilize international relations but also how a common culture of shared values could provide a basis for stability. In this second respect, Malcolm points out that, when it came to culture, Hobbes thought it just as important that the sovereign make political education part of the internal project of achieving stability within the state.[28]

Malcolm does not conclude that we should change our picture of Hobbes in a radical fashion. Hobbes's "famously low opinion of human nature" survives. Nevertheless, Hobbes must be seen as holding out hope for improvement, not on the basis of some sense of an ultimate good for mankind but on the basis of a natural law theory derived from the principle of individual self-preservation. According to that theory, there are moral rights and duties in international relations, as there are in the state of nature. However, the difference between those states and civil society is that only in the latter can rights and duties be presumed to be in harmony. Hobbes is then a Realist, though not in the sense that he thinks that no moral rights and duties exist in international relations. He is a Realist in that, unlike Rationalists, he does not think that international relations can ever achieve the "presumed" "harmony" of civil society.[29]

In the following sections, I want to pick up on Malcolm's idea of the transition from one level to the others, from the psychological through the moral to the jural, in order to show how this idea of transition provides an attractive account of transitional justice. I will suggest that we can take the idea of transition from level to level quite literally, as marking stages in a transition from T_1 through T_2 to T_3. But we have to see that it is possible, albeit rare, for particular individuals to transcend the subjective and, in so doing, to trigger transition to the moral level. In addition, the moral level is not simply moral. The morality that Malcolm finds to provide objective standards is a special kind of morality—the morality of the laws of nature. It is what we can think of as the morality of legality, akin to what Lon L. Fuller would later term the "internal morality of law."[30] Moreover, this morality is not purely formal; it has substantive content that conditions and regulates the process of transition.

Sovereignty by Institution in Action

Assume that the state of nature is one in which there are at least two contending factions—an actual or threatened civil war. While Malcolm's view is that international relations presents the most realistic actual example of a state of nature, we should recall that Hobbes was addressing an audience that had just experienced an actual civil war, a fact frequently adverted to though never dwelt on in *Leviathan*.[31] It is therefore plausible to suppose that Hobbes did not have to go to very great lengths to convince readers of the reality and nastiness of a state of nature, since they had all come close to experiencing such a state. Moreover, the immediate aftermath of a civil war is in fact much closer to the state of nature than international relations. As Malcolm points out, Hobbes does not think that states are compelled to attack each other in the cause of an imperialist desire to grab more resources.[32] In contrast, unless one side in a civil war has been totally vanquished and its support virtually obliterated, the chances that the tensions will escalate into a new outbreak of hostilities are high. So I will make a further assumption that what puts the two factions into T_2—the time of transition—is that one has performed in such a way that it makes itself vulnerable to the other but that at the same time makes it possible for the other to reciprocate, thus laying the basis for a transition to civil society.

To give some particularity to the example, suppose that the situation is that of South Africa in the last years of apartheid and that the performance is President F. W. de Klerk's unbanning of the South African Communist Party and the African National Congress (ANC), as well as the unconditional release from imprisonment of Nelson Mandela and other leaders of the liberation struggle. From that time on, the National Party (NP), the ruling political party of white Afrikaners, which still controlled the police force and the military, and the ANC, which had its military wing but, more important, the support of a radicalized black youth, ever ready to take to the streets, faced each other as do two nations in the state of nature, "in continuall jealousies, and in the state and posture of Gladiators; having their weapons pointing, and their eyes fixed on one another."[33] Moreover, they faced each other as do two nations that are trying to conclude a peace after a war, with the difference that neither could be said to be internally sovereign. Rather, both sides were committed to getting to the point where they could agree on a set of moves at the conclusion of which a political entity would come into existence that they agree in advance to obey —the sovereign.

On the Hobbist view, the ANC and the NP were in a state of nature until T_3, which could be the first post-apartheid election or, perhaps more likely, whatever time one could say that the ANC had successfully consolidated power to the point where a coup by right-wing white groups no longer looked feasible. In addition, de Klerk's performance could be seen as one that pushed the country decisively into T_2 and through which he, contrary to the prescriptions of Hobbism, relinquished his grip on sovereign power and brought about a situation in which the "notions of Right and Wrong, Justice and Injustice" have "no place."[34]

These observations raise an interesting problem for theories of transitional justice—the problem of deciding when a transition starts and stops. I recall reading at first with disbelief but then with growing agreement the obituary in the London *Times* of John Vorster, one of apartheid's strong men, which pointed out that his attempts to establish diplomatic links with Africa in the 1970s should be seen as the first steps in the dismantling of apartheid, in other words, as putting South Africa into T_2. In addition, as South Africans still struggle with questions about the role and scope of affirmative action, about the redistribution of land and other economic resources, about the reform of the judiciary, as well as about other transition-like issues,[35] it strikes me that there is an excellent case to be made that South Africa has not yet moved into T_3, if, that is, we accept, with theorists of transitional justice, that there is radical discontinuity between T_2 and T_3. But, while these observations raise problems for theories of transitional justice, they might not seem as problematic for a Hobbist, since all a Hobbist is concerned with is the consolidation of power to the point where it can be said that there is a sovereign. Until that point is reached, justice talk and morality talk are futile.

However, if Malcolm is right about the place of morality and justice in international relations, then there is likely a place for them in transitions. And I will now argue that we can better understand that place in attending to the transition that we have seen Malcolm sketch, from the psychological through the moral to the jural.

In my own work on Hobbes's legal theory, I have argued that
Hobbes's laws of nature can be divided into roughly three groups.
Laws 1, 2, and 3 are fundamental.[36] They tell us to seek peace, to
give up as much our right of nature as is necessary to achieve this
end, and to obey our covenants. Laws 4 to 10, from the law that
requires gratitude through to the law against arrogance, which requires that no individual seek to retain a right that he thinks others should give up, set out what I call the moral psychology of the
"Just man," the individual whose will is "framed by the Justice" of
his actions, rather than by the benefit they will bring him.[37] The
remaining Laws, 11 to 19, are about the institution of legal order,
for example, the requirement of impartial adjudication in Laws 17
and 18, or about the kinds of positive law that the sovereign must
make, most notably Law 11 on equity, which requires that the sovereign deal equally with individuals if he is to retain their trust as
the ultimate judge of right and wrong.

Hobbes's point about the individual whose will is framed by justice occurs in between his discussion of the fundamental laws and
his discussion of the laws that set out the moral psychology of the
just man, as do the rather difficult paragraphs where he sets out
his response to the Foole, who states publicly that, if one's guiding
principle is to pursue self-interest, there can be "no such thing as
Justice," since one's calculations of what is in one's interest should
always trump any standards set by another.[38] The placing suggests
that one who is not yet in a civil society but who is resolved to follow the first three laws has to have the moral psychology of the
just man, set out in laws 4–10, and must understand Hobbes's argument against the Foole in order to continue down the path of
reason. But not only is it surprising to find Hobbes suggesting that
both morality and justice talk have a place before a sovereign has
been established, but it seems that there is a deep tension in his
account of rationality. In order to continue down the path of rationality, one has to act irrationally, since, as we have seen, according
to Hobbes, in the state of nature one betrays oneself if one performs first.

Recall that the individual whose will is framed by justice does
not act because he is assured of securing a benefit. As Hobbes
goes on, this individual's actions have the "relish of Justice,"
which comes from a "certain Nobleness or Gallantness of cour-
age, (rarely found,) by which a man scorns to be beholding for the

contentment of his life, to fraud, or breach of promise."[39] The only
discussion of this passage of which I am aware is Michael Oakeshott's, and he suggests that it may provide the solution to the
problem of the impossibility of exit from the state of nature.[40]

I think there is much to this suggestion. Following it, Hobbes
would give the following description of de Klerk's precipitation of
South Africa into T_2. On the one hand, de Klerk, in making this
first performance, was under no *in foro externo* obligation to do so.
In addition, in relaxing the NP's grip on power through this performance, he acted irrationally, at least in the sense that his act was
irrational from the perspective of his faction. That is, not only did
de Klerk have no guarantee of reciprocity, but he betrayed his faction, both because he turned them from the group that held sovereign power into a mere faction and because their very survival as a
distinct cultural and ethnic group—white Afrikaners—was imper-
iled by this step.[41] However, despite the fact that de Klerk's actions
were irrational, they were both in fact and in purpose in accordance with his *in foro interno* obligation to seek peace. They had, at
the least, the "relish" of justice: they provided the anticipation or
taste of what could be brought into being.

On the other hand, once de Klerk had performed, Mandela was
under an obligation to reciprocate and moreover an obligation
that was *in foro externo* as well as *in foro interno*. While there was no
common power over the two factions to guarantee performance,
no such guarantee was needed, since performance had occurred.
Thus, while de Klerk's performance was in a sense irrational, it
also created a situation of *in foro externo* obligation for Mandela.
Indeed, it created a situation in which *in foro externo* obligation was
generally possible, because, once Mandela had reciprocated, de
Klerk was under an obligation to respond to his performance, and
so on.

Now, the sense in which de Klerk was irrational—call it "factional irrationality"—is a rather specialized sense. From another
perspective, that of an individual seeking to maximize his chances
of survival qua individual, as well as the survival of all the individuals qua individuals in his faction, it might seem perfectly rational
in the circumstances of the early 1990s for de Klerk to seek to compromise with the enemy in a way that would bring to an end a
conflict that could only get worse. In addition, Mandela was not

Genghis Khan. He, as well as other senior figures in the ANC, had a track record of willingness to negotiate, indeed, a political program for the creation of a society organized along nonracial lines, governed under the rule of law, and so on.

Moreover, the negotiations that ensued ushered in a set of compromises on both sides, all of which can be explained by prudential, self-interested calculations about how to avoid the abyss of a renewed and intensified civil war. The leaders of white South Africans gave up their grip on political power. The ANC accepted constitutional guarantees of the property rights of white South Africans and conceded both that white civil servants would keep their jobs and that there would be a process of amnesty for the crimes of the white regime, rather than criminal trials.[42]

Hence, my claim about factional irrationality might seem vacuous in the face of a challenge that both de Klerk and Mandela acted perfectly rationally from the perspective of individual self-interest. It would follow that a Hobbist account of purely prudential political calculations not only explains what happened in the South African situation but also probably suggests the most effective recipe for success in any transition. The correct description of the process from T_1 through T_2 to T_3 is that the leaders forsake factional loyalty for fear of the consequences, and that allows them to adopt the perspective of individual self-interest, from which it is possible to make appropriate prudential calculations.

On this view, *Leviathan* is a textbook of prudential calculation for individuals who are no different from the Foole. The Foole is, after all, not only someone who assesses his options and tries to maximize self-interest. That is also all he does. Moreover, that he makes, according to Hobbes, some mistakes when it comes to the calculation of the chances of getting caught does not make him different from any other calculator, since Hobbes is clear that we are all prone to making such mistakes.

Besides the fact that Hobbes wants to refute the Foole, there are at least two problems with the view that *Leviathan*, despite Hobbes's wants, is a textbook for this figure. First, Hobbes nowhere says that fear is either necessary or sufficient to trigger rationality in the context of the state of nature. At most, fear, along with other passions, can "encline men to Peace."[43] Indeed, when he says that fear is the passion that "enclineth men least to break the Lawes," even "the onley thing . . . that makes men keep them," he adds that this claim is not true of "some generous natures" and, more important, that fear can cause men to commit crimes.[44] Thus, not only is fear neither sufficient nor necessary to put men on the path of reason, it also can lead to unreason. The point about lack of necessity brings us back to Oakshott's emphasis on the individual whose will is framed by justice and thus to the thought that some of those rarely found generous natures are at the least helpful to, but perhaps even a necessary ingredient of, a transition.[45]

Second, the relevant Fooles in a transition are the political leaders of factions, and so their calculations are about what will advance the interests of the faction. They will either fail to enter negotiations or resile from them as soon as cost-benefit analysis seems to them, on their individual estimate, to indicate that this is the right choice. Thus, their ability to detach themselves from the interest set of the faction and to calculate what is in the interests of all individual members of the society is subverted by the feature that makes them Fooles in the first place—their denial that there is such a thing as justice. And Hobbes makes it clear that one is just as much a Foole when one fails to perform when the other party has performed but there is no civil power as when there is a civil power but neither party has performed.[46]

Put differently, the kind of rational perspective that Hobbes thinks it is necessary for individuals to take up, whether to make a first performance or to respond appropriately to one, is not available to the Foole, since that perspective includes the ability to understand the force of the laws of nature. It is the perspective of someone whose will is framed by justice. Even if one concedes that fear is the passion that gets the process going, the perspective it drives an individual to is one not of pure prudential calculation but of reason, where reason involves reasoning in accordance with the convenient Articles of Peace, "otherwise . . . called the Lawes of Nature."[47] The space of reason one enters differs from the space that one left not only in that one is now making long term enlightened calculations of self-interests but also in that the space is structured or disciplined by the laws of nature.

The difference is clearly brought out in Hobbes's discussion of "Free-gift,"[48] an act that is even more irrational than a first performance, since it is done without any expectation of a reciprocal performance. Yet, according to Hobbes, a free gift does create an obligation—set out in Law 4, the natural law that commands gratitude—not to give the giver "reasonable cause to repent of his good will." Hobbes likens the injustice of breaking a covenant to the failure to respond appropriately to the act of grace involved in a voluntary gift and observes that the resulting frustration means that:

> there will be no beginning of benevolence, or trust; nor consequently of mutuall help; nor of reconciliation of one man to another; and therefore they are to remain still in the condition of *War*, which is contrary to the first and Fundamentall Law of Nature, which commandeth men to *Seek Peace*.[49]

In sum, while de Klerk's acts were irrational in only a very specialized sense, this is the relevant sense in the state of nature that Hobbes primarily has in mind in chapter 13, a fact rather obscured by the description of that state of a war between individuals rather than a situation in which political factions are either engaged in or are on the brink of a civil war. It follows not only that one can have and follow obligations in the state of nature—the *in foro interno* obligations one has to obey the laws of nature—but also that following such obligations can be precisely what generates *in foro externo* obligations for others and at the same time makes it possible for them to generate similar obligations for oneself. In order for such a process to continue to unfold, the factions have to follow the laws of nature, for example, the law against arrogance, which precludes an insistence on giving up less of the right of nature than the other faction. In following these laws, the factions will find themselves drawn into an increasingly structured set of expectations around their obligations until they get to the point where they can agree on a set of moves at the conclusion of which a political entity will come into existence that they have agreed in advance to obey—the sovereign.

Until the sovereign comes into existence, the factions' agreement is unenforceable and so fragile. But it is not as fragile as an agreement based purely on calculations of self-interest. Rather, the agreement is built on an ever more secure foundation of obligations that are binding, not because there is a common authority to enforce them but because the obligations following from the very first performance have continued to be met in a pattern of mutually reinforcing reciprocal performances. If either faction were to resile at any point, it would display itself to be an irrational "Foole," an entity not to be trusted within or without civil society. Moreover, the costs of resiling become greater as both parties become more enmeshed in these patterns of reciprocity, because the greater the degree of trust that has built up between them, the less the resiling party will be deemed worthy of trust should it wish at a later stage to renew the process.

It follows that SBI, sovereignty by institution, is not impossible.[50] Formerly warring factions can covenant to create a new sovereign, as long as at least one faction has a leader willing to make the first performance or to give a free gift. Of course, this kind of situation differs from the state of nature described in chapter 13 of *Leviathan* in some respects. T_1 was a period when there was a sovereign, and that means that in T_2 the factions find themselves with a legacy that can be both a help and a hindrance. It is a help if, as in the South African transition, the legacy includes institutions, traditions, and cultures such as those that make up the rule of law, as well as political leaders who have manifested a will framed by justice, and that can be relied upon during the transition as building blocks for the future. It is a hindrance, as already indicated, to the extent that those same institutions have during T_2 to be staffed by the officials who made them the instrument of the ideology that prevailed during T_1. In addition, the legacy of bitterness from a T_1 of oppression inflicted by a sovereign might be thought to be greater than if one were escaping a chapter 13 state of nature in which individuals fear each other as self-seeking individuals. However, I do not think one should make too much of these differences, especially if it is plausible to suppose that what Hobbes had primarily in mind in *Leviathan* is a transition from a civil war.

Now it might be thought that, even on this non-Hobbist view of Hobbes, there is a clear difference between civil society and the transitional period, between T_3 and T_2, because in civil society one can count on more than the normative basis of obligations; one can also count on the sanctions that the sovereign will inflict on noncompliance. Further, it is just because one can so count that civil society is stable, whereas transitions and international relations are more akin to a state of nature.

But Hobbes does not in fact think that the stability of civil society is secured mainly by the ability of the sovereign to make the consequences of law-breaking likely more painful than beneficial to one who is tempted to break the law to secure his own desires. His answer to the Foole includes but does not rely mainly on the argument that the Foole has the wrong cost-benefit account of the consequences of law-breaking. More accurately, the cost that the Foole fails properly to take into account is not so much the cost that he will likely be punished by the sovereign, for the Foole has already taken that likelihood into account when he makes his claim. Rather, as already pointed out, it is the cost of being stigmatized as someone unfit to live in civil society because he can't be trusted to carry out his obligations even when he has complete assurance of performance.[51] Thus, when Hobbes continues his analysis of the irrationality of the Foole in chapter 27, he describes the civil law as "Cob-web Lawes" and worries that Fooles might conclude from the fact that others have benefited by breaking the law that "Justice is but a vain word."[52]

Hobbes takes up this same theme in chapter 30, "Of the OFFICE of the Soveraign Representative," where he emphasizes the duty of the sovereign to instruct his subjects "diligently" in the "grounds of these Rights":

> because they cannot be maintained by any Civill Law, or terrour of legall Punishment. For a Civill Law, that shall forbid Rebellion, (and such is all resistance to the essential Rights of Soveraignty,) is not (as a Civill Law) any obligation, but by vertue onely of the Law of Nature, that forbiddeth the violation of Faith; which naturall obligation if men know not, they cannot know the Right of any Law the Soveraign maketh. And for the Punishment, they take it but for an act of Hostility; which when they think they have strength enough, they will endeavour by acts of Hostility, to avoid.[53]

So here, as elsewhere, the antidote Hobbes offers is not increased sanctions or police powers but public education.[54]

In chapter 30, Hobbes claims that there is "no difficulty" in teaching all men the laws of nature.[55] He does see that the medium of instruction might have to be tailored to the beliefs of its audience, and so he suggests that the instruction should be in the vernacular of Scripture. Following this suggestion, he sketches the principles of a civic education that form a kind of bridge between the laws of nature and the understanding in which subjects should be instructed in order that they can adopt an appropriate stance of fidelity to law.[56] These principles track the Ten Commandments, requiring, for example, that people should not covet the form of government of another nation, that they should not hold any of their fellow subjects in as high esteem as they hold their sovereign, that they should not speak ill of their sovereign representative, and that they should have a day set apart for learning their duty to their sovereign.[57] In short, Hobbes seems to require a kind of civic religion that is consistent with his reputation as an authoritarian and that will make his theory of justice even more antithetical to liberal democrats.

I do not think that one can rescue Hobbes altogether from the charge of authoritarianism. But one can go a long way to moderating that reputation through a better understanding of his idea of civic education and through seeing that the worship of the sovereign is the worship of an artificial, not a natural, person. Moreover, once moderated, his authoritarianism might seem not too many degrees removed from the authoritarianism considered appropriate in the most stable liberal democratic societies.

As I will now show, in order to understand the content of that education, we have to unpack what is involved in Malcolm's claim that the category of the jural cannot be reduced to the content of an actual sovereign's commands—it is, as he put it, "both universal and analytic." But, as we will also see, Malcolm himself does not quite follow through on the implications of this claim. In particular, he does not see why the universality and analyticity of the jural precludes his suggestion that, strictly speaking, "an instituted monarch in Hobbes's theory remains in a state of nature" in his relationship with his own subjects: "he is jurally entitled to treat them just as he would treat his enemies."[58]

While that suggestion is true of the situation in which the sovereign is about to inflict punishment on the subject, it is not true of the other sorts of relations in which sovereign and subject find themselves, because these relationships are not between natural individuals in a state of nature but between natural individuals who understand how to live in civil society. And, to understand how to live in civil society, one must understand the nature of one's role as an artificial person, whether the person be that of the sovereign or the subject.

My argument is thus that Hobbes's understanding of legality is the most plausible theory of transitional justice. Put differently, T_2, which is most likely the state of nature Hobbes has in mind, arises because of a breakdown in order at T_1. The problem for political actors in T_2 is how to reestablish order. They are the architects who have to design a "firme and lasting edifice" given the confines of the "crasie building" they inhabit.[59] And, in order to do that, they have by their actions to educate the future subjects of the sovereign they hope to create in the virtues of life in a jural community.

EDUCATION IN LEGALITY

Jonathan Allen has argued, in my view correctly, that the kind of justice achieved by South Africa's Truth and Reconciliation Commission (TRC) should not be understood in terms of a model of restorative justice. Rather, it should be understood in terms of what he calls "justice as recognition" and "justice as ethos."[60]

In regard to the first, the work of the Committee that heard from victims—the Committee on Human Rights Violations—supports the restoration of the rule of law by drawing attention to the "evil consequences resulting from apartheid and the officially sanctioned transgressions of the rule of law." The hearings "demonstrate the consequences of a lack of public commitment to justice and the rule of law and thus show the importance of such a commitment. In this sense the TRC supports legal recognition in a context where law's equal recognition of all responsible agents has been grossly distorted."[61]

In regard to the second, justice as ethos involves the demonstration of how under apartheid people's sense of justice was corrupted. Justice became equated with the ideology of the group one happened to belong to, rather than serving as a standpoint from which any particular ideology might be criticized. This equation, in turn, led to an impoverished view of public discourse—politics is either a dirty business or a noble calling in which the end justifies the means. But neither of these views permits any operation for a sense of injustice, and that sense is required if the transitional government is to preserve legitimacy and a commitment to the constraints of the rule of law, constraints that make it possible for citizens to call government to account for injustice.[62]

As I understand them, Allen's ideas of justice as recognition and justice as ethos are not meant to be discoveries of new kinds of justice. Rather, they are labels for processes that serve the transformation of an unjust society into a just one. But the justice they serve is little more than the justice of the rule of law, the kind of justice that has to be in place before order becomes something worth having and that also makes it possible for a society to decide other kinds of political issues in a civil fashion. If that is right, then most of the debate about transitional justice should be boiled down to one about how to achieve the rule of law.[63]

This boiling down, even deflation, might cause disappointment not only to those who see in transitional justice and the work of truth commissions something altogether new and exciting but also to the political activists who risked much to bring about the transition. As one such activist, Bärbel Bohley, from the former German Democratic Republic, famously complained of the transition that followed German reunification, "We expected justice, but we got the *Rechtsstaat* instead."[64] I will come back to this point later. For the moment, I want to note that, on the Hobbist interpretation of Hobbes, justice as recognition seems feasible, but not justice as ethos. That is, if justice as recognition amounts to an education in what goes wrong when legality or the rule of law is not respected, a Hobbist might regard a process that drives this lesson home as most valuable. But justice as ethos is an education in the claim that justice transcends the ideology of the particular group that happens to be in power and is thus to be able to use law to achieve its ends, which to a Hobbist must appear as an education in treason. However, if an education in legality cannot be other than an education in how justice transcends particular ideologies, it must be the case that an education in the first kind of justice entails an education in the second.

Of course, the claim about transcendental justice and legality is controversial. For example, the central theme of a recent collection of essays on democracy and the rule of law is the distinction between rule by law and the rule of law, where the former means the use of law as a brute instrument to achieve the ends of those with political power while the latter means the constraints that normative conceptions of the rule of law place on the instrumental use of law.[65] The contributors argue that the normative conception, which is the one adopted by jurists, is a "figment of their imagination."[66]

Law, they say, is not an autonomous constraint on actions but a constraint that those with political power will accept or not, depending on their relative strength. If accepting the constraint is the only way to maintain their power, they will, otherwise not. Not only is the choice to abide by the rule of law a matter of political incentives; the same is true of the choice to use rule by law to achieve one's ends. It follows that the weaker one's relative position, the closer one will find oneself to the normative rule-of-law end of the continuum between rule-by-law and rule-of-law. One who is in a very powerful position will submit to ruling at various points on that continuum only when it is expedient to do so, for example, when it is convenient to have public attention and thus possible hostility deflected onto officials such as judges. Machiavelli is the chief theoretical inspiration for this collection, but Hobbes is one of the secondary sources of inspiration, usually cited for the point that ultimately the sovereign is unconstrained by law. Even if the sovereign agrees to being bound by his own positive law, he can always unbind himself or change the bonds simply by exercising his supreme law-making power.[67]

Their argument assumes, as does Malcolm, that the political entity we call the sovereign is prior to law so that it can choose to accept legal constraints and can also choose to break free of those that it has in the past chosen to accept. It also assumes, though it is not clear exactly what Malcolm's position on this point would be, that the kind of legal order a sovereign puts in place could, depending on his strength, be one in which there is rule by law with hardly any rule of law. Not only is legal order optional, in other words, but the kind of legal order one adopts if one so chooses is optional, depending, of course, on one's relative power. Moreover, one who has that option will exercise it against the normative conception of the rule of law.

However, for Hobbes, the sovereign must govern through legal order. And, while the sovereign is the direct author of the civil laws and so can change any particular civil law, he still has to follow whatever public criteria exist for change in order for his changes to be recognized and so is bound by what H. L. A. Hart would later call the rule of recognition.[68] Even more important is that the sovereign cannot change the laws of nature. The latter, as we have seen, are immutable and eternal.

Hobbes thus comes at least close to adopting and, in my view, adopts what Hans Kelsen would later call the Identity Thesis, the thesis that the sovereign is entirely constituted by law.[69] This thesis leads to the conclusion that for the sovereign to act as a sovereign, his acts must be consistent with law. But, since, for Hobbes, "law" includes both the civil law and the laws of nature, his version of the Identity Thesis is stronger than Kelsen's.

Recall that Hobbes says that, while it is possible to say that a sovereign has acted against equity, it is not possible to say that he has acted unjustly, since justice is simply the justice of the law: "the Lawes are the Rules of Just, and Unjust; nothing being reputed Unjust, that is not contrary to some Law."[70] But, in order for legal subjects to receive the justice of the law, law has to deliver that justice. And it is far from clear that for Hobbes a positive or civil law that is clearly in violation of the laws of nature has a sound claim to be law.

First, as we have seen, he is clear that the laws of nature are intrinsic to legal order: "The Law of Nature and the Civill Law, contain each other, and are of equal extent."[71] Second, as we have also seen, it is his view that the sovereign "is as much subject, as any of the meanest of his People" to equity and to all other laws of nature.[72] Third, it is also clear that judges are under a duty to interpret the civil law as if it were intended to comply with the laws of nature. If they did not, Hobbes says, they would insult the sovereign.[73] In other words, rule by law for Hobbes—the rule of the positive or civil law of the sovereign—requires the rule of law; it must be in accordance with the transcendent laws of nature.

There is an interpretive strategy that empties this line of argument of any content. Its textual basis has already been mentioned. Hobbes, after saying that the laws of nature and the civil law contain each other, immediately goes on to say that in the state of nature the laws of nature are not "properly Lawes, but qualities that dispose men to peace, and to obedience" and that they become laws properly so called only in civil society where it is the task of the sovereign to give them content and to make them binding.[74] That is, the content of the laws of nature in civil society is to be read off the content of the positive law. It follows from this line of argument that, were the sovereign to enact a law requiring that all subjects must kill on sight any person passing through his realm on his way to mediate peace in some other land, subjects must take that positive law as the correct interpretation of Law 15 of the laws of nature: "That all men that mediate Peace, be allowed safe Conduct."[75]

This would be an absurd result. By far the better interpretation, in my view, is that the enactment of such a law might take the sovereign outside what Malcolm calls the jural community, where the sovereign risks facing his subjects not in the relationship of sovereign and subject but in the relationship of individual and individual, that is, within the state of nature. Here we need to see that Hobbes does distinguish between power and authority.

Helpful to understanding this distinction is the one clear exception Hobbes makes to the claim that we have a general duty to obey the law of our sovereign, whatever its content—the right we have to resist our sovereign when he threatens us with death. Because the point of the contract that establishes or institutes sovereignty is to ensure survival, Hobbes is adamant that a contract that gives the sovereign the authority to put one to death is void, and so an individual who is threatened with death has the right to resist the sovereign or his agents. So Hobbes does set one clear limit on the sovereign's authority.

Armed with this distinction between sheer power and authority, we can better understand another aspect of Hobbes's concept of the public sphere, what he calls the "publique Conscience" of the law.[76] As I have suggested, Hobbes is quite clear that there are internal constraints of legality on sovereign power, and these are listed in the catalogue of the laws of nature. Consider, for example, a sovereign who commands that his judges give judgment to the party who can offer the biggest bribe. This command is not only in violation of Law 18, which requires that judges be impartial.[77] It also subverts the office of Judicature and so contradicts what Hobbes concedes, rather reluctantly, to be a "Fundamentall Law" of sovereignty, one whose violation is likely to destroy the foundation of the Commonwealth.[78]

In my view, Hobbes is reluctant to make such concessions because he fears that the common lawyers will seize on any alleged fundamental laws as the basis for a doctrine that will legitimate the idea that judges are entitled to use the reason of the common law to control the sovereign. But not only is he unable to avoid the concession, he is also, as I have indicated, adamant that judges must bend over backward to show that any particular command of the sovereign is compatible with the laws of nature, especially Law 11, which requires that the sovereign deal equitably with his subjects.[79]

Hobbes does not tell us precisely what a judge should do when confronted by a technically valid law that violates the substantive content of a law of nature, though he does seem to suggest that the judge should stay judgment and consult a higher authority.[80] And he also does not say what a subject should do when faced with such a law.[81] It does not, however, matter as much what institutional solution to such predicaments works best for Hobbes as that he clearly recognizes them as predicaments that arise within a legal order because of the role of the laws of nature in conditioning the content of the positive law. They arise when the sovereign seems to have overstepped the limits of his authority, limits that are set by universal jural criteria, many of which have a content that goes beyond what Malcolm seems to have in mind when he calls the laws analytic, as well as universal. That content makes it clear when a command is inconsistent with the laws.

Hobbes clearly does not favor judicial invalidation of such commands; nor does he believe that individual subjects should be given a right to disobey them. Rather, he seems to want institutional mechanisms that will provide a judge or a subject with an opportunity to get a remedy from a higher authority. That he sees the need for such mechanisms tells us that here, as in the situation of actual or threatened punishment, the sovereign has stepped out of his artificial role and governs by power, rather than by authority. The difference is that, in the case of the technically valid but jurally suspect law, the tension arises within the legal order and so cannot be met by a moral right of resistance. Rather, the case requires some mechanism internal to legal order.

In other words, that a law lacks authority for a legal subject does not have the result that that subject is automatically entitled to disobey it, as he is in the case of a clash between the positive law and the right of nature. The difference comes about because, in the case of the clash between positive law and the right of nature, the clash happens because a moral right that is external and prior to jural community comes into conflict with the execution of a valid law of that community. In contrast, the category of jurally suspect but technically valid laws is created by tensions that arise within a jural community.

The more a sovereign puts the subject into the kinds of predicaments that result from this latter category, the more the subject will find it difficult to maintain the moral psychology necessary to be a just man, one who follows the law not out of fear of sanctions but because he understands the argument why the sovereign rightly claims authority over him. And this situation will be exacerbated to the extent that the sovereign has not put in place the institutional mechanisms that permit recourse to a higher authority to resolve the predicaments.[82] When Hobbes says at the end of *Leviathan* that the whole point of the book is to set out to his readers the "mutuall Relation between Protection and Obedience,"[83] he is not giving up his claim that there is no contract between the sovereign and his subjects. Rather, he is emphasizing that there is a relationship of reciprocity between sovereign and subjects whose maintenance requires constant observance by both of the constraints on their respective roles.

The so-called rebel's catechism—the passage where Hobbes says that one is at liberty to disobey the sovereign when his commands frustrate "the End for which the Soveraignty was ordained"[84]—might seem to undermine the whole of Hobbes's argument until one takes into account that commands that do this are only those commands that clearly put a great deal of strain on the sovereign's constitutional commitment[85] to abide by the laws of nature. If the class of commands is limited in this way, then it is possible for Hobbes to achieve the aim he set out in the dedication of *Leviathan*: to show how it is possible to pass "unwounded" between those who contend "for too great Liberty, and on the other side for too much Authority."[86]

CONCLUSION

I have argued that legality provides standards against which the positive law can be measured and found wanting. It is a kind of justice, not the justice to which an ideology lays claim but the justice intrinsic to a regime of legality. If a sovereign uses the law as an instrument of a political ideology that puts great strain on his constitutional commitment to comply with those standards, then the idea that Allen calls justice as ethos becomes corrupted. Such corruption undermines the sovereign's claim to provide protection in return for obedience, which requires him to rule more by terror than by the rule of law, until he puts his society at risk of deteriorating into civil war. If that happens but the society manages to pull back from the brink and enter a time of transition toward T_3, it will be the task of the architects to educate their audience through the measures they take in the related matters of justice as recognition and justice as ethos. Their task is to make a jural community possible, which involves securing, renovating, and adding to the building in which they find themselves, even to the extent of attempting to change its foundations. The legal institutions they propose to put in place, the laws they enact, and the measures they propose and adopt to deal with the legacy of the past should be guided primarily by the aim of achieving a condition of legality that makes it possible for the new sovereign to get on with a different task, providing "commodious living"[87] for his subjects. Whether such an education requires a truth and reconciliation commission or criminal trials or some combination is, in my view, dictated not by a theory of transitional justice but by an evaluation of particular contexts.

It is at this stage that we can fruitfully return to the topic of the extent of Hobbes's authoritarianism, in particular, his advocacy, to put things at their harshest, of a civic religion of veneration for the sovereign. This civic religion is not, however, a cult of personality, nor, as much of Hobbes's argument in *Leviathan* makes clear, can it be a cult based on claims by a leader to have a hotline to some source of divine revelation. As the Introduction to *Leviathan* tells us, the soul of the sovereign, what gives the whole body of the state its "life and motion," is not natural but artificial.[88] It follows that the awe in which subjects are supposed to hold the sovereign is not the awe in which we might hold someone who claims to be able to work miracles. Rather, the awe is based on the fact that the artifice of formerly masterless men, who might previously have been divided by bitter ideological disagreements and violent deeds, is able to provide civic order. The awe of the subjects is ultimately awe of themselves.

It might be that to become involved in the process of SBI, of creating a sovereign by institution, the principal actors need to be impelled by self-interest based on fear, although I have suggested, following Oakeshott, that Hobbes quite plausibly entertains a different scenario, one in which it is the presence of some more generous individuals, whose will is framed by justice, that gets the process started. That is, the actors who take the initiative and those who respond have to have the relish of justice, and that requires an understanding of and a commitment to the laws of nature. Should they follow through on that commitment, a civic order will begin to emerge that will make, as we have seen Hobbes say, trust and even reconciliation possible,[89] though these goods will come about as by-products of the actors' focus on the logic of reciprocity.

Further, if liberal democrats think of their own attitude when a new political party whose illiberal ideology we despise wins power, they might find that they are not that distant from Hobbes. That is, until the going gets really rough, they maintain their stance of obedience to the person of the sovereign, on the basis that their duty of loyalty to the state and its laws generally trumps even strongly held views about the obnoxious content of the laws. The main difference is that they reject Hobbes's claim that they should not criticize the people who hold sovereign power because, unlike him, they do not think that unrestrained political debate risks a slide into the state of nature.

That difference should not be underestimated, nor the fact that Hobbes's fears of the divisive nature of debate in a parliamentary system and of the threat to stability posed by judicial review have proved unfounded. But, however wrong he was on these issues about optimal institutional design, he was right that what makes successful experiments in institutional design as well as in political and social justice possible is the morality of legality, which must be given institutional expression and find support in a public, civic culture.

I also do not want to claim that there are no differences between the situation of civil society where the political task is the maintenance of a jural community and the problem of transition from a state of disorder verging on civil war, where the task is to create a jural community. But, if we go back to Malcolm's sketch of the distinction between the jural community of nations—the international order—and the jural community of a civil society, we should see why my discussion of *Leviathan* as a theory of transitional justice might lead us to soften the distinction between an established state of civil society on the one hand and more unsettled states, societies in T_2 or the state of international relations, on the other.

Recall that Malcolm's conclusion is that Hobbes's Realism resides not in the fact that Hobbes thinks that moral rights and duties have no place in international relations but only in that he does not think that international relations can ever reach the state of presumed harmony that characterizes civil society. My suggestion is that the idea of presumption has to be taken very seriously. Hobbes contemplates that, even in the most stable societies, the sovereign's ideological experiments in justice might unsettle the presumption, not merely because subjects happen to disagree with the sovereign but because the experiments strain or even contradict the sovereign's commitment to the laws of nature. The difference is that the presumption does exist in civil society. But it exists when and only when the relationship between sovereign and subject is one of reciprocity, which in turn requires that subjects generally find that they are treated as full members of the jural community.

Establishing such a presumption is a much more difficult task, and perhaps in some states, notably the state of international relations, it is one of those ideals to which one has to strive in the knowledge that it will always be well beyond reach. But the task is not impossible in transitions, though much depends on the precise legacy from T_1.[90] And, as in international relations, the task can be begun in T_2 only if those who undertake it treat one another as if they are already full members of a jural community in order that such a community might have a real chance of being established.[91]

I have tried to show that Hobbes's theory of justice, while universal, is quite modest, but not so modest that it has no bite. I suspect that we should not expect more of a universal theory, one that is meant to apply to all societies. And that is in part because such a theory must, to succeed, be a theory of transitional justice. No universal theory of justice can afford to be anything other than a theory of transitional justice, since all societies are in transition. Of course, in stable societies we are entitled to expect much more of our sovereigns than legality—government in accordance with the laws of nature; we are also entitled to expect a good-faith effort to focus on providing us with commodious living. But neither the difficulty in achieving legality nor the significance of that achievement should be underestimated.[92] It might be that societies that find themselves in dramatic transitional moments should focus almost exclusively on that task.

NOTES

I thank Bernard Boxill and Eric Posner for their critical commentaries on my initial draft.

1. Thomas Hobbes, *Leviathan*, ed. Richard Tuck (Cambridge: Cambridge University Press, 1997), chap. 13, [63] 90. Hereafter, *Leviathan*.

2. See further, ibid., chap. 26 "Of Civill Lawes," [137] 184: "Lawes are the Rules of Just, and Unjust."

3. Ibid., chap. 13, [63] 90.

4. In chap. 20 of *Leviathan*, Hobbes discusses sovereignty by acquisition, where one consents to the authority of an already existing sovereign who has vanquished one. However, logically speaking, at least one sovereign has to have been established by institution before there can be sovereignty by acquisition, so sovereignty by institution is the primary mode of establishing sovereignty.

5. Ibid., chap. 19.

6. David Dyzenhaus, "Transitional Justice," *International Journal of Constitutional Law* 1 (2003): 163–75. For an argument to similar conclusions, see Eric A. Posner and Adrian Vermeule, "Transitional Justice as Ordinary Justice," *Harvard Law Review* 117 (2004): 762–825.

7. Of course, my typology here is controversial. Some who have been attracted to the idea of transitional justice as the theory appropriate to transitions also wish to argue that attention to transitions might change our understanding of what is appropriate in our own societies. So they assume discontinuity with T_1 but not with T_3. See, for example, Elizabeth Kiss, "Moral Ambition Within and Beyond Political Constraints: Reflections on Restorative Justice," in *Truth v. Justice: The Morality of Truth Commissions*, ed. Robert I Rotberg and Dennis Thompson (Princeton: Princeton University Press, 2000), 9. Others seem to vacillate between assuming radical discontinuity and hence the need for a special theory and recognizing that there is neither such discontinuity nor anything particularly special about transitional justice; for example, Ruti G. Teitel, *Transitional Justice*

(New York: Oxford University Press, 2000). Jon Elster's recent work stands apart because he seeks to uncover the dilemmas posed by problems that arise within transitions while disclaiming any ambition to provide a theory of justice: *Closing the Books: Transitional Justice in Historical Perspective* (Cambridge: Cambridge University Press, 2004), xi.

8. I discuss this issue in "Justifying the Truth and Reconciliation Commission," *Journal of Political Philosophy* 8 (2000): 470–96.

9. See especially Posner and Vermeule, "Transitional Justice as Ordinary Justice."

10. For example, in the debate about the appropriate reaction to the supposedly new threat of global terrorism since 9/11, political and legal theorists often work with the assumption that the kinds of information on which intelligence services rely in making decisions about who poses a risk to security cannot be tested in a judicial forum. But this assumption about institutional incapacity to deal with a problem is false. (See David Dyzenhaus, *The Constitution of Law: Legality in a Time of Emergency* (Cambridge: Cambridge University Press, 2006).) Moreover, it presupposes the same dichotomy between the normal and the exceptional situation that is at work in much of the debate about transitional justice.

11. *Leviathan*, chap. 18, [94] 128–29.

12. Quentin Skinner, "Hobbes and the Purely Artificial Person of the State," in *Visions of Politics: Vol. III: Hobbes and Civil Science* (Cambridge: Cambridge University Press, 2002), 177, 232–37.

13. *Leviathan*, "Introduction," [2] 10. For further discussion, see Kinch Hoekstra, "The *De Facto* Turn in Hobbes's Political Philosophy," in *Leviathan After 350 Years*, ed. Tom Sorell and Luc Foisneau (Oxford: Oxford University Press, 2004), 33.

14. *Leviathan*, chap. 29, [167] 221, quoted in Duncan Ivison, "Pluralism and the Hobbesian Logic of Negative Constitutionalism," *Political Studies* 47 (1999): 95.

15. Noel Malcolm, "Hobbes's Theory of International Relations," in *Aspects of Hobbes* (Oxford: Clarendon Press, 2004), 431, 435. 16. *Leviathan*, chap. 13, [62] 88–89.

17. Ibid., chap. 13, [63] 90.

18. Ibid.

19. Ibid., chap. 30, [185–186] 244.

20. Ibid., chap. 15, [79] 110.

21. Ibid.

22. Ibid., chap. 26, [138] 185.

23. Malcolm, "Hobbes's Theory of International Relations," 436.

24. Ibid., 437. *Leviathan*, chap. 16, [79] 110.

25. Ibid., chap. 18, [90] 24.

26. Ibid., chap. 15, [73] 102. Malcolm, "Hobbes's Theory of International

Relations," 438. Note that immediately following the distinction between *in foro interno* and *in foro externo*, Hobbes says that one who fails to reciprocate in the situation where there is assurance "seeketh not Peace, but War; & consequently the destruction of his Nature by Violence"; *Leviathan*, chap. 15, [79] 110.

27. Malcolm, "Hobbes's Theory of International Relations," 445–46.

28. Ibid., 449–55.

29. Ibid., 455–56.

30. Lon L. Fuller, *The Morality of Law*, rev. ed. (New Haven: Yale University Press, 1969).

31. I do not wish to suggest that Hobbes was being coy about discussing the civil war, as in *Behemoth* he had addressed that topic.

32. Malcolm, "Hobbes's Theory of International Relations," 448.

33. *Leviathan*, chap. 13, [63] 90.

34. Ibid.

35. Consider for example the offer some years ago by the government of amnesty for those who had illegally and criminally moved money out of the country. In return for full disclosure, the government gave one immunity from criminal sanctions and imposed a tax on the money. This measure seems quintessentially one about transitional justice, but it was introduced at a time when the ANC had consolidated its power to the point where it had no serious political opposition in Parliament or in the country more generally.

36. David Dyzenhaus, "Hobbes and the Legitimacy of Law," *Law and Philosophy* 20 (2001): 461–98. I attempt to take that argument further in "Hobbes's Constitutional Theory," in *Leviathan*, ed. Ian Shapiro (New Haven: Yale University Press, 2010).

37. *Leviathan*, chap. 15, [74] 103–4. These laws express what Hobbes speaks of in *De Cive* as an obligation in the state of nature to a "readiness of mind" to observe the laws of nature "whensoever their observation shall seem to conduce to the end of which they were ordained." Hobbes, *De Cive*, in *Man and Citizen*, ed. Bernard Gert (Indianapolis: Hackett Company, 1991), paragraph 27 at 149.

38. *Leviathan*, chap. 15, [72–74] 101–3.

39. Ibid., chap. 15, [74] 104.

40. Michael Oakeshott, "The Moral Life in the Writings of Thomas Hobbes," in *Rationalism in Politics and Other Essays* (Indianapolis: Liberty Press, 1991), 295–350, at 344–50.

41. Note that the NP formally disbanded after some years as a clearly spent force and that white Afrikaners are experiencing what one without exaggeration can term an identity crisis.

42. In this paragraph, I set out the main challenge posed to my argument by both my commentators.

43. *Leviathan,* chap. 13, [63] 90.

44. *Leviathan,* chap. 27, [155] 206.

45. While I do not want to make too much of this line of thought, it is intriguing, to say the least, to speculate about the difference Rabin's assassination made to the prospects of peace in the conflict between Israelis and Palestinians.

46. *Leviathan,* chap. 15, [73] 102.

47. Ibid., chap. 13, [63] 90.

48. Ibid., chap. 15, [75–76] 105–6. See Malcolm, "Hobbes's Theory of International Relations," 446–47, for a discussion of the importance of this law in Hobbes's general scheme, though in the context of the relationship between sovereign and subject within civil society. Note that "free gift" might more accurately than "first performance" describe de Klerk's first move, but this would not affect my argument.

49. *Leviathan,* chap. 15, [75] 105.

50. Compare Jean Hampton, *Hobbes and the Social Contract Tradition* (Cambridge: Cambridge University Press, 1988), chap. 6. Hampton does think that sovereignty by institution is possible, but her solution to the problem of the apparent impossibility of escape from the state of nature is bounded by an assumption which I reject—that escape has to be possible on the basis of short-term calculations of interest.

51. *Leviathan,* chap. 15, [73] 102–3.

52. Ibid., chap. 27, [153] 204.

53. Ibid., chap. 30, [175–176] 232.

54. Ibid., chap 30, [179–180] 236–37.

55. Ibid., chap. 30, [177] 233.

56. See Mary G. Dietz, "Hobbes's Subject as Citizen," in *Thomas Hobbes & Political Theory,* ed. Dietz (Kansas: University Press of Kansas, 1990), 91.

57. *Leviathan,* chap. 30, [177–178] 233–35.

58. Malcolm, "Hobbes's Theory of International Relations," 446.

59. *Leviathan,* chap. 29, [167] 221.

60. Jonathan Allen, "Balancing Justice and Social Unity: Political Theory and the Idea of a Truth and Reconciliation Commission," *University of Toronto Law Journal* 49 (1999): 315, 328–32, 335–38.

61. Ibid., 330–31.

62. Ibid., 336–38.

63. For more argument, see Dyzenhaus, "Justifying the Truth and Reconciliation Commission."

64. A. James McAdams, *Judging the Past in Unified Germany* (Cambridge: Cambridge University Press, 2001), 7.

65. José María Maravall and Adam Przeworski, eds., *Democracy and the Rule of Law* (Cambridge: Cambridge University Press, 2003).

66. José María Maravall and Adam Przeworski, introduction to ibid., 1.

67. See ibid., 10, 190, 193–94, 217, 244–45.
68. H. L. A. Hart, *The Concept of Law* (Oxford: Clarendon Press, 1961), chap. 5. Howard Warrender explained just why Hobbes must allow for rule-of-recognition-type constraints before Hart had articulated the idea for which his legal theory is famous; Warrender, *The Political Theory of Hobbes: His Theory of Obligation* (Oxford: Clarendon Press, 2000), 258–63. For discussion of Hobbes and the rule of recognition, see Robert Ladenson, "In Defense of a Hobbesian Conception of the Rule of Law," *Philosophy and Public Affairs* 9 (1990): 134; Jean Hampton, "Democracy and the Rule of Law," in *Nomos XXXVI: The Rule of Law*, ed. Ian Shapiro (New York: New York University Press, 1994), 13; Jeremy Waldron, "Legal and Political Philosophy," in *The Oxford Handbook of Jurisprudence & Philosophy of Law*, ed. Jules Coleman and Scott Shapiro (Oxford: Oxford University Press, 2002), 352, 366–68. Note that Hobbes does permit the subject to challenge the sovereign in court for violating the law; *Leviathan*, chap. 21, [113] 152–53. The lines that immediately follow about the result of the sovereign demanding or taking anything "by pretence of his Power" are in some tension with my claim in the next paragraph in the text about Hobbes and the Identity Thesis.
69. See Hans Kelsen, *Introduction to the Problems of Legal Theory: A Translation of the First Edition of the Reine Rechtslehre or Pure Theory of Law*, trans. S. L. Paulson and B. Litschewski-Paulson (Oxford: Oxford University Press, 1992). I am indebted here to discussions with Lars Vinx. See Vinx, *Hans Kelsen's Pure Theory of Law: Legality and Legitimacy* (Oxford: Oxford University Press, 2007), for the argument that Kelsen's conception of legality has the kind of substantive content to it that I claim is also to be found in Hobbes. Hobbes, of course, says things that seem inconsistent with this claim; for example, in chapter 30 of *Leviathan*, in a discussion of why the sovereign should not give away the essential rights of sovereignty, Hobbes suggests that an acknowledgment by the sovereign that he is subject to the civil law would amount to giving away one of these rights; [175] 231. But, in chap. 26, [137–138] at 184, he makes it clear that what he means by not being subject to the civil law is that the sovereign is able to change the civil law and thus free himself from subjection, and he emphasizes that the sovereign is not free to change the laws of nature. Some other discussions in *Leviathan*, notably that of David and Uriah in chap. 21, [109–110] 148, are also problematic for my argument, but, as I try to show in "Hobbes's Constitutional Theory," they are no less problematic for Hobbes himself.
70. *Leviathan*, chap. 26, [137] 184.
71. Ibid., chap. 26, [138] 185.
72. Ibid., chap. 30, [180] 237.
73. Ibid., chap. 26, [145] 194.
74. Ibid.
75. Ibid., chap. 15, [78] 108. See Mark C. Murphy, "Was Hobbes a Legal

Positivist?" *Ethics* 105 (1995): 846–73 at 857, arguing for precisely this position. Of course, subjects would be entitled to disobey the positive law because obedience to it would imperil them. But the point in the text is different—the status of the law as law.

76. *Leviathan*, chap. 29, [169] 223.

77. Ibid., chap. 15, [78] 109.

78. Ibid., chap. 26, [150] 200.

79. Ibid., chap. 26, [145] 194.

80. Ibid.

81. There is a suggestion in a different context that the subject is under an *in foro interno* obligation to obey a suspect though technically valid law —it would be a sin though not a crime to fail to do so. In addition, the subject should not resist a public official who wishes to enforce the law, and here the obligation is an *in foro externo* one; indeed, Hobbes says that it is a crime to resist. The reason Hobbes gives for the latter obligation is that the subject should be able to count on being "righted upon complaint," again one might assume to a higher authority. Ibid., chap. 27, [157] 209. The passage is a difficult one, since Hobbes seems to suppose an example where the sovereign grants the subject a liberty inconsistent with the rights essential to sovereignty and then issues a command that is inconsistent with that liberty.

82. Hobbes's hostility to judicial review thus creates problems for his theory because it severely limits the scope of mechanisms. Note that Bentham, who was perhaps even more hostile, thought that judges should be able to continue applying a law that led to injustice and that they should then be able to inform a special legislative committee. See Gerald Postema, *Bentham and the Common Law Tradition* (Oxford: Clarendon Press, 1986), 453–59. The United Kingdom's Human Rights Act (1998) is a kind of Hobbesian solution to statutes that are in violation of human rights since it permits the courts to make only a declaration of incompatibility with the Act and leaves it to government and the legislature to decide whether and how to respond.

83. *Leviathan*, "A Review, and Conclusion," [395–396] 491.

84. Ibid., chap. 21, [112] 151.

85. See my "Hobbes's Constitutional theory" for elaboration of this idea.

86. *Leviathan*, 3.

87. Ibid., chap. 13, [63] 90, read with the opening paragraph of chap. 30, [175] 231.

88. Ibid., "The Introduction," [1] 9. Indeed, it was this very lack of natural personality that made Carl Schmitt doubt that Hobbes's sovereign could ever awe his subjects: Carl Schmitt, *The Leviathan in the State Theory of Thomas Hobbes: Meaning and Failure of a Political Symbol*, trans. George Schwab and Erna Hilfstein (Westport, CT: Greenwood Press, 1996).

89. See text to note 50.

90. See Alexandra Barahona De Brito, Carmen Gonzalez-Enriquez, and Paloma Aguilar, eds., *The Politics of Memory: Transitional Justice in Democratizing Societies* (Oxford: Oxford University Press, 2001), 314.

91. For very fruitful arguments in this regard, see P. F. Strawson, "Freedom and Resentment" in *Freedom and Resentment and Other Essays* (London: Methuen, 1974), 1.

92. For example, consider Adam Tomkin's arguments about the failures of the contemporary British constitution: *Our Republican Constitution* (Oxford: Hart, 2005).

8

TRANSITIONAL PRUDENCE:
A COMMENT ON DAVID DYZENHAUS,
"*LEVIATHAN* AS A THEORY OF
TRANSITIONAL JUSTICE"

ERIC A. POSNER

David Dyzenhaus's interesting chapter argues that Hobbes's theory of justice provides insights into questions of transitional justice faced by modern societies such as South Africa and the successor states in eastern Europe. I am no expert on Hobbes, so I will not comment on Dyzenhaus's interpretation of *Leviathan*. I will also not dwell on large areas of agreement. I will, however, express some doubts about whether Dyzenhaus's interpretation of Hobbes's thought, or the "Hobbist" alternative, can provide much practical guidance for evaluating the transitional measures that we have observed in recent years. I conclude that the most valuable Hobbesian insight on transitions is psychological, rather than philosophical.

Let me begin with Dyzenhaus's recurrent example—the transition in South Africa. In the 1980s, it became clear to the white-dominated ruling class that apartheid was no longer sustainable in light of international pressure and internal discontent. F. W. de Klerk replaced P. W. Botha as president of South Africa in 1989, and in 1990 he freed Nelson Mandela and legalized the ANC and other opposition parties. Over the next few years, the government entered negotiations with the opposition parties over a new constitution and repealed some apartheid-era laws. In 1994, an election was held, and Nelson Mandela became president.

The eventual settlement provided for a shift to a democratic system, though one designed, in part, to protect the white minority from black majority rule. The settlement also provided for a truth and reconciliation commission whose task was to ferret out the truth of the apartheid system. Although frequently lauded for its humane goal—to seek the truth without seeking revenge —it was clearly a compromise between the black majority, which wanted justice, and the white minority, which wanted amnesty. The compromise was that those who spoke the truth would not go to prison. The unsurprising consequence was that, although the atrocities of the apartheid regime were widely publicized, virtually none of the wrongdoers was punished.

The debate about the TRC and other elements of the South Africa transition followed a pattern that goes back to much earlier transitions. One typical argument is that transitional justice can be achieved only if the leaders of the old regime are punished for committing atrocities, even if their actions were not formal crimes under positive law, at least to the extent that it is possible to do this and maintain order. The opposite argument is that the leaders of the regime cannot be punished without violating principles of legality—including the prohibition on retroactive criminal punishment—and in any event this is morally suspect because nearly everyone was complicit in the crimes of the old regime. These are all important arguments, and the morally and practically correct transitional measures must vary considerably from setting to setting, just as criminal and civil law vary greatly from non-transitional society to society without raising any great suspicion that injustices routinely occur. There is no particular reason to think that one or the other extreme is always and everywhere just; in some transitions, the just measures will approximate one extreme, in other transitions the other extreme, and in many others, perhaps most, a middle path will be just. Local conditions, beliefs, and mores determine what is just and practical in any given case.

At any rate, this is my view.[1] Theorists of transitional justice think that these questions have general, perhaps universal, answers; they think that a theory could tell us whether a particular transitional regime should opt for one extreme or another or choose a middle path. Dyzenhaus does not believe that theories of transitional justice are different from ordinary theories of justice, but he does believe that an ordinary theory of justice can serve the same function. He thinks that Hobbes's theory of justice applies as much to transitional as to non-transitional societies, and he thinks that it is universally valid; therefore, he argues that Hobbes's theory can provide guidance to a society choosing among transitional measures. If Dyzenhaus is right, then Hobbes's theory of justice should help us evaluate the transitional measures used in South Africa and should help future leaders guide and structure the transitions in their countries.

What are Hobbes's insights for transitional justice? Dyzenhaus identifies two. First, Hobbes teaches us that "a theory of transitional justice is an account of the importance of civic education in legality or the rule of law" (p. 187).[2] Second, the task of the architects of a transition is "to make a jural community possible. . . . The legal institutions they propose to put in place, the laws they enact, and the measures they propose and adopt to deal with the legacy of the past, should be guided primarily by the aim of achieving the condition of legality that will make it possible for the new sovereign to get on with a different task, providing 'commodious living' for his subjects" (p. 208). There are two separate ideas here: establishing the principle of legality (the second) and teaching people (including the designers of the transition themselves) about the importance of the principle of legality (the first).

Dyzenhaus begins his argument with Hobbes's theory of international relations. The conventional reading of Hobbes, I believe, is that Hobbes thinks that international relations are like the state of nature; that therefore between sovereigns there is no (positive) law, no justice, no right and wrong; that the laws of nature bind only the conscience of sovereigns (*in foro interno*); and that they are free to violate these laws (*in foro externo*) when doing so advances self-preservation. This is the "Hobbist" version of Hobbesian thought.

Yet, drawing on Noel Malcolm, Dyzenhaus says that "Hobbes states that one is bound *in foro externo* as long as one has assurance of performance from the other party to a contract, which means that if the other party performs his part of the contract in the state of nature, one is bound to reciprocate. In other words, *in foro externo* obligation is not confined to the situation in which state coercion follows failure to perform; it also arises when failure to perform is immoral because one is under an obligation to respond to another's first performance" (p. 189). For Dyzenhaus, this modification of the Hobbist view is of great significance; it shows that Hobbes believes in a kind of general moral code, one that is universally binding and that affects behavior, as well as feeling.

Dyzenhaus then claims for all of Hobbes's nineteen laws of nature what he claims for promise-keeping. Even though Hobbes says that they do not bind people's behavior except when backed by state coercion and that therefore they cannot bind the sovereign himself (except internally), nonetheless Hobbes really means that the sovereign must obey them, for the sovereign can't count on loyalty from his subjects unless those subjects believe that the sovereign respects the laws of nature. The reason for this claim is that subjects are all motivated by self-preservation, the laws of nature all advance self-preservation, and therefore subjects who believed that the sovereign violated the laws of nature would think themselves better off in the state of nature, where they can fend for themselves.

Dyzenhaus is right that there is a tension between Hobbes's claims that the laws of nature advance self-preservation, that people submit to a sovereign because they fear death, but that the sovereign can do what he likes, including ignoring the laws of nature. Hobbes acknowledges that people have the right to resist the sovereign when he tries to execute them (lawfully); so why don't people have the right to resist the sovereign when he violates the laws of nature, like the rule that "all men that mediate Peace, be allowed safe Conduct"? Hobbes's answer, I think, is that no sovereign would violate the laws of nature because doing so would be irrational—it would lead to disobedience by subjects who realize that the sovereign is not protecting them. The phenomenon that concerns Dyzenhaus is "off the equilibrium path," to borrow the jargon of game theorists.

To be sure, a sovereign could make a mistake. But it is more likely that subjects will make a mistake; given this, they ought to obey all laws and orders. Dyzenhaus argues that the law of nature that "all men that mediate Peace, be allowed safe Conduct" would clearly be violated by an order from the sovereign to kill such men, and so subjects of that sovereign would have reason to rebel. But suppose that the sovereign issues this order because it knows (or

suspects) that the man in question will create peace between the
sovereign's two worst enemies, who will then together make war
against the sovereign. Hobbes thinks that everyone is better off if
he accepts the sovereign's orders than if he questions them, so the
value of the laws of nature for evaluating the sovereign is minimal. As Dyzenhaus observes, a court might be reluctant to believe
that the sovereign really intended to issue an order that appears
to violate a law of nature and for that reason ought to seek further
guidance, but in the end the court must defer to the sovereign's
authority.

Dyzenhaus calls the "morality of the laws of nature" the morality of "legality" (p. 190). The point here is to make a distinction
between morality in the full-blown sense and a subset of any given
moral system. Moral systems differ from culture to culture, but the
subset—legality—remains constant. So the morality of legality is
both thin and universal. At this point in the argument, it's not entirely clear why Dyzenhaus thinks that the subset has anything to
do with legality; one could alternatively have called it something
like "the morality of minimal cooperation"—the amount of cooperation necessary to ensure that a society does not lapse into
the Hobbesian civil war. Although Hobbes's laws of nature refer to
courts and laws, there doesn't seem to be any reason in principle
why they have to exist in Hobbes's scheme, as opposed to, say, a
system based on a unitary executive that makes, interprets, and
enforces administrative orders. But as Dyzenhaus's reference to
Fuller suggests, he wants to claim that justice requires all societies
to supply a package of rights intermediate between the minimalist
Hobbist view and the full-blown liberalism of theorists like Dwor-
kin. Dyzenhaus attributes this claim to the non-Hobbist Hobbes,
though of course it could stand on its own even if Hobbes himself
did not hold it.

The two versions of Hobbes have different implications for understanding transitions and transitional justice. For a "Hobbist,"
transitional justice and ordinary justice are the same; ordinary
justice means whatever the sovereign says it means; thus, transitional justice occurs when the transitional government issues laws
that are obeyed. If the transitional government is sovereign, that is
the end of the matter. If the transitional government is not sovereign, then we are in the state of nature, and its laws have no larger

authority based on the consent and self-interest of the people. In such a condition, there is no point in talking about justice.

Dyzenhaus's Hobbes also believes that transitional justice and ordinary justice are the same. But ordinary justice has more content—it means that the sovereign's orders comply with the laws of nature, maximizing the likelihood that all subjects will be spared violent death—and, indeed, universal content that applies even in the state of nature. When the state of nature exists, no one has any *in foro externo* obligations except the conditional obligation not to take advantage of others who make themselves vulnerable by (for example) performing a promise. The transitional government—which apparently exists even in the state of nature—acts justly by complying with these conditional obligations, which are actuated by the relinquishment of power by its opponents. Both the transitional sovereign and the non-transitional sovereign (which differ in degree only, anyway) must comply with the laws of nature because or to the extent that people have yielded power to them, thus making absolute the sovereign's (otherwise) conditional *in foro externo* obligation.

Consider how these approaches might be applied to a real transition such as the one that occurred in South Africa.

According to Dyzenhaus, the "Hobbist" interpretation of the South Africa transition is that the ANC and the NP were in a state of nature until the first post-apartheid election or perhaps later. Thus, de Klerk, by releasing Mandela and other leaders and entering into negotiations with the ANC, relinquished his power in violation of the Hobbist injunction to engage in self-preservation, and what he did was morally neutral or perhaps even morally wrong if one believes that the state that he destroyed created the rules of morality by positive law.

Dyzenhaus thinks this view is wrong. One problem is that it seems self-contradictory: why would de Klerk give up his power and, in doing so, bring about a state of nature? Another problem is that it seems wrong to say that de Klerk's actions were morally neutral or that, in the transitional stage, no rules of political morality governed the actions of de Klerk, Mandela, or anyone else. The latter point seems to be the focus of Dyzenhaus's critique: power does not determine morality.

One reaction to Dyzenhaus's argument that the Hobbist view is wrong is to agree, but on the ground that it is not helpful to use Hobbes or the Hobbist version of his thought to evaluate a modern transition. I don't see much value in trying to decide whether the ANC or the NP was in the state of nature, and the exercise of fitting real events in the Hobbesian (or Hobbist) framework seems artificial.

But we shouldn't allow questions of Hobbesian interpretation to distract us from Dyzenhaus's real concern, which is whether the South African transition succeeded (to the extent that it did) because the major players refrained from acting in their self-interest but instead obeyed the laws of nature—that is, sought to comply with and advance the principle of legality, even as they tried to obtain a political victory. That this is Dyzenhaus's claim is clear from the following passage:

> On the one hand, once de Klerk had performed, Mandela was under an obligation to reciprocate and moreover an obligation that was *in foro externo* as well as *in foro interno*. While there was no common power over the two factions to guarantee performance, no such guarantee was needed, since performance had occurred. Thus, while de Klerk's performance was in a sense irrational, it also created a situation of *in foro externo* obligation for Mandela. Indeed, it created a situation in which *in foro externo* obligation was generally possible, because, once Mandela had reciprocated, de Klerk was under an obligation to respond to his performance, and so on. (p. 194)

This interesting and complex passage requires extended comment.

Some readers might be puzzled that Dyzenhaus insists that de Klerk was "irrational." We rarely think that successful statesmen are irrational, even if they are moral; Lincoln was not irrational; nor was FDR, Churchill, or Wilson. Even more peculiar is the claim that de Klerk acted irrationally since there was no guarantee of reciprocity and that de Klerk "betrayed his faction." I will say more about these claims later, but for now one needs to understand that Dyzenhaus's claim that de Klerk was irrational follows from his agenda of discrediting the Hobbist view. According to Dyzenhaus, de Klerk was irrational on the Hobbist account because he did not act in his narrow self-interest, which would have meant declining to move first in the state of nature and refusing to betray his faction.

But what are we to make of this? A true Hobbist, I suppose, would, if he accepted Dyzenhaus's interpretation, just shrug his shoulders. De Klerk was lucky that Mandela did not take advantage of him, but stranger things have happened. The apparent success of the South African transition does not disprove Hobbism. Leaders of the next transition should ignore the South Africa experience as an anomaly and, in Hobbist fashion, act in their narrow self-interest.

But there is a more serious objection to Dyzenhaus's argument: this is that de Klerk and Mandela's behavior was fully consistent with the Hobbist prescription. De Klerk did not act irrationally. The ruling class had, by 1989, realized that the apartheid system could not survive internal unrest and external pressure without significant reform and that bold moves had to be made. Even P. W. Botha had recognized this state of affairs as early as the mid-1980s, and his refusal or inability to seek significant reform contributed to his ouster. De Klerk did not betray his "faction"; he understood that his faction wanted him to try to effect a reconciliation with the black majority. To be sure, the faction contained many views, and de Klerk's position was probably not that of the median faction member, but he received strong support both before and after he released Mandela and made clear that he wanted a genuine constitutional settlement that was agreeable to all sides. It is true that de Klerk had no guarantee of reciprocity. Mandela would not renounce armed struggle, and so de Klerk knew that the black majority might respond to his tentative steps with a violent revolution. But politicians never have guarantees; they always weigh the risks. De Klerk weighed the risks and decided, plausibly, that liberalization was less dangerous for his own hide and the hides of the white minority than was continuation of the status quo.

Dyzenhaus does not say whether he thought Mandela acted "irrationally" in the narrow instrumental sense, but clearly he does not believe that Mandela was a Hobbist. Here, too, we can express some doubts. Mandela emerged from prison with immense moral authority and prestige but no formal power. The white ruling class controlled the government, the economy, the military, and the bureaucracy. Mandela could have called for a revolution, but no one at the time thought that such a revolution could be won. The failed states in Africa hardly supplied an attractive model, and in the early 1990s it was becoming clear in eastern Europe that a peaceful transition with amnesty and power sharing was a viable alternative. In sum, Mandela reciprocated not because he had an *in foro externo* obligation; he reciprocated because self-preservation and the preservation of the lives of his people would be more effectively advanced by negotiation and compromise than by civil war.

Dyzenhaus argues that the Hobbist interpretation cannot really explain what happens during a successful transition.

> Until the sovereign comes into existence, [the parties'] agreement is unenforceable and so fragile. But it is not as fragile as an agreement based purely on calculations of self interest. For the agreement is built on an ever more secure foundation of obligations that are binding not because there is a common authority to enforce them but because the obligations following from the very first performance have continued to be met in a pattern of mutually reciprocal performances. If either faction were to resile at any point, it would display itself to be an irrational "Foole", an entity not to be trusted within or without civil society. Moreover, the costs of resiling become greater as both parties become more enmeshed in these patterns of reciprocity, because the greater the degree of trust that has built up between them, the less the resiling party will be deemed worthy of trust should it wish at a later stage to renew the process. (pp. 197–198)

It might be true that cooperation is more robust when the parties do not act solely on the basis of self-interest, but that doesn't mean that the Hobbist interpretation is an incorrect account of the South African transition or any other. People might simply be unable to rise above narrow self-interest. But narrow self-interest is consistent with reciprocity, as countless game theoretic models show.

In arguing that de Klerk and Mandela's actions may have been consistent with Hobbism, I am not making an argument about their actual motivations or character. They may not have cared much about their own safety and comfort, for example. But I think we can productively, albeit speculatively, reverse Dyzenhaus's formulation. Botha was no Hobbist. He realized that the status quo was unsustainable; if he had been a good Hobbist, he would have negotiated a settlement with the opposition. But he could not overcome his emotional attachment to apartheid and the ideology of white superiority; by failing to overcome his ideology, he acted irrationally and betrayed his faction. De Klerk comes across in the historical treatments of this period as a skilled politician who played the hand dealt him as best he could—a genuine Hobbist. What makes him deserving of praise is that, although, like Botha, he was emotionally attached to the ideology of white superiority, he was able to suppress his distaste for black people in general[3] and for Mandela in particular and reach a settlement that reflected the Hobbist goal of self-preservation for all involved. Mandela, unlike the other two men, was an exceptional person; what made him exceptional was that he overcame powerful emotional reasons for seeking vengeance that might have destroyed South Africa and instead acted in his rational self-interest. He, too, was a Hobbist. The contrast between Mandela and Botha could not be clearer. What made Mandela praiseworthy was that he placed Hobbism over his extremely powerful reasons for seeking personal justice.

I offer the Hobbist interpretation of the South African transition as a plausible alternative version of Dyzenhaus's; I do not know whether it is true.[4] No doubt motivations were complex, and many players acted for moral rather than self-interested reasons. One reason to offer this interpretation, though, is to show how adherence to the Hobbesian framework can only distort historical understanding. Dyzenhaus claims that the transitional period was a state of nature; on this assumption, moving first is irrational on the Hobbist view and thus must have reflected something else —statesmanlike compliance with the laws of nature despite the absence of an *in foro externo* obligation to do so. But it is unhelpful to call the transitional period a state of nature: there were working institutions, including a more-or-less effective government, and a more-or-less coherent opposition. By agreeing to an armistice, the ANC was provisionally pledging loyalty to the transitional government. Foreign countries dangled rewards and threatened punishments to encourage South Africa along the path of peaceful transition. Thus, actions that might seem surprising or irrational in the hypothetical state of nature can be understood as predictable expressions of self-interest and political prudence in the actual historical settings.

But, even if the Hobbist interpretation is wrong and the reason that the South Africa transition succeeded was that de Klerk and Mandela complied with the laws of nature, there is another problem with Dyzenhaus's argument: the exceedingly minimal content of the laws of nature provides virtually no guidance on the design of the transition. Consider Mandela's perspective after de Klerk moves first. His obligation now is to reciprocate, but what does it mean to reciprocate? Comply with promises he made to de Klerk while in prison? But he did not make any promises, and, even if he had, he has no moral obligation to comply with promises made while being held by force. Does he have to reciprocate on the "gift" theory (p. 197) because de Klerk provided him a benefit? But wasn't imprisonment unjust, in which case release entitled de Klerk to nothing in return? And, supposing Mandela did have some obligation toward de Klerk, what did it consist of? Not to prosecute the torturers of the old regime? To make sure that whites would retain a veto in a new political order? To preserve property rights and white wealth in a country with millions of impoverished blacks? To establish a liberal democracy? Or to establish anything better than a tyranny?

Dyzenhaus does not say much about the content of legality, so it is hard to answer these questions. Legality is expounded in the laws of nature, but the laws of nature are themselves ambiguous, and in any event they are subordinate to the goal of self-preservation. But consider two possible interpretations of Dyzenhaus's position: robust and thin. If Dyzenhaus's interpretation of legality is robust —so that, for example, it forbids caste systems—then it supplies Mandela with plenty of guidance, but it is difficult to find such a position in Hobbes's thought. If Dyzenhaus's interpretation of legality is thin—so that it allows anything but tyranny and chaos —then it supplies Mandela with no guidance and so fails as a useful theory of transitional justice.

In other work, Dyzenhaus makes the interesting argument that the robust interpretation of legality (or perhaps an intermediate version) can be derived from the thin.[5] The argument is made in the context of a defense of the Truth and Reconciliation Commission, and it reappears in less explicit form in the chapter in question. Dyzenhaus argues that the function of the TRC was not to expose the evils of apartheid (which were well known) or to effect racial reconciliation (which was in tension with exposing the truth) but to show that the apartheid regime could be sustained

only through extralegal violence—that is, government or govern-
ment-approved action that violated the principle of legality. Here
is the move from thin to thick.

This strikes me as a puzzling argument. Many states have caste
systems—in the broad sense that includes institutionalized discrimination against ethnic and religious groups or women—and
are reasonably stable. They do not rely on extralegal violence or
extralegal violence greater than what is to be expected even in a
just society. Thus, if Dyzenhaus's claim is an empirical one, it seems
dubious. Suppose that the TRC had discovered that the apartheid
system had been sustained without such violence, that institutionalized discrimination was possible within the rule of law (narrowly
construed). Security forces tortured and killed people, but they
had prior legal authorization to do so. On this interpretation, the
TRC would be forced to close shop and admit that the apartheid
regime was just, at least as far as the TRC's mandate ran. This can't
be right: a regime of legalized torture and killing of black people would have been just as objectionable as (more objectionable
than?) a regime that formally prohibited torture and killing but
nonetheless depended on them. A TRC would be as proper in the
first case as in the second.

In any event, this argument threatens to collapse the distinction between order and justice, a distinction that Dyzenhaus otherwise insists upon. If self-preservation implies thin legality and thin
legality implies robust legality, then liberalism or something close
to it can be justified as a way of avoiding the war of all against all.
The logic carries Dyzenhaus to the conclusion that the TRC's function is to show that thin legality implies robust legality, but, again,
the alternative view is that the TRC's function is to show that some
forms of order are worse than civil war.

The history of the TRC supports the latter view, I think, not
Dyzenhaus's argument. The TRC was a compromise between the
desire to achieve substantive justice for the victims of apartheid
and the exigencies of power sharing. It had little to do with legality. The ANC would have liked to punish the supporters and
perpetrators of apartheid regardless of whether their behavior was
formally legal and regardless of whether punishing them would violate or advance the principle of legality. It just wanted justice. But
it could not obtain justice without alienating whites who continued

to hold most of the levers of power and would for the foreseeable future, so it settled on exposure and public humiliation. Even the tone and procedures of the TRC had little to do with the principle of legality. Some lawyers served on the TRC, but, partly because of the dominant role of religious figures such as Archbishop Tutu, its proceedings had "an overridingly religious and emotional tone rather than a legal one."[6] This contrasts interestingly with the Nuremberg trial, which used legal form, albeit while seriously compromising it, in order to advance new legal understandings. The TRC abandoned legal form but also disclaimed any legal effect. Outlawing apartheid could be taken care of by the new South African legislature.

One other lesson of the history of the TRC is the difficulty of deriving useful transitional guidance from Hobbes. Consider a standard question of transitional justice: should the leaders of the old regime be punished? Dyzenhaus's implicit answer is that punishment should occur to the extent that it advances the principle of legality (and educates the public about this principle). But the decision to punish leaders of the old regime cannot be made on the basis of the principle of legality, which points in both directions: punish them because they failed to comply with the principle of legality during the old regime or amnesty them because punishing them would violate the principle of legality. So, instead, societies rely on local feelings and conditions: how bad was their behavior? How many people did they harm? Were they culpable or not? Do they show remorse? Did they harm the types of people that society admires or cares about (religious officials, peaceful dissidents, children)?

Let me conclude by returning to my earlier discussion of Botha's, de Klerk's, and Mandela's motivations. Mandela famously suppressed his resentment and his desire for vengeance as he walked out of prison. De Klerk suppressed his commitment to the ideology of white supremacy when he realized that apartheid could no longer be sustained and, by entering good-faith negotiations with Mandela, bound himself to eventually yield power. Botha's failure to abandon the ideological underpinnings of apartheid undermined his political effectiveness. What separates Mandela and de Klerk from Botha (and other transitional failures like Milosevic and Ceausescu) is not, as Dyzenhaus argues, that Mandela and de Klerk acted "irrationally" but in compliance with the principle of legality while the others did not but that they acted in their rational self-interest (or in the rational self-interest of their group), while the others were constrained by ideology or perhaps, in Milosevic's case, simply miscalculated. The distinction, then, is between self-interest and passion, rather than between narrow self-interest and enlightened or constrained or legality-respecting self-interest.

This distinction is not a moral distinction but a psychological distinction. The lesson of *Leviathan* is perhaps that we can expect transitions to succeed and ordinary politics to succeed when leaders and followers act according to rational self-interest, not according to ideology, the desire for glory, resentment, the thirst for vengeance, religious zealotry, or higher ideals (including the ideal of legality).[7] This argument is not based on political theory; it is based on political psychology. As such, it is better interpreted as prudential advice rather than as moral direction. The advice is that, in designing a transition, the best we can do is support self-interested, politically skillful leaders and hope their self-interest leads them to conclude that they will survive and prosper in a system that is just, rather than merely ordered. Call this "transitional prudence." Those who evince a passion for justice are best kept on the sidelines. As far as advice goes, transitional prudence is less than inspiring, but nonetheless it seems to be advice that every transitional society is in need of.

NOTES

Thanks to David Dyzenhaus and Adrian Vermeule for very helpful comments.

1. See Eric A. Posner and Adrian Vermeule, "Transitional Justice as Ordinary Justice," *Harvard Law Review* 117 (2004): 762–825.

2. Unless otherwise indicated, all page references refer to this volume.

3. I don't know whether de Klerk was a racist at the time of his presidency or whether, as some claim, he had a "conversion" at the time of his inauguration or just modified his views in the 1980s, but certainly his longtime support for apartheid prior to that time suggests as much.

4. Dyzenhaus does not think it is true, as his disapproving citation to

José María Maravall and Adam Przeworski, ed., *Democracy and the Rule of Law* (Cambridge: Cambridge University Press, 2003) makes clear.

5. See David Dyzenhaus, *Judging the Judges, Judging Ourselves: Truth, Reconciliation and the Apartheid Legal Order* (Oxford: Hart, 1998).

6. Leonard Thompson, *A History of South Africa*, 3rd ed. (New Haven: Yale University Press, 2001), 275; Martin Meredith, *Coming to Terms: South Africa's Search for Truth* (New York: Public Affairs, 1999), 17–18.

7. This distinction is Albert Hirschman's, of course, though he emphasizes the thought of post-Hobbesians like Hume and Smith; see Albert O. Hirschman, *The Passions and the Interests: Political Arguments for Capitalism Before Its Triumph* (Princeton: Princeton University Press, 1997). I thank Adrian Vermeule for suggesting this line of argument.

9

WHAT IS NON-IDEAL THEORY?

GOPAL SREENIVASAN

Derek Parfit concludes his seminal analysis of egalitarianism with the rueful observation, "Taxonomy is unexciting, but it needs to be done."[1] No doubt every taxonomer harbors secret hopes that his taxonomy will still prove useful, despite being tedious, though few succeed on anything like Parfit's scale. In a field as neglected as that of non-ideal theory, one might think that greater optimism in this regard could survive without a protective guard of caution. But it is difficult to know, since tedium can be such a challenge to surmount.

Any analysis of the category of the "non-ideal theory of justice" should begin with John Rawls's division of non-ideal theory into two branches,[2] partial compliance theory and transitional theory.[3] What emerges on the second branch of this division is something aptly called "transitional justice." But the label has quite a different meaning here from its meaning in the political science literature burgeoning under the same name (and, indeed, from its meaning in the rest of the present volume). It has nothing in particular to do with the "aftermath of regime change." However, it is not merely a coincidence that the same label is used in these two contexts. Moreover, there is something to be learned from considering each topic in the context of the alternative background frame. Vindicating this suggestion will be my first order of business.

After setting the philosophical stage a little in §1, I proceed in §2 to articulate the change in perspective on the aftermath of regime change afforded by seeing it in the context of the non-ideal theory of justice. Thereafter, I pursue a more resolutely taxonomic agenda. In §3, I defend Rawls's division of non-ideal theory against those who neglect its transitional justice branch. It is here that we shall reap the benefit to be gained from considering the non-ideal theory of justice in the context of the aftermath of regime change, namely an improved defense. I close by arguing, in §§4–5, for an extension of the category of non-ideal theory beyond the terms of Rawls's division.

§1. On Rawls's account of justice, ideal theory describes a well-ordered institutional arrangement: institutions are well ordered when they are both just and known to be just and when individuals both accept and comply fully with the requirements these institutions impose on them.[4] This suggests two rather different ways in which circumstances may fail to be ideal. On the one hand, background institutions may not be just; on the other hand, individuals may not fully comply with the standing requirements placed on them. For each kind of defective case, there is a corresponding branch of non-ideal theory.[5]

To prescribe for the case in which individuals do not fully comply with the requirements of justice, there is non-ideal theory as partial compliance theory. Partial compliance theory embraces several different kinds of question. Let me give three examples. To begin with, partial compliance theory specifies what happens to an individual's obligations when others fail to do their fair share within some distributive scheme.[6] Next, it includes the theory of punishment and restitution, since a good deal of the criminal law is plausibly regarded as articulating requirements of justice. Finally, not all of the (legal) requirements that agents actually face in the real world are themselves fully just. Hence, partial compliance theory also includes the question of civil disobedience:[7] of when justice permits (or even requires) non-compliance with standing requirements that are less than fully just.

To prescribe for the case in which background institutions are not just, there is non-ideal theory as transitional theory. Transitional theory specifies the obligations that individuals have to bring just institutions into existence. There are also two ways in which background institutions may fail to be just: they may be unjust, or they may not exist at all. An individual may therefore be obligated to do her part either to reform existing institutions or to introduce just ones from scratch (e.g., in the state of nature).[8]

Of course, the distinction between these branches of non-ideal theory is merely an analytic convenience. While the case in which background institutions fail to be just and individuals fail to comply fully with the requirements of justice is thereby made to appear logically "special," everyone knows that in our actual circumstances it is all too ordinary. This means that partial compliance theory and transitional theory often apply together.

I should like to suggest that, at least up to a point, theorizing about the aftermath of regime change can usefully be seen as an instance of this joint application of non-ideal theory. In particular, it combines the theory of punishment and restitution (from partial compliance theory) with the reform of existing but previously unjust institutions (from transitional theory). This combined category plausibly contains the two main questions that Jon Elster discusses, for example, as part of his taxonomy of the "decisions of transitional justice" (in the political science sense), namely the questions of whether and how to punish old wrongdoers and of whether and how to compensate old victims.[9]

Now, properly to accommodate these questions from the aftermath of regime change within the combined category of non-ideal theory I have just constructed requires that we mildly complicate Rawls's account in two respects, once for each branch. Let me spell these complications out before we turn to consider what light the resultant framework throws on theorizing about the aftermath of regime change. (Strictly speaking, the first complication is better understood as a clarification, since Rawls himself is well aware of the point.)[10]

In the first instance, then, we should recognize explicitly that institutions, and not simply individuals, can be in partial compliance. It follows that we should also allow for the possibility that punishment and restitution may be called for in response to institutional injustice (and not only to individual injustice). Examples of punishment for institutional injustice can easily be given if we are prepared to count the punishment of individuals for crimes committed in an official capacity (e.g., at Nuremberg). But, even if we are not, clear examples are available in the international arena, such as an aggressor nation's being prohibited from maintaining an army (e.g., article 9 of Japan's constitution).

In the second instance, we should explicitly distinguish two moments in the reform of previously unjust institutions. On the one hand, there is a forward-looking moment, in which just institutions—or at least more just institutions—are introduced.[11] However, the introduction of just institutions may not suffice to inaugurate a steady-state of ideal justice. This is not simply because the newly introduced institutions are themselves likely to be only imperfectly just. Rather, even if the new institutions were perfectly just (assuming that is possible), achieving a steady-state of ideal justice might still require some sort of collective reckoning with what went before—require it, that is, in addition to introducing the new institutions. Whether some such reckoning is in fact required is doubtless something best decided on a case-by-case basis. But, in the absence of some guarantee that the answer will always be negative, transitional theory has at least to provide for the possibility that punishment or restitution for previous institutional injustice(s) will be required. It therefore needs a second, backward-looking moment, in which to ask whether that possibility is realized in the case at hand.[12]

§2. Let me illustrate what the framework of non-ideal theory might have to offer the political science literature by first engaging with some of the details of Elizabeth Kiss's instructive analysis[13] and then distilling two conclusions that pertain to the aftermath of regime change more generally.

Kiss defines "transitional justice" as "a systematic effort to right the wrongs of a prior political regime or era and, in so doing, to create a more just and humane society."[14] Her definition already highlights the combination of forward- and backward-looking moments. But the special importance of the backward-looking moment emerges even more clearly when she identifies the two salient alternatives in relation to which the political choice to pursue transitional justice (in her sense) is made. For the second of these alternatives is the choice "to move on, to build a more humane and democratic polity and establish the rule of law without any systematic effort to right the wrongs of the past."[15] That is, the second alternative is purely forward-looking: simply to introduce new (and more just) institutions and to leave reform at that. To employ Kiss's terminology, it was to accommodate the possibility that "transitional justice" may be a better choice than (merely) "moving on" that we added a backward-looking moment to the transitional theory branch of non-ideal theory.

Kiss herself does not concentrate so much on the question of whether "transitional justice" is better (e.g., than "moving on") as she does on the question of how to pursue it. As she puts it, proponents of transitional justice "confront a choice between two moral visions and two institutional models."[16] The two moral visions are those of "retributive justice" and "restorative justice," while the two institutional models are centered respectively on the International Criminal Court and the Truth Commission. For my own purposes, the important point here is that the choice said to confront proponents of transitional justice is constructed as a pair of package deals—either the "vision of retributive justice, leading to the International Criminal Court" or the "vision of restorative justice, leading to a Truth Commission." It seems to me that this construction is too rigid and that the framework of non-ideal theory can help us to see as much. More specifically, I claim that one can arrive at each of these institutional models along a variety of argumentative paths, some of which are anchored in the "opposite" vision of justice (relative to Kiss's construction) and others of which are anchored in neither vision. We should therefore resist the attempt to categorize the institutional options during the aftermath of regime change in terms of a single "vision of transitional justice."

To illustrate these claims (and thereby substantiate them), I shall describe three different argumentative paths leading to the choice of a Truth Commission as an institution of transitional justice (in all senses).[17] The categories of non-ideal theory will help us to keep the paths, as well as the steps along them, distinct. To simplify the dialectic, let me stipulate that the International Criminal Court is the favored institutional expression of retributive justice in these contexts.

The first path starts at the beginning, with the fundamental question: what is the best response, in principle, to wrongdoing? The institutional choice between a Truth Commission and the International Criminal Court can certainly be debated on this basis, that is, from first principles. José Zalaquett, for example, argues along these lines, anchoring his argument for the Truth Commission in the claim that retribution is not the best response to wrongdoing.[18] So I hardly want to deny that there can be (indeed, have actually been) argumentative paths that correspond to Kiss's "restorative justice" package.

Notice, however, that if Zalaquett is right, then the preference in justice for a Truth Commission does not turn out to be any kind of special truth of the aftermath of regime change. Rather, it is a general truth of the theory of punishment (or, better, theory of how best to respond to wrongdoing).[19] In other words, the operative conclusion here is a result in partial compliance theory—albeit, a result that can be borrowed by transitional theory (or, perhaps, shared with it), since the two branches of non-ideal theory overlap to an extent when the partial compliance in question is institutional.[20]

A second path starts with the best theory of responding to wrongdoing in the background. For the sake of the illustration, let us say that the best response is retributive. It follows from my stipulation that the preferred institutional choice is therefore the International Criminal Court. But it does not follow that this is also the choice that is actually warranted under the circumstances. After all, the option to use the International Criminal Court may not be available in a given context, or it may not be feasible or it may not be worthwhile all told. Any number of factors may impede the otherwise favored institutional expression of retributive justice in a given context. If that is how the circumstances have turned out, then a case might still be made for a Truth Commission as a second-best substitute for the International Criminal Court. As Kiss reports, that is more or less how the early proponents of Truth Commissions did argue for them (not, of course, as a substitute for the International Criminal Court, which did not yet exist, but as a substitute for some form of punishment).

Here again, the conclusion of the argument (ultimately favoring a Truth Commission) is not a special truth of the aftermath of regime change. It might be most happily described as a general truth about the line of institutional succession, as it were, within the best theory of how to respond to wrongdoing.[21] More important for present purposes, however, is the fact that, along this second path, the choice of a Truth Commission is not in the least a repudiation of retributive justice (the assumed content, recall, of the best theory). On the contrary, it represents a second-best implementation of retributive justice. Hence, this is an example of an argumentative path to a Truth Commission that is anchored in (what Kiss would regard as) the "opposite" vision of justice.

Finally, consider a third path. Let us retain the assumption that the best response to wrongdoing is retributive. Let us also assume that a Truth Commission is neither the favored institutional expression of retributive justice nor its second-best substitute (or, indeed, any kind of acceptable substitute). From the standpoint of responding well to wrongdoing, a Truth Commission is simply out of the question. For all that, it may still be possible morally to justify the choice of a Truth Commission. That is because, even when retributive justice represents the best response to wrongdoing, there is more to morality than retributive justice. In fact, there is more to justice than retributive justice.

Suppose, in particular, that forward-looking (moral) considerations ground a duty on the victims of the previous institutional injustice to forgo having the perpetrators punished (or to accept reduced punishment for them). If this duty also outweighs the victims' claim to retributive justice, then the path remains open to conclude that the morally best institutional choice, all things considered, is a Truth Commission. The special burden of the argument, along this third path, is explicitly to justify the moral trade-off in favor of the forward-looking duty. But this is by no means an impossible task. Jonathan Allen, for example, offers a version of this kind of argument for a Truth Commission.[22]

As Allen emphasizes, nothing in this argument recommends a compromise between justice and expediency. In his version of the argument, the compromise occurs instead between justice and other moral values (e.g., reconciliation). But even that modest degree of compromise with justice is unnecessary. The argument can plausibly be structured so that its trade-off (or compromise) takes places entirely within justice. Notably, if the victims' forward-looking duty to forgo punishment is grounded in the duty to do one's part to bring just institutions into existence[23]—a duty the transitional branch of non-ideal theory imposes on everyone, including victims—then the forward-looking duty will itself count as a duty of transitional justice (in my sense). In that case, the trade-off takes place specifically within non-ideal justice, either between its partial compliance branch and its transitional branch or, perhaps better, between the backward- and forward-looking moments of transitional theory. Seen in this light, the third path to a Truth Commission is actually the only one that yields a special truth of transitional justice; it is also the only one anchored in neither of Kiss's visions of transitional justice.

We can distill two conclusions from this discussion that may be of wider relevance to theorizing about the aftermath of regime change, understood now as an instance of non-ideal theory. First, even if the best response to wrongdoing is retributive, there is no immediately compelling objection to partial punishment or restitution for previous institutional injustice(s). In particular, the objection that partial punishment (say) is not the best response to wrongdoing is not necessarily compelling. In non-ideal theory, one naturally turns to assess the next-best option if the previously-best option is not available.[24] One naturally slides down the (best theory's) line of institutional succession, as the obstructions of circumstance require. Hence, to make the objection compelling, one would have to show that partial punishment is not even the next-best option or that the first-best option remains (unproblematically) available.

Second, victims may actually have a duty to accept partial punishment or restitution. This duty may be a consequence, under the circumstances, of the victims' duty to do their part to bring just institutions into existence. Hence, the bottom-line assessment of a given institutional option may have to weigh valid considerations of justice against each other and not simply against the exigencies of cost and actual circumstance.[25]

§3. As I mentioned at the outset, the enterprise of non-ideal theory has been sadly neglected, at least in philosophy.[26] Such attention as non-ideal theory has received has mostly been directed to the theory of punishment or of civil disobedience.[27] That is, it has mostly been directed to topics that are subjects in their own right, in addition to falling within the scope of non-ideal theory.

The major exception to this generalization is Liam Murphy's book, *Moral Demands in Nonideal Theory*. Murphy is concerned with the first question among the three examples I gave earlier of questions addressed by partial compliance theory. He asks "what a given person is required to do in circumstances where at least some others are not doing what they are required to do."[28] To illustrate

Murphy's question, let us follow him in supposing that the ideal requirements of justice are given by (roughly) utilitarianism: individual agents are required to maximize everyone's total well-being to the best of their individual ability. Under circumstances of partial compliance (i.e., usually), other agents will shirk their responsibilities under this principle. The predictable consequence is that total well-being will remain at a sub-optimal level. However, if a given individual can relieve some of the shortfall by contributing still more to total well-being (i.e., by sacrificing more), then utilitarianism requires (even) more of that agent under partial compliance than it does under full compliance. Murphy claims, very plausibly, that this is not fair.

Consider an example. In 2002, there were more than 43 million people without health insurance in the United States, and the cost of funding primary-care physician services for this group was about US$9.68 billion annually.[29] Suppose that ideal theory (somehow) singled out a million people to foot this bill at an annual cost of US$9,680 each. Now, if only half of the designated million contributors actually paid up, it would seem unfair to respond by asking the half who paid to pay another US$9,680 each. Moreover, it would be unfair even if they could "afford it," in the sense that losing US$19,360 would not disqualify them from the requirement to contribute, as defined by whatever criteria of justice had singled them out in the first place.

Partial compliance theory should therefore insulate responsible agents from the unfairness of having to pick up the slack caused by the noncompliance of others. To this end, Murphy introduces a "compliance condition," which holds (roughly) that the costs to an agent of complying with requirements of beneficence should not be higher under partial compliance than they are under full compliance.[30] While the details he adds in interpreting this condition need not concern us, the general idea is certainly plausible.[31]

Unlike Rawls, however, Murphy seems to identify non-ideal theory wholly with its partial compliance branch.[32] Now, it would be natural to suppose that the issue of whether or not non-ideal theory has a transitional justice branch as well depends on a recent dispute about the role of institutions within a theory of justice.[33] Roughly, the dispute concerns whether some fundamental principles of justice apply to institutions alone—and, therefore, to individuals only mediately via institutions—or whether instead fundamental principles of justice always apply simply and directly to individuals. Since Murphy and Rawls take different sides in this dispute, one might think that Murphy's narrow view of non-ideal theory flows from his skepticism about institutions as the primary subject of justice.[34] However, while entirely plausible, this conjecture is mistaken.

One way to see that it is mistaken is to restrict our attention to the relations in which individuals stand to fundamental requirements of justice that apply directly to them (if need be, we can add the assumption that there are some). Suppose that, by and large, individuals do not fully satisfy these requirements. Two quite distinct questions can be raised against this background. The first question takes the violations themselves as given and asks what kinds of response to them are warranted (e.g., how should violators be treated, or how should the requirements for non-violators be adjusted, if at all?). By contrast, the second question focuses precisely on the violations themselves and asks how they can be permissibly eliminated or at least reduced. I take it that the first question operates on what is recognizably the territory of partial compliance theory. But, while perhaps less easily recognized (given Rawls's formulations), the territory on which the second question operates is effectively that of transitional theory. For what it asks is how justice can be (more) fully achieved, beginning from circumstances where it is at best incompletely achieved.

A different way to see the mistake in the plausible conjecture is to distinguish two relations in which institutions may stand to the requirements of justice. The first relation is the topic of the dispute between Murphy and Rawls. Let us call it "institutions as subject." The second may be introduced by considering the extent to which institutions facilitate the implementation of the requirements justice imposes on individuals. In particular, consider whether certain institutions are effectively compulsory to implement justice fully. If they are, there is a distinct relation in which institutions may stand to the requirements of justice. Let us call it "institutions as (compulsory) handmaiden." To illustrate, recall the administration of justice in Locke. According to Locke, the law of nature applies directly to individuals in the state of nature, who are also authorized to enforce it. However, the pre-political enforcement of this law (i.e., of justice) is defective: it suffers from three famous "inconveniences." Fully to remedy these inconveniences requires individuals to introduce political institutions (i.e., to leave the state of nature).

Suppose we agree with Murphy that institutions are not the primary subject of justice. This still leaves open the possibility that they are its (compulsory) handmaiden. It is implausible to deny institutions this weaker role. But then justice actually requires certain institutions to be introduced, at least for its full implementation. Hence, non-ideal theory has to assign transitional obligations that refer explicitly to institutions (as in Rawls's original formulation), even if only in the service of achieving full compliance with requirements of justice that apply directly to individuals.[35]

Moreover, on the plausible assumption that introducing supporting institutions has certain one-time start-up costs, in addition to the cost of continuing maintenance, non-ideal theory will have to assign some one-time transitional costs. Taking account of these costs contradicts the generalization of Murphy's compliance condition that results from explicitly identifying non-ideal theory with partial compliance theory: the costs to an agent of complying with the requirements of beneficence should not be higher under non-ideal theory than they are under ideal theory. The contradiction follows from the fact that costs under ideal theory do not include transitional costs. Indeed, in the special case of the administration of justice, this point goes through without assuming that there are one-time start-up costs, since under full compliance there would be no need for the relevant institutions (and, hence, for their maintenance costs).

In fact, we can make this argument from still weaker premises. So far, the strongest premise we have employed is that some institutions are effectively compulsory (and not simply instrumentally useful) for the full implementation of justice. As it happens, the complications we introduced into our taxonomy of non-ideal theory earlier (to accommodate the aftermath of regime change as an instance) allow us to dispense with even this premise.

Let us assume, instead, that institutions make no necessary contribution to justice, not even an instrumentally necessary contribution. Ideal justice, then, can be fully achieved without any institutions at all.[36] But imagine that, despite being superfluous in this sense, institutions nevertheless exist. Finally, suppose that these existent institutions are unjust. None of these premises violates any of Murphy's strictures, since he allows that fundamental principles of justice can apply to institutions: he insists only that such principles be the same principles that apply to individuals.[37]

The brute existence of institutional injustice suffices to raise questions corresponding both to transitional theory's forward-looking moment (how to pursue institutional reform) and to its backward-looking moment (whether to seek punishment and restitution for institutional injustice). But the backward-looking question alone suffices to raise the prospect of one-time transitional costs that cannot be dismissed from the standpoint of justice.[38] If there is restitution to pay, for example, then non-ideal theory will need a principle of (transitional) justice to assign the one-time costs;[39] the previous generalization of Murphy's compliance condition will fail again, since the costs it counts under ideal theory do not include the costs of restitution, either.

I conclude that even skeptics about institutions as the primary subject of justice should broaden their conception of non-ideal theory. Specifically, they should recognize a transitional justice branch, in addition to the partial compliance branch.

§4. To illustrate the transitional justice branch with a philosophical example, we have to turn to Rawls's late work, *The Law of Peoples*.[40] The only example of an obligation to transfer resources that Rawls accepts in the international case belongs to this second branch of non-ideal theory. His "duty to assist burdened societies" is explicitly an obligation of transitional justice, since its aim is to assist "burdened societies" to become "well-ordered."[41] Moreover, from Rawls's point of view, this has a crucial consequence, namely that the duty toward a given society expires once that society has become well ordered. One of his main objections to principles of global distributive justice is that they lack a "target and a cut-off point."[42] In other words, the objectionable principles are proposed in ideal theory and so entail permanent obligations. We shall return to the subject of international distributive justice.

But I should now like to suggest a more radical expansion of the category of "non-ideal theory," one that goes beyond either Murphy or Rawls. To begin with, we should notice an assumption they both share, namely that ideal theory is prior to non-ideal theory. On their conceptions, non-ideal theory proceeds by reference to the content of an ideal theory of justice and thereby presupposes it. Rawls is explicit on this point:

> Nonideal theory asks how this long-term goal might be achieved, or worked toward, usually in gradual steps. It looks for policies and courses of action that are morally permissible and politically possible as well as likely to be effective. So conceived, nonideal theory presupposes that ideal theory is already on hand. For until the ideal is identified, at least in outline—and that is all we should expect —nonideal theory lacks an objective, an aim, by reference to which its queries can be answered.[43]

The rough idea is that, before we can take any steps forward, we need to know where we are supposed to end up. Otherwise, we cannot know whether any given step is a step in the right direction.

This priority assumption operates on both the partial compliance branch and the transitional justice branch of non-ideal theory, as Murphy and Rawls understand them. Under partial compliance, we need to know what the ideal principle of justice is —in Murphy's case, the principle of beneficence—and what fair shares it assigns, in order to know how the "compliance condition" operates. Otherwise, we will be unable to specify the limits it sets on individual sacrifice. Similarly, in transitional justice, we need to know what the ideal institutions are—in *Law of Peoples*, some description of a "well-ordered society"—in order to know what agents are obligated to introduce (and how). Otherwise, we will be unable to specify the cutoff point on the duty of assistance.

Of course, I do not deny that non-ideal theory can work like this. But I want to suggest that it need not. More strongly, there exists a kind of non-ideal theory for which the priority assumption fails. On this conception, non-ideal theory functions as an anticipation of ideal theory. Its prescriptions anticipate the ideal requirements of justice, rather than presupposing them. To do so, non-ideal theory has to make assumptions about the minimum requirements that any plausible and complete ideal theory of justice will include. In this vein, it can define targets for practical action before a complete ideal has been worked out, even in outline. Furthermore, if our assumptions about the minimum demands of justice are defensible, we can be confident that steps toward these targets are steps in the right direction.

Let us call this third conception of non-ideal theory "anticipatory theory."[44] A comparison with supervaluationism about vague predicates may be instructive.[45] What the two theories have in common is that, in each case, the subset of what all the disagreeing contenders agree upon is counted as correct. With supervaluationism, the contenders are "precisifications" of some vague predicate. With an anticipatory theory of justice, the contenders are plausible and complete specifications of the requirements of ideal justice. Both approaches reach a core of agreement by circumventing existing disagreements instead of resolving them.[46]

I take it that non-ideal theory so conceived is coherent and distinctive. What remains to be seen is whether it has any significant instantiations. Elsewhere I have proposed an anticipatory theory of international distributive justice:[47] it holds that any plausible and complete ideal theory of international distributive justice will minimally include an obligation on the richest nations to transfer one percent of their Gross Domestic Product (GDP) to the poorest nations. For concreteness, I specify this as an obligation incumbent on the "major seven" (G7) countries of the Organization for Economic Co-operation and Development (OECD). For 2007, this amounts to an obligation to transfer some US\$280 billion.[48] In fact, in 2007, official development assistance from the G7 was 0.23 percent of GDP or US\$69.446 billion.[49] So even a one percent transfer would clearly be a step of some kind. The question is whether we can know that it is a step in the right direction.

To establish the one percent proposal as an instance of anticipatory theory, we would have to show that it can be secured without having to resolve various debates in ideal theory about international distributive justice.[50] The aim would be to demonstrate that a one percent transfer is philosophically and not simply intuitively secure as a step toward justice between nations and to do so before an ideal theory is settled or in hand.

A good start on this demonstration can be made by observing that a one percent obligation belongs to the core of agreement already shared among a significant coalition of rival moral theories and positions. For instance, it can be endorsed by utilitarians,[51] by global egalitarians and prioritarians of various kinds,[52] and by decent humanitarians[53]—not to mention by many decent, ordinary people.[54] Each of these groups can endorse the proposal for its own reasons.

Unlike supervaluationism, however, anticipatory theory does not simply rest content with the core of such agreement as it happens to find ready made. It also aims to expand the scope of existing agreement among plausible and complete ideal theories. There are at least two strategies by which anticipatory theory can expand this scope. To begin with, it can seek to demonstrate that certain disagreements in ideal theory do not need to be resolved for the purposes of non-ideal theory. In the next section, we shall see how an application of this strategy suffices to bring Rawls and his followers into the one percent coalition.

In addition, anticipatory theory can seek to demonstrate that other disagreements or objections are actually resolvable on the basis of premises that are not controversial in ideal theory. In effect, this strategy aims to make latent agreement manifest. Elsewhere I argue that applications of this second strategy suffice to resolve disagreements about the magnitude of the proposed obligation and about how to spend the money.[55] Both arguments refer to a more specific version of the proposal, which divides one percent of the G7's GDP into quarters, with one quarter allocated to cover existing development commitments and the remaining three quarters spread over three fundamental determinants of health in developing countries—health care and public health; education (especially for girls and women); and basic nutrition and income support.

For example, what the argument about magnitude seeks to show is that, so targeted, the G7's transfer would very plausibly yield a disproportionate "bang for the buck" in terms of individual well-being. It thereby offers to explain, on empirical grounds, how an obligation can be both light enough in its burden (on the G7) to avoid being "too demanding" and yet also bountiful enough in its effects (on the well-being of the globally worst off) to be worthy of the status of "minimum obligation."

§5. Altogether I have distinguished three different kinds of non-ideal theory: partial compliance theory, transitional theory, and anticipatory theory. Naturally, there may be still others. But, as these three are all consistent, one might pursue non-ideal theory along any one of these branches or along any combination of them. Earlier I illustrated how partial compliance theory might combine with transitional theory. Let me close by illustrating how anticipatory theory might combine first with transitional theory and then with partial compliance theory.[56]

Recall the disagreement between Rawls and his cosmopolitan critics about whether obligations to transfer resources between nations are permanent obligations of ideal theory or temporary obligations of transitional non-ideal theory. I myself think the one percent obligation is plausibly regarded as a part of ideal theory and so as a permanent obligation. But, for the purposes of anticipatory non-ideal theory, it makes no sense to insist on this. Hence, we may begin by regarding it as a transitional obligation. To this end, it suffices to add a suitable cutoff point to the one percent obligation. In keeping with the more specific version of the proposal mentioned earlier, we can say that the obligation cuts off when no country (better still: or Indian state or Chinese province) has an average life expectancy of ten years or more below the global average.[57] When the final cutoff point has been reached, the question of whether or not the G7's obligation to transfer one percent of GDP annually to the poorest nations is a permanent obligation will acquire practical purchase. But, until then, non-ideal theory can safely ignore the question, and Rawls and his followers can participate fully in the one percent coalition.

Under full compliance by the G7, US$210 billion (0.75 percent of GDP) would be transferred annually to improve the fundamental determinants of health in poor countries. If this transfer were directed to the world's poorest quintile (1.316 billion people), it would fund a per capita package of almost US$160. Unfortunately, in the real world, not a single G7 nation spends (anything like) one percent of GDP on official development assistance (ODA)— in 2007, France was closest, at 0.39 percent.[58] However, Murphy's basic observation in partial compliance theory retains its force here, even though its beneficiary must be identified hypothetically: it would be unfair to require a "fully compliant G7 nation" to transfer more than one percent of GDP so as to pick up some of the slack caused by the rest of the G7's partial compliance.[59]

To insulate "full compliers" against this unfairness, we should therefore regard one percent of GDP as a fixed ceiling on each G7 nation's obligation under partial compliance by other G7 nations. That is to say, the non-ideal theory of justice would require nothing further of any G7 nation that managed to raise its ODA to one percent of GDP annually. One percent constitutes a G7 nation's "fair share" of improvements, in anticipatory non-ideal theory, to the fundamental determinants of health in poor countries.

Now, since anticipatory theory centrally proceeds by avoiding unnecessary disagreements, we should actually distinguish our conclusion here—that one percent is fixed as the ceiling on a G7 nation's obligation under partial compliance—from the rationale that fair distributive shares are fixed under partial compliance. While I myself find the rationale very plausible, it is not wholly uncontroversial. However, there is no need to rely on it, either. For, in anticipatory theory, the ceiling on a G7 nation's obligation winds up being fixed at one percent anyhow, as a side effect of avoiding controversies about the magnitude of obligations of international distributive justice under full compliance (i.e., of escaping the objection of being "too demanding"). Thus, full compliers with obligations of anticipatory theory are insulated against the unfairness Murphy identifies, but without presupposing that partial compliance theory requires them to be so insulated.

Finally, we should consider separately whether the "floor" is fixed under obligations under partial compliance, as well as the ceiling. The floor is fixed under a G7 nation's obligation under partial compliance when that nation remains responsible for no less than its "full" obligation, even when no other G7 nation complies. Even if the ceiling on a G7 nation's obligation is fixed, it does not follow that the floor is fixed under that obligation, as well. Nevertheless, one percent of GDP has the further advantage of being small enough that no G7 nation can plausibly claim that solitary compliance will put it at any serious relative disadvantage within its peer group (i.e., the G7). Hence, noncompliance by the rest of the G7 does not relieve a given G7 nation of its obligation to transfer the full one percent of GDP.

The tenability of this solitary compliance scenario helps to answer an important practical objection to the one percent proposal, namely that there is no obligation to line the pockets of the corrupt. Let me illustrate and then explain. I shall take Canada as my

example, since it is my own country. In 2007, Canadian ODA was
0.28 percent of GDP and 0.72 percent of Canadian GDP (one percent minus existing ODA) was US$9.068 billion.[60] Under full com-
pliance (by the G7), Canada would be responsible for transferring that US$9.068 billion at a rate of US$160 per capita. In other
words, in anticipatory non-ideal theory, Canada's fixed share of
improvements to the fundamental determinants of health among
the world's poorest quintile would cover a population of 56.68 million people.

Since partial compliance by the rest of the G7 does not relieve
Canada of its obligation to transfer a full one percent of GDP, Canada should simply go it alone if need be and transfer US$9.068
billion annually at the full compliance rate of US$160 per capita.
To do so, Canada would have to choose a mix of jurisdictions
where life expectancy is ten years or more (our cutoff point, recall) below the global average, up to a total population of 56.68
million people.

Transferring its one percent on this basis would enable Canada
to cover the same fixed share of the world's poorest quintile as it
would cover under full compliance by the G7—neither more nor
less. Yet, in that case, corruption is relevant to Canada's action only
if it is so prevalent that insufficient noncorrupt (and badly off) jurisdictions exist to allow Canada to reach its fixed share of 56.68
million people effectively. To put it the other way round, if there
are enough noncorrupt (and badly off) jurisdictions that Canada
can still reach its fixed share effectively by simply avoiding corrupt
jurisdictions altogether, then corruption is no impediment to Canada's action on its one percent obligation. At worst, it is an impediment to later full compliers, which is not Canada's problem.

NOTES

For helpful comments, I am very grateful to Melissa Williams and Joe
Millum.

1. Derek Parfit, "Equality or Priority?" (Lindley Lecture, University of
Kansas, Lawrence, KS, November 21, 1991), 34.
2. John Rawls, *A Theory of Justice*, rev. ed. (Cambridge, MA: Harvard
University Press, 1999). I shall abbreviate references to Rawls's A Theory
of Justice as *TJ*.

3. As we shall see in §3, this claim is actually controversial, though nevertheless correct.

4. *TJ*, §§2, 39, 69.

5. For completeness, I should note that Rawls also adds that ideal theory "works out the principles that characterize a well-ordered society *under favorable circumstances.*" *TJ*, 216; emphasis added. This suggests a further branch of non-ideal theory, to prescribe for the case in which circumstances are *un*favorable. However, I shall not pay much attention to this idea myself. While the circumstances addressed by non-ideal theory are obviously less favorable than those addressed by ideal theory, it is not clear to me how much more weight this way of drawing the contrast will bear. On the one hand, given Rawls's stipulation of the "circumstances of justice" (*TJ*, §22), there is a limit both to how "favorable" the circumstances assumed by ideal theory can be and to how "unfavorable" those assumed by non-ideal theory can be. On the other hand, insofar as non-ideal theory is still *theory*, rather than policy or administration (say), its assumptions and precepts will inevitably remain simplified and idealized to some extent. I am indebted here to Alex Tuckness, "Non-ideal Theory and Justice" (paper presented at the Association for Political Theory Conference, Colorado Springs, CO, October 29–31, 2004), which emphasizes the quoted passage.

6. Liam B. Murphy, *Moral Demands in Nonideal Theory* (New York: Oxford University Press, 2000). I expand on this example further later.

7. *TJ*, §§53, 55–59.

8. *TJ*, 99, 293–94.

9. Jon Elster, *Closing the Books: Transitional Justice in Historical Perspective* (New York: Cambridge University Press, 2004), 116–29. Elster subdivides the "how" questions into "six types of substantive political decisions." Ibid., 118.

10. *TJ*, 215–16.

11. I take it that this is the moment one naturally associates with an obligation to reform existing institutions.

12. This is not exactly the same as the question interjected by the first complication, for here the question operates with a wider scope than its counterpart has in partial compliance theory. Under partial compliance, the concern is limited to how far institutional injustice *merits* punishment or restitution (or both), either in general or in a particular case. By contrast, in this backward-looking moment, the case for punishment or restitution can extend beyond the (de)merits of an institutional injustice to include various instrumental requirements of achieving a steady-state of ideal justice.

13. Elizabeth Kiss, "Righting Wrongs: Two Visions of Transitional Justice" (paper presented at the annual meeting of the American Political

Science Association, Washington, D.C., September 1–3, 2005). See also Kiss, "Moral Ambition Within and Beyond Political Constraints," in *Truth v. Justice: The Morality of Truth Commissions,* ed. Robert I. Rotberg and Dennis Thompson (Princeton: Princeton University Press, 2000), 68–98.

14. Kiss, "Righting Wrongs," 2.

15. Ibid., 3.

16. Ibid., 7.

17. For clarity's sake, I should perhaps emphasize that the paths I describe are merely *recipes* for arguments. The point is to distinguish various distinctive sequences of possible steps, not to assert (let alone vindicate) any particular step.

18. José Zalaquett, "Commissions of Truth and Reconciliation: Chile," in *The Healing of a Nation?,* ed. Alex Boraine and Janet Levy (Cape Town: Justice in Transition, 1995), 44–55.

19. Strictly speaking, the precise preference for a Truth Commission may not have sufficient generality to count as a general truth about response to wrongdoing. But the essential point is that, along this first path, the *operative* conclusion—if not the final conclusion—in the argument for a Truth Commission will be a general truth, that is, one that transcends the context of regime change, such as the conclusion "not retribution."

20. If the argument for a Truth Commission actually turns in some significant way on the fact that the partial compliance is institutional, then its conclusion will at least be closer to a special truth of the aftermath of regime change. We might say, in that case, that its conclusion belongs equally to transitional theory and to partial compliance theory.

21. There may well be a high correlation between the particular terms of succession that favor a Truth Commission and a change of regime. That depends on the details of the theory.

22. Jonathan Allen, "Balancing Justice and Social Unity: Political Theory and the Idea of a Truth and Reconciliation Commission," *University of Toronto Law Journal* 49 (1999): 315–53.

23. To illustrate, consider the simple case in which insistence on meting out punishment straightforwardly prevents a change of regime (or, more generally, obstructs the introduction of more just institutions).

24. Notice that even the *first-best* response to wrongdoing is not "ideal," for the ideal here is full compliance (i.e., no wrongdoing to begin with).

25. One way to see the difference, then, between the second and the third paths is as follows. Both share the assumptions that the best response to wrongdoing is retributive and that the favored institutional expression of retributive justice here is the International Criminal Court (ICC). Moreover, neither path terminates with the ICC. But, on the second path, it is the exigencies of actual circumstance that force us away from the ICC, by moving us *down* retributive justice's line of institutional succession,

whereas on the third path, it is conflicting (and superior) considerations of justice that move us away from the ICC by breaking the alignment between retributive justice and morality, all things considered (thereby making its line of institutional succession *irrelevant*).

26. For a thoughtful account of how considerations of partial compliance and of unfavorable circumstance might factor in moral reflection on the problems of migration, see Joseph Carens, "Realistic and Idealistic Approaches to the Ethics of Migration," *International Migration Review* 30 (1996): 156–70. Carens frames his analysis in terms of a contrast between "idealistic" and "realistic" approaches to morality, instead of a contrast between "ideal" and "non-ideal" theory (for that matter, he does not use the expressions "partial compliance" or "unfavorable circumstances," either). It seems to me that Carens's contrast is actually better suited than Rawls's to capturing the theoretical relevance of variation in how "favorable" actual circumstances are (cf. note 5). Among other reasons, Carens's contrast saliently applies to the enterprise of *ideal theorizing*, in Rawls's sense, taken all by itself. Indeed, Rawls's own ideal theory aims to strike some kind of balance between the terms of Carens's contrast, as Rawls's aspiration to a "realistic utopia" makes clear. See John Rawls, *The Law of Peoples* (Cambridge, MA: Harvard University Press, 1999), §1; henceforth, *LP*.

27. We could add just war theory to this list, which Rawls includes under partial compliance theory. *TJ*, 8; see also *LP*, 91–105.

28. Murphy, *Moral Demands in Nonideal Theory*, 5.

29. Avraham Astor, Marion Danis and Gopal Sreenivasan, "Providing Free Care to the Uninsured: How Much Should Physicians Give?," *Annals of Internal Medicine* 139, no. 9 (2003): W-78.

30. Murphy, *Moral Demands in Nonideal Theory*, 77.

31. For some skepticism, see Richard J. Arneson, "Moral Limits on the Demands of Beneficence?," in *The Ethics of Assistance: Morality and the Distant Needy*, ed. Deen K. Chatterjee (New York: Cambridge University Press, 2004), 33–58. I accept that, as baldly formulated in the text, the compliance condition is subject to counterexamples. For example, if two children are drowning in the proverbial pond and one can save both of them at little cost or risk to oneself, then one is obliged to save both; this remains the case even if there is another bystander, equally capable of saving the children, who refuses to help. But I am simply taking it for granted that the compliance condition can be refined to accommodate such cases.

32. Murphy, *Moral Demands in Nonideal Theory*, 5, 135. Murphy is not alone in neglecting the transitional justice branch of non-ideal theory. For example, see Joel Feinberg, "Duty and Obligation in the Non-Ideal World," *Journal of Philosophy* 70, no. 9 (1973): 263–75; Kai Nielsen, "Ideal and Non-Ideal Theory: How Should We Approach Questions of Global Justice?," *International Journal of Applied Philosophy* 2 (1985): 33–41; and

Michael Phillips, "Reflections on the Transition from Ideal to Non-Ideal Theory," *Noûs* 19, no. 4 (1985): 551–70. But my defense of Rawls's division of non-ideal theory concentrates on Murphy, since in his case a plausible explanation can be conjectured for the neglect. George Sher, *Approximate Justice: Studies in Non-Ideal Theory* (Lanham, MD: Rowman and Littlefield, 1997), 1–2, also treats "non-ideal theory" and "partial compliance theory" as interchangeable, but then he goes on to include transitional questions in his illustrative list of questions falling within their ambit.

33. See Murphy, "Institutions and the Demands of Justice," *Philosophy and Public Affairs* 27 (1998): 251–91, and G. A. Cohen, "Where the Action Is: On the Site of Distributive Justice," *Philosophy and Public Affairs* 26 (1997): 3–30; *Rescuing Justice and Equality* (Cambridge, MA: Harvard University Press, 2008), opposing Rawls (e.g., *Political Liberalism* [New York: Columbia University Press, 1993], lecture VII). Other contributions to the debate include Thomas W. Pogge, "On the Site of Distributive Justice: Reflections on Cohen and Murphy," *Philosophy and Public Affairs* 29, no. 2 (2000): 137–69, and Samuel Scheffler, "Is the Basic Structure Basic?," in *The Egalitarian Conscience*, ed. Christine Sypnowich (New York: Oxford University Press, 2006).

34. Murphy himself makes no such claim.

35. Both of the diagnoses I have offered treat "transitional" obligations as requiring individuals to do something to *improve* compliance with principles of justice that apply directly to individuals. The second diagnosis takes the "something" to involve introducing or reforming facilitating institutions. It would be reasonable to ask, in relation to the first diagnosis, what distinctive steps individuals might take to improve compliance by others, that is, steps that are not tantamount to introducing or reforming institutions. But profitably to discuss this question requires a tolerably clear account of what counts as an "institution." I have offered two diagnoses partly in order to avoid that thicket.

36. Of course, in one sense, this is an extremely strong assumption. However, since it is all grist to Murphy's mill, it makes for a dialectically weak premise.

37. Murphy, "Institutions and the Demands of Justice," 252–53.

38. This prospect cannot be dismissed as long as it is safe to assume that punishment or restitution *is* sometimes warranted for institutional injustice.

39. The relevant principle most clearly counts as a principle of transitional justice if the ground for paying restitution is not (or not only) a matter of an intrinsically warranted response to institutional injustice but rather (or also) a matter of what is instrumentally required to maintain justice as the new steady state. Compare note 12.

40. This section excerpts from Sreenivasan, "International Justice and

Health: A Proposal," *Ethics and International Affairs* 16 (2002): 81–90, and "Health and Justice in our Non-Ideal World," *Politics, Philosophy, and Economics* 6 (2007): 218–36.

41. *LP*, 106, 111, 118.

42. *LP*, 115–19. Rawls has Charles R. Beitz, *Political Theory and International Relations*, rev. ed. (Princeton: Princeton University Press, 1999), and Thomas W. Pogge, "An Egalitarian Law of Peoples," *Philosophy and Public Affairs* 23 (1994): 195–224 in mind.

43. *LP*, 89–90; cf. *TJ*, 8, 216, and Beitz, 170–71.

44. If it is compulsory to model conceptions of non-ideal theory as "theoretical responses to" some set or other of "non-ideal circumstances," then anticipatory theory can be modeled as responding to the *absence of a (settled) ideal theory of justice.*

45. Kit Fine, "Vagueness, Truth and Logic," *Synthese* 30 (1975): 265–300.

46. Alternative comparisons might be to Cass R. Sunstein, "Incompletely Theorized Agreements," *Harvard Law Review* 108, no. 7 (1995): 1733–72, or to Rawls, *Political Liberalism*, lecture IV. But, since their subjects are closer to home, those comparisons may also distract and mislead. For example, there is no commitment in anticipatory theory to Rawls's idea of "public reason" or its attendant strictures.

47. Sreenivasan, "International Justice and Health," and "Health and Justice in our Non-Ideal World."

48. Organization for Economic Cooperation and Development, *OECD in Figures* (Paris: OECD, 2008), 13.

49. Ibid., 61.

50. For an overview, see Simon Caney, *Justice Beyond Borders: A Global Political Theory* (Oxford: Oxford University Press, 2005), chap. 4.

51. E.g., Peter Singer, *One World: The Ethics of Globalization* (New Haven: Yale University Press, 2002), 192.

52. E.g., Thomas W. Pogge, *World Poverty and Human Rights* (Oxford: Blackwell, 2002), chap. 8.

53. E.g., Jeffrey D. Sachs, *The End of Poverty: Economic Possibilities for our Time* (New York: Penguin Press, 2005), chap. 15; and Bono.

54. Singer and Pogge explicitly endorse a one percent minimum; Sachs and Bono endorse the United Nations' Pearson target of 0.7 percent.

55. Sreenivasan, "Health and Justice in our Non-Ideal World."

56. This section includes excerpts from Sreenivasan, "Global Health and Non-Ideal Justice," in *Cambridge Textbook of Bioethics*, ed. Peter A. Singer and A. M. Viens (Cambridge: Cambridge University Press, 2008), 369–75.

57. Of course, progress toward this goal will also raise the global average. So let us say that the obligation "finally cuts off" when the global average is ten years below the top national average and the condition given in the text is satisfied.

58. OECD, *OECD in Figures*, 60.

59. Anticipatory theory leaves open the possibility that, in the ideal theory of justice, rich nations will be obligated to transfer *more than* one percent of GDP to poor nations. But, for its non-ideal purpose of setting interim targets for practical action, anticipatory theory ignores this possibility and simply concentrates on the minimum requirements of ideal justice.

60. OECD, *OECD in Figures*, 60, 12.

10

WHEN MORE MAY BE LESS: TRANSITIONAL JUSTICE IN EAST TIMOR

DAVID COHEN AND LEIGH-ASHLEY LIPSCOMB

I. INTRODUCTION

In this volume, Jon Elster argues that it is wrong to assume that the development of each of the core objectives of transitional justice—truth, justice, and peace—is synchronous and complementary. In fact, more of one does not necessarily lead to more of the other.[1] This chapter uses the case of East Timor[2] to challenge the notion that the accumulation of transitional justice mechanisms in any one post-conflict context necessarily leads to a better result for the population for whose benefit these mechanisms are purportedly deployed. To put it somewhat simplistically, more may actually mean less if scarce resources are dispersed rather than concentrated; if a new, equally flawed program is implemented to make up for the shortcomings of another; and if the expectations of the victimized population are unrealistically raised and then disappointed. As we will see, all of these features inform the case of East Timor.

Ruti Teitel has characterized the current state of transitional justice development as expansive and normalized after decades of growth and change.[3] Yet, despite the many advances in our abilities to perceive and enact transitional justice along multiple dimensions (retributive and restorative, local and global), what has been achieved in most post-conflict situations is at best an approximation of the justice owed to victims of human rights abuses.

Adrian Vermeule in this volume discusses these limitations on our ability to fully enact justice in terms of "rough justice." The following case study also touches upon this concept where it documents the effects of transitional justice institutions that collectively and individually adopt the "something is better than nothing" philosophy. Unlike the work of Vermeule and Eric Posner, our case study does not focus on the continuities with domestic or so-called ordinary justice systems.[4] Instead, it highlights some of the particular features operating in a multinational context involving the United Nations, a nascent national legal system, a fully developed national judiciary, and a variety of other institutional actors.

There has been a recent movement toward an inclusive and broad-based approach to transitional justice that integrates a variety of instruments in a way that aims to avoid a choice between justice and truth. Pablo de Greiff's contribution to this volume proposes a theory of transitional justice that supports the holistic application of transitional justice where the coordinated use of multiple types of transitional justice tools provides better outcomes.[5] Although East Timor implemented a transitional justice policy that on paper appeared to be coherent and coordinated between multiple judicial and non-judicial programs and restorative and retributive measures, in practice East Timor's experience of a multifaceted transitional justice approach may act as a useful case study to demonstrate the key challenges to studying and implementing such a holistic vision of transitional justice in certain kinds of post-conflict environments.

In many ways, East Timor provides a unique opportunity to test our theoretical claims against the messy details of the implementation of transitional justice. Cases such as this one, where many transitional justice mechanisms have been deployed intensively in a short period of time (in this case, eight years) and in a small country (East Timor's total population is about nine hundred thousand) offer the opportunity to examine some of the key and too often unstated assumptions on which some theoretical propositions about transitional justice rest. The challenges presented by the East Timor case are by no means unique. Rather, they are unfortunately all too typical of the experience in contemporaneous transitional justice settings, as the examples of Kosovo, Sierra Leone, Cambodia, Serbia, Bosnia, Rwanda, and, most recently, Lebanon all attest.

Like each transitional justice setting, East Timor possesses distinctive characteristics. The first outstanding feature of the East Timor context is a dual transition. This study examines the shift from authoritarianism to democracy in two countries at the same time—the newly independent East Timor and the reformist regime after the end of dictatorship in Indonesia. It was the incipient Indonesian movement of post-Suharto *Reformasi* that created the opportunity for the end of Indonesian rule in East Timor, yet it was the incompleteness of that same reform movement that doomed Indonesia's attempts to provide justice and accountability for its failures. Second, East Timor is one of the few contexts in which the United Nations acted as sovereign, where it could create the transitional justice regime and the domestic judiciary in which it was embedded, and make many of the key transitional justice decisions.[6] Because of this degree of direct authority over the transitional justice process, East Timor may be an example of one of the best opportunities to implement a holistic program of transitional justice that could be designed and initiated from the start as part of single, overarching concept for creating truth, justice and peace. Finally, East Timor is the only place where a hybrid tribunal, a national tribunal from another country, a national truth commission, and a bilateral truth commission have all been deployed. While these features of the East Timor case are unique, East Timor is not unusual among transitional societies in terms of the challenges it faces: a severe lack of financial and human resources and its weak post-conflict state, judiciary, and economy.[7]

We have already noted the intensity of the investment in transitional justice in East Timor. These processes were undertaken by two national governments (Indonesia and Timor-Leste), the United Nations, and various other national actors (e.g., Portugal and Australia). Substantial capital expenditures, as well as training, mentoring, and other capacity-building programs, were incorporated into these projects, purportedly to assist in the reconstitution of the judiciary and to promote the rule of law for the future.

Collectively, these institutions have to various degrees attempted the full range of transitional justice measures, including diplomatic peacemaking, judicial accountability, truth-seeking, national and local-level reconciliation, amnesties, memorialization, reparations, and lustration.

Despite this multitude and diversity of transitional justice schemes, many victims in East Timor still report a high degree of dissatisfaction with the justice system.[8] Why? There appears to be a wide gap between the perceived benefits of using multiple institutions and the quality of justice felt by the people who experienced them. Further, the repeated turmoil and civic disorder in East Timor has shown that, despite ten years of capacity-building in the institutions dedicated to the administration of justice and public security, these still have a long way to go before they will be able to prevent and respond to violence. While Kofi Annan celebrated the end of the UN mission in East Timor in 2005 as the UN's greatest success in nation building, the military mutiny, an outbreak of mass civic violence, and renewed international intervention less than a year later gave the lie to this rose-tinted assessment.

The East Timor case suggests that the mere addition of more institutions to a transitional justice scheme may not create better opportunities for justice. Even when there are agreements and legislation to coordinate the work of multiple transitional justice institutions, as there were in East Timor, they may not perform in smooth conjunction. In theory, a holistic approach is desirable; in practice, combining multiple institutions may produce very unsatisfactory results. This is particularly the case where all, or most, of the institutions suffer from the same underlying problems: lack of resources, incompetence, politically motivated compromise on essential elements, failure to adhere to minimum international standards, and, above all, lack of political will on the part of national governments and the United Nations. Unless *each* institution cooperates in closing gaps of impunity at the highest levels of responsibility, complies fully with international human rights standards, and implements outreach effectively, rather than "more being more," "more" may in fact provide "less."

This chapter proceeds by providing historical background to the events that led to the political transition in East Timor, followed by an introduction to its transitional justice institutions. In this way, we hope to orient the reader who is not familiar with East Timor. Next, we discuss the standards and methodology that lead to our evaluation and comparison of the performance of the individual institutions. We conclude with reflections on the lessons that can be learned from the sum of these institutions' limitations and achievements.

II. HISTORICAL BACKGROUND

East Timor is a former Portuguese colony. In 1974, the authoritarian regime in Portugal fell, spawning a period of civil conflict in Portuguese Timor between political parties with different philosophies regarding decolonization and independence. On December 7, 1975, Indonesia invaded East Timor. The territory continued to be ruled by Indonesia until 1999.[9] East Timor remained on the UN's non-self-governing territory list throughout this period as it continued its campaign for independence. After the fall of the Indonesian dictator Suharto, the UN, Portugal, and Indonesia reached an agreement in May 1999 that provided for a UN-monitored popular vote to decide the sovereignty of East Timor. The population voted by an overwhelming majority for independence, despite the campaign of terror to which it had been subjected for many months.

Although the referendum secured East Timor's independence, the popular vote was accompanied by grave violations of human rights throughout 1999, including murder, torture, sexual violence, forced transfer, deportation, and illegal detention committed on a massive scale. The Indonesian military, police, civilian government, and their proxy local militias committed the vast majority of these crimes.[10] East Timor was administered by the UN from October 25, 1999, until May 20, 2002, when it officially gained its independence and became the state of Timor-Leste.[11]

During the period of UN administration, a Timorese council, which took various forms and sizes, acted in an advisory capacity to the United Nations and was allowed to debate proposed UN regulations; however, the UN maintained the final authority to govern until independence. After 2002, the UN downsized its mission incrementally as part of a plan to leave East Timor, but, after the outbreak of violence in 2006, it reverted to a large-scale peacekeeping mission. The UN no longer exercises sweeping political authority in East Timor, but it continues to play a significant role, particularly in the justice and security sectors.[12]

Indonesia has continued to enact democratic reforms since the beginning of its political transition in 1998 and has successfully completed several rounds of local and national elections. Although its powers have been formally curbed, the military remains a strong influence on politics and has not yet completed the agenda of reforms meant to bring it into compliance with international standards, in particular, holding its personnel accountable for human rights violations.[13] Within a ten-year period, Indonesia has emerged from dictatorship to become one of the most democratically governed countries in Asia.

III. Transitional Justice in East Timor: An Overview

The periods of political transition in East Timor and Indonesia have been accompanied by the establishment of the multiple transitional justice institutions mentioned earlier. To help guide the discussion, Table 10.1 summarizes the transitional justice institutions formally established in East Timor and their essential components.

The East Timor transitional justice system was composed of two main types of institutions: trials and truth commissions. In addition, the United Nations conducted several short-term commissions of inquiry to assess the scale of human rights abuses and the performance of the trials. The UN inquiries—the International Commission of Inquiry (CIET) and the Commission of Experts (COE)—are not included here due to space limitations and because they did not engage directly in any programs of transitional justice in East Timor or Indonesia.

Indonesia established the first transitional justice institution in this system when it created the Commission for the Inquiry on Violations in East Timor (hereafter KPP-HAM). Established under the Indonesian Human Rights Law 26/2001, the Commission's mandate was to document human rights abuses that had occurred in 1999 as a first step toward criminal prosecution by the Indonesian Attorney General's Office. The KPP-HAM was a fully independent body affiliated with the National Human Rights Commission in Indonesia (KOMNAS-HAM). Its leadership included some of the most prominent human rights activists and civil society representatives in Indonesia. The recommendations of the KPP-HAM Report led to an Indonesian domestic trial process before the Jakarta Ad Hoc Human Rights Court.[14]

Initially, an international tribunal was proposed for East Timor in the Security Council, but the UN eventually agreed to Indonesia's proposal to conduct its own trials. Under Law 26/2000, the jurisdiction of the Indonesian Ad Hoc Human Rights Court in Jakarta was limited to gross violations of human rights.

The decision to conduct trials in Indonesia was taken, however, with the knowledge that the UN could also create a hybrid international-domestic tribunal that would operate simultaneously in East Timor. In 2000, the UN established the Special Panels for Serious Crimes (Special Panels, or SPSC) within the Timorese judiciary at the Dili District Court. The jurisdiction of the Special Panels for Serious Crimes in East Timor was defined by UNTAET Regulation 2000/15 Art. 1.3 as encompassing genocide, crimes against humanity, war crimes, murder, torture, and sexual offenses. These two courts were established without official agreement on the distinctions between their prosecutorial strategies or jurisdictions. The lack of jurisdictional definition may have been intentional and not necessarily an oversight in planning. Given this transitional justice structure, if one tribunal failed to prosecute effectively, the other could fulfill the prosecutorial function. However, the consequence of this strategy was that, in effect, the two tribunals had jurisdiction over the same crimes committed in 1999, and neither was able to adequately fulfill the demands for prosecution.

There were mechanisms to coordinate the work of the tribunals and to alleviate the problem of overlapping jurisdictions. For example, Indonesia and East Timor signed a Memorandum of Understanding to allow KPP-HAM and the two courts to cooperate in investigation and extradition. However, in practice, neither side fulfilled this agreement. Some of the same perpetrators were indicted by both tribunals, and neither tribunal successfully convicted any of those considered "most responsible" for gross violations of human rights in East Timor.

The Indonesian court process was entirely domestic, and the Special Panels were composed of a mix of international and Timorese staff. The Indonesian court prosecuted some high-level

TABLE 10.1 SUMMARY OF TRANSITIONAL JUSTICE INSTITUTIONS FOR HUMAN RIGHTS ABUSES COMMITTED IN EAST TIMOR

YEAR ESTABLISHED— END OF OPERATIONS	ACRONYM	NAME OF INSTITUTION	ESTABLISHED BY AUTHORITY OF	TYPE OF INSTITUTION	TEMPORAL SCOPE OF INQUIRIES	BASED IN
Nov. 1999– Jan. 2000	KPP-HAM	Commission of Inquiry on Violations of Human Rights in East Timor	Indonesian National Human Rights Commission	Inquiry	1999	Indonesia
Nov. 1999– Jan. 2000	CIET	International Commission of Inquiry	UN Commission of Human Rights	Inquiry	1999	New York
2000–2003	Ad Hoc Court	Jakarta Ad Hoc Human Rights Court	Presidential Decree	National Court	1999	Indonesia
2000–2005	SCU	Serious Crimes Unit	UN Regulation*	Hybrid Prosecution Unit	1999	East Timor
2000–2005	DLU	Defense Lawyers Unit	UN Regulation*	Hybrid Legal Defense Unit	1999	East Timor
2000–2005	SPSC	Dili District Court— Special Panels for Serious Crimes	UN Regulation*	Hybrid Court	1999	East Timor

2001–2005	CAVR	Commission for Truth, Reception and Reconciliation (Comisão de Acolhimento, Verdade e Reconciliacão de Timor-Leste)	UN Regulation with East Timorese CNRT Congress Resolution	Truth Commission	1974–1999	East Timor
2005–present	Post-CAVR	Post-CAVR Secretariat	Presidential Decree	Education/Truth Commission	n/a	East Timor
2005	COE	Commission of Experts	UN Secretary General	Inquiry	1999	New York
2005–2008	CTF	Commission of Truth and Friendship of East Timor and Indonesia	Diplomatic agreement between 2 States	Truth Commission	1999–present	Indonesia/East Timor
2008–present	SCIT	Serious Crimes Investigation Team	UNMIT with Security Council Endorsement	Inquiry	1999	East Timor
1999–present	none	Dili District Court—Ordinary Crimes Panels	UN Regulation*	National Court	1999	East Timor

* The UN exercised all legislative powers at this time, but in consultation with a representative Timorese advisory body appointed by the UN.

Indonesian commanders and Timorese perpetrators, but all convictions were subsequently overturned on appeal or judicial review. In contrast, the Special Panels for Serious Crimes (SPSC) in East Timor tried only the Timorese "little fish" (very low-level militia members) but convicted nearly everyone.[15]

In East Timor the SPSC was part of the national judicial system, even though it had international elements as part of its inherent structure. SPSC had jurisdiction over what were labeled as "serious crimes" (crimes against humanity, war crimes, genocide, murder, torture, and sexual violations). The "Ordinary Panels" of the Dili District Court had jurisdiction over all other crimes, referred to as "less serious crimes," with the exception of those crimes that were processed through the CAVR reconciliation process, discussed later.

The Serious Crimes Unit (SCU) was the prosecutorial arm of the hybrid court, or Special Panels, in East Timor. It conducted investigations and prosecuted cases brought before the Special Panels. The SCU also operated under a hybrid structure, with the General Prosecutor of East Timor as its figurehead and an overwhelmingly international staff, led by a UN-appointed Deputy Prosecutor for Serious Crimes. A hybrid Defense Unit of the Special Panels was also established, called the Defense Lawyer's Unit (DLU), but it does not feature as prominently in our discussion below largely because of its neglect throughout the transitional justice process.[16]

In 2001, the United Nations established the first truth commission in East Timor—the Commission for Reception, Truth and Reconciliation (Comisão de Acolhimento, Verdade e Reconciliacão de Timor-Leste, hereafter CAVR)—as a complement to the judicial system. The CAVR was established with the consent of the Timorese advisory body created by the UN. The Commission was governed by a committee of appointed Timorese political elites and human rights activists and was administered by a mix of local and international staff. International staff played a strong role in advisory and management capacities, but the majority of the staff was local. The CAVR was mandated by law to institute processes for truth-seeking, reconciliation, and healing in relation to human rights abuses that had occurred from 1974 to 1999.[17]

The CAVR's activities included a non-judicial traditional justice mechanism, referred to as Community Reconciliation Processes

(CRPs), that heard cases of lower-level crimes such as theft and arson.[18] In exchange for truthful testimony and the fulfillment of a restitution agreement determined by the local community, a perpetrator could receive immunity from prosecution. The CAVR's ability to hear and make decisions about the commission of crimes resulted in effective amnesties for low-level perpetrators that required the formal consent of and an ongoing relationship with the Special Panels/Serious Crimes Unit. Because of the inclusion of the Community Reconciliation Processes in the CAVR mandate, the law that established the CAVR also stipulated in detail a process by which the judicial and non-judicial elements of the transitional justice system (in this case, the SCU and the CAVR) would be linked to share information and coordinate their activities. This coordinating mechanism was defined by law so that, at least in theory, the institutions would not contradict or interfere with each other in terms of temporal mandates, prosecutorial priorities, or reconciliation.[19] Following the closure of the CAVR, in 2005, the Post-CAVR Secretariat (Post-CAVR) institution was created to disseminate the Final Report and to engage in legacy activities.

As the CAVR's work was nearing completion, the governments of Indonesia and East Timor together created the bilateral Commission of Truth and Friendship (CTF), in 2005. The Commission's members were appointed by the two Presidents and consisted of political elites from both countries, representing, from the perspective of the two governments, civil society, victims' groups, the Foreign Ministries, the legal community, and the militaries. The Timorese delegation to the CTF contained a number of former CAVR Commissioners and local staff. Over the course of about two years, this truth commission reviewed the work of all the previous transitional justice mechanisms (KPP-HAM, SCU/Special Panels, CAVR, Jakarta Ad Hoc trials) in both countries and conducted its own truth-seeking process. Its mandate required the identification of institutional responsibility for gross human rights violations committed in 1999 and recommendations for preventative and healing measures that would enable the two states to live together peacefully.[20]

In 2008, the UN mission in East Timor reconstituted a limited version of the Serious Crimes Unit that had been disbanded in May 2005 when the UN Missions were beginning to close. The mandate

of the Serious Crimes Investigation Team (SCIT) is to complete
the more than four hundred investigations that were left unfinished by the Serious Crimes Unit. Under its negotiated agreement
of cooperation with the Prosecutor General of East Timor, it can
only investigate and recommend cases for indictment.

To summarize this astonishing multiplicity of transitional justice mechanisms deployed in an eight-year period, two courts assumed jurisdiction over serious offenses committed in 1999: the
Jakarta Ad Hoc Human Rights Court and the Special Panels for
Serious Crimes.[21] The Ordinary Panels of the Dili District Court
and the CAVR's Community Reconciliation Program were del-
egated the task of dealing with non-serious crimes committed in
and before 1999, but only 10 percent of the CRP cases heard involved pre-1999 offenses, and the Ordinary Panels of the Dili District Court in practice heard only cases involving crimes committed after 1999. The bilateral truth commission (CTF) also dealt
only with crimes committed in 1999, and it was not permitted to
recommend prosecutions. The CAVR could initiate truth-telling
for events that occurred before 1999 but had no powers to compel legal action. Both the CAVR and the CTF found that the Indonesian military and other institutions had committed crimes
against humanity in East Timor in 1999. The overall result of this
narrowing of the temporal jurisdiction of these institutions to the
year 1999 was that the largest number of serious offenses, as well
as many lesser crimes, were left out of the accountability plans and
processes because they were committed before 1999.

IV. STANDARDS OF EVALUATION

Much literature has evaluated the performance of the truth commissions and trials in East Timor introduced here as independent
systems.[22] However, to date, there has been limited critical discussion of how all of these mechanisms in East Timor worked together
as part of a multipronged transitional justice strategy.[23] It is not
difficult to understand why analysis of the entire system of institutions in narrative form, as we undertake in this chapter, is rare: it
is an extremely complex undertaking to evaluate the performance
of a sector that proposes to provide so many different kinds of justice (e.g., punishment, reconciliation, truth, history, healing) for

a wide variety of people with different sets of expectations (victims, perpetrators, national and international governments). Apart from the fact that the research materials we draw on are in four languages (English, Portuguese, Indonesian, and Tetum) and are often accessible only with special permission,[24] the difficulty lies in creating an evaluative system that can adjust to each institution and different actors, while maintaining consistency and establishing standards sufficient to bring about genuine insights into the best way to implement transitional justice programs that are linked to one another.

Yet, this kind of evaluation is necessary because, for participants in the process, "justice" is not experienced in isolated parts but as a whole. Exactly whose standards and expectations should be used for evaluation, and what are the benchmarks that cut across all institutions and all the different types of justice pursued within each of these institutions? In East Timor, as elsewhere in transitional justice settings, relatively little thought has been given to such issues. They are of vital importance, however, because, as our research reveals, one of the core weaknesses of the transitional justice regime in East Timor is that, despite the existence of a multifaceted "plan" for the transitional justice scheme, there was a failure on the part of the multiple institutional leaders to agree upon performance criteria and outcomes that the overall transitional justice program should yield.

As Elster's chapter in this volume explains, the area in which there is most consensus about what the outcomes of transitional justice should be is what we may call the "aspirations of transitional justice." The satisfaction of justice, the full truth, and a sustainable peace are all lofty goals that transitional justice institutions work to attain and where they are most often accused of falling short. Elster's contribution helps us to understand why these goals are difficult to balance, but how we measure what a system has satisfactorily achieved in any or all of these areas is another question, one that we cannot examine in any depth here. We try to contribute to that discussion, however, by looking at how the East Timor institutions measured themselves in these areas, while also assessing their performance against these same aspirations.

For example, the satisfaction of justice could be understood in a variety of ways. From a quantitative perspective one may measure it by the number of convictions of perpetrators or the number of victims who receive reparations. A qualitative assessment may focus more on the question of how people feel about those convictions or, in a more general sense, the notion of justice (drawing on survey research, interviews, and media commentary, for example). Qualitative and quantitative assessments are also concerned with how well institutions fulfilled their specific mandates, but mandates are often full of vague aspirational criteria[25] that require another set of measures. In this case or in the rare case when mandates are more specific, qualitative independent standards of evaluation, not necessarily part of the publicly declared mandate, may play this role.

A body of literature is developing that lays out the international best practices for specific institutions or areas of transitional justice.[26] The standards that cut across all transitional justice institutions include effective prosecutions for war crimes, crimes against humanity, and genocide; prompt and efficient reparations programs; outreach and legacy efforts commensurate with the needs of the affected population; and comprehensive witness/victim protection and support. Further standards include the degree of public access to the justice system, gender balance, and therapeutic programs for traumatized groups.

This discussion of the need for balancing qualitative and quantitative standards may seem obvious, but the application of this understanding has not proved to be the norm in transitional justice practice. Our research has noted the way in which primitive quantitative standards (e.g., numbers of cases investigated, numbers of indictments and convictions) have had an ill-fated tendency to fill the gaps in our ability to understand the performance of transitional justice institutions. In the case of East Timor, we will show how quantitative criteria (i.e., a higher number of convictions, greater numbers of statements taken) and instincts (the desire to do "more") determined institutional assessments of the transitional justice scheme and examine some of the consequences of decisions made on the basis of those assessments. For this study, we have attempted to contrast these quantitative views with a more qualitative evaluation of each of the transitional justice mechanisms and of the system as a whole. On the basis of this comparison, we argue that the urge to do "more" in quantity may not provide greater qualitative results in regard to justice, truth, and peace for victimized populations.

The framework for evaluation we employ includes the following criteria:

   i. *Aspirational goals (justice, truth, peace)*. This discussion includes the institutions' individual performances in these areas and their ability to complement each other to enhance these goals across the board. Part of our assessment includes victims' perceptions of the achievement of these goals.
   ii. *Adherence to institutional mandates*. This discussion makes references to the clarity and quality of the mandates of the institutions themselves, as well as how effectively and accurately the institutions implemented the mandate.
   iii. *Adherence to international fair trial standards and best practices* (including procedural due process, independence and impartiality, gender balance, access to justice, effective outreach, protection and support for victims, witnesses, and perpetrators).

These standards will be woven throughout our narrative discussion of the institutional performances, and the overall performance in these areas will be clarified in our analysis and final reflections. It is the task of the next section to put these standards into a more detailed and local context.

V. INSTITUTIONAL PERFORMANCE

Our analysis considers the paradox that, despite the plethora of institutions, one feature they all shared was a lack of political will to make them succeed. While one might somewhat naively assume that the creation of institutions is a reflection of a political commitment by policymakers, the Timor case reveals that this is not the case. By "political will" we refer to the determination of those responsible for creating transitional justice mechanisms to ensure that they receive the resources (human and financial) and the political backing to make them work effectively. The failure of political will involves the failure to provide those necessary resources; the failure to address crippling problems that are known to have arisen; the failure to provide political support when it is needed to enable an institution to carry out its mandate; the failure to hold individuals accountable for gross mismanagement, corruption, or incompetence; and the failure to insist that an institution meet the minimum applicable standards for fairness and due process.

The failure of political will, in the end, basically involves the failure to ensure that the outcome of a process actually fulfills the mandate and meets the needs of those in whose name it was created. In the transitional justice process arising from the 1999 violence in East Timor, all of these failures were manifest. They involved some of leading figures in the UN Mission and in the various components of the justice institutions, the Timorese and Indonesian national leadership, and, ultimately, the UN leadership in New York in both the Secretariat and the Security Council. While many individuals dedicated years of their lives to making transitional justice in East Timor work for the benefit of the Timorese people, their efforts were too often thwarted by indifference, denial, and lack of accountability at higher levels

From this perspective, the East Timor case study raises the question of whether the sum of the individual efforts of multiple under-resourced and deeply flawed institutions was greater than what would have been achieved by any one mechanism backed by real political will to ensure its success. In the East Timor case, increasing investment basically functioned as a band-aid in response to institutional failures, rather than expressing a proactive commitment to achieving the goals of truth, justice, and peace. The UN and the government of Indonesia typically lauded the quantitative appearance of the process, rather than assessing what all of these efforts collectively achieved. From the foregoing perspective, it is perhaps not surprising that one of the most successful institutional efforts in the East Timor saga was driven by civil society, rather than governmental actors. We now turn to the Indonesian investigative commission for East Timor.

A. Commission of Inquiry on Violations of Human Rights in East Timor (KPP-HAM)

As noted earlier, the Indonesian investigation aimed to provide the basis for a report recommending criminal prosecution for the violence that had occurred in East Timor from January to September 1999. The Commission, co-chaired by two respected human rights activists, Asmara Nababan and Mulya Lubis, identified fourteen priority cases and pursued its investigation in both Indonesia and East Timor. The Commission questioned victims, international observers, and members of the Indonesian military and police forces. Despite having only four months in which to complete their investigation and write their Report, the commissioners assembled a large database of testimonial and documentary evidence. They also obtained invaluable physical evidence through the exhumation of mass graves and forensic analysis.

The KPP-HAM Report argues for the massive nature of the violations by revealing the number of victims and the geographical range of the violence perpetrated during the period under investigation. Building upon this evidence, the Report shows that these gross violations of human rights constituted crimes against humanity because the incidents constituted a massive, intensive series of attacks against a civilian population. This demonstration provided the basis for the Attorney General of Indonesia to proceed with prosecution in the newly formed Jakarta Ad Hoc Human Rights Court. That prosecution, as we will see, unfortunately did not proceed with the commitment, energy, and competence displayed by KPP-HAM.

Indonesian government officials' accounts of the violence universally portrayed the Army and security forces as helpless bystanders unable to intervene or prevent the sudden outbreaks of spontaneous violence between civilian groups.[27] At the most, it was averred, they had not properly prepared for the possibility of large-scale violence following the Popular Consultation on independence. Even in this regard, however, the supposedly spontaneous nature of the outbreak of violence was put forward as an excuse for their failure to take the steps necessary to maintain security. This version of events was widely accepted, both by the Indonesian media and within the general population. The KPP-HAM Report rejected such accounts and provided evidence showing that the violence was not perpetrated by civilian groups that spontaneously formed but rather was the work of Indonesian-backed militias that had been trained and equipped for just such a role. KPP-HAM detailed the deliberate involvement of Indonesian

274 DAVID COHEN AND LEIGH-ASHLEY LIPSCOMB

institutions in various phases of the planning, organization, financing, and perpetration of the violence by the "pro-autonomy" (i.e., pro-Indonesian) militias and by Indonesian army personnel.[28]

In addition to demonstrating the involvement of Indonesian institutions in the violence, the KPP-HAM Report also explored individual accountability in accordance with its mandate. On the basis of evidence that revealed patterns of perpetration and institutional cooperation, they recommended prosecution of twenty-two persons and further investigation of more than one hundred whom they suspected also bore responsibility for the crimes. These individuals included the most senior military officers at the high command echelon of the Indonesian Army. Eighteen of these twenty-two individuals were subsequently prosecuted before the Jakarta Ad Hoc Court. The Attorney General did not investigate the remaining individuals named in the Report, however. In terms of seeking justice and contributing to individual accountability, the KPP-HAM process made a significant contribution.

Apart from investigating the hundreds of murders that had taken place during the 1999 violence, KPP-HAM also turned its attention to other categories of crimes. This work stood in contrast to the inattention to gender-based crimes of judicial processes in both Jakarta and Dili (the Special Panels). From the beginning of the transitional justice process, KPP-HAM discussed the violence directed against women, including sexual slavery. Its Report cited evidence that young women had been forced to sexually serve militias and the military, sometimes in the form of forced "marriage" or enslavement. Further, the Report documented how sexual slavery and rapes had also occurred in civilian settlements, military stations, and refugees' settlements, before and after the referendum.[29] Although the investigation of KPP-HAM in this area was by no means exhaustive because of the Commission's statutorily limited temporal scope, it provided a sufficient basis for both UN and Indonesian prosecutors to conclude that crimes of sexual violence had in all likelihood been perpetrated systematically and on a large scale. This could also have provided the basis for more effective prosecutions of crimes against humanity for sexual violence had this been a priority in either the UN prosecution unit in Dili or the Indonesian Attorney General's office.

KPP-HAM also concluded that the massive population displacement in 1999 constituted forcible transfer and deportation. It estimated that the number of refugees forcibly displaced reached around 250,000 persons in East Nusa Tenggara. The Report indicated that this forcible transfer was accomplished by Indonesian-backed pro-autonomy militias that attacked and burned settlements. This campaign of terror and intimidation was not random, on its account, but especially targeted pro-independence supporters. The pattern of this campaign strengthened the Commission's conclusion that, contrary to official accounts, the violence had been carefully planned and orchestrated by Indonesian institutions, utilizing Timorese militias as the direct perpetrators.[30] Part of the pattern of this orchestrated violence included a scorched-earth policy that targeted many districts in East Timor and that, through arson and looting, destroyed approximately 70 percent of civilian settlements.[31]

KPP-HAM's careful documentation of the role of Indonesian institutions was vital in countering another aspect of the official story promulgated by the Indonesian government and in laying the foundation for institutional responsibility. Defenders of Indonesian policy pointed to various documents and actions that, in their view, showed that the higher echelons of government and the military had pursued a peaceful solution in East Timor. For this reason, they argued, they were innocent of the violence that might have been organized at the local level by what the Indonesian military commonly referred to as "rogue elements." The KPP-HAM Report did list official efforts and proclamations designed to promote peace among parties of opposing political beliefs;[32] however, it drew a sharp contrast between these initiatives and the policies that were being implemented by Indonesian armed forces on the ground.[33] Clear evidence of continuous support for and involvement in the criminal activities by the pro-autonomy militias aimed at pro-independence supporters substantiated this conclusion, as did the language contained in reports of and communications between governmental and military officials.[34]

While KPP-HAM accomplished a great deal in its Report, with more time and resources it could have done much more. The time limitations, mandated by the legal framework under which it operated, were one of the Commission's inherent weaknesses. While KPP-HAM assembled a substantial document database, it appears

that it did not have sufficient time to evaluate all of these documents and to integrate them into its Report. Some areas, such
as the mechanism used to channel funding to the militias, could
have been examined in much greater detail. The Commission also
would have benefited from greater cooperation by the military, but
this lack of cooperation is hardly surprising, given that the military
structures of political dominance and influence established under
the Suharto regime remained to a significant degree intact. While
political reform had occurred rapidly and was already well under
way, during the period of KPP-HAM's investigation and the subsequent trials, military reform and, in particular, the establishment
of civilian control of the military and the rule of law lagged significantly behind. From 2001 to 2005, the military remained one
of the most powerful political and economic forces in Indonesia,
capable of exerting its influence, whether through intimidation,
corruption, or other means, in every arena of judicial and political activity. As in the earlier Chilean transition, the incomplete
state of political transition in this case can be seen to shape the
parameters within which national transitional justice institutions
must operate.[35]

Perhaps the single greatest contribution of the KPP-HAM Report is that it succeeded in capturing the broader context of the
gross human rights violations that had occurred in East Timor in
1999, setting a high standard both for truth and for the scope of
prosecutions in judicial settings. In this regard, despite the limitations with which it had to operate, KPP-HAM went further than
either the UN or Indonesian justice processes.

While, as will be seen, the Report of the Timorese Truth and
Reconciliation Commission (CAVR) also discussed this broader
context, KPP-HAM's conclusions in this area were distinctive in
that they were based upon the Commission's own independent
investigation and analysis of testimonial, documentary, and physical evidence. It is a confirmation of KPP-HAM's contribution
that, rather than introducing their own evidence to support the
contextual elements of crimes against humanity charges, the UN
prosecutors in Dili simply introduced the KPP-HAM Final Report
into evidence. Because the Report had already been disseminated
and had gained the high regard of activist communities in both
Indonesia and East Timor, the UN prosecutors felt that the Report

could stand on its own as the strongest evidence available to describe the overall patterns of human rights abuses that had occurred in East Timor.

B. The Jakarta Ad Hoc Human Rights Court

Following the submission of the KPP-HAM Report, with its recommendations for formal criminal investigation, the Attorney General of Indonesia issued a decree establishing an investigation team to look into gross violations of human rights in East Timor.[36] This investigation began in April 2000, and in 2001 twelve cases were brought before the new human rights tribunal, the Jakarta Ad Hoc Human Rights Court.[37] The Attorney General's investigation team largely ignored all of the evidence collected by KPP-HAM and essentially began anew, largely out of disdain for the "civilian" process that had produced the Report. Its decision to ignore the KPP-HAM database and areas of investigation such as gender violence resulted in a trial process far narrower in scope than what would have resulted from implementing the case strategy laid out in KPP-HAM's Report.

While the Attorney General's investigation team assembled case files ("Dossiers" or BAPs) that contained substantial evidence demonstrating "probable cause" for crimes against humanity, as we will demonstrate, the investigation and trial phase of the formal criminal justice process was deeply marred by incompetence at every step. In some ways, the Jakarta trials can be regarded as a mirror image of the KPP-HAM process. In the latter case, despite severe limitations of time and resources, the result was as good as could have been hoped for under the circumstances. In the former, despite having the full resources of the state at its disposal and significantly more time, the institution made errors in all areas of evaluation.

The Investigation Phase and Its Case Files (BAPs)

In total, the investigation brought forward twelve cases involving eighteen defendants.[38] Collectively, the defendants represented a cross-section of the Indonesian political, military, and security structures in East Timor. The inclusion of three generals, in particular, in the indictments (including the regional [Udayana] commander, two-star general Adam Damiri) would seem to indicate the seriousness of the investigation. Yet, none of the higher-level commanders in the Indonesian military's high command in Jakarta were investigated, despite the specific recommendations of KPP-HAM concerning their potential involvement in the violence.

The investigative team assembled the case files on the basis of the theory of command responsibility. While this theory of liability was a plausible starting point, its deployment was flawed. Two of the fundamental conceptual shortcomings had to do with a lack of comprehension of the legal requirements for establishing command responsibility and crimes against humanity. While these categories from the Rome Statute of the International Criminal Court had been incorporated into the Indonesian human rights law, they were imperfectly understood by prosecutors, who had had no training or educational background in international law and no practical experience in the prosecution of such complex cases. For example, with regard to command responsibility, the case files alleged that the commanders had failed to prevent the violence in question, but they did not establish a superior-subordinate relationship between these commanders and the Timorese militias alleged to have been the direct perpetrators. They also did not focus on the cognitive element requiring the commander to have known or to have had information on the basis of which he should have known that these crimes were being or were about to be committed by his subordinates.[39] Such evidence was available, but a lack of understanding of the concept of command responsibility and of the required elements of proof undercut its use as a theory of liability. The prosecutors' failure to properly use the legal tools at their disposal resulted in part from a lack of training but also from an ingrained resistance, still manifest in the Attorney General's Office today, to the application of international law in the sovereign state of Indonesia. This again reflects a mindset inherited from the previous regime.

An even more serious shortcoming, and one far more difficult to explain on the basis of incompetence, had to do with the fact that, in nine of the twelve case files, the accused were charged only with omissions, that is, with having failed to prevent the crimes from occurring. In only three cases was there any attempt to use a theory of complicity or other means to link the accused to the actual perpetration of the crimes. This was the case despite the fact that the case files contained ample evidence of such link-ages, particularly in the form of aiding and abetting.[40] Thus, while all twelve case files concluded that crimes against humanity had been committed, almost all of the investigations failed to provide evidence or to clearly explain how the particular accused had any substantive link with the specific crime alleged. Here is one of the many examples where a quantitative assessment of an institution's success could lead to a flawed judgment: the files may have consti-tuted the highest possible number of crimes against humanity, but the quality of the evidence supporting those conclusions was so weak that it rendered effective prosecutions nearly impossible.

The prosecution's failure to comprehend the full context in which the crimes were committed also critically affected its abil-ity to build a successful case proving crimes against humanity. The fundamental weakness resided in a lack of comprehension of the structure of the law of crimes against humanity, which requires proof of the larger attack against a civilian population as an in-dependent prerequisite to proving the specific offense.[41] In these cases, however, the investigation adopted a purely case-based ap-proach, looking at the incident as an isolated event that did not have any relation to the incidents investigated in the other case files. There was no attempt to do what KPP-HAM had already pro-vided a roadmap for, that is, to portray the full context of the vio-lence in East Timor and to analyze the underlying patterns and organization. Even more damaging to the ultimate success of the cases was that so little of the inculpatory evidence that was ob-tained by investigators was put in the case files or presented to the court at trial.[42]

What accounts for these failures? Of particular relevance here are general problems that may arise in transitional justice inves-tigations by national institutions in close temporal proximity to regime change. First, there is the manifest lack of competence in the body of law being applied. Without the provision of spe-cial training for the prosecutors involved in the cases, this could hardly have been otherwise, as international criminal law was not part of the law school curriculum. Since this was also the first hu-man rights case prosecuted under the new law in Indonesia, the prosecutors had no experience in the investigation of such cases and apparently did not develop the special skills and expertise necessary to do so in an adequate manner in the course of their work. It must also be noted that, from the standpoint of political will, the Attorney General, well aware of these weaknesses, made absolutely no attempt to mobilize the necessary resources to offset them (e.g., assigning the most capable prosecutors; providing training and adequate funds; accepting offers of assistance from the Serious Crimes Unit to provide evidence).[43]

The second, more prominent feature involves the continuity of the mindset within the public prosecution service, starting at the very top with the Attorney General, who set the tone for those assigned to these cases. Under Suharto, there was a deliberate and highly successful attempt to militarize the Attorney General's Office at the expense of professional investigatory and prosecutorial competence.[44] The legacy of that militarization will long be felt in the public prosecution service, despite ongoing efforts at training and reform. The entrenched lack of prosecutorial independence, coupled with a deep commitment to the institutional values inculcated by the previous regime, inevitably was felt in the prosecution of the East Timor cases at the Jakarta trials.[45] Here, the contrast with the independence and integrity of the KPP-HAM investigation could not be more striking. As a result of this lack of common values between the National Human Rights Commission and the Human Rights Directorate of the Attorney General's Office, the entire system of human rights prosecutions had come to a standstill by 2009. Thus, in this case we can see how the addition of another institution system, which in theory should have built on the achievements of the first institution, KPP-HAM, instead functioned to undermine them. Finally, there is the issue of political interference in the investigation of these cases. This topic is dealt with in the following section.

The Trial Phase Before the Jakarta Ad Hoc Human Rights Court

In the trial phase, the twelve cases resulted in the conviction of six individuals: three members of the Indonesian military, two civilians, and one police official. One of the civilians convicted was a Timorese citizen, Eurico Gutteres, the commander of the notorious Aitarak militia in Dili District and the Deputy Commander of the PPI (Pasukan Pejuang Integrasi) umbrella organization for pro-Indonesian militias. In the end, Gutteres was the only one of those convicted who was not acquitted on appeal and who served part of a prison sentence.[46] It is beyond the scope of this chapter to discuss all of the twelve trials. It will suffice here to summarize some of their features, those most pertinent to issues of transitional justice.[47]

Like the professionals involved in the investigation phase, the trial judges also lacked expertise in the body of law they were applying. This resulted in final judgments—leading to both convictions and acquittals—that in some cases reveal fundamental errors in the interpretation and application of the law of command responsibility and crimes against humanity.[48] Moreover, the judges did not have the experience or the training to prepare them to deal with many of the issues that arise in human rights trials, particularly involving the protection and proper treatment of potentially traumatized victim witnesses. The presence of large numbers of uniformed and often armed members of the Indonesian Special Forces (Kopassus) in the visitor's gallery of the courtroom every day was intimidating to witnesses and judges alike, especially given the lack of any form of security.[49] The continuing power of the military was evident throughout the proceedings. The atmosphere in the courtroom was a problem for victim protection but also for effective prosecutions, because it had the potential to impinge on judicial independence.

These problems are linked to another grave defect of the trials from the perspective of transitional justice: the lack of victim witnesses called to testify in court. Without victim witnesses, the quality of truth obtained in such proceedings is questionable and the accessibility of the process to victims is also compromised. Although numerous victim witnesses had testified in the investigative stage, the prosecution chose to call very few of them to testify at trial. In all twelve trials, only seven persons appeared as victim witnesses. The more activist judges in some of the trials repeatedly requested that the prosecution produce more witnesses with relevant testimony, especially victim witnesses; however, the prosecution consistently ignored these requests.[50] The failure to produce adequate numbers of victim witnesses had a serious negative impact on the legitimacy and effectiveness of the trials.

Indeed, the prosecution's selection of witnesses proved to be one of the most curious aspects of the trial and illustrates the many shortcomings of the public prosecution service noted earlier. Those witnesses whose testimony at the investigative stage was the most probative and inculpatory typically were not called by the prosecution. Instead, the prosecution called as witnesses defendants from the other cases, who predictably defended the accused in blatantly self-serving ways. The bulk of the other witnesses called by the prosecution were subordinates of the accused who also testified in favor of the defendant and contradicted the prosecution's case as set out in the case file. Their testimony was often irrelevant and of questionable credibility. The prosecution, rather than subjecting such self-serving and exculpatory testimony to rigorous examination, instead encouraged it. It was above all this aspect of the trials that led some commentators to denounce them as a sham.[51] That the prosecution proceeded this way in nearly all of the twelve trials indicates the lack of political will at the highest level of the Attorney General's Office to ensure their success. It was clear from the outset that, from the standpoint of the public prosecution service, the strategy in all except the Eurico Gutteres case was to go through the motions of a trial while doing everything possible to negate the possibility of guilty verdicts.[52] In a highly hierarchical and militarized institution such as the Attorney General's Office, such a consistent pattern of conduct extending over months of trial and in the face of both national and international criticism can only be taken to indicate official policy.

The prosecution's clear failure to discharge its function in most of the twelve cases provides the clearest evidence of political influence on the trials.[53] While it is also true that some of the prosecutors assigned to these cases appeared blatantly incompetent, the selection of such personnel only goes to underscore the lack of political will on the part of the Attorney General to prosecute the cases fairly. Another indication of political influence on the trials came in the form of witnesses who withdrew their previous sworn testimony when called at trial. Other witnesses, notably from the military and police, suddenly proved unable to recall facts to which they had testified in great detail during the investigation.

In short, the seemingly deliberate incompetence of the prosecution, coupled with pressure on witnesses and the failure to call victim witnesses or adduce other important documentary or other evidence, severely undercut the weight of the prosecution's case.[54] While it is true that some of the panels convicted in spite of these shortcomings, these verdicts were all overturned on appeal, save for that against Eurico Gutteres. The appellate judgments manifested, in many cases, a far greater lack of professionalism and knowledge of the applicable legal doctrines than the worst of the trial judgments. In the case of the reversal of the conviction of General Adam Damiri, the judgment is so poorly crafted that one must suspect that the result was determined by other factors.[55] While it may be true that if the conviction was founded upon an inadequate evidentiary basis reversal upon appeal would be proper, the Adam Damiri case indicates that this was not the basis on which the High Court reversed the decision. The High Court's appellate judgment reveals no careful examination of the evidence or analysis that discusses the relevant legal principles. It instead indicates an appellate panel ignorant of the applicable legal standards and unwilling to analyze the evidence contained in the trial court judgment and upon which the conviction was based.[56]

Despite these failures, this attempt at transitional justice in Indonesia may be seen as a partial success. Of course, the failures in terms of the aspirations for justice were overwhelming: there was a failure to provide accountability; a failure to give victims a voice and a meaningful role in the proceedings and to protect them; a failure to establish the truth; and a failure to achieve any sort of peace. On the other hand, it could hardly have been expected that, some three years after the fall of Suharto, an intact and politically influential military and a public prosecution service and judiciary that had scarcely changed since the Suharto era would permit what they saw as the humiliation of the Indonesian Armed Forces and the nation with which they were still so closely identified. The strength of the continuity from the previous political order indicates how difficult it is to leave the process of accountability to national institutions when there has not been a sufficient interval for genuine reform to take place. Thus, insofar as the Ad Hoc courts submitted TNI (Tentara Nasional Indonesia) generals to a civilian court for the first time and applied a framework of international law to their prosecution, it was a watershed in Indonesian politics. The extent to which international mechanisms were more successful in fulfilling transitional justice goals is explored in the next section.

C. Serious Crimes Unit (SCU)/Special Panels

The Serious Crimes Unit (SCU) was established by the United Nations during its period of transitional authority in East Timor to investigate and prosecute serious crimes committed in East Timor during the Indonesian occupation. The Special Panels for Serious Crimes adjudicated these cases.[57] The SCU opened investigations in more than four hundred cases. In total, it issued ninety-five indictments that included allegations against 440 individuals. Both East Timorese and Indonesians were indicted. However, of those accused, 339 were living outside East Timor's geographic jurisdiction, mostly in Indonesia. When the SCU closed, in 2005, eighty-seven defendants had been tried before the Special Panels in a total of fifty-five cases. Eighty-four of these eighty-seven defendants were convicted.[58]

All levels of perpetration were indicted by the SCU, from the highest level of military command to farmers who held no rank or membership in militia groups. During its five-year tenure beginning in 2000, the unit's reach in each of these investigations in terms of level of responsibility and volume of cases is highly unusual and impressive for a relatively small and modestly funded prosecution unit in a transitional justice setting. Yet, the Serious Crimes Unit and the Special Panels have been harshly criticized by the populace of East Timor and experts.[59] Given this quantitatively outstanding record of indictments leading to a high number of trials and convictions, how is it that the serious crimes process failed to meet international standards and public expectations? For reasons of length, we focus on the Serious Crimes Unit and only summarize our findings with respect to the Special Panels trials.[60]

While the SCU clearly did not receive all the resources it needed, it is important to compare what it did receive with the resources accorded other justice institutions within East Timor and other tribunals that have operated in response to a larger volume of atrocities. For example, in 2001, the Special Panels' budget was US$300,000, the Defense Lawyers Unit (DLU) received no UN budget at all, and US$6 million was allocated to the SCU. The results of this imbalance produced a situation that clearly violated the principle of equality of arms, a key element of international fair trial standards.[61] The following analysis therefore focuses on the consequences of decisions about the allocation and management of resources, particularly with regard to the effectiveness of prosecution efforts.

From the beginning of the investigations, in 2000, the SCU's mandate was ambiguous, both in terms of priorities and, as seen earlier, over the historical period under scrutiny. Due to factors such as pressure exerted by victims to indict lower-level perpetrators who were returning from West Timor, immediate needs at times conflicted with the SCU's pursuit of a mid- or long-term strategy to target those who were most responsible for human rights violations. This conflict between short-term and long-term demands on the judicial system and shifting priorities due to frequent replacement of key personnel were never sufficiently resolved and resulted in a constantly evolving, ad hoc approach to investigations and prosecutions.

In January 2002, the SCU came under new and far more competent leadership in the person of Siri Frigaard from Norway, appointed as Deputy Prosecutor-General. The result was a significant clarification of prosecutorial priorities and strategy, as well as an increase in resources for investigations. On the one hand, this resulted in a greatly expanded focus and increased staffing that allowed the allocation of significant resources to develop a case against the Indonesian command structure. On the other hand, just as this process was gathering momentum in spring 2002, UN Headquarters ordered the SCU to begin downsizing and to complete its investigations by 2004. According to this time frame, all trials were to be completed by May 2005, when all work was to be handed over to the Timorese Prosecutor General.

The challenging task of investigating the Indonesian military high command demanded substantial resources. Yet, because the Indonesian military personnel under investigation could not be brought into the custody of the court, none of these individuals was ever brought to trial. At the same time, cases of low-level Timorese perpetrators continued through the pipeline. With a change in leadership again after the departure of Frigaard, in mid-2003, the priorities that brought cases forward to trial became even more obscure. Because the SCU was never given adequate resources to both investigate the Indonesian high command and prosecute the very large numbers of low-level perpetrators against whom investigations had been opened, the result was that a large majority of the cases investigated could not be brought to trial. This situation was exacerbated by two factors. First, the SCU was unable to develop a coherent prosecution strategy that was commensurate with its resources and limitations and to implement that strategy consistently over the period of its operation. Second, the inefficiency and under-resourcing of the Special Panels, until a key change in personnel in early 2004, greatly increased the difficulty of moving cases through the system. While the UN Mission and Secretariat were aware of these difficulties, they failed to act decisively to address the problems in the first three and a half years of the process. It was only in its last year of operation, for example, that the administrative structure of the Special Panels was reorganized so as to improve its performance. Other issues, such as the lack of an adequate witness and victim protection and support regime, were never addressed.[62]

As a case study of the way in which SCU strategies were developed and resources allocated, we may consider the haphazard prioritization of gender crimes.[63] Both the KPP-HAM and the CAVR set a specific priority on gender-based violence from the beginning of their mandates. The SCU, for its part, at no point chose a gender-based crime in itself as one of its priority cases and failed to develop a coherent strategy involving the investigation of such crimes. The few cases where gender-based violence led to an indictment arose from investigations into murder that led to evidence of sexual violence. In some of these cases, this led to further investigation directed at sexual violence, but in almost all instances this further investigation did not result in prosecution, despite the discovery of compelling evidence involving significant numbers of victims.

When she took over the SCU in January 2002, Frigaard determined that the SCU should appoint a gender investigation team. This team's work, however, did not result in a significant redefinition of prosecutorial priorities over the long term. Frigaard explained to the public that the main reason for this obstacle was the lack of witnesses who were able to provide sound evidence and were willing to testify in public.[64] However, our own research in the SCU archives disclosed that SCU investigations collectively yielded a significant amount of strong evidence to prosecute gender-based violence as a crime against humanity and that at least several key witnesses had indicated their willingness to testify publicly and did so before the CAVR.[65] These cases included systematic rape and sexual enslavement directed against significant numbers of victims who were targeted because of their connection to the pro-independence movement. If the evidence was there, why, then, did the SCU not pursue this as a prosecutorial priority, and what was the impact of this decision on the overall achievements of the institution and the transitional justice system as a whole?

Evidence uncovered by our research team as part of our work with the Commission on Truth and Friendship revealed that gender-based violence was consistently overlooked in SCU investigations until the end of the period of investigations, in 2004. For example, a memorandum from an SCU prosecutor to an investigator who had been pursuing evidence regarding serious allegations of systematic rape in conjunction with a murder case "complains that there is 'superfluous evidence' in the file and states that the evidence of rape is not relevant to the investigation and might not be 'called priority offenses at all.' "[66]

Our research also revealed that the SCU failed to include charges of sexual violence in several other cases where the evidence was readily at hand in the case file. One case, for example, was left unprosecuted because of the perpetrator's claim that the victim was a prostitute. Not only was there no support in the case file for this allegation, but the investigators and the prosecution did not appear to find it relevant that at the time of the first of the series of acts of alleged sexual violence the victim was twelve years old and, hence, under the age of consent. This perpetrator was released based on a "lack of evidence," despite the fact that the investigators had provided documentation proving that the victim was in fact twelve years old at the time.

The indictments issued by SCU for rape as a crime against humanity included at least four systematic attacks of sexual violence on communities resulting in large numbers of victims: multiple women from Suai were raped,[67] multiple women in Cailaco were raped,[68] multiple women from Lolotoe were raped,[69] and multiple women in Atabae were raped.[70] The remaining indicted cases involve individual cases of rape followed by murder, but, as in all the cases, they provide very strong evidence that specific women were targeted for sexual violence precisely because of their pro-independence beliefs. The sexual violence was not random but rather a weapon used for political intimidation and repression. The acts alleged in these indictments occurred across multiple districts within West Timor (three in these indictments) and within multiple communities within these districts (three different locations in Bobonaro and two in Covalima) and were perpetrated by different militia groups (Laksaur, Mahidi, Halilintar, DMP, KMP) and by members of the Indonesian armed forces.[71]

Despite the clear magnitude of these crimes, the Serious Crimes Process resulted in only one successful conviction of rape as a crime against humanity and one successful conviction of rape as an "ordinary" crime.[72] Indeed, forms of gender-based violence other than rape were never prosecuted by the SCU, even, for example, cases that included evidence of abduction, enslavement, forced sterilization and forced marriage that might have led to further investigation and prosecution.[73]

What lessons can be learned from these aspects of the SCU's work? The Serious Crimes Unit consistently argued that it had to give priority to murder cases because it had to make choices, given its limited resources. However, by focusing on murders that happened in 1999, the justice process failed to adequately prosecute some of the most heinous and systematic crimes, particularly those committed against women. At the same time, a significant number of the murders investigated and tried involved low-level perpetrators charged with single acts of violence. This high degree of prosecutorial selectivity greatly inhibited the ability of the SCU and of the justice process as a whole to provide the Timorese people with a full and accurate account of the violence in 1999. The successful pursuit of the truth, including the truth of gender-based crimes, was therefore stymied by a specific interpretation of what it means to pursue effective prosecutions. Although the mandate for the SCU and SPSC clearly included the power to investigate sexual violations, in practice the body overwhelmingly prioritized murder investigations (which are far easier to investigate), rather than thoroughly investigating a smaller number of crimes that covered the range of their mandate and revealed the systematic terrorization, through a variety of means, of the Timorese civilian population associated with pro-independence groups.

The serious crimes process has been lauded as a success in quantitative terms on the basis of the volume of evidence com-

piled, indictments issued, and convictions achieved in relation
to the very modest expenditure on the justice process. There is
also no doubt that many individuals at the SCU and Special Panels worked with dedication and against the odds to achieve some
measure of accountability, despite their lack of access to the majority of the perpetrators they targeted. They experienced a daily confrontation with "rough justice."[74] However, the selectivity shown
in establishing prosecutorial priorities and the lack of a coherent
prosecution strategy to effectively allocate limited resources too
often overshadowed these good intentions and the unit's best accomplishments. For the SCU, the result was that resources were
expended to investigate some four hundred cases that could not
be brought to trial in time, while at the same time not enough
resources were devoted to many of the fifty-five cases that did go
to trial. The lack of sound and consistent management severely
and unnecessarily hindered the investigation and prosecution
processes. A weak, shifting, and incomplete prosecution strategy
also inherently skewed the representation of the conflict for the
historical record and may have decreased the likelihood that certain types of victims, for example victims of gender-based violence,
will receive justice through the courts in the future, as the likelihood that effective investigations can be completed in these cases
wanes with time. The failure to develop a coherent prosecution
strategy, to implement it fully, and to convey it to the Timorese
people through an integrated outreach program represents a key
source of victim dissatisfaction with the transitional justice process
in East Timor.

D. Serious Crimes Investigative Team (SCIT)

In early 2008, in East Timor, the UN-appointed Serious Crimes
Investigative Team (SCIT) began to address its mandate of com-
pleting the nearly four hundred open and incomplete investigations that remained from the original Serious Crimes Unit. These
case files had been left incomplete because of the UN decision to
terminate the justice process in May 2005. Perhaps in response to
widespread criticism for this decision, and with a large majority of
investigations incomplete, the UN created the SCIT.

The SCIT's task, still ongoing as of this writing, is to complete these investigations or to recommend the closure of cases. Because this team is working as an independent section of the United Nations Mission in East Timor (UNMIT), it has no authority to initiate a prosecution process or to compel the Timorese Prosecutor General to draft or file an indictment. Indeed, the government of East Timor has made it abundantly clear that it has no interest in seeking further prosecutions in its domestic justice system for crimes committed during the 1999 violence. The question arises whether the allocation of more resources for more investigations is going to result in more justice or, indeed, any tangible benefit for the Timorese people.

This issue is particularly pressing with regard to a process that is limited to investigation. Because of the confidentiality of investigations, the information gathered in these investigations cannot be made public unless there is an indictment or trial. How, then, can these investigations assist Timorese society in coming to terms with the violence of 1999?

The answer to these questions will depend on SCIT's strategy and the response of the Timorese government. The SCIT has already announced a "priority case" strategy so that it can complete the greatest number of investigations possible in a short period of time with its very limited resources. To date, fifty "priority" cases have been chosen for further investigation, far more than the approximately ten priority cases pursued by the SCU.[75] Twenty cases have already been submitted by SCIT to the Prosecutor General for consideration; however, these twenty cases are not from the group of uninvestigated cases remaining from 2005 but are cases that had already been indicted by the original SCU.[76] In this scenario, the target *number* of investigations is determining a large part of the judicial process, not necessarily the quality, in part because of the UN's unwillingness to assign the SCIT the full resources it needs to pursue the highest quality of investigations.

The specific insistence by the UN on including full-time Outreach and Gender Officers at SCIT and the recruitment of an international investigator who previously investigated sexual violations for the SCU suggests that sexual violence cases may be a higher priority for SCIT than they were for the SCU. However, staff indicate that murders will remain the top priority.[77] Therefore, the strategy and organization of the SCIT in terms of investigations appear largely the same as the SCU.

The degree of closure provided to victims by the SCIT will remain dependent on how effectively witnesses and families receive targeted information about their cases and on the support provided. Early, proactive public outreach efforts by the SCIT show some promise for this aspect of the process,[78] but more specific and consistent follow-ups will also need to be carried out by the individual investigation teams, as well as by civil society groups that provide support services, in order to have a lasting impact on the families who become part of the process. Previously, the SCU had extremely limited witness protection services and no formal victim relief or compensation programs.[79] The SCIT has been assigned no special victim support officers or unit: they will use the existing Vulnerable Person's Unit (VPU) within the East Timorese police system. A serious fault in this approach is that victims of mass murder or mass rape have very different needs from victims supported by the domestic judicial system's victim support teams, which specialize in crimes such as domestic violence and in the protection of children. Further, if indictments and trials do not ensue, as it appears they will not, how can the results of confidential investigations be disclosed to the public and victims' families?

It says quite a lot about the prospects for future accountability that, while the SCIT is working to enable future prosecutions, the East Timorese President, Jose Ramos Horta, has been pursuing an amnesty agenda. For example, in 2008, he issued a number of pardons to those who were convicted by the Special Panels and remained in jail. These included individuals who had been convicted of the most serious crimes brought before the Special Panels. More recently, President Horta pursued this policy by proposing a blanket amnesty law to Parliament in June 2009.[80] For all the reasons indicated earlier, even if SCIT is able to complete a large number of investigations, the current Timorese government has not shown any willingness to support further prosecutions. The Timorese government's public statements explaining this policy cite lack of capacity and resources and a desire to leave the past behind.[81] Whatever the real reasons may be, despite the efforts of the SCIT, there is no apparent political will on the part of the current Timorese leadership to address the demands of victims and to seek accountability.

In summary, although there are a number of improvements in the new SCIT institution, the majority of the limitations that faced the SCU remain intact. Political will, jurisdictional limitations, limited mandate, and a lack of resources and highly specialized expertise in all areas of the unit's operations will continue to hinder the prospects for effective prosecution of grave human rights violations in East Timor. The SCIT could become yet another institution whose quantitative achievements are overshadowed by its qualitative limitations.

E. Commission for Truth, Reception, and Reconciliation (CAVR)

The scale of the CAVR's activities sets it apart from other transitional justice institutions in the East Timor case.[82] No other institution dealt with such a large volume of victims and cases or at such an intimate level—in the local communities, in former sites of atrocity, and at the direction of the former victims who made up the Timorese Board of Commissioners. The question is to what degree this heavy allocation of responsibility, along with a high volume of activity and broad reach, allowed the Commission to achieve its goals and provide victims with the promised truth, justice, and reconciliation. A brief overview of some of the core activities for each of the mandated areas of the CAVR's work—truth, reconciliation, and healing—may assist in assessing how effective this institution was in achieving the aspirational goals stated in its mandate (truth and reconciliation), as well as contributing to some overall independent indicators of justice—effective prosecution and victim protection.

Truth Telling

The CAVR's truth-telling project was based on four methods of inquiry: statement taking, statistical data collection and analysis, public hearings, and document and secondary source analysis. The vast majority of this work was invested in statement taking, which resulted in the collection of nearly eight thousand statements. In addition to the collection of testimony and statistical data, the CAVR conducted public hearings organized around human rights themes. These hearings received widespread coverage on radio throughout the country.

The truth-seeking activities collectively formed the basis for the writing of the Commission's Final Report. The Final Report describes the Commission's work and contains thematic chapters with findings for various categories of violations, as well as an historical overview and a legal framework. An additional report was amended to the report that describes the human rights violations in 1999. Overall, the Final Report records compelling witness testimony and provides the only reliable statistical analysis of the human rights violations that occurred during the period of civil war in East Timor and the Indonesian occupation. The CAVR's Final Report is also the first and only comprehensive account of this period of history as told from the East Timorese perspective, and it deserves credit for reporting human rights abuses committed by Timorese, as well as Indonesian, parties to the conflict. Combined with other public educational and outreach activities, the CAVR contributed to the "truth-telling" function of transitional justice. On the other hand, the Post-CAVR follow-up institution has been engaged in dissemination for nearly three years now, and its results have been limited.[83]

Access to the "truth" produced by the CAVR is relevant to all areas of the Commission's work. For example, the Final Report is more than two thousand pages long and is written in a complex manner. The Commission created a shorter Executive Summary of the Report, but even this version is more than two hundred pages long. The Report was originally published only in English and Indonesian and then translated into Portuguese. A Tetum[84] version has not yet been produced.[85] Literacy rates are extremely low in East Timor, a problem that the CAVR has tackled with film and radio broadcasts, but this strategy does not convey the full extent of the institution's historical project and may not reach the broadest audience.[86] Therefore, a large proportion of the population may not be able to access the parts of the Final Report that are most relevant to their individual needs.

Finally, while the Final Report is generally regarded as credible and independent, as with any rendering of history, it is debatable to what degree it represents a complete or impartial truth. The uncontested nature of the truth-telling process and the lack of any verification or analysis of witness statements means that some parts of the Report may be more accurate than others. Although the Report acknowledges and describes human rights abuses committed by all sides of the conflicts, some participants have accused the Commission of not being inclusive enough of non-FRETILIN[87] and pro-autonomy supporters.[88] More important, until the history contained in the Final Report is accessible to all Timorese citizens in a language they can comprehend, the CAVR's mandate to provide truth and reconciliation will remain unfulfilled. The witness statements themselves remain confidential and are not accessible to the public or to researchers.

Reception and Reconciliation

The Community Reconciliation Process (CRP) was introduced earlier in order to explain the accountability framework of the transitional justice system as a whole. Now we will look more closely at this part of the CAVR's work to ask how it complemented the transitional justice system's overall task of pursuing effective prosecutions and also to what degree it contributed to peace through reconciliation and the protection of victims.

The CRP process was initiated by perpetrators, and the benefits were most tangibly theirs. They received immunity from prosecution without going through an extensive investigation process. Perpetrators also exerted greater control than victims over the CRP process in three respects:

1. Perpetrators initiated the process, and victims could not stop it once initiated, although they could individually choose not to participate in the proceedings.
2. Because perpetrators were themselves responsible for initiating their participation in the process, rather than participating in response to evidence or accusations from villagers, in any one village a mere handful of perpetrators may have chosen to come forward, while the rest remained silent.
3. The CAVR could not compel the truth from perpetrators about their violations. If a particular perpetrator told only partial truths and these were accepted as sufficient by the CRP panel appointed by the CAVR, the perpetrator could still receive immunity.[89]

Victims' views of the CRP process call into question the degree to which reconciliation, understood in terms of resolving and preventing conflict over past human rights abuses to preserve peace in the future, occurred. Victims have reported that their main motivation for participating in the process was to get information about the more serious crimes committed against their loved ones in order to fuel demands for accountability, rather than to contribute to a reconciliation process. Other victims report not being sufficiently informed by the CAVR because they did not adequately understand the process and their rights. Finally, the most common criticism of the process is that victims participated in CRPs with the expectation that the judicial process would prosecute offenders of serious crimes.[90] Without this complementary trial process, the victims may have granted immunity for the crimes that most directly affected them while receiving nothing in return. While the CAVR undoubtedly made a contribution to the short-term normalization of relations at the community level, the question remains whether this process then also qualifies as a legitimate contribution to justice, at least in its restorative form, and if it does, then how evenly and fairly this kind of justice was distributed to all members of Timorese society.

Victim Healing

Following its mandate, the CAVR also conducted the most extensive healing activities in the nation. These victim support activities were integrated into all aspects of the CAVR's public activities. For many victims, the CAVR's thirty-six-person victim support team may be the only organization that they will ever encounter that supports them because they have experienced grave human rights abuses. This aspect of the organization's work lends great credibility to the CAVR's claims that it was victim centered. However, the quality and quantity of support that these teams could provide was very small in proportion to the great numbers of victims who participated in the CAVR process. The victim support unit operated heroically but on meager resources that could never have been sufficient to cover the physical and psychological needs generated by such a large-scale truth-telling and reconciliation process.

Victim support staff acted in both reactive and proactive roles. During the statement-taking and CRP processes, staff responded to referrals when the CAVR identified individuals who demonstrated severe trauma or other forms of physical or mental vulnerability. Victim support staff also provided support to witnesses who participated in the public hearings. In addition, the victim support unit collaborated with several local nongovernmental organizations (NGOs) to administer an informal reparations program to approximately two hundred of the most vulnerable victims.[91] In addition to these reactive services, the Commission conducted its own research program in conjunction with its healing workshop series, called the Community Profiles.

In all the truth-telling forums of the CAVR, victims were asked to share their stories—a practice known to have the consequence of evoking traumatic memories and grief. The victim support team's primary task was to assist victims in this process so that the communal and individual exercise of remembrance and mourning could occur without re-traumatization. This is a delicate process, usually handled in clinical settings and incorporating both group and private therapies. In total, the team was responsible for at least fifteen thousand persons who participated in CAVR programs.[92] Yet, for this great responsibility, staff members (who were not required to have prior medical or counseling experience or qualifications) received only about two weeks of full-time training. The victim support team was assigned a Herculean task for which, despite the best of intentions, it was hardly equipped and that it could not adequately fulfill under the circumstances. This inadequate training and support system may explain why a common critique among victims is that the CAVR forced them to relive their trauma, but offered no concrete benefits to give them hope for the future. Local victim support staff members expressed awareness of the fact that they were not prepared to provide for the needs of many of their clients, and the staff still feel guilt and remorse about not being able to help victims more.[93]

Again, this circumstance raises the question of whether something is better than nothing and if more is necessarily more. In trying to address the needs of more victims, these activities contributed to the emotional harms of some victims, rather than offering them cautious protection. At the same time, while the number of persons involved in CAVR programs is significant,[94] it is a small fraction of the total number of victims, which includes some 250,000 Timorese who were forcibly transferred or deported from their home villages, typically accompanied by the destruction of all or most of their property and concomitant violence, terror, and intimidation.

The CAVR can justifiably claim that it made contributions to the truth and peace aspirations of transitional justice. Some may argue that the CRPs at the community level provided some justice when the only other option was none, and others may contend that the CRPs required too great a compromise because they sacrificed justice and a complete form of the truth. As with the SCU and Special Panels process, the limitations of the CRPs' work are many and the tangible benefits felt by victims have been few. The scope and depth of the CAVR's work were ambitious and admirable in many ways, but perhaps it is precisely the expansiveness of the institution's vision in relation to its resources that compromised the quality of the provision of some of its basic services. A number of publications, cited in this chapter, have documented the shortcomings of the judicial processes for East Timor, but there has been insufficient scrutiny of the truth commission's role in the overall effectiveness of the transitional justice system. However, this evaluation of the CAVR shows that the responsibility for the inadequacies of the transitional justice system is shared among all the transitional justice institutions in East Timor and cannot be attributed to the limitations of the judicial process alone.

F. Commission of Truth and Friendship of East Timor and Indonesia (CTF)

In 2005, Timor-Leste and Indonesia jointly embarked on a new turn in transitional justice—a bilateral truth commission with a diplomatic mandate. The Commission of Truth and Friendship of East Timor and Indonesia (CTF) conducted "truth-seeking" activities for the purpose of promoting reconciliation between East Timorese in East Timor and those who were still living estranged in West Timor and between the two states of Indonesia and Timor-Leste. The Commission's ostensible goal was to promote sustainable peace between the two countries.

The Commission of Truth and Friendship was the most controversial mechanism within the transitional justice schema. Denounced by the UN and by local and international human rights activists, the Commission was criticized because its mandate contained specific prohibitions against recommendations for prosecution and enabled it (like many truth commissions) to recommend amnesty and legal rehabilitation. Many observers accused the CTF of either being repetitive or denigrating the CAVR's work in establishing the truth about Indonesia's participation in human rights abuses. In short, the Commission of Truth and Friendship had the potential to undo all the work done by all the previous transitional justice mechanisms by recommending amnesties for the most senior Indonesian military and government leaders and the most active Timorese militia leaders. The CTF therefore raises the question once again: is more actually more? Did the transitional justice system in East Timor need another truth commission?

Institutional Responsibility and Moral Reparations

The unique powers of the CTF within this schema resided in its ability to incorporate all the previous processes into its review of their documentary record (Document Review) and to fully integrate the Indonesian, pro-autonomy perspective into the historical record and reconciliatory efforts. Because of its mandate to establish the truth about the institutions responsible for gross human rights violations in 1999, it was also positioned to correct some of the incompleteness and inaccuracy of the historical record left by the trials before the Jakarta Ad Hoc Human Rights Court. Finally, because its mandate to address institutional responsibility was far broader than the task of the Special Panels in trials involving low-level perpetrators, it was better positioned to examine the systematic nature of the violence perpetrated in East Timor and to assess the roles of the different institutions involved. The constructive participation of certain Indonesian commissioners who had expert knowledge of these institutions was an asset not enjoyed by any of the previous transitional justice mechanisms and enabled the Commission to contribute to an understanding of the role of these institutions in the violence.

All of the previous transitional justice mechanisms in both countries addressed institutional responsibility and reparations; however, the CTF was the only one to achieve certain tangible outcomes: (1) the creation of a framework for long-term institutional responsibility, particularly for the reform of military and security forces in both countries, and (2) a public and formal apology by both governments to victims of human rights abuses.

Underlying these achievements was the acceptance by both governments of uncomfortable "truths" about the commission of human rights abuses as delineated at length in the Report and based mostly on the more detailed evidence and analysis compiled in the results of the Commission's Document Review process.[95] In the case of Indonesia, the government accepted the Commission's findings that the Indonesian military and civilian institutions were responsible for the vast majority of grave violations of human rights committed in East Timor in 1999, specifically in the form of crimes against humanity, and for the systematic perpetration of murder, torture, unlawful detention, sexual violations, forced transfer, and deportation. The Indonesian government also had to expressly accept responsibility for all the crimes committed by the Timorese armed pro-autonomy militia groups that the Commission found it had created, supported, and controlled for its own political purposes. The government of Timor-Leste, on the other hand, had to accept responsibility for human rights violations committed by pro-independence groups in East Timor in 1999, in particular illegal detention.[96]

These uncomfortable truths were not surprising to the Timorese public, but the admission of these truths for an Indonesian audience was especially meaningful because, for the many Indonesians who, prior to 1998, had received only censored news, it was the first real exposure to the truth about the atrocities committed in East Timor during Indonesian rule. It was certainly the first time that the Indonesian government had in any way accepted its involvement in such crimes, let alone assumed full responsibility for them, as the President of Indonesia did when he accepted the Report without qualification. In the context of Indonesia's era of democratic reforms, this acceptance of responsibility for systematic gross human rights violations and of recommendations that call for far-reaching reform of the military, police, and state accountability mechanisms has the potential to be transformational. Whether this potential will be fulfilled rests on the fate of ongoing fundamental reform processes aimed at ending the military's continued influence on the democratic system and its operation outside the rule of law. Initial signs have not been promising, and some members of the Timorese government appear to regard these recommendations as applying only to Indonesia, despite the instability within Timor-Leste's own armed forces and police institutions.

Aside from these abstract political and military calculations of potential reforms, what did the victims gain from this process? The CTF can make no claim to being a victim-centered or protective process. Procedurally, its efforts to incorporate victims' perspectives in the truth-telling process were weaker than those of any of the other transitional justice mechanisms except the Jakarta Ad Hoc Court, and it made no efforts to provide for victim support, witness protection, or reparations measures in its activities. The Commission did not include a single victim (other than the commissioners themselves) in its closing ceremony, and not a single victim has received a copy of its Final Report to date.[97]

On the other hand, the CTF Final Report may be seen as a catalyst to move collective forms of reparatory justice forward, and there are signs that this has indeed already been the case.[98] The existence of future programs for victims will require significant input of political will by both nations. How well these forms of reparations respond to victims' needs will again be contingent on the subsequent bilateral bodies that design and implement these programs and, ultimately, on the political will of the governments that create them.

The CTF's contributions to justice, truth, and peace can be secured only if it is used to deepen knowledge about and to improve systems of accountability, as opposed to promoting the already persistent culture of impunity in both Indonesia and East Timor. It is also important to bear in mind that the CTF addressed only violations committed in 1999, and all the human rights violations committed between 1974 and 1999 in East Timor remain uninvestigated and unpunished.

The CTF's achievements in terms of institutional responsibility and moral reparations may seem to have added something "more" to the transitional justice accomplishments in East Timor. Its ability to build upon the previous transitional justice institutions' accomplishments may have enabled its own research process to achieve its mandate of fixing institutional responsibility for gross human rights violations in East Timor. Although it lacked any substantial investigative resources of its own, its ability to access and incorporate the evidence compiled by the other bodies was key to this successful aspect of its work. These achievements, however, have been severely compromised by its failures to incorporate victims and other forms of outreach into its work and its lack of transparency and follow-through. Furthermore, as demonstrated with the earlier transitional justice mechanisms, the CTF could not cooperate with the other institutions or develop a plan that could compensate fully for the impunity gaps created by the relationship among the other institutions. Although it added something new to the transitional justice scheme, "new" does not necessarily mean "more" to victims. Victims have not felt any radical change in the pervasive state of impunity, and it remains an open question to what extent the contents of the CTF Report will ever be communicated to them in a meaningful way.

VI. Final Reflections

How did the transitional justice system as a whole perform in comparison to the standards enumerated earlier? In terms of aspirational goals—truth, justice, and peace—there were many outcomes that at times complemented but at other times conflicted with each other.

Taken in its entirety, the transitional justice system in East Timor demonstrates the inherent resistance of all of these institutions to provide closure through truth, justice, and peace working in orchestration. In every case, a new mechanism was added, but these aspirational goals of transitional justice remained elusive or incomplete and created yet another opening for another try at a more acceptable outcome. Along the way, many truths were revealed, but these, too, remain incomplete in the absence of thorough investigations. Accountability also remains elusive in that the trials in East Timor focused only on the conviction of low-level perpetrators who were ultimately released before serving their full minimum sentences, while trials in Indonesia ultimately resulted in acquittals. The trials in both countries failed to meet minimum international fair trial standards in significant respects. The senior leadership of the Indonesian military has enjoyed complete impunity.

Formal peace between the nations has been maintained, but the quality of both national and local reconciliation remains in question. Do these collective experiments in justice amount to something that justifies the expense, the frustrations, and the continuing impunity? Not in the instances demonstrated in each mechanism where the institution failed fully to complete its tasks due to willful incompetence or greed, lack of political will, misguided good intentions, or blatant political manipulation.

One victim who was involved in at least three of the transitional justice mechanisms discussed in this chapter characterized the problem of justice in East Timor as follows: "*Ami koalia, koalia, koalia konaba justisa, maibe realidade . . . la iha,*" or "We talk and talk and talk about justice, but the reality is . . . there isn't any."[99] This woman's observations must act as a cautionary tale to all those who participate in the collective process of theorizing, designing, choosing, and supporting transitional justice mechanisms. East Timor's case study may provide an example to executives and governments who make the final decisions about what kinds of transitional justice mechanisms will be adopted. East Timor may also provide valuable lessons for administrators of either judicial or non-judicial accountability mechanisms. Donor communities may also look to the experience of East Timor to frame discussions about how and where their money could best be distributed within transitional justice programs. In the case of East Timor, these elaborate designs have obviously failed to provide the quality of satisfaction of justice and protection that victims deserve. But, what is the alternative?

The alternative would be to decide on a limited regime of mechanisms commensurate with the available resources, the political will of key players, and the difficulty of the challenges in the particular post-conflict context. The evaluation of these factors and of the prospects for the transitional justice regime must be made on the basis of a careful and realistic assessment of the actual circumstances, rather than on the basis of wishful thinking, empty promises, and cosmetic responses to international pressure and outrage that are likely to diminish as time passes and new crises emerge. The alternative is thus to create mechanisms where the conditions (resources, commitment, appropriate circumstances) exist to carry the process through to its mandated conclusion. Above all, it requires being honest in the face of the demands and the suffering of victims who clamor for justice and redress by not promising them more than can with certainty be delivered. The irresponsible raising of victims' expectations by UN personnel unwilling to explain thoroughly to the Timorese the truth about the inevitably limited outcomes of the transitional justice process in terms of its ability to hold accountable the perpetrators who acted in their localities or even those "most responsible" within the Indonesian military and government, to find out the complete truth or even to create sustained peace is one of the most tragic—and one of the most easily avoidable—outcomes of the ten years of transitional justice in East Timor.

The implementation of such an alternative to transitional justice mechanisms growing out of a realistic assessment of what it is actually possible to achieve requires a concentration of resources commensurate with an appropriately narrow and clearly defined mandate. It requires an absolute commitment to furnish the human and other resources necessary to ensure fulfillment of applicable international standards and complete the mandate, no matter how long it takes.

The success of an institution that would avoid these failings depends on establishing very limited priorities and tasks that it realistically can competently accomplish. In the case of a country like East Timor, where investment of resources on the scale of tribunals like the International Criminal Tribunal for the former Yugoslavia (ICTY) is obviously unlikely, a realistic mandate would inevitably involve the acceptance of a symbolic justice and a serious consideration of the limitations of a holistic model that tries to meet all of the goals that tribunals and truth commissions are said to fulfill. At the very least, it would require a degree of oversight and consensus among institutions that are operating in the same system that has not yet been experienced in East Timor or elsewhere. It would also depend upon an adequate degree of political will, including the will to provide necessary resources that have been notably lacking not only in East Timor but probably in every other transitional justice institution except the "showcase" model, the ICTY.

But such a process, as indicated earlier, would leave the work of justice incomplete. It will never be the case that all of the hundreds of thousands of victims find the closure, meaning, healing, and justice they seek. That is the brute fact of the limits of transitional justice in the face of mass atrocity. The question is how to define what can be done in each individual context and best bring into balance the competing goals of transitional justice. If this task is honestly faced, it will inevitably involve hard and uncomfortable choices.

The case of East Timor provides a valuable lesson in humility to us all: the logic of "more" transitional justice is incompatible with the logic of mass violence. Sadly, "more" will never be "enough" to respond to the scale of inhumanity entailed by the commission of grave human rights violations. The acceptance of this reality does not mean the abandonment of hope. Rather, our job may be best redefined to create more modest transitional justice systems that are streamlined, realistic, competently implemented, and able to do at least one job well—in all areas of evaluation—whether in the form of a tribunal, a truth commission, an investigative body, or some other mechanism. The deployment of multiple mechanisms may sound promising but is far more difficult to implement in a world of limited resources, "donor fatigue," uncooperative national institutions, difficult operational conditions, and conflicting political interests.

The real issue is not the format but rather the ability to carry through on the promises made to victims in the concrete transitional context that the international community has decided to address. These promises are made in myriad ways but most concretely in the implicit and explicit content of transitional justice institution mandates. Fulfilling any one of these promises, whether through accountability, truth, or reconciliation, requires a degree of sustained effort that has only rarely been evidenced in transitional contexts. This suggests that "less may be more," in that limited focus and concentration of resources and competencies may permit the achievement of more modest but, perhaps to victims, more meaningful goals.

As the East Timor case study reveals, achieving even modest goals depends not upon decisions made in the abstract about transitional justice but rather upon clear-eyed and realistic analysis of what is achievable in the circumstances at hand, including the degree of political will of international and national actors. This further requires the establishment of clear priorities and evaluative standards in light of available resources, the development of a coherent plan for implementation, the recruitment of adequate numbers of properly qualified staff, and the development of effective training and capacity-building programs so that the effort can be sustained by national actors. Above all, however, it requires the honest and effective communication of those goals, and the means to achieve them, to the victims, the general population, and the relevant national institutions. It further requires a steady commitment to outreach and legacy, that is, to the communication of the progress and results of the process, particularly to those who have been most affected by the violence. Without the ongoing understanding, cooperation, and approval of these groups, the best of efforts, as we have seen in East Timor, are likely to remain ineffective, misguided, or misunderstood.

NOTES

1. See also Bronwyn Anne Leebaw, "The Irreconcilable Goals of Transitional Justice," *Human Rights Quarterly* 30 (2008) 95–118.

2. "East Timor" is conventionally used to denote the country prior to independence. "Timor-Leste" is the preferred term for after independence. Because our study discusses both of these time frames, for simplicity we use primarily "East Timor."

3. For a summary and analysis of the development of the transitional justice field, see Ruti G. Teitel, "Transitional Justice Geneology," *Harvard Human Rights Journal* 16 (2003): 69–94.

4. East Timor's case also adds a new dimension to their discussion by featuring a supranational transitional justice system in a contemporary Southeast Asian setting, which was not included in their previous set of cases for analysis. See Eric A. Posner and Adrian Vermeule, "Transitional Justice as Ordinary Justice," *Harvard Law Review* 117 (2004): 761–825.

5. See also UN Secretary General's Report, "The Rule of Law and Transitional Justice in Conflict and Post-Conflict Societies," S/2004/616, 2004; Laurel Fletcher and Harvey Weinstein, "Violence and Social Repair: Rethinking the Contribution of Justice to Reconciliation," *Human Rights Quarterly* 24 (2002): 573–639; Eric Stover and Harvey Weinstein, eds., *My Neighbor, My Enemy: Justice and Community in the Aftermath of Mass Atrocity* (Cambridge: Cambridge University Press, 2004); Paul Gready, "Reconceptualising Transitional Justice: Embedded and Distanced Justice," *Conflict, Security and Development* 5, no. 1 (2005): 3–21.

6. Kosovo would provide a similar framework for discussion.

7. One should note that its degree of poverty and the total absence of judicial professionals were severe in contrast to some other contexts. During the Indonesian occupation, East Timorese were banned from holding

positions of high legal authority. This meant that in 1999, after Indonesia withdrew, there were no East Timorese judges or prosecutors, although there was a group of Indonesian-trained East Timorese lawyers. In terms of poverty, East Timor currently ranks 141 out of 178 on the Human Development Index, which marks it as the poorest country in Asia. The countries ranking below East Timor on this index include many of the African nations where transitional justice programs are ongoing and Haiti.

8. For a survey of East Timorese opinions about transitional justice, see Piers Pigou, *Crying Without Tears: In Pursuit of Justice and Reconciliation in Timor-Leste: Community Perspectives and Expectations* (New York: International Center for Transitional Justice, 2003).

9. For further background on the political history of East Timor up to 1999, see James Dunn, *A Rough Passage to Independence* (Double Bay, N.S.W, Australia: Lougueville Books, 2003); Brad Simpson, "'Illegally and Beautifully': The United States, the Indonesian Invasion of East Timor and the International Community, 1974–1976," *Cold War History* 5, no. 3 (2005): 281–315; John Taylor, *East Timor: The Price of Freedom* (New York: St. Martins Press, 1999); Helen Hill, *Stirrings of Nationalism in East Timor: FRETILIN 1974–1978* (Otford, N.S.W.: Otford Press, 2002).

10. The best academic account of the history of violence in East Timor in 1999 is Geoffrey Robinson, *East Timor 1999: Crimes Against Humanity* (Geneva: United Nations Office of the High Commissioner for Human Rights, 2003). This Report was an addendum to the CAVR's Final Report and can be accessed at http://www.cavr-timorleste.org.

11. For further information on the postindependence period, see James Fox and Dionisio Babo Soares, eds., *Out of the Ashes: Destruction and Reconstruction in East Timor* (Adelaide, S. Aust.: Crawford House, 2000), and Damien Kingsbury and Michael Leach, eds., *East Timor: Beyond Independence* (Caulfield East, Vic.: Monash University Press, 2007).

12. For further reading on the UN administration of East Timor, see Hansjoerg Strohmeyer, "Collapse and Reconstruction of a Judicial System: The United Nations Missions in Kosovo and East Timor," *American Journal of International Law* 95, no. 1 (2001): 46–63; Simon Chesterman, *Justice Under International Administration: Kosovo, East Timor and Afghanistan*, Transitional Administrations (New York: International Peace Academy, 2002); Anthony Goldstone, "UNTAET with Hindsight: The Peculiarities of Politics in an Incomplete State," *Global Governance* 10 (2004): 83–98; Jaret Chopra, "The UN's Kingdom of East Timor," *Survival* 42, no. 3 (2000): 27–39; Paulo Gorjão, "The Legacy and Lessons of the United Nations Transitional Administration in East Timor," *Contemporary Southeast Asia* 24, no. 2 (2002): 313–36.

13. For further reading on Indonesia's political transition, see Marco Bunte and Andreas Ufen, eds., *Democratization in Post-Suharto Indonesia*

(New York: Routledge, 2008); Marcus Mietzner, *The Politics of Military Reform in Post-Suharto Indonesia: Elite Conflict, Nationalism and Institutional Resistance* (Washington, DC: East West Center Washington, 2006); Arief Budiman, Barbara Hatley, and Damien Kingsbury, eds., *Reformasi: Crisis and Change in Indonesia*, Monash Papers on Southeast Asia, no. 50 (Melbourne: Monash Asia Institute, 1999).

14. See the Executive Summary of the report at http://www.etan.org/news/2000a/3exec.htm. For further information on the KPP-HAM process, see David Cohen, *Intended to Fail: Trials Before the Jakarta Ad Hoc Human Rights Court* (New York: International Center for Transitional Justice, 2004); *The CTF Final Report*, 75–87; and *Report of the Expert Advisor*, chap. 2, all available on the Berkeley War Crimes Center website, http://socrates .berkeley.edu/~warcrime/East_Timor_and_Indonesia.

15. For further information on the Jakarta Ad Hoc trials, see Cohen, *Intended to Fail*, and Suzannah Linton, "Unravelling the First Three Trials at Indonesia's Ad Hoc Court for Human Rights Violations in East Timor," *Leiden Journal of International Law* 17 (2004): 303–61.

16. For more background on the SPSC, SCU, and DLU, see David Cohen, "Seeking Justice on the Cheap: Is the East Timor Tribunal Really a Model for the Future?," *East-West Center, Asia Pacific Issues*, no. 61 (2002); Caitlin Reiger and Marieka Wierda, *The Serious Crimes Process in Timor-Leste: In Retrospect*, Prosecutions Case Studies 48 (New York: International Center for Transitional Justice, 2006); Suzannah Linton, "Prosecuting Atrocities at the District Court of Dili," *Melbourne Journal of International Law* 2 (2001): 414–58; Megan Hirst and Howard Varney, *Justice Abandoned? An Assessment of the Serious Crimes Process in East Timor*, Occasional Paper Series 33 (New York: International Center for Transitional Justice, 2005); David Cohen, *Indifference and Accountability: The United Nations and the Politics of International Justice in East Timor* (Honolulu, HI: East West Center, 2006); Suzanne Katzenstein, "Hybrid Tribunals: Searching for Justice in East Timor," *Harvard Human Rights Law Review* 16 (2003): 245–78.

17. For further information on the CAVR, see Patrick Burgess, "Justice and Reconciliation in East Timor: The Relationship Between the Commission of Truth, Reception and Reconciliation and the Courts," *Criminal Law Forum* 15 (2004): 135–58; Carsten Stahn, "Accommodating Individual Responsibility and National Reconciliation: The UN Truth Commission for East Timor," *American Journal for International Law* 95, no. 4 (2001): 952–66; Monika Schlicher, *East Timor Faces Up to Its Past: the Work of the Commission for Reception, Truth and Reconciliation* (Aachen, Germany: Pontifical Mission Society, Human Rights Office, 2005).

18. For more information on the CRPs, see Ben Larke, "'And the Truth Shall Set You Free': Confessional Trade-Offs and Community Reconciliation in East Timor," *Asian Journal of Social Science* 37, no. 4 (2009): 646–76;

Lia Kent, *Unfulfilled Expectations: Community Views on CAVR's Community Reconciliation Process* (Dili: Judicial System Monitoring Programme, 2004); Piers Pigou, *The Community Reconciliation Process of the Commission for Reception, Truth and Reconciliation* (New York: UN Development Programme, 2004); Spencer Zifcak, *Restorative Justice in East Timor: An Evaluation of the Community Reconciliation Process of the CAVR* (Asia Foundation, 2004).

19. On the relationship of the CAVR to the SCU, see Burgess, "Justice and Reconciliation in East Timor."

20. For further information on the CTF, see its *Final Report* at the Berkeley War Crimes Studies Center website, http://warcrimescenter.berkeley.edu, and Megan Hirst, *Too Much Friendship, Too Little Truth: Monitoring Report on the Commission of Truth and Friendship in Indonesia and Timor-Leste* (New York: International Center for Transitional Justice, 2008); Hirst, *An Unfinished Truth: An Analysis of the Commission of Truth and Friendship's Final Report on the 1999 Atrocities in East Timor* (New York: International Center for Transitional Justice, 2009).

21. Under UNTAET regulations, the exclusive jurisdiction of the Special Panels applied only to crimes committed from January 1 to October 25, 1999 (UNTAET 2000/15 Art. 2.3). Under UNTAET 2001/25 (amending UNTAET 2000/11), the District Courts of East Timor could exercise jurisdiction over serious crimes committed outside the dates defining the exclusive jurisdiction of the Special Panels. There was no jurisdictional bar to the Special Panels hearing cases involving crimes committed before 1999. In practice, however, no such cases were ever brought.

22. See the citations in the previous section to review some of the critical studies for each institution.

23. A recent study by Elizabeth Stanley evaluated the impact of the collective transitional justice institutions from the perspective of torture survivors. Her study can act as another kind of model for examining holistic approaches to justice. See Elizabeth Stanley, *Torture, Truth and Justice: The Case of Timor-Leste* (London: Routledge, 2009).

24. Our access to these materials arose from our engagement in a variety of capacities over the past eight years with the Special Panels for Serious Crimes, the Jakarta ad Hoc Human Rights Court, the KPP-HAM, and the Commission on Truth and Friendship.

25. For example, in the case of East Timor, the most specific mandate the Security Council gave the hybrid tribunal system was to hold accountable those "most responsible" for human rights abuses. The SCU had difficulty defining its prosecution strategies in part because of the vagueness of this mandate (author's field notes from observation at "The Legacy of the Serious Crimes Process" Conference, Bangkok, May 2006).

26. See the "Rule of Law Tools for Post-Conflict States" series available on the website of the UN High Commissioner for Human Rights and the

various manuals published by the International Center for Transitional Justice.

27. For such accounts, see "I Tried to Build a House of Peace, Interview with General Wiranto," *Time Asia*, February 28, 2000, http://www.time.com/time/asia/magazine/2000/0228/indonesia.wiranto.html. The testimony given to the CTF by Indonesian military and government officials in 2007 maintained the same arguments. See Hirst, *Too Much Friendship, Too Little Truth*.

28. National Commission of Inquiry into Human Rights Violations in East Timor (KPP-HAM), *Report of the Indonesian Investigative Commission into Human Rights Violations in East Timor*, Jakarta, January 2000, p. 21, no. 72. Hereafter, *KPP-HAM Final Report*.

29. With regard to sexual violence, the KPP-HAM Report largely relied on the investigations of other bodies and for the most part did not go beyond their findings.

30. *KPP-HAM Final Report*, p. 21, no. 72.

31. Ibid., no. 75.

32. Ibid., no. 86.

33. See "Executive Summary," *KPP-HAM Final Report*, available online at http://www.etan.org/news/2000a/3exec.htm.

34. Ibid.

35. For more details on the transition to democracy and transitional justice choices made in Chile, see Jorge Correa Sutil, " 'No Victorious Army Has Ever Been Prosecuted': The Unsettling Story of Transitional Justice in Chile," in *Transitional Justice and the Rule of Law in New Democracies*, ed. A. James McAdams (Notre Dame, IN: University of Notre Dame Press, 1997), 123–54, and Greg Grandin, "The Instruction of Great Catastrophe: Truth Commissions, National History and State Formation in Argentina, Chile and Guatamala," *American Historical Review* 100, no. 1 (2005): 46–58.

36. Decree KEP-070/JA/04/2000.

37. Established under Law 26/2000 to hear cases of gross human rights violations.

38. The Indonesian system is based on a civil law model. Unlike the common law system, the judges already have the evidence before them when the trial begins in the form of a case dossier, the BAP. The case file is thus the key element in determining the course of the trial. The judges may, however, request the production of additional evidence, whether in the form of witnesses or physical evidence.

39. These elements are contained in the law establishing the Jakarta Ad Hoc Court, RI Law no. 26/2000, Article 42.

40. For further analysis of the case files, see the sections on the BAPs in "Expert Advisor's Report to the CTF: Seeking Truth and Accountability," *CTF Final Report*.

41. On the Chapeau Elements required for crimes against humanity, see ICTY Appeals Chamber Judgment in the Kunarac Case, paragraphs 88–106.

42. "Expert Advisor's Report to the CTF."

43. For a detailed account of the problems, see Cohen, *Intended to Fail*, 37–50.

44. Cohen, *Intended to Fail*.

45. For more background on judicial independence in Indonesia, see Tim Lindsey and Mas Achmad Santosa, "The Trajectory of Law Reform in Indonesia: A Short Overview of Legal Systems and Change in Indonesia," in *Indonesia: Law and Society*, 2nd ed., ed. Tim Lindsey (Sydney: Federation Press, 2008), 2–22.

46. Gutteres was acquited and released in 2008 by the Supreme Court of Indonesia on the basis of new evidence. A judge involved in the decision, Supreme Judge Joko Sarwoko, told reporters Gutteres "was not proven to have structural command to coordinate attacks, even if he was the leader of the militia, so he could not be held responsible for the violence." "Indonesia Releases Former East Timor Militia Leader," *Jakarta Post*, April 5, 2008, http://www.etan.org/et2008/4april/05/05court.htm.

47. For a discussion of each of the trials, see Cohen, *Intended to Fail*, and Linton, *Unravelling the First Three Trials*.

48. It is to their credit, however, that, during the course of the trials, a group of judges requested that David Cohen organize a training seminar in international criminal law for them and made the most of the opportunity when it took place in 2003.

49. During the first three trials, uniformed members of the Aitarak Militia were often present at the trial of their commander, Eurico Gutteres. Gutteres himself and some followers attended the two other trials under way at the same time. The judges felt unable to prevent such behavior.

50. It must be added, however, that part, though only part, of the problem involved the reluctance of some Timorese to travel to Indonesia to testify.

51. "East Timor Human Rights Trials: All Just a Game," *Jakarta Post*, December 26, 2002; Aboeprijadi Santoso, "Jakarta Rights Tribunal Buries East Timor Atrocities," *Jakarta Post*, August 21, 2003; Jill Jolliffe, "Jakarta's Timor Trials a Sham," *The Age*, June 19, 2005.

52. The most capable prosecutor to appear in any of the twelve trials, Mohamed Yusuf, was assigned to the Eurico Gutteres Case. One might speculate as to whether this was coincidence or whether it was due to the fact that Gutteres was the only accused who was not an Indonesian citizen and government official or military officer. In other words, he was the most easily expendable.

53. This was manifested most blatantly in the fact that nearly all of the

witnesses called by the prosecution actually testified in favor of the defense. No attempt was made by the prosecutors to rebut this highly damaging testimony. These witnesses were subordinates, colleagues, and co-defendants of the accused, all still on active duty.

54. Most of the significant evidence contained in the case files was never brought into court. See Cohen, *Intended to Fail.*

55. For an analysis of the Damiri Appeals Judgment, see David Cohen, *International Law and Command Responsibility in the Adam Damiri Case at the Indonesia Ad Hoc Human Rights Court* [in Bahasa Indonesia] (Jakarta: ELSAM, 2007).

56. On the Damiri trial, see Cohen, *Intended to Fail*, 23–28 and 62–64. On the failings of the appellate review, see *CTF Final Report*, 99–105.

57. Appeals were heard by the Court of Appeal, which functioned both as the highest court (and only appellate body) in the Timorese justice system and as the appellate body for the Special Panels.

58. All of these statistics were taken from: Judicial Systems Monitoring Program (JSMP), "Overview of the Timor-Leste Judicial Sector 2005," JSMP, http://www.jsmp.minihub.org/Reports/.

59. See Cohen, "Seeking Justice on the Cheap" and *Indifference and Accountability*; Hirst and Varney, *Justice Abandoned?*; Linton, "Prosecuting Atrocities at the District Court of Dili"; and Reiger and Wierda, *The Serious Crimes Process in Timor-Leste.*

60. For more details regarding the Special Panels as a separate entity, see David Cohen, *Indifference and Accountability.*

61. The due process legal principle guarantees the procedural equality of the defense and the prosecution in criminal proceedings. This principle implies that the defense should never be placed at a substantial disadvantage relative to the prosecution in a way that would jeopardize the fairness or effectiveness of the trial. The principle can be explicitly stated in court statutes or regulations, but it does not have to be in order to apply based on international customary law and the rights of the defendant stipulated in Article 14 (d) of the ICCPR.

62. In 2003–2004, the entire witness protection unit consisted of one low-level international staff member, one local staff member who served as a driver, and one vehicle. Despite the repeated requests by the international staff member for more resources to deal, for example, with reported cases of witness intimidation, such needs were never addressed.

63. The SCU also did not prioritize the investigation of crimes committed by pro-independence groups. There is some justification for this imbalance because it was clear to all observers that the vast majority of crimes were perpetrated against pro-independence supporters. But, since the SCU decided to prosecute mostly individual murders rather than crimes against humanity, the justification for not fully investigating allegations

of murders by pro-independence groups is unclear. There were some attempts to do so, such as in the notoriously botched Victor Alves case (see Cohen, *Indifference and Accountability*), but no systematic examination of the scope of such crimes.

64. Hirst and Varney, *Justice Abandoned?*

65. For a full account of this evidence, see David Cohen, Aviva Nababan, and Leigh-Ashley Lipscomb, "Seeking Truth and Accountability: The Report of the Expert Advisor to the CTF: Parts I and II," Appendices to *CTF Final Report* (April 2008).

66. Cited in Cohen and Lipscomb, "Seeking Truth and Accountability," Part II.

67. See Indictment, Case #9/200.

68. See Indictment, Case #15/2003.

69. The Lolotoe cases were tried in three separate trials. See Indictments and Judgments for Cases #4a/2001, #4b/2001, and #4c/2001.

70. See Indictment, Case #8/2002.

71. *CTF Final Report*, 229–231.

72. In January 2010, a Special Panels panel was reconvened in the Dili District Court to hear a case involving a defendant who came into Timor-Leste's jurisdiction and was indicted by the SCU on charges of rape and murder as crimes against humanity (Case #8/2004). The defendant, Domingos Noronha (aka Mau Buti), was convicted of three counts of murder as a crime against humanity by the court of first instance, but not on the rape charges. He is currently serving a sixteen-year prison sentence.

73. In total, the SCU issued eight indictments (out of ninety-five) for gender-based crimes. Six of these indictments charged rape as crimes against humanity. Of these six, only one case went to trial, and it yielded the only conviction for rape as a crime against humanity. The SCU issued the other two indictments for "simple" rape. One of these cases was dismissed for lack of jurisdiction (the crime took place in West Timor), and the other, for a single act of rape, resulted in a conviction of four years of imprisonment.

74. See Adrian Vermeule, "Reparations as Rough Justice," in this volume.

75. Although there were ten priority cases designated by the SCU, which ten cases were classified as such shifted throughout the SCU's mandate. Therefore, in real terms, more than ten cases were pursued by the SCU as priority, but fewer than ten were pursued consistently.

76. UNMIT, "Transcript of Press Briefing, 2008," http://unmit.un missions.org/Default.aspx?tabid=216&ctl=Details&mid=628&Itemid=355.

77. SCIT staff members, personal communication with Leigh-Ashley Lipscomb, July–August 2008.

78. SCIT has held a number of town hall meetings throughout the country and met with victim advocacy groups to explain the SCIT process.

Many of these meetings included representatives of the former SCU and CAVR, who explained those institutions' roles in the transitional justice system, as well. SCIT also disseminated an information pamphlet in the local language of Tetum.

79. Some personnel at the SCU provided victims with assistance on a personal basis, but an institutional program to support victims, such as the one at the ICTR, did not exist. The SCU did participate in a memorial project for victims, however. SCIT is administering a program to provide small grants to pay for traditional funeral rites for families of victims whose bodies are exhumed in the course of their investigations.

80. For a comparative perspective on East Timor's politics of amnesty, see "Burying Asia's Savage Past," *The Economist*, June 25, 2009.

81. As only one example of this kind of rhetoric, see Simon Roughneen, "East Timor: Justice in the Dock," *ICTJ in the News*, July 16, 2009, http://www.ictj.org/en/news/coverage/article/2829.html.

82. The website of the CAVR and its Final Report can be accessed at http://www.cavr-timorleste.org/.

83. Many individuals who participated in the truth-telling process complain that they never received any follow-up from the CAVR. As one example, in one set of interviews conducted by Leigh-Ashley Lipscomb on behalf of the International Center for Transitional Justice (ICTJ), a woman in Suai stated that she had given a statement to CAVR but had never seen any of the products of the CAVR's work. Two weeks later, at a public viewing of the CAVR film in Dili, this same woman's testimony was featured in the film. She apparently has no knowledge that her testimony was used in the film or of how her contribution relates to the CAVR's work.

84. Tetum, along with Portuguese, is an official language of Timor-Leste. It is spoken and read by the majority of people in East Timor, whereas Portuguese speakers make up a very small minority.

85. The CAVR website advertises a simplified version of the Report in Tetum. As of July 2009, this publication still had not been completed or disseminated (authors' on-site visits to the Post-CAVR as well as to communities and groups that participated in the dissemination process). A multivolume comic book version of the Final Report in Tetum has been drafted but has not yet been finalized or published (Pat Walsh and Hugo Fernandes, personal communication, June and July 2009). An exhibition at the CAVR office, created in November 2008, presented standup displays in Tetum that explain the Report, but to access this version of the Report people had to come to the CAVR during scheduled visitation hours.

86. For example, the radio broadcast currently takes place once a week on Saturday mornings at 7:30 A.M. and does not reach the broadest listening audience.

87. FRETILIN (Frente Revolucionária de Timor-Leste Independente)

was the dominant political party in East Timor that supported independence from 1974 until independence. It remains one of the main political
parties in East Timor today.

88. Former CAVR staff and Commissioners, discussions with Leigh-
Ashley Lipscomb, July 2008.

89. Kent, *Unfulfilled Expectations*, and Schlicher, *East Timor Faces Up to Its
Past*. In contrast, although limited in its sample size, Lia Kent's excellent
study of participant attitudes toward the CRP process shows that perpetrators perceive that they benefited from the CRP process.

90. Ibid.

91. For more detailed information regarding the CAVR Reparations
program, see Galuh Wandita, Karen Campbell Nelson, and Manuela
Leong Pereira, "Learning to Engender Reparations in Timor-Leste:
Reaching Out to Female Victims," in *What Happened to the Women? Gender
and Reparations for Human Rights Violations*, ed. Ruth Rubio-Marin (New
York: International Center for Transitional Justice, 2006), 284–335.

92. This number is a rough estimate based on the total pool of participants in the statement taking, community profiles, public hearings, perpetrators, and victims directly involved in the CRPs. This figure does not include the much larger number of people, including victims, who attended
the CRPs or public hearings as audience members.

93. Comments by staff members such as these further call into question
the degree to which the CAVR was able to provide for its own staff's mental
health needs. In more than fifteen interviews conducted by Leigh-Ashley
Lipscomb with former CAVR staff members, nearly all reported multiple
symptoms of well-developed secondary trauma, and multiple Timorese
staff members stated explicitly that they did not receive sufficient training
or support from the institution to deal with this element of their work.

94. Although there is not an exact official figure available yet, on the basis of the number of people who participated in the individual programs,
it is possible that as many as fifty to sixty thousand Timorese participated
in some aspect of the CAVR's work (*CAVR Final Report* and program reports
in CAVR archives).

95. The Commission entrusted the Document Review research process
to its Expert Advisor and his research teams in Dili and Jakarta. The decision by the Commission to permit a fully independent group to conduct
this highly contentious and central aspect of its work meant that Commissioners from both countries would have to accept the evidence that
research uncovered, no matter how uncomfortable the revelations might
be. For the full results of the Document Review process, see Cohen, Nababan, and Lipscomb, "Seeking Truth and Accountability," and Cohen and
Lipscomb, "Addendum."

96. The findings of the Commission with regard to the crimes com-

mitted by pro-independence groups were more tentative concerning the scope and number of gross human rights violations because there had been little investigation of reported pro-independence violations.

97. The Foreign Ministries of both countries have posted the Report on their websites for public access. Since the majority of vulnerable victims in Timor-Leste do not have internet access or computer skills, this is a some-what futile gesture.

98. In July 2009, the Timorese and Indonesian Foreign Ministries held a highly publicized round of negotiations in East Timor to discuss the Rec-ommendations of the CTF Report. These negotiations were accompanied by a public debate on Timorese TV with two former CTF Commissioners (one Indonesian and one Timorese). The talks were followed by a free public rock concert to honor the CTF Report and to celebrate peace with Indonesia. However, there are no credible reports yet of any specific, sub-stantive recommendations materializing. Progress so far has been limited to this kind of superficial and symbolic event.

99. Member of Rate Laek, discussion with Leigh-Ashley Lipscomb on behalf of ICTJ, August 22, 2008. All translations by Leigh-Ashley Lipscomb.

11

RECONCILIATION, REFUGEE RETURNS, AND THE IMPACT OF INTERNATIONAL CRIMINAL JUSTICE: THE CASE OF BOSNIA AND HERZEGOVINA

MONIKA NALEPA

Standard definitions of transitional justice identify its context (transitions from authoritarian regimes to rights-respecting rule-of-law regimes), its core institutions (of which the most prominent are criminal tribunals and truth commissions), and its broadest aspirations (establishing historical truth, achieving retributive justice for human rights abuses, and, ultimately, establishing peace or reconciliation among the citizens of the new regime). Commonly, truth commissions are identified with the aspiration to truth and reconciliation, and criminal tribunals are associated with the goal of retributive justice and accountability. Some scholars pose the choice between truth and justice as dilemmatic;[1] however, most scholars now acknowledge that, while there may be heuristic value in contrasting the goals of truth commissions and criminal proceedings, in practice both can serve the goals of truth, justice, and reconciliation. Truth commissions, for example, involve testimony about individual crimes as wrongful and thus provide some justice to victims through the acknowledgment that they were unjustly treated. Trials depend for their integrity on a detailed and precise factual record and so contribute to the reconstruction of a public history of human rights abuse.[2]

Empirical political science, however, has yet to clearly establish whether and how criminal prosecutions can contribute to what is arguably the highest goal of transitional justice institutions: reconciliation. Ultimately, one might argue, a crucial test of transitional institutions is whether they establish a foundation for members of societies that were deeply torn by violence to live peacefully together. This is not to deny that truth and justice are intrinsic goods; nor does the achievement of a measure of truth or justice always contribute positively to the goal of peace or reconciliation.[3] But some transitional mechanisms may contribute to reconciliation by promoting truth, and others may do so by promoting justice and accountability. Research in the transitional justice field has only recently begun to inquire into the particular institutional features of criminal tribunals that can contribute to reconciliation. How do different institutional strategies affect citizens' willingness to live together on peaceful terms? Does the contribution of criminal trials to reconciliation stem from their contributions to *justice* through the prosecution and conviction of guilty perpetrators or from their contributions to *truth* through the creation of an authoritative and condemnatory public record of human rights abuses?

This chapter employs the methods of empirical political science to help answer these questions. The motivation comes from observing distinct patterns in refugee returns to two municipalities that were the sites of egregious human rights violations during the civil war: Prijedor and Srebenica. An in-depth analysis of the prosecutorial strategies of the International Criminal Tribunal for the Former Yugoslavia (ICTY) reveals that international prosecutors employed contrasting approaches in dealing with perpetrators of war crimes in the two municipalities. The tale of two cities allows us to focus on the mechanism linking ICTY prosecutorial strategies to refugee returns. The detailed analysis of Prijedor and Srebenica that I develop in a later section suggests that paying the price of plea bargaining in order to reconstruct the chain of command and reach order-giving perpetrators depresses reconciliation. I conjecture that reconciliation may be lacking because justice awarded to victims of plea bargaining perpetrators is severely constrained. I notice, however, that limiting the analysis to these two municipalities alone does not allow us to test simultaneously competing explanations for reconciliation, because Prijedor and Srebrenica are not identical in some important respects that could be responsible for returns, as well. Acknowledging the limitations of a comparison between two municipalities that diverge on more dimensions than just the prosecutorial strategies used by the ICTY, the chapter sets out to explore the relationship between prosecutorial strategies and reconciliation for the set of all municipalities in Bosnia and Herzegovina. I have combined census and electoral data with information on the actions taken by the ICTY's prosecutors and justices on perpetrators of war crimes in specific municipalities. This dataset allows for rigorous micro-level tests of the purported relationship against competing explanations. Using multivariate statistical analysis, I explore the relationship between one measure of reconciliation (explained further later) and a range of independent variables, including rates of conviction, plea bargaining, the intensity of nationalist sentiments, ethnic diversity, and economic conditions. Surprisingly, the relationship suggested by the isolated comparison of Prijedor and Srebrenica is reversed by the multivariate analysis.

One of the difficulties in amassing empirical evidence for the effects of different transitional justice practices on reconciliation lies in deciding how to conceptualize "reconciliation" as a measurable empirical phenomenon. In its most ambitious formulation, reconciliation would go far beyond the cessation of civil conflict to capture the establishment of strong patterns of social trust and cooperation across ethnic lines. In contexts with deep histories of conflict, it is unlikely that this goal will be reached in the short or medium term. Moreover, even putting aside the difficulties of gathering reliable data on different measures of social trust and cooperation, the longer the road to full reconciliation, the greater the number of intervening factors that might contribute to explaining it. As a starting point for empirical investigation of the impact of criminal tribunals on reconciliation, I argue here for a more modest approach—one that focuses on the return of refugees to their home regions in the wake of gross human rights abuses. While refugee returns fall short of full reconciliation, they are one of its preconditions: social trust and cooperation across ethnic lines cannot begin until populations have been resettled in the aftermath of violent conflict. The present study proceeds by examining the impact of different ICTY prosecutorial strategies on refugee returns. Specifically, I contrast the impact of (truth-producing) plea bargaining with that of (justice-producing) criminal convictions. Through micro-level time-series cross-sectional analysis, I show that establishing a detailed historical record at the local level has a greater impact on refugee returns than the full prosecution and punishment of high-ranking perpetrators. Truth and justice both matter for reconciliation, but truth appears to matter more.

1. The Functions of International Criminal Tribunals

The International Criminal Tribunal for the Former Yugoslavia (ICTY) was created to prosecute those responsible for serious violations of international humanitarian law in the territory of the former Yugoslavia in the period after 1991. This tribunal is the most prominent example of the international community's involvement in the peace and democratization process in the Balkans.[4] As summarized on its official website, the ICTY's mandate consists of spearheading the shift from impunity to accountability, establishing the facts, and giving voice and bringing justice to thousands of victims.[5] There is little doubt that the ICTY has fulfilled the fact-finding part of its mandate; it has produced massive evidence of war crimes committed in the territory of the former Yugoslavia. For instance, the late Slobodan Milosevic's trial generated thousands of pages of evidence (which, incidentally, were not used to render a verdict because Milosevic died before his trial concluded). According to a former ICTY staffer, the evidence accumulated by the ICTY in all of its trials by 2006 supports the prosecution of a further nine hundred war criminals.[6] In terms of delivering accountability, however, the ICTY's output has been strikingly low—particularly if this output is measured relative to the costs of maintaining the tribunal. In January 2004, the ICTY's budget totaled US$135.9 million.[7] By the end of 2008, the ICTY had indicted 161 individuals and proceedings were still ongoing for 116 of them. The ICTY found 57 people guilty and sentenced them collectively to a little over eight hundred years.[8]

It is tempting to conclude that the tribunal has produced very little justice at a very great expense. This would, however, be a hasty conclusion if the tribunal's proceedings buttressed a popular sense of justice and the rule of law and promoted reconciliation in ways that we have not yet learned to measure adequately. A substantial conviction rate—when obtained through criminal proceedings that meet high standards of due process—does signal the end of a culture of impunity, but it is a crude measure of whether the tribunal's larger mandate has been fulfilled.

The ICTY's mandate reflects a broad consensus that a central goal of international criminal justice is putting high-ranking leaders responsible for war crimes on trial.[9] Many advocates of international tribunals are attracted to them because of their perceived effect in deterring future war crimes. They believe that such tribunals dissuade leaders from issuing criminal orders. From Nuremberg to the establishment of the International Criminal Court, international war crimes tribunals have concentrated their efforts on reaching the top commanders responsible for war crimes, crimes against humanity, and genocide.

Putting aside the question of whether deterrence is a reasonable expectation of international criminal tribunals,[10] transitional justice advocates advance a number of further justifications for them. Most important for our purposes, there are several reasons for thinking that criminal prosecutions of human rights violations in transitional societies can contribute significantly to the aim of reconciliation. First, it seems reasonable to believe that restoring citizens' trust in political institutions requires that rights abusers, especially those in positions of political power, be held accountable for their actions. This logic underlies lustration, as well as criminal prosecutions. Further, public confidence in rule of law institutions is likely to be deeply undermined if a culture of impunity prevails in post-conflict societies. A key argument for focusing on the prosecution of high-ranking decision makers is that prosecuting order-takers without going higher up the chain of command is so great a failure of justice that it jeopardizes the very possibility of law-governed political community.[11]

The challenge, however, is that, in order to reach the high-ranking perpetrators, prosecutors first need to reconstruct the chain of command and the chronology of events. One strategy is to obtain information about the chain of command or chronology of events by building the case record from low-ranking perpetrators through medium-ranking ones up to the top-echelon commanders responsible for issuing the orders. Another strategy proceeds through plea bargaining with medium-ranking perpetrators who are offered reduced sentences in exchange for their testimony. Both techniques, once effected, make it possible to reach many perpetrators, including mid-level and low-ranking ones.

International tribunals—such as the ICTY—typically pursue low-level prosecutions with the primary purpose of building the evidentiary record to facilitate successful high-level prosecutions. To be sure, plea bargaining produces a fair amount of truth by way of the testimony of certain perpetrators who have been offered reduced sentences, but international criminal tribunals treat obtaining this truth as instrumental to the superseding objective of prosecuting high-ranking perpetrators. The implication of this strategy that is problematic from the standpoint of justice is that most low-level perpetrators will not be prosecuted at all and will receive de facto amnesty.[12] It is possible, however, that, inasmuch as trials fail to deliver justice to a wide range of perpetrators, they make up for this loss by producing truth in the process of hearing testimony from plea bargaining defendants.

If this is the case, then the supposed choice between trials and other forms of transitional justice (such as truth commissions or amnesties) is not really a choice between truth and justice. As noted earlier, truth commissions obviously deliver goods that we associate with justice: they establish that some actions are morally wrong and shame perpetrators who are exposed as part of the truth commissions' proceedings. But trials can also produce some goods that we associate with truth. They create a public record of atrocities, an official account of what happened, thereby acknowledging victims' suffering. The Nuremberg trials, over and above their seminal significance in applying international law to crimes committed by a state, also served the purpose of educating the global public about the Holocaust. Plea bargains, in particular, yield enough truth about the past that this benefit may outweigh the loss of justice in bypassing low-rank perpetrators who would need to be prosecuted in order to reconstruct the chain of command.

Although these theoretical reflections set out plausible accounts of the relationship between the impact of criminal tribunals' truth and justice functions on reconciliation, ultimately these are empirical questions. Regrettably, empirical research on these questions is still in its infancy.

2. EMPIRICAL RESEARCH ON INTERNATIONAL CRIMINAL TRIBUNALS

Empirical studies of the consequences of international criminal tribunals in transitional contexts are still relatively few in number.[13] In part because of the difficulty of operationalizing the concept of reconciliation, which I shall discuss further later, it is even rarer for scholars to investigate the impact of international tribunals on reconciliation. Clearly, it is impossible to assess the relative effectiveness of alternative institutional strategies available to tribunals without first identifying some measure of reconciliation as the dependent variable of one's study. Studies that have focused on variables that are closely related to reconciliation (democratization, post-conflict peace, deterrence of future violence, and respect for human rights) have tended to yield inconclusive findings. This is in part because each of these concepts resists easy operationalization. To date, the empirical evidence does not support a strong claim for the impact (positive or negative) of international criminal tribunals on reconciliation or related outcomes.[14]

A further limitation of existing research on international tribunals is that scholars tend to focus on the impact of prosecutions of high-ranking officials without exploring in any detail prosecutorial strategies toward mid-level or low-ranking officials. Distinguishing the effects of prosecutorial strategies at different levels of the decision-making hierarchy is important for two principal reasons. First, an exclusive focus on high-ranking prosecutions fails to account for the possibility that victims' demands for justice may be directed toward low-ranking perpetrators. Suppose that victims prefer that justice be done to perpetrators who directly inflicted harm on them, rather than to perpetrators who issued orders. If this is so, greater reconciliation will occur when large numbers of low-ranking perpetrators are prosecuted than when fewer high-ranking perpetrators are brought to trial. In the aftermath of war, high-ranking perpetrators—the order-givers—are geographically removed from the victims' residence, while low-ranking perpetrators—the order-takers—often have a glaring presence in their victims' lives.

Consider as an illustration the following excerpt from Ed Vulliamy's story about Srebrenica ten years after the atrocities were committed there: "As she [Sija Mustafic] speaks, a man walks by the window, checking electricity meters. 'He is doing that now,' says Sija. 'But during the war, he was burning houses. I know they killed my husband and my son. I know that my neighbors were involved in this.' "[15] It may be that victims would prefer to see these direct oppressors put on trial, rather than the perpetrators residing at the commanding heights. My research in this chapter takes seriously the possibility that truth- and justice-seeking processes contribute most effectively to reconciliation when they target the most localized human rights abuses. [16]

Second, as noted earlier, prosecutorial strategies toward mid- and low-ranking perpetrators may involve an aggressive policy of plea bargaining aimed at building evidence against high-ranking decision makers. Although not at the center of transitional justice debates, plea bargaining has captured the attention of some students of transitional justice.[17] Despite a fair number of theoretical studies and numerous anecdotes illustrating the effects of plea bargaining in transitional justice contexts, however, no transitional study has yet undertaken a systematic investigation into the effects of plea bargaining on reconciliation. This gap makes it impossible to judge whether plea bargaining's truth-gathering function can have a positive impact on reconciliation or whether plea bargaining's compromise with justice may have a negative impact. Thus, one contribution of the research presented in this chapter is to build the body of evidence concerning plea bargaining as a prosecutorial strategy. My research reveals that prosecutions of low-rank perpetrators do not contribute to reconciliation as much as confessions extracted from medium-rank perpetrators in the process of plea bargaining.

Finally, let me return to the vexing challenge of operationalizing "reconciliation." Theorists of transitional justice remain far from consensus on a definition of this difficult concept.[18] Empiricists, for their part, have yet to come up with a universal operationalization of the concept. Consider as an illustrative example, Africa's Reconciliation Barometer, an annual public opinion survey, which measures "South African attitudes towards the country's social transformation process, with particular emphasis on national reconciliation."[19] It is not clear how easily this method of operationalization can be exported to other contexts, given that, as the researchers behind the South African Reconciliation Barometer effort admit, "[t]he notion of reconciliation has firmly rooted itself in the parlance of South African society."[20] What they are referring to are the Christian origins of the concept of reconciliation. Although religion was not a dividing cleavage in South Africa, it was in other transitional justice contexts. Consider, for instance, the former Yugoslavia, where victims are often deeply ambivalent about the idea of reconciliation as the ultimate goal of transitional justice. In particular, Bosnian Muslims tend to associate this view of reconciliation with Serb Christian heritage.[21] Their reluctance can be especially pronounced when the concept of reconciliation is identified with Christian theology and characterized as a relationship between victims and perpetrators: perpetrators accept blame and apologize, while victims embrace them in an act of forgiveness. One member of a nongovernmental organization (NGO), when asked about the prospects for reconciliation in the former Yugoslavia, suggests that this model is too idealistic to be practical: "Reconciliation? I don't want reconciliation, I want accountability! There are people with whom I will not reconcile and that's it!"[22]

Yet, if empirical research is to generate evidence concerning the effectiveness of international criminal justice in advancing reconciliation, finding appropriate empirical indicators of the concept is clearly an inescapable task. One approach, exemplified by James Meernik's insightful study of the ICTY, is to address the impact of tribunal proceedings on conflict and cooperation between members of ethnic groups that were previously at war (he calls this "societal peace").[23] Meernik finds that ICTY indictments, trials, and sentencing decisions had almost no effect on societal peace as operationalized in the study, but his study measures societal peace at the aggregate level of the entire country. This research strategy does not detect whether victims direct their demand for justice toward specific perpetrators—those individuals who committed war crimes in the victims' own city or village (by, for instance, forcing them to flee their homes). If demand for transitional justice is individualistic, not collective, then victims will respond to trials of perpetrators who committed crimes in areas close to the victims' residence and may be indifferent to the trials of those who committed war crimes in other places. Indeed, one might expect that they might even react adversely to such other trials. An alternative strategy to Meernik's is the one I adopt in the present study, which reaches to the micro level of specific municipalities, starting with Prijedor and Srebrenica, and then extends to a multivariate analysis of the data in all of the municipalities of Bosnia and Herzegovina.

By analyzing data that link war crimes to the specific municipalities where they were committed, I investigate the possibility that Meernik's finding that the ICTY had little effect was generated by his focus on the prosecution of high-ranking perpetrators and his use of an aggregated societal, rather than a disaggregated local, level of analysis. In doing so, I use data on refugee returns to specific locales as a less ambitious but more easily measurable proxy for reconciliation. When Louise Arbour, Justice and President of the ICTY from 1993 to 1999, was asked about the prospects for reconciliation in the former Yugoslavia, she responded, "First you need a will to live together."[24] I take this notion of living in the same neighborhoods as their perpetrators' co-ethnics as my working definition of reconciliation; I operationalize it as victims' decisions to return home to live in cities or villages whose majority population is of the same ethnicity as the perpetrators from whom victims suffered abuse during the civil war. Even though returning home may not reflect the achievement of complete reconciliation with one's victimizer, it may well be a necessary prerequisite of reconciliation. Long before victims can start sharing democratic institutions with their perpetrators, not to mention living in the same neighborhoods as their perpetrators' co-ethnics, they must start returning to their homes. Consequently, I use the return of minority refugees to the places where they were the subjects of human rights violations as a proxy for reconciliation. In other words, the refugee returns are used to operationalize reconciliation.

In sum, this chapter fills some of the existing gaps in the empirical literature by investigating how the prosecutorial strategy of the ICTY affects the reconciliation of victims with perpetrators of war crimes and their co-ethnics. Intriguingly, I find that, although justice was the ICTY's ostensible goal, it has produced as an unintended, incidental consequence truth through plea bargaining. The truth produced in the plea bargaining process has brought about more reconciliation than straightforward sentencing would have.

3. A Tale of Two Cities: Prijedor and Srebrenica

The 1992–1995 war in Bosnia-Herzegovina inflicted massive human suffering on the population. All three of the major population groups in the region—Bosniaks,[25] Serbs, and Croats—sustained significant casualties. Scholars agree that it is very hard to estimate the number of civilian deaths and especially hard to disaggregate them into Serb, Croat, and Bosniak casualties. In 1994, the CIA estimated there had been 156,600 civilian deaths in Bosnia and Herzegovina and an additional 81,500 combatant deaths. Of the combatant deaths, 45,000 were on the Bosnian government side, 6,500 on the Bosnian Croat side, and 30,000 on the Bosnian Serb side.[26] Eric D. Weitz maintains that, in estimating the final tally of civilian deaths in the entirety of Yugoslavia, the figure of "200,000 deaths, around 50 percent Muslim, 30–35 percent Serb, and 15–20 percent Croat is probably correct."[27] Patrick Ball and his collaborators from the Households in Conflict Network research group assessed the quality of the "Bosnian Book of Dead" database; they confirmed 96,895 documented deaths in Bosnia and Herzegovina, of which 66.1 percent, or approximately 64,003, were Bosniaks. Of the total deaths, 39,199 were civilian.[28] Other sources report that among the civilian deaths, Bosniaks represented 83.3 percent, Serbs 10.2 percent, and Croats 5.4 percent.[29] The massive scale of violence was generated by policies of "ethnic cleansing" carried out by multiple means, including genocidal killing and rape. As people fled the violence in their home regions, the number of refugees grew dramatically. By the end of the war, relative to projections from the 1991 census, 49 percent of the population in Bosnia had been displaced.[30] The UN High Commissioner for Refugees, specially appointed by the United Nations to coordinate the return of displaced minorities, estimates that the war generated approximately 2 million refugees from a prewar population of 4.4 million.[31]

Although the right of refugee return was a central pillar of the Dayton Accords, which officially ended the fighting, the process of returning refugees to their homes has been slow and partial. A decade after the end of the war, about half of the original refugee population had returned to the country.[32] But fewer than half the total number of returnees have returned to where they are currently in a minority. Across Bosnia, returns began to increase significantly in 2000, when approximately sixty-seven thousand people returned to areas in which their ethnic group was a minority of the population. Minority refugee returns peaked in 2002; more than one hundred thousand people returned that year, but returns fell off significantly thereafter. Over the ten-year period between 1996 and 2006, a total of 446,795 people returned to areas in which they were an ethnic minority.[33] It is specifically minority refugee returns that I use to operationalize reconciliation.

No two cases represent the dilemma of refugee returns as well as Prijedor, in the northwest of Bosnia-Herzegovina and Srebrenica in the east. Both places were sites of unspeakable atrocities. In 1992, as war was unfolding in the east of the county, Serbs in Prijedor gradually started establishing institutions parallel to the official Bosniak ones. In March of that year, they took over the television station, and, by April, they already controlled the police and military. By the end of the month, an alternative Serbian enforcement apparatus had taken over the town under the pretext of protecting Serbs from Bosniak "rebels." In the meantime, Bosniaks and Croats living in villages of the municipality of Prijedor fled their homes while the area was under siege by Serb troops. More than three thousand refugees (mostly men) were captured by the Serbian army and marched into the specially established camps. Political leaders and intellectuals from the towns of Prijedor and Kozerac were kept in Omarska, while the Keraterm and Trnopilje camps were set up as investigation centers for screening out undercover participants in the Bosniak and Croatian rebellion from regular civilians. In practice, Omarska and Keraterm were death camps, where inmates, primarily men, suffered severe beatings and malnourishment. Eventually, these people were executed. Trnopilje was a concentration camp mostly for women, many of

whom were sexually abused. As a result of actions carried out by
the Serb army, out of a population of fifty thousand Bosniaks living in the Prijedor municipality before the war, only slightly more
than six thousand remain there today.[34]

The Red Cross was not admitted into the camps near Prijedor
because they were run by civilians, not the army.[35] The first witness
to discover these sites was Ed Vulliamy of *The Guardian*. Vulliamy's
and Roy Gutman's reports[36] dramatically contributed to the awareness of the camps among members of the international community.[37] Within months, the U.S. ambassador to the UN established
a commission of experts to prepare a report on the atrocities in
the Balkans.[38] The commission, chaired by Cherif Bassiouni, provided a 131-page report that systematically documented the ethnic cleansing in the former Yugoslavia. The report recommended
the creation of a Nuremberg-style tribunal to prosecute war criminals.[39] The ICTY's first indictments, issued on February 13, 1995,
were those of two Omarska and Keraterm perpetrators, Dusko Tadic and Goran Borovnica. These two had supplied the Serb army
with death lists of intellectuals living in Kozarac (a major town in
the Prijedor municipality) and then personally supervised acts of
torture in the camps.

Many scholars, including Cherif Bassiouni, believed that establishing an international tribunal would end the interethnic violence in the territory of the former Yugoslavia, but, within four
months of the initial indictments, another massacre took place,
this time in Srebrenica, in the eastern part of Bosnia. Ironically,
the massacre occurred while the ICTY was preparing to indict two
Bosniak Serbs, Radovan Karadzic and Ratko Mladic.[40]

During the Balkan wars of the 1990s, Srebrenica became the
site of one of the most embarrassing failures of the international
peacekeeping community. The area had been marked off as one
of the "safe zones" protected by the United Nations Protection
Force troops (UNPROFOR).[41] For this reason, Bosniaks from the
eastern part of the Republic flocked into Srebrenica. But, in the
summer of 1995, Serbian fighters from the Army of Republika
Srpska under the command of Ratko Mladic shelled the UN posts.
North Atlantic Treaty Organization (NATO) forces protected the
peacekeepers with air strikes. In retaliation, the Serbian fighters
took thirty Dutch UNPROFOR troops hostage. NATO, however,

refused to intervene. Shortly afterwards, an agreement was struck between Mladic and the Dutch Defense Minister, Joris Voorhoeve, which freed the troops under the condition that the Muslim refugees would be deported from Srebrenica after all adult men were screened for possible war criminals. As a result, men between the ages of sixteen and sixty were isolated and detained in an area within the municipality of Srebrenica called Potocari. At the same time, another column of refugees—a third of whom were Bosniak fighters—began to make their way towards Tuzla, northwest of Srebrenica. They were intercepted by other units of the Serb enforcement apparatus, and the entire group of refugees was captured and sent to the Potocari detention center. From there, all the refugees were gradually relocated to places of execution. According to the most recent estimates, more than seven thousand Bosniak men and boys were summarily executed and buried in mass graves. The women were victimized through programmatic rape, an ethnic-cleansing policy recognized by the ICTY years later as a war crime.[42]

The truly horrific events in Prijedor and Srebrenica during the war caused massive suffering in both regions; however, the rates of minority refugee returns in the two regions were significantly different. In this section, I use case studies of Prijedor and Srebrenica to explore whether any part of the difference in refugee return rates might be explained by differences in the ICTY's prosecutorial strategies in the two regions. Prijedor and Srebrenica were both sites of gross human rights violations during the war. Both places are similar in terms of their proximity to the border, size of the Serbian population, ethnic composition, economic development before the war, and intensity of nationalism. The aggregate output of the ICTY regarding war crimes committed in the two municipalities is also strikingly similar. They exemplify very different rates and patterns of minority refugee returns, however. Figure 11.1 presents the annual minority refugee returns to Srebrenica and Prijedor after the Dayton accord and compares them to the number of minority refugees returning on average to municipalities in Bosnia.

These data reveal that, while the number of returns to Prijedor was consistently well above average, the number of returns to Srebrenica was consistently below that average. Moreover, most

FIG. 11.1   REFUGEE RETURNS TO PRIJEDOR AND SREBRENICA
BETWEEN 1996 AND 2005
*Source: Statistical Yearbooks of the UNHCR, UN Refugee Agency for Bosnia and
Herzegovina, http://www.unhcr.org/cgi-bin/texis/vtx/page?page=49e48d766.*

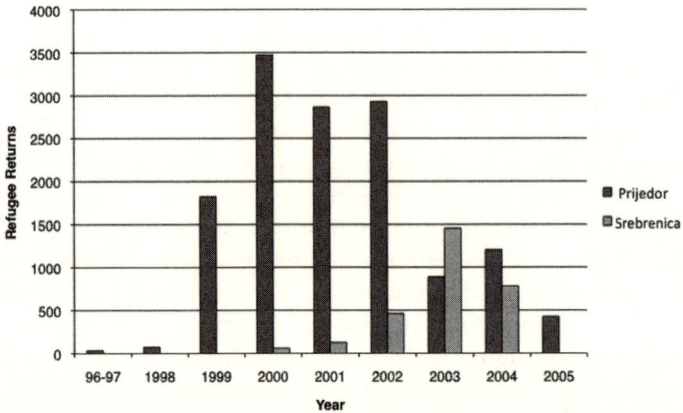

of the returns to Prijedor occurred in the early aftermath of the
war, whereas returns to Srebrenica have been more recent. Could
different degrees of attention from the ICTY explain these differences? In what follows, I consider this explanation, along with alternative theories that might explain different patterns of minority
refugee returns.

I begin with the central hypothesis of this chapter: the prosecutorial strategies of the ICTY can offer a partial explanation for the
divergent patterns of refugee returns to Prijedor and Srebrenica.

3.1. The Central Hypothesis: ICTY Prosecutorial Strategy

At first glance, the ICTY appears to have accorded similar levels of
attention to both Prijedor and Srebrenica. They are comparable
in terms of aggregate sentencing decisions. Table 11.1 contains
data with the aggregate output of the ICTY between 1996 and
2005 for the prosecution of war crimes committed in Prijedor and
Srebrenica.

In trials of defendants accused of war crimes committed in Prijedor and Srebrenica, the ICTY sentenced those found guilty to a

total of more than 120 years in prison for each municipality. Yet, despite the similarity in aggregate sentencing decisions, the numbers of minority refugees returning to Prijedor and Srebrenica are dramatically different. Figure 11.1 points to Prijedor as one of the leading municipalities to which minority refugees have returned, with 13,728 returns by 2005. Srebrenica is among the last, with only 2,884.[43] Thus, if the ICTY's operations did have an impact on different rates of refugee returns, this impact must have been through mechanisms at the micro-level of prosecutorial strategies. These differences in prosecutorial strategies can be observed in the different numbers of defendants, counts, and indictments. I discuss them in detail later.

To reconstruct the chain of command in Prijedor, the ICTY was forced to put low-ranking perpetrators on trial. Dusko Tadic, the ICTY's first defendant, was identified in Munich, where he had escaped to avoid being drafted into the Bosnian Serb Army. The person who identified him was a victim of his from the Omarska concentration camp. His case brought 153 other victims to the Hague to testify. This stands in stark contrast with Srebrenica, where Drazen Erdemovic, a medium-ranking perpetrator, confessed his role in the Srebrenica massacre even before he was indicted.[44] His voluntary revelation, followed by a guilty plea, enabled the tribunal to avoid prosecutions at the lowest level. By revealing his accomplices, Erdemovic helped the court reconstruct the chain of

TABLE 11.1 AGGREGATE OUTPUT OF THE ICTY BETWEEN 1996 AND 2005 FOR THE PROSECUTION OF WAR CRIMES COMMITTED IN PRIJEDOR AND SREBRENICA

VARIABLE	PRIJEDOR	SREBRENICA
Indictments	23	17
Counts	21	12
Genocide Counts	13	13
Crimes Against Humanity	90	61
No. of Defendants	12	6
Sentence in Years	125	127

Source: ICTY's Official Website, United Nations, International Criminal Tribunal for the former Yugoslavia, "The Cases," UN ICTY, http://www.icty.org/action/cases/4 (accessed February 9, 2009).

command, as well as the chronology of events. His sentence for participation in the massacre amounted to ten years and was reduced to five in 1998. Upon release from prison, he was covered by the witness protection program. According to an anonymously interviewed former ICTY staffer, the Erdemovic case was very damaging to the image of the Tribunal but was crucial to achieving further indictments.[45] A total of nineteen persons—mostly high-ranking perpetrators—were prosecuted in the Srebrenica case.

How did the victims respond to the ICTY's work? They did not begin returning to their homes until 2003.[46] Victims of the Srebrenica massacre did not see the low-ranking order-takers—those who committed the crimes directly—prosecuted. Instead, they saw the prosecution of high-level perpetrators who could be reached more easily because of Erdemovic's confession. A similar trend became visible in Prijedor when the ICTY stopped prosecuting lower-level perpetrators. After the events and chain of command had been fully reconstructed, such prosecutions were no longer needed. In response, refugee returns peaked in 2000 and then gradually started falling (see Figure 11.1).

The Tribunal's reputation in the Srebrenica investigation was undermined not only by its failure to prosecute low-ranking perpetrators but also by Erdemovic's plea bargain. That Erdemovic's revelation was crucial to issuing other indictments did little to comfort his victims. Furthermore, Erdemovic's sentence reduction induced other perpetrators to come before the court before being indicted, to plead guilty, and to offer information in exchange for sentence reductions. Critics of the ICTY claimed that, from the point of view of victims, this led to a very undesirable outcome: not only were the medium- and low-ranking perpetrators who had directly inflicted harm upon them prosecuted selectively, but, when the perpetrators did stand trial, they received shockingly soft sentences.

Eventually, the court stopped offering incentives for plea bargaining because it no longer needed the information that low- or medium-ranking perpetrators had to offer. Thus, by the time Deputy Commander Drago Nikolic decided to come before the court and plead guilty, the chain of command in Srebrenica had already been reconstructed, and the court knew all the facts. Nikolic was a medium-ranking perpetrator who had coordinated the transportation of the captured Bosniaks to concentration camps around

Srebrenica. The prosecutor asked for a twenty-year sentence; however, in order to reverse the trend of reducing sentences, the judge sentenced Nikolic to twenty-seven years. The perpetrators' response was immediate: the self-revelations stopped instantly, as did the trials of many low- and medium-ranking perpetrators.

Despite similarities in the aggregate ICTY outputs, there appears to be a marked difference in the prosecutorial strategies employed for prosecuting war crimes in the two municipalities. War crimes committed in Prijedor were followed by intensive prosecutions at the lowest level. War crimes in Srebrenica resulted in almost no prosecutions at the lowest level, but the ICTY engaged in extensive bargaining with mid-level perpetrators to reach the high-level perpetrators. Prijedor had significant rates of minority refugee returns, but Srebrenica saw very few minority refugees returning home.

The low level of minority refugee returns to Srebrenica contrasted with the high level of minority refugee returns to Prijedor suggests the following hypothesis: prosecuting low-level perpetrators increases refugee returns, while non-prosecution and plea bargaining decrease refugee returns. In other words, the prosecutorial strategy of bypassing low-rank order-takers and engaging in plea bargaining with a few medium-rank perpetrators to ultimately focus prosecutions on high-rank order-givers undermines victim reconciliation; increasing the number of low-ranking prosecutions has a positive impact on reconciliation. Before accepting this hypothesis, though, we must consider other differences between the two municipalities that could have generated such distinct patterns of returns. It is possible that we have neglected some important difference between Prijedor and Srebrenica that affected refugee returns. Among such alternative explanations, I consider the proximity to the border, ethnic composition, macroeconomic conditions, virility of nationalism, and the magnitude of the atrocities committed.

3.2. Alternative Explanation 1: Proximity to the Border

The first competing explanation for the divergent patterns of refugee returns is the proximity to the border with Serbia. One could argue, for instance, that, because Srebrenica is closer to the

Serbian border than Prijedor, minority refugee returns should be lower. But returning to Prijedor could be just as risky as returning to Srebrenica because of Prijedor's proximity to Krajina, a Serb-inhabited part of Croatia marked by the most virulent nationalism at the war's onset. Prijedor's distance from Krajina, past the border with Croatia (14.87 miles),[47] is not much greater than Srebrenica's distance from the border with Serbia (6.12 miles). Thus, proximity to the border does not plausibly account for the differing refugee patterns.

3.3. Alternative Explanation 2: Demography

A related alternative explanation is the ethnic composition of the two municipalities before and after the war. The population of Prijedor before the war (113,000) was divided almost evenly between Serbs and Bosniaks (with a population of a little under 50,000 for each). As of 2010, it was 105,000, but most of these inhabitants were Orthodox Serbs. What was once an ethnically diverse community has become a relatively homogenous one in the wake of ethnic cleansing.[48]

Srebrenica's transformation was even more dramatic. According to the 1991 census, 36,600 people lived in the Srebrenica district. Of these, 25,000 were Bosniak Muslims and 8,500 were Serbs. As of 2008, the total population was 10,000, of whom 4,000 were Serb returnees and 2,000 were Serbs displaced from elsewhere in Bosnia. Although about 4,000 displaced Muslims have returned to the area, they live mainly in the surrounding villages, leaving Srebrenica itself an almost entirely Serbian town. Before the war, Serbs made up only a third of the town of Srebrenica.[49]

Available census data, however, indicate that the two municipalities experienced similar changes in their ethnic composition as a result of the war. In Srebrenica, before the war, Bosniaks made up three-quarters of the municipality; after the war, they made up only a third. In Prijedor, Bosniaks made up almost 44 percent of the population; after the war, they constituted only 16 percent. So, in both places, Bosniaks' minority status deepened. In Srebrenica, Bosniaks went from being a majority to becoming a minority: after the war, the Bosniak presence in Srebrenica was only 43 percent of what it had been before the war. In Prijedor, from a sizable minority almost equal in size to the Serb population, Bosniaks became a small minority: after the war, the Bosniak presence in the population of Prijedor was only 36 percent of what it had been before the war.

Population growth rates before the war were considerably higher in Srebrenica than in Prijedor (13.2 percent versus 6.1 percent).[50] This can be attributed to the fact that there was a larger urban population in Prijedor than in Srebrenica, because natural growth rates in urban areas tend to be lower than in rural communities. Prewar economic conditions in the two municipalities were remarkably similar, with a per capita income of 4,857 dinars in Prijedor and 4,460 dinars in Srebrenica.[51] The differences in natural resources and potential for economic development between Prijedor and Srebrenica are also not great enough to explain the dramatic gap in refugee returns.[52]

3.4. Alternative Explanation 3: Intensity of Nationalism

I now turn to the political and ideological differences between the two municipalities and whether they can explain different patterns of refugee returns in Prijedor and Srebrenica.

Before the war, communist Yugoslavia did not organize competitive multiparty elections; thus, unfortunately, we cannot use electoral data to compare the intensity of nationalism in each case. Note, however, that in Bosnia there were two cleavages: religion (Christian Orthodox, Catholic, and Muslim) and ethnicity (Serb, Croat, and Bosniak). One can interpret the extent to which these cleavages were cross-cutting rather than overlapping as an indication of the intensity of nationalism. The strength of the nationalism that developed over the course of the war forced these qualitatively distinct cleavages to overlap and the distinctions to sharpen. We can use prewar census data to examine whether the overlap of ethnic and religious cleavages in Prijedor and Srebrenica before the war was markedly different from the present situation, which would indicate a difference in the potential for outbreaks of nationalism.

Before the war, 43 percent of Prijedor's population self-identified as Muslim and 39.38 percent claimed to speak Bosnian, while 40.5 percent identified as Orthodox and 26.36 percent claimed to speak Serbian. In Srebrenica, 75.5 percent identified as Muslim and 72.89 percent claimed to speak Bosnian, while 22.56 percent identified as Orthodox and 19.63 percent claimed to speak Serbian.[53] These numbers suggest that, in both municipalities, self-reported linguistic identities only roughly reflected religious identities. There is therefore little reason to suspect that the pre-existing ethnic cleavage structure predisposed Srebrenica to have a greater potential for ethnic violence than Prijedor.

3.5. Alternative Explanation 4: Magnitude and Timing of Atrocities

The "Bosnian Book of Dead" assessed by the Households in Conflicts Network puts the total number of documented deaths that occurred in Srebrenica in 1992–1995 at 9,377 and the number for Prijedor at less than half of that, 4,792; yet, in the overall ranking of war victims by municipality, Prijedor and Srebrenica rank third and second, respectively. Only Sarajevo, the capital, suffered more casualties.[54] Furthermore, a comparison of victims by municipality of origin makes the difference in population losses between the two municipalities much smaller, with Srebrenica at 7,591 and Prijedor at 5,285, again with both municipalities occupying second and third rank in the total number of deaths.[55] When considered in conjunction with the two earlier figures, this suggests that victims from Prijedor perished beyond the borders of the municipality, while victims from outside Srebrenica were transported to that municipality to die.

Direct comparisons of population losses across the two municipalities are complicated by the fact that concentration camps in Prijedor were discovered three years before the Srebrenica massacre started. This suggests that some refugees may have been fleeing Srebrenica while others were already returning to Prijedor. Thus, comparing the population losses in the two municipalities at the same point in time would ignore the difference in the timing of the genocide and the fact that Bosniaks from all over the area came to Srebrenica to meet their deaths.[56]

The tale of these two cities has left us with an unresolved puzzle: it is not clear whether the difference in minority refugee returns to the Prijedor and Srebrenica municipalities (above average in Prijedor and below average in Srebrenica, as shown in Figure

11.1) should be more strongly attributed to the difference in the magnitude of atrocities than to the different prosecutorial strategies employed in the two places. A comparison limited to just two cases cannot serve as evidence that a prosecutorial strategy that concentrates on order-takers better contributes to reconciliation than one that focuses on high-ranking officials. To draw more definitive conclusions, we need to extend our analysis beyond the comparison of two illustrative cases; we need to expand the universe of cases to more municipalities in the state of Bosnia and Herzegovina. In the next section, my central hypothesis is tested against alternative explanations (ethnic composition, war suffering, economic conditions, intensity of nationalism, and magnitude of suffering) with data from a ten-year period across all municipalities in Bosnia and Herzegovina. This analysis shows that the magnitude of atrocities measured by the numbers of killed and missing does not have an independent effect on minority refugee returns, controlling for effects of prosecutorial strategies. In contrast to what we would expect to find on the basis of the Prijedor and Srebrenica case studies, however, plea bargaining has a positive, not negative, effect on minority refugee returns. In the discussion of the results, I attribute the significance of plea bargaining to the truth-revealing feature of this mechanism.

4. Refugee Returns Beyond Prijedor and Srebrenica

So far, I have used the Prijedor and Srebrenica studies to discuss certain explanations for different patterns of refugee returns. While some of these explanations could be refuted by using the two cases of Prijedor and Srebrenica, others—such as the magnitude of suffering—require a broader set of cases to be tested. In this section, I build on these two cases and adopt a more systematic approach to analyzing the connection between the prosecution strategies of the ICTY and the readiness of refugees to return home.

In order to rigorously test whether the intuitive relationships suggested by the Prijedor and Srebrenica cases hold more broadly, I have collected data on all municipalities in Bosnia over the twelve-year period following the Dayton Accords that ended the war. I evaluate this data using multivariate statistical analysis. Appendix

11.1 contains the technical details of the statistical model and the operationalization of the dependent and independent variables. It presents the results and explains the tests I conducted to ensure the results' robustness. The following section informally describes the data I used to operationalize the prosecutorial strategy and presents the findings.

4.1. Operationalization of Dependent and Independent Variables

This section explains the empirical analysis I conducted to obtain the results of this study. It discusses the data, the operationalization of the variables, and the results of the multivariate analysis.[57]

The data for the dependent variable, returns, comes from the UNHCR. Specifically, the UNHCR has tracked all Bosniak, Croat, and Serb minority returns at the level of municipalities in Bosnia and Herzegovina, Republika Srpska, and the Brcko district.

The main independent variables, representing the ICTY's prosecutorial strategy, have been coded by extracting key information from indictments, transcripts, and ICTY decisions between 1994 and 2006.[58] I coded variables from three stages of the trial: the indictments, the trial stage, and the sentencing process.

The indictment stage contains (1) the number of indicted persons; (2) the number of counts on which each defendant was indicted; (3) the counts of crimes against humanity; and (4) the counts of crimes of genocide on which they were indicted. The dataset includes amended indictments and amended sentencing through appeals, if any. The trial stage includes information about (1) the initiation of the trial; (2) the number of defendants; (3) whether or not plea bargaining took place; and (4) the number of witnesses who testified for the prosecution and for the defense. The sentencing stage includes data on (1) the number of years of imprisonment to which the defendants were sentenced and (2) the number of defendants. Notice that the data on the number of indicted persons, counts, counts of genocide, and counts of crimes against humanity can be used to signify differences between low- and high-ranking perpetrators: where the ICTY focused on low-rank perpetrators in order to reconstruct the chain of command, the number of prosecuted perpetrators is high, while the number of counts, particularly counts of genocide and crimes against humanity, is low. On the other hand, where the ICTY focused on a few medium-ranking perpetrators to get as quickly as possible to the high-ranking perpetrators, there are fewer defendants. Municipalities for which this prosecutorial strategy was adopted are also characterized by large numbers of counts, plea bargaining, and long sentences.

The complete dataset is a cross-section time series of 136 municipalities with considerably fewer time periods (only ten) than municipalities. The unit of analysis is a municipality in a given year. A row in the dataset is a municipality-year. The columns include the following data:

1. Three dependent variables—minority refugee returns: how many Bosniak, Croat, or Serb minority refugee returns were recorded in a given year in a given municipality?
2. Five independent variables of interest that operationalize the ICTY's prosecutorial strategy in a given year for a given municipality:
   (a) How many indictments were issued?
   (b) How many counts were included in the indictments?
   (c) How many defendants were put on trial?
   (d) How many years of sentencing were pronounced?
   (e) How many witnesses were called in cases against suspected war criminals?
3. Data operationalizing alternative explanations for refugee returns:
   (a) Economic development and unemployment rate
   (b) Size of the ethnic group of the returnees
   (c) War suffering and population growth rate
   (d) Postwar nationalism

A brief explanation of how these variables operationalize factors that could affect the return rates of minority refugees follows.

Economic Development and Unemployment Rate

A plausible variable for predicting minority refugee returns is the economic differential between the place from which refugees are coming and the place to which they are returning. Unfortunately, the UNHCR did not collect data on returning refugees' points of origin. When this research was conducted, the Bosnian statistical office did not have detailed data on economic growth at the municipality level either. I was able, however, to obtain data on unemployment for most of the time periods and municipalities under consideration.

Size of the Ethnic Group of the Returnees

The size of the ethnic group of a returning minority group relative to the other ethnicities residing in the municipality is an important factor for refugees deciding to return home. Returning refugees should be more likely to return if they know they will be part of a larger, rather than smaller, ethnic minority. Thus, the regression includes a set of independent variables that measure the size of each ethnic group for each municipality. I obtained these census data from the State Statistical Office of Bosnia and Herzegovina.

War Suffering and Population Growth Rate

We would expect minority refugees who experienced considerable suffering before they fled to be, all things being equal, less likely to return to their homes than refugees who experienced relatively little suffering. War suffering is one of the competing explanations for patterns in minority refugee returns that we were not able to refute with the tale of two cities, which is why it is particularly important to include this variable in the multivariate analysis. The "Bosnian Book of Dead" database[59] contains municipality-level data about war casualties, but these data provide only an aggregate figure for the 1992–1995 war years for each municipality. Our cross-country time series dataset, however, requires a distinct figure for each of the ten years (from 1996 to 2006) *following* the war, because these are the years for which we have data on returning minority refugees.[60] In other words, because we need a figure that changes between 1996 and 2006, we cannot use as a measure of war suffering a constant of deaths that occurred during the war in 1992–1995 in each municipality. Thus, we need some measure of relative deprivation resulting from the war for each municipality that changes over time, one per year for each of the ten years following the war. Although the Correlates of War (CoW) project provides direct measures for assessing the consequences of war for the entire state of Bosnia and Herzegovina,[61] it does not give us cross-sectional figures that vary by municipality. Thus, the "Bosnian Book of Dead" offers a measure of war suffering that varies across cases but not over time, while the CoW project offers data that varies over time but not across cases. We need a variable that addresses both types of variation simultaneously. For this reason, I have decided to use population growth rate as a proxy for capturing the factors associated with war destruction.[62]

Nationalism

Finally, a nationalistic political climate may discourage minorities from returning home. In the aftermath of war, this can be measured with electoral behavior. One would expect minority refugees to return more willingly to municipalities in which cosmopolitan rather than nationalistic parties win elections. I have coded votes in general and municipal elections for eight main political parties that are classified and ordered on a scale from most cosmopolitan to most nationalistic, using Kenneth Benoit and Michael Laver's *Party Policy in Modern Democracies* expert survey.[63] The survey asks experts to place parties on a scale from 1 to 20, with 1 representing "Strongly promotes a cosmopolitan rather than a Bosniak/Serbian national consciousness" and 20 representing "Strongly promotes a Bosniak/Serbian national rather than cosmopolitan consciousness." I operationalized the nationalism of a municipality as the percentage of votes for parties that were more nationalistic on this scale than average. I obtained data from general and municipal elections from the Electoral Commission.[64]

The main hypotheses I tested were as follows:

Hypothesis 1: Refugees are less likely to return to areas where war crimes were committed but the guilty have not been held accountable by the ICTY.

The alternative explanations are represented by the following hypotheses:

Hypothesis 2: Refugees are less likely to return to areas that are economically underdeveloped.
Hypothesis 3: Refugees are less likely to return to areas where they would be in a small minority.

Hypothesis 4: Refugees are less likely to return to areas that suffered intensive destruction during the war.

Hypothesis 5: Refugees are less likely to return to areas where nationalistic parties win elections.

4.2. Why Do They Return?

In the results reported in the tables of Appendix 11.1, the variable that has the greatest predictive power is the number of guilty pleas. Although "counts pleaded guilty" reduces returns, "defendants pleading guilty" increases the return of refugees. Importantly, the absolute effect of defendants pleading guilty is greater than the effect of the number of counts to which the defendant has pleaded guilty. Including two independent variables to describe guilty pleas (the number of counts pleaded guilty and defendants pleading guilty) allows us to conceptually separate two types of defendants (those who issued orders and those who followed orders). Note that for any fixed number of counts pleaded guilty, the smaller the number of defendants who pleaded guilty, the higher the profile of their crimes (order-givers were charged with more counts). A negative sign on counts pleaded guilty combined with a positive sign on defendants pleading guilty suggests that the ICTY's transitional justice is producing effects in the form of refugee returns not through harsh sentencing in high-profile convictions but rather by cutting deals with perpetrators who were responsible for following orders. Furthermore, obtaining guilty pleas from lower-rank perpetrators (with fewer counts to plead) increases refugee returns more than procuring pleas from high-rank perpetrators. Guilty pleas involve revealing information about the wrongdoing of other perpetrators. Perpetrators who plead guilty offer truth about the character of the war crimes in which they were involved. In order to induce such pleas, however, testifying perpetrators must receive reduced sentences, as Drazen Erdemovic did. Guilty pleas may seem to undermine justice, interpreted in the most legalistic sense; however, information provided by pleading perpetrators leads to new indictments. Guilty pleas do contribute to justice, in the sense evoked in this chapter: the confessions of perpetrators who disclose full information about the nature of their crime as part of the plea bargain increase refugee returns.

The findings of this chapter are surprising in that they undermine the intuitive relationship between prosecutorial strategy and refugee returns suggested by the Prijedor and Srebrenica cases. In Srebrenica, plea bargaining led to fewer refugee returns. The Prijedor case showed that the prosecution of many low-ranking perpetrators resulted in larger numbers of refugee returns.

Statistical analysis of a larger dataset involving another 134 municipalities revealed that our initial hypothesis is not universally valid. On the contrary, plea bargaining turns out to have a positive impact on reconciliation, operationalized as refugee returns. This finding holds even after we control for other competing explanations: economic development, war suffering, the intensity of nationalism, and the size of the returning minority relative to the two remaining ethnicities. I have also included in the multivariate analysis variables that operationalize these competing explanations for refugee returns (see the tabulated results in Appendix 11.1).

Neither wartime suffering (operationalized through measures of demographic growth or decline) nor the intensity of nationalism (operationalized as voting for nationalistic rather than cosmopolitan parties) nor even economic development (operationalized as unemployment) had a significant influence on returns. The prevailing finding is that, contrary to what the Prijedor and Srebrenica examples suggest, it is not the sheer volume of ICTY prosecutions but the extent of plea bargaining that induces refugee returns. But why does plea bargaining contribute to reconciliation in the aftermath of a civil war? It may well be that the revelations of truth by order-givers pleading guilty are what victims want more than seeing order-takers prosecuted.

The ICTY has always been reluctant to embrace plea bargaining as part of its general prosecutorial policy. It has also been very explicit about the priority it gives to reaching high-ranking perpetrators and its readiness to bypass prosecuting low- and medium-ranking perpetrators unless their trials are instrumental to reaching the order-givers. Recall Prijedor's perpetrator, Dusko Tadic, the ICTY's first defendant, who was identified by a random victim. Of his indictment, Cherif Bassiouni observed, "He [Tadic] was a nothing." The Chief ICTY Prosecutor, Richard Goldstone, was so severely criticized for initiating the Tribunal's work with the indictment of such a low-ranking perpetrator that he had to publicly explain that the prosecutorial strategy was to build effective cases against military and civilian leaders. He also admitted that the tribunal's success would have to be judged by the degree to which the most guilty were adequately punished. Since Tadic was not among the high-level perpetrators, Goldstone admitted that "If in two years time Tadic is all we have to show, then clearly we have failed."[65]

Implicit in these comments is the fact that the ICTY had no reason to prosecute more low-ranking perpetrators than was necessary to determine the chain of command leading to medium-ranking perpetrators. After the proceedings had reached the level of medium-ranking perpetrators and the bottom part of the chain of command had been revealed to the ICTY, it had no further need to prosecute low-rank perpetrators. The numbers that had been prosecuted were sufficient to reveal the chain of command leading to the top order-givers. Bringing about reconciliation through truth (revealed in plea bargaining) as opposed to justice (heavy sentencing) was an unintended consequence of the ICTY's strategy. Truth revelation was included in the ICTY's prosecutorial strategy for only as long as it could be reconciled with the ICTY's ultimate goal, that is, prosecuting the highest-ranking perpetrators.

5. CONCLUSION

Plea bargaining leads neither to pure truth nor to pure justice. It is a by-product of a justice procedure that is ostensibly developed to reach high-ranking perpetrators. International war crimes tribunals can reach high-rank perpetrators effectively when they permit the occurrence of plea bargaining. The value of plea bargaining in producing truth is underappreciated by the international community engaged in prosecuting war crimes.

Providing an arena for perpetrator confessions has worked in other transitional justice processes, however. In her book *Unsettling Accounts*,[66] Leigh Payne analyzes confessions of human rights violators in Chile, Argentina, Brazil, and South Africa. She considers in her analysis a variety of motivations for confessions. Some are institutional, as in South Africa, where perpetrators had to publicly disclose before the truth commission the full details of the political crimes they had committed in order to apply for amnesty. This had an effect very similar to that of plea bargaining. Payne notes that perpetrators frequently use such incentives to further their self-interested goal of avoiding a tougher sentence, and victims are often disgusted by the comportment of the perpetrators, as well as by the rationalizations and excuses they devise. She notes, however, that, although these confessions should never be treated as distilled accounts of what happened in the past, by putting contentious truths into the public domain, they provoke a response and generate debate about the atrocities of former regimes. Such debates are by nature democratic and foster, on Payne's account, a climate of reconciliation and democratic consolidation.[67]

If provoking confessions—much more contentious than the strategies that accompany plea bargaining—induces widespread debates about the past and ultimately leads to reconciliation between formerly warring sides, plea bargaining may certainly have a similar reconciling effect. Reconciliation on the local scale requires that truth be told on the local scale, and plea bargaining can help to serve this function.

APPENDIX 11.1: MULTIVARIATE DATA ANALYSIS

Analyzing cross-section time series data calls for deciding whether to use fixed effects (using dummy variables for each time period and each municipality) or random effects (using additional error terms to account for time-specific and municipality-specific errors). It is quite plausible that I have omitted variables that vary across cases but are constant over time (leading to contemporaneous correlation), as well as variables that are common to all cases but vary with time (leading to serial correlation). Thus, wherever Hausman tests made it possible to avoid fixed effects, I used random effects models. In a model not presented here, I also ran OLS models with the same set of variables but with panel corrected standard errors. Neither the coefficient values nor their significance turned out to be considerably different. Table 11.2 contains results from regressing minority refugee returns on the independent variables of interest in a random effects model. There are two models presented in this table. The first model (with coefficients in columns two and standard deviations in column three) includes sizes of

Table 11.2   DV: PERCENTAGE OF MINORITY RETURNS TO
MUNICIPALITY/YEAR; N = 200 (MODEL 1), N = 365 (MODEL 2)

INDEPENDENT VARIABLE	COEFFICIENT	STD. ERROR	COEFFICIENT	STD. ERROR
Bosniak population	.505	(.796)		
Serb population	10.12**	(1.99)		
Croat population	.497	(.847)		
Years sentenced	−.0508	(.06)	.0564	(.063)
Number of defendants	2.36**	(.75)	1.97**	(.833)
Indicted individuals	−.203*	(.123)	−.047	(.114)
Counts	.039	(.061)	.0102	(.065)
Crimes against humanity	.0947	(.166)	.0259	(.183)
Crimes of genocide	−1.456	(.4)	−1.0852**	(.43)
Counts pleaded guilty	−10.23**	(2.35)	−6.996**	(2.22)
Defendants pleading guilty	18.12**	(3.35)	13.54**	(3.13)
Defense witnesses	−.085	(.028)	−.1024**	(.031)
War suffering	−.001	(.002)	−.0015	(.004)
Nationalism	.015	(.052)	.0252	(.18)
Economic development	−.003	(.01)	−.1627**	(.043)
constant	−.008	(1.28)	8.807	(3.67)
within	.092	.338	.3679	2.67
between	.622	1.45	.0175	1.434
overall	.27	.051	.0534	.776

the ethnic populations other than the ethnic group of returning minorities. However, since data on relative sizes of ethnic groups were not available for all municipalities, the number of cases was small enough to justify running a separate model with the ethnic group variables dropped. I present these results in columns four and five. In both models, the dependent variable is the percentage of refugee returns in the population of the municipality in a given year. Ethnic minorities in the first model are also measured as the percentage of the population of the municipality in a given year. Variables that are statistically significant at the .05 level are marked with one star; variables significant at the .005 level are marked with two stars.

By far, the largest effect on refugee returns is that of guilty pleas. Each defendant who pleads guilty for crimes committed in a given municipality contributes to the return of more than eighteen refugees. In the case of perpetrators who have been indicted on multiple counts, that is, for severe crimes, the effect is somewhat reduced (indicated by the negative sign on the significant coefficient on counts pleaded guilty). This is consistent with the theory that the truth from low-rank perpetrators that leads to reconstructing the chain of command contributes to reconciliation more than guilty pleas from high-rank perpetrators.

What about other variables operationalizing the ICTY prosecutorial strategy? These variables do have statistically significant effects, albeit not always in the direction anticipated. Whereas the number of defendants standing trial before the ICTY increases refugee returns, the number of indicted individuals does not (both figures are significant, although the indictment effect stops being significant in the second model). This could be explained by poorly prepared indictments generating too many counts for the prosecution to support with evidence. As a result, perpetrators with excessively long lists of indictments may end up being acquitted. In essence, the baby gets thrown out with the bath water. More realistic or streamlined indictments have proved to be much more effective in contributing to successful convictions. This explains the negative coefficient on counts.

The variable of counts of crimes of genocide decreases refugee returns. In order to account for this, note that the counts of crimes against humanity and crimes of genocide were handed down quite sparingly. Hence, this negative coefficient could be driven by the Srebrenica case alone: crimes of genocide are so egregious that refugees do not want to come back to the places where they were committed. We do observe the opposite pattern in the case of crimes against humanity, which were also rare but with a high concentration of perpetrators from Prijedor—the municipality with unusually high refugee returns (see Figure 11.1).

Note also that in the second model (columns four and five), the effect of unemployment becomes significant, while in the first model (columns two and three), it was not. This can be attributed to the fact that areas with larger Bosniak populations tend to have higher unemployment rates, and, after dropping the Bosniak population variable, unemployment is picking up variation explained in model 1 by the removed variable.

TABLE 11.3 MINORITY RETURNS BY ETHNICITY, FIXED EFFECTS

RETURNS	BOSNJAKS	SE	CROATS	SE	SERBS	SE
Bosniak/Serb majority	239.8*	136.3	−250.3**	86.16	−31.198	100.5
Years sentenced	5.538	6.907	−5.134	3.943	−.0733	6.668
Number of defendants	−90.16	66.79	10.4	40.88	73.19	54.26
Indicted individuals	−19.64	40.2	28.5*	16.78	25.37	32.4
Counts	8.373	6.878	2.34	2.927	11.71**	5.347
Crimes against humanity	−27.26	27.18	−5.46	10.74	−76.99**	20.52
Crimes of genocide	185.9	58.75	−38.27	24.21	330.99**	50.35
Guilty pleas (counts)	510.9	160.2	179.3**	83.7	570.1**	193.95
Guilty pleas (defendants)	−218.9**	74.84	−65.52**	30.5	27.76	56.151
Defense witnesses	2.517	3.129	1.944	1.46	−3.265	2.505
Prosecution witnesses	−2.204	1.961	−.0794	.848	2.136	1.432
constant	229.1**	62.39	305.9**	51.04	225.8**	68.3
within	.135	599	.07	255.02	0.215	456.3
between	0	744	0	296.64	0.05	532.3
overall	.09	.39	.04	.338	0.11	.423

Finally, note that the relative size of the Serb population positively affects returns. One does not find similar effects for the respective sizes of the Bosniak and Croat populations. This may be a result of conflating reactions of different ethnic groups, however. For instance, the size of the Serb population may induce returns of Serb minorities but discourage the return of Bosniaks.[68]

In order to verify how robust the finding about guilty pleas is, I used a fixed effects model. The dependent variable here is the number of returnees of a given ethnicity to a given municipality in a given year. Table 11.3 contains results from three regressions: one for returning Bosniaks, one for Croats, and one for Serbs. Separate regressions for each of the three ethnic groups allow one of the coefficients (in each regression, I have included an ethnic majority dummy) to account for whether refugees are returning to municipalities with a Serb, a Bosniak, or a Croat majority. Because each ethnicity can return as a minority to a municipality containing two different majorities (for instance, a Bosniak minority to a Croat majority or to a Serb majority), we need use only one dummy variable per ethnicity, with the remaining possible majority as the base category. In the case of Bosniaks, I use Croats as the base category; in the case of Croats, the base category is Bosniaks; in the case of Serbs, I use Croats. Each model includes a complete set of variables measuring the prosecutorial strategy. Fixed effects use considerably more degrees of freedom than random effects. Splitting up total returns by ethnicity further decreased the number of cases. Thus, in order to preserve a sufficient number of cases to run the regression model, I have eliminated from the set of independent variables nationalistic voting, unemployment, and natural increase. The omission does not produce bias in estimation because the fixed effects model already controls for any omitted variables that characterize specific municipalities.

Columns two, four, and six in Table 11.3 contain the coefficients of the regression, while columns three, five, and seven contain their standard errors. Significant coefficients at the .05 level are marked with a star, and coefficients significant at the .005 level are marked with two stars.

There are some significant differences in predicting returns of refugees from different ethnicities;[69] however, the persistently significant effect in models 3–5, just as in models 1 and 2, is the impact of guilty pleas. Counts of guilty pleas significantly increase returns of Serbs and Croats. In the case of Serb returns, the co-efficient for defendants pleading guilty is also positive. Although having guilty-pleading defendants reduces returns of Bosniaks and Croats, the coefficient for guilty-pleading defendants is considerably smaller than for guilty plea counts in the case of both ethnicities. Hence, even in the case of Bosniaks and Croats, overall, guilty pleas still contribute to an increase in refugee returns.

APPENDIX 11.2

ICTY OUTPUT THROUGH THE END OF MARCH 2010
Source: UN ICTY, "The Cases: Key Figures," UN ICTY,
http://www.icty.org/sid/24.

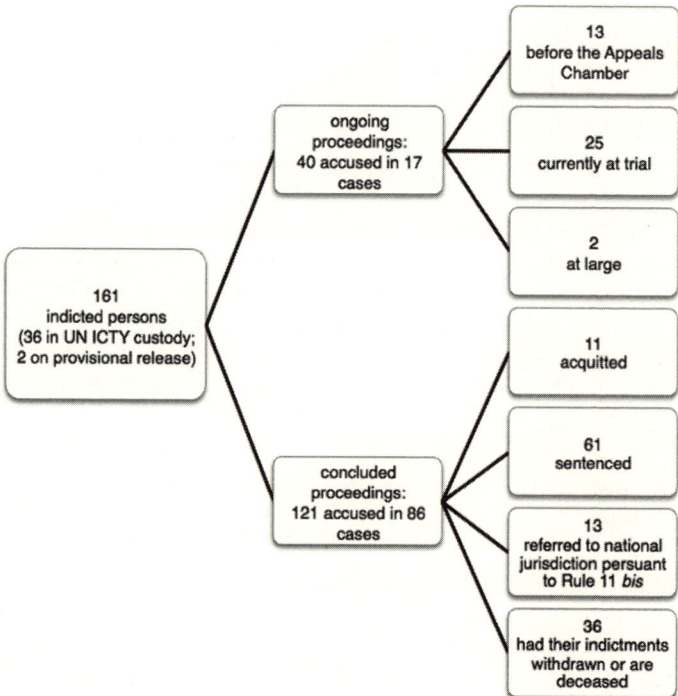

NOTES

I thank Refik Hodzic, Natasha Kandic, Iavor Rangelov, and Marianna Toma for conversations leading up to this project and Bruce Hemmer, Nathan Pohlman, Sergali Adilbekov, and Alexander Roinesdal for help in compiling the dataset. I thank participants in the 2006 Peace Science Society meeting in Columbus, Ohio, especially Ben Fordham and Pat Regan, Jon Elster, Jim Fearon, Scott Gates, and Gary Bass; participants in the PRIO workshop on Transitional Justice in the Settlement of Civil Conflicts in Bogota, Colombia, including Harris Mylonas, Stathis Kalyvas, and Betsy Paluck; and participants in the Order, Conflict, and Political Violence workshop at Yale University for feedback. I owe special thanks to Erica Frederiksen, Rosemary Nagy, and Melissa Williams for written comments and suggestions on how to revise the paper. Financial support from the Undergraduate Researchers Program at the Political Science Department of Rice University and from the Weatherhead Center for International Affairs and Area Studies at Harvard University is also gratefully acknowledged. All problems and mistakes are my own responsibility.

1. For a skeptical view of truth commissions' contribution to justice, see, in particular, the contributions of Elizabeth Kiss, David A. Crocker, Amy Gutmann and Dennis Thompson, and Rajeev Bhargava to the volume *Truth v. Justice: The Morality of Truth Commissions*, ed. Robert I. Rotberg and Dennis Thompson (Princeton: Princeton University Press, 2000). For a more optimistic interpretation of truth commissions, see the chapters by Alex Boraine, Dumisa B. Ntsebeza, Ronald C. Slye, and Kent Greenawalt in the same volume.

2. Morten Bergsmo stresses the International Criminal Court's role in the public documentation of crimes in his work on the ICTY, "The Theme of Selection and Prioritization Criteria and Why It Is Relevant," in "Criteria for Prioritizing and Selecting Core International Crimes Cases," ed. Morten Bergsmo, *FICHL Publication Series* No. 4 (2009): 15–21. See also Morten Bergsmo and Pablo Kalmanovitz, eds., "Law in Peace Negotiations," *FICHL Publication Series* No. 5 (2009).

3. For a discussion of the possible tensions between these goals, see Jon Elster's essay in this volume.

4. United Nations Security Council, *Resolution 827*, adopted May 25, 1993.

5. "ICTY-TPIY: Achievements," United Nations International Criminal Tribunal for the Former Yugoslavia, http://www.icty.org/sid/324.

6. B1, interview with author, July 2005. Information from NGO members interviewed by the author in the summer of 2005 is used throughout

this chapter; to preserve their anonymity, I have coded their identities as follows. The first letter refers to their nationality. Numbers have been assigned chronologically, as they appear in the text.

7. Brett D. Shaefer, "Why the U.S. Is Right to Support an Ad Hoc Tribunal for Darfur," Heritage Foundation, Web Memo 665, February 15, 2005, http://www.heritage.org/Research/InternationalOrganizations/wm665 .cfm (accessed March 24, 2010).

8. At the time of writing, in March 2010, five cases are currently being reconsidered by the Appeals Chamber. For ICTY output, see Appendix 11.2.

9. Naomi Roht-Arriaza, *Impunity and Human Rights in International Law and Practice* (New York: Oxford University Press, 1995).

10. For a discussion of the deterrence aspect of international criminal tribunals, see Martha Minow, *Between Vengeance and Forgiveness: Facing History After Genocide and Mass Violence* (Boston, MA: Harvard University Press 1998), and Minow, "The Hope for Healing: What Can Truth Commissions Do?," in Rotberg and Thompson, *Truth v. Justice*, 235–60, quoted in James Meernik, "Justice and Peace? How the International Criminal Tribunal Affects Societal Peace in Bosnia," *Journal of Peace Research* 42, no. 3 (2005): 271–89.

11. Hitomi Takemura, "Big Fish and Small Fish Debate: An Examination of the Prosecutorial Discretion," *International Criminal Law Review* 7, no. 4 (2007): 677–85.

12. I am far from saying that the defendant with whom the prosecution plea bargains receives amnesty, but the perpetrators that the prosecutor, pursuing high-ranking perpetrators, can bypass thanks to the information received in the plea bargaining process translates into de facto amnesty for a lot of low-ranking perpetrators. For a discussion of when amnesty offered in the context of transitional justice is just, see Kent Greenawalt, "Amnesty's Justice," in *Truth v. Justice*, 189–210.

13. For a literature review of these early works, see Oskar N. T. Thomas, James Ron, and Roland Paris, "The Effects of Transitional Justice Mechanisms: A Summary of Empirical Research Findings and Implications for Analysts and Practitioners," working paper, Centre for International Policy Studies, University of Ottawa, Ottawa, April 2008. Other authors who have contributed to this genre of transitional justice research are Laurel E. Fletcher and Harvey M. Weinstein, "Violence and Social Repair: Rethinking the Contribution of Justice to Reconciliation," *Human Rights Quarterly* 24 (2002): 573–639, and Meernik, "Justice and Peace?"; Meernik, "Victor's Justice or the Law? Judging and Punishing at the International Criminal Tribunal for the Former Yugoslavia," *Journal of Conflict Resolution* 47, no. 2 (2003): 140–62; Meernik, Kimi Lynn King, and Geoffrey Dancy, "Judicial Decision Making and International Tribunals: Assessing the Impact of

Reconciliation, Refugee Returns, and International Criminal Justice 353

Individual, National, and International Factors," *Social Science Quarterly* 86, no. 3 (2005): 683–703.

14. Thomas, Ron, and Paris, "The Effects of Transitional Justice Mechanisms."

15. Ed Vulliamy, "Srebrenica: Ten Years On," openDemocracy.net, http://www.opendemocracy.net/conflict-yugoslavia/srebrenica_2651.jsp.

16. Note that the issue here is not whether the human rights violations under prosecution are more or less serious. From the victim's perspective, local crimes are more egregious than crimes committed by those who issue orders to kill, although international law considers giving orders a more serious crime. Paul Gready refers to the prosecution of neighbor-on-neighbor killings as "embedded justice" and to the limiting of prosecutions to individuals issuing orders as "distanced justice," suggesting that the conviction of order-givers is too "distanced" from locales where the crimes were committed. He then employs the analysis of case studies from South Africa, Rwanda, and Sierra Leone to discuss the normative and practical aspects of both types of justice. See Paul Gready, "Reconceptualising Transitional Justice: Embedded and Distanced Justice," *Conflict, Security and Development* 5, no. 1 (2005): 3–21. I am indebted to Rosemary Nagy for this suggestion.

17. In previous work, I have drawn a comparison between certain types of lustration laws and plea bargaining. Lustration, known also as vetting or screening, refers to the purging of the state administration of members of and collaborators with the prior regime in the aftermath of the transition to democracy. Monika Nalepa, "To Punish the Guilty and Protect the Innocent," *Journal of Theoretical Politics* 20 (2008): 221–45. See also Jon Elster, "Coming to Terms with the Past," *European Journal of Sociology* 39 (1998): 7–48. Sanford Levinson, in a chapter on due process, explicitly compares amnesty granted by truth commissions, such as the South African Truth and Reconciliation Commission (TRC), to the plea bargaining strategy of U.S. courts. He notes that in cases where courts have to deal with large numbers of cases, allowing defendants to opt out of their due process rights (by choosing to plea bargain) may be the only way to ensure that the court system functions efficiently. Levinson, "Trials, Commissions, and Investigating Committees: The Elusive Search for Norms of Due Process," in *Truth v. Justice*, 211–34. Martha Minow, for her part, describes how the trade of amnesty for truth offered to perpetrators by the South African TRC induced General Johan van der Merwe, who had authorized the use of firearms against demonstrators in 1992, to testify against two cabinet-level officials who had authorized the violent crackdown. Minow, "The Hope for Healing," 240. Kent Greenawalt in his chapter on the justice of amnesties argues that, even if the granting of amnesty is politically prudent, it does not render the amnesty just. Thomas, Ron, and Paris provide

an instructive example of a politically wise, albeit morally unjust amnesty: Uganda's refusal to hand Joseph Kony, the former dictator, over to ICC prosecutors: "The Effects of Transitional Justice Mechanisms," 9–10.

18. Consider, for instance, the theorists who contributed to the volume *Truth v. Justice*, who understand reconciliation as a secular concept, rather than as the spiritual exchange of apologies and forgiveness. Rajeev Bhargava, for example, takes issue with the claim that forgiveness is morally appropriate and argues that it may not be consistent with the dignity and self-respect of the victim. He argues that truth commissions cannot bear the burden of bringing about forgiveness by individuals and suggests turning to an idea of societal reconciliation instead. Bhargava, "Restoring Decency to Barbaric Societies," in Rotberg and Thompson, *Truth v. Justice*, 51. David Crocker goes even further than Bhargava in saying that to force people to agree about the past and forgive the sins committed against them is morally objectionable. Crocker, "Truth Commissions, Transitional Justice, and Civil Society," in Rotberg and Thompson, *Truth v. Justice*, 103, 108. Gutmann and Thompson, for their part, claim that too broad an interpretation of reconciliation may go against principles of liberalism, when an entire society is expected to embrace one and the same moral approach to the past. Gutmann and Thompson, "The Moral Foundations of Truth Commissions," in Rotberg and Thompson, *Truth v. Justice*, 22–44. A notable exception to this trend is Daniel Philpott, who claims that religion and reconciliation still enjoy what Max Weber calls an "elective affinity." Philpott, *The Politics of Past Evil: Religion, Reconciliation, and the Dilemmas of Transitional Justice* (Notre Dame, IN: University of Notre Dame Press, 2006).

19. Institute for Justice and Reconciliation, "Reconciliation Barometer," Institute for Justice and Reconciliation, http://www.ijr.org.za/publications/archive/reconciliation-barometer.

20. Ibid.

21. B1, B2, B3, interview with author, July 2005.

22. C2, interview with author, July 2005.

23. Meernik, "Justice and Peace."

24. Aldin Arnautovic and Refik Hodzic, *Justice Unseen*, DVD (Sarajevo: XY Films, 2002).

25. I use the term "Bosniaks" to refer to Bosnians with a Muslim heritage. Since many or most of them are not actually practicing Muslims, the term is not equivalent to Muslim. It is also worth mentioning—to correct likely imaginings otherwise—that, even though Serb nationalists like to call them "Turks," Bosniaks are also Slavic and speak Serbo-Croatian and thus generally look and sound the same as Bosnian Serbs, and Bosnian Croats.

26. Quoted from Eric D. Weitz, *A Century of Genocide: Utopias of Race and Nation* (Princeton: Princeton University Press, 2003), 229–30, who notes

that the figures for civilian casualties do not include the genocides of Srebrenica and Zepa, as in 1994 those killed there were still considered missing.

27. Ibid., 186.

28. Patrick Ball, Ewa Tabeau, and Philip Verwimp, "The Bosnian Book of Dead: Assessment of the Database," Households in Conflict Network, Research Design Note 5, The Institute of Development Studies at the University of Sussex, Brighton, UK, June 17, 2007.

29. "Bosnian Atlas of War Crimes," Research and Documentation Center, Sarajevo, http://www.idc.org.ba/index.php?option=com_content&view=category&layout=blog&id=112&Itemid=144&lang=bs. See also Ewa Tabeau and Jakub Bijak, "War-Related Deaths in the 1992–1995 Armed Conflicts in Bosnia and Herzegovina: A Critique of Previous Estimates and Recent Results," *European Journal of Population* 21 (2005): 187–215.

30. Murat Prašo, "Demographic Consequences of the 1992–95 War," *Most*, no. 93, April 1996, http://www.barnsdle.demon.co.uk/bosnia/dem.html.

31. UNHCR figure drawn from UNHCR, "Returns to Bosnia and Herzegovina Reach 1 Million," *Briefing Notes*, September 21, 2004, http://www.unhcr.org/414ffeb44.html.

32. Ibid.

33. UNHCR Statistics Package, Sarajevo, September 30, 2006, Table 5, data provided to author by Bruce Hemmer.

34. John Hagan, *Justice in the Balkans: Prosecuting War Crimes in the Hague Tribunal* (Chicago: Chicago University Press, 2003).

35. In order to avoid such inspections, they were called centers, as opposed to camps.

36. Human Rights Watch, "War Crimes in Bosnia–Hercegovina, Volume I," Human Rights Watch, August 1, 1992, http://www.hrw.org/en/reports/1992/08/01/war-crimes-bosnia-hercegovina-volume-i; Human Rights Watch, "War Crimes in Bosnia-Hercegovina, Volume II," Human Rights Watch, April 1, 1993, http://www.hrw.org/en/reports/1993/04/01/war-crimes-bosnia-hercegovina-volume-ii.

37. Ed Vulliamy, "Shame of Camp Omarska: Starvation and Human Rights Abuses as Detention Camps," *The Guardian*, August 7, 1992.

38. United Nations Security Council, Resolution 780, S/RES/780, 1992.

39. Hagan, *Justice in the Balkans*, 51.

40. Karadzic was President of the Bosnian Republika Srpska and head of the Serbian Democratic Party; he was indicted for genocide by the ICTY and removed from office by the Dayton Accords. General Ratko Mladic served as Karadzic's military chief. Twice indicted for crimes against humanity and genocide, Mladic was arrested in Serbia in May 2011 after years in hiding.

41. The status of Srebrenica was regulated by a special resolution of the UN, in which it demanded that all parties to the conflict in the Republic of Bosnia and Herzegovina treat Srebrenica and its surroundings as a "safe area" free from any armed attack or other hostile act. United Nations Security Council, Resolution 827, S/RES/827, 1993.

42. Olivera Simic refers to this policy using the term "gendercide" and says that "eliminating the male population made procreation with the remaining females easier"; he points out that what makes Bosnian women particularly vulnerable in a wartime environment is that in Muslim society, children are born with their father's ethnic identity. In addition, "the dominant image of women was based on patriarchal norms." Simic notes also that the women of Srebrenica were "regarded as unworthy without their male protectors and breadwinners. It was perceived that cultural humiliation would follow the women who were punished to live without their men. Indeed, it may be the fact that ironically gender images based on patriarchal norms saved lives of the Srebrenica women." Simic, "What Remains of Srebrenica? Motherhood, Transitional Justice and Yearning for Truth," *Journal of International Women's Studies* 10, no. 4 (2009): 224.

43. Note that the increase in returns to Srebrenica after 2002 is largely dependent on support from international agencies, such as the project run by Charlie Powell in Suceska, a peasant hamlet in the Srebrenica municipality. Vulliamy, "Srebrenica Ten Years On," 6.

44. Specifically, Erdemovic testified about his duties as a member of the tenth sabotage unit of the Bosnian Serb army. He had been responsible for the transportation of Bosnian Muslims to military farms, where they were to be killed.

45. Erdemovic's testimony was critical in the trials of Dragan Obrenovic, Chief of Staff of the Zvornik brigade in Srebrenica; Radoslav Krstic, a general of the brigade; Vidoje Blagojevic, a colonel during the massacre; and Jokic, an engineer who masterminded the transfer of mass graves to secondary graves. The tribunal's extensive investigation not only focused on the week of the massacre that took place in mid-July 1995 but researched the development of the ethnic cleansing policy, which began in 1992. The investigation was very precise in reconstructing the chain of command and the chronology of the crime. B1, interview with author, July 2005.

46. Many NGO workers in the field attribute these returns not to any activities carried out by the ICTY but to the report published in 2002 by the Srebrenica Commission. This report, produced by a commission appointed by the authorities of Republika Srpska, was remarkably sincere and remorseful in attributing blame to Serb participants in the massacre.

47. Calculated using GIS systems, using Prijedor's and Srebrenica's geographical coordinates from Google satellite maps.

48. Official website of Prijedor municipality, http://www.opstinaprijedor
.org/content.php?content_category=41.

49. Federation of Bosnia and Herzegovina, Federal Office of Statistics
(*Drzavni Zavod za Statistiku*), *Census of the Republic of Bosnia and Herzegovina*,
1991, http://www.fzs.ba/Eng/population.htm.

50. Population growth rate (PGR) is defined in demographics as the
fractional rate at which the number of individuals in a population increases over a unit period of time. Here, the period is equal to a year, and
PGR is expressed as the percentage of the number of individuals in the
population at the beginning of the year: (end-of-year population − population at the beginning of the year)/population at the beginning of the year.

51. *Census of the Republic of Bosnia and Herzegovina*, 1991.

52. Literally, Srebrenica means "silver mine." Historically, the municipality's main sources of revenue were gold, lead, and zinc mines, along
with a metal factory.

53. Ibid.

54. Ball, Tabeau, and Verwimp, "The Bosnian Book of Dead," Table 33.

55. Ibid., Table 11. One can report casualties by municipality in two different ways: (1) by assigning the deaths to the municipality where the victim was born or (2) by assigning the death to the municipality where the
victim died. Understandably, the latter figure is higher for Srebrenica, as
victims were transported to that area to meet their death.

56. The idea of one occurrence of genocide being milder than another
strikes one as odd, if not disrespectful; however, it would be inaccurate to
say that the sheer amount of suffering in Prijedor and Srebrenica was the
same. Perhaps Srebrenica was destroyed in the civil war to the point that
refugees were unable to resettle there even if they wanted to.

57. Data for operationalized variables were drawn from several sources;
the sources used for each variable are indicated in the body of the text.
The entire dataset on which this analysis is based is housed with the author.

58. This information can be accessed on the ICTY's official website,
United Nations, International Criminal Tribunal for the Former Yugoslavia, "The Cases," UN ICTY, http://www.icty.org/action/cases/4.

59. Referred to in section 3.

60. Note that, although we could have included the same variable for
each year for the same municipality, that variable would be perfectly correlated with the variable created by our fixed effect model (explained in
the appendix). In other words, our statistical technique does not allow us
to use it.

61. See A. F. K. Organski and Jacek Kugler, *The War Ledger* (Chicago:
University of Chicago Press, 1980), and Hugh Wheeler, "Postwar Industrial Growth," in *The Correlates of War*, ed. J. David Singer (New York: Macmillan, 1980), 258–84. CoW uses prewar measures of economic growth

and industrialization to make projections of economic development and compares the projections to the actual postwar levels to create a measure of war destruction. In order to create CoW type measures for particular municipalities, we would need measures of economic growth and industrialization from periods preceding the war, which were not available from the census.

62. I also tried to use the number of births available from the 1991 census in the Bosnian Republic of Yugoslavia and to compare these to the numbers of children enrolled in primary and high schools after the war, which have been recorded by the Statistical Offices of the Federation of Bosnia and Herzegovina and Republika Srbska, but this proxy did not work as well as population growth rate. Although we cannot measure war destruction at the level of municipalities directly, such destruction should be correlated with population growth rates.

63. Kenneth Benoit and Michael Laver, *Party Policy in Modern Democracies* (New York: Routledge, 2007).

64. BiH Central Election Commission, "Election Statistics," BiH Central Election Commission, http://www.izbori.ba/eng/default.asp.

65. Hagan, *Justice in the Balkans*, 72. Goldstone had higher hopes when in the winter of 1995, on Hagan's account, "two senior Serb officers, General Djordje Djukic and Colonel Aleska Krsmanowic, made the wrong turn into Bosnian-controlled territory outside of Sarajevo and were taken into custody by the Bosnian Muslim army. Goldsone hoped that these senior officers could be part of a leadership case of the kind Bassiouni had favored, leading up the chain of command to General Ratko Mladic, whom the tribunal had indicted on charges of genocide." Ibid., 73.

66. Leigh Payne, *Unsettling Accounts: Neither Truth nor Reconciliation in Confessions of State Violence* (Durham, NC: Duke University Press, 2008).

67. One finds support for this claim more generally in some of the literature on the Truth and Reconciliation Commission. See James Gibson, *Overcoming Apartheid: Can Truth Reconcile a Divided Nation?* (New York: Russell Sage Foundation, 2004). Some authors are skeptical about the TRC's ability to provoke both sides of the conflict in the same way, however. Rosemary Nagy, for instance, describes the pressure the TRC exerted on victims to forgive their perpetrators, rather than demand retribution: "The legitimacy of anger, and its role in psychological progress, is undermined by the call to turn the other cheek." Rosemary Nagy, "Reconciliation in Post-Commission South Africa: Thick and Thin Accounts of Solidarity," *Canadian Journal of Political Science* 35, no. 2 (2002): 333.

68. The next three models, presented in Table 11.3, allow us to parse out the ethnic identities of the returnees.

69. Most notably, Bosniaks are more likely to return to areas with Serb majorities than to areas with Croat majorities. Croats, on the other hand

are less likely to return to areas with Serb majorities than to areas with Bosniak majorities (both effects are significant). This could be explained by the fact that relatively more Bosniaks fled from areas with Serb majorities, while more Croats fled from areas with Bosniak majorities. Whereas this does not necessarily gauge the mechanism we were looking for, it undermines the claim of repatriation skeptics that what gets measured as refugee returns is in fact attempts at colonization. An interesting factor separating Serbs from the two other ethnicities is the significance of crimes against humanity and crimes of genocide. While counts of crimes of genocide increase returns, however, counts of crimes against humanity decrease returns. Notably, the magnitude of the coefficient is much smaller in the case of crimes against humanity. Thus, if the two types of counts often appear in the same indictment, one may be correcting for the other. The positive coefficient is a sad finding, suggesting that the policies of ethnic cleansing may have accomplished the goal of the war criminals: to rid Bosnia of Muslims so that Serbs could settle it.

INDEX

Estonia, 91
Ethic cleansing: International Criminal
 Tribunals, 3; reparations, 136; Yugo-
 slavia, 326, 334, 356, 359
Ethnic composition: transitional justice
 consideration, 24; Prijedor and Sre-
 brenica, 318, 327, 329, 333–34, 337,
 340, 346
Europe, 74n69; Eastern, 3, 89, 110, 130,
 218, 226; Franco-German axis, 172;
 Marshall Plan, 171; post-War, 118;
 West Germany, 170

Forgiveness, 5, 85, 105, 358n67; Chris-
 tian, 169–70, 324, 354n18; Yom Kip-
 pur, 166
France: Bosnia, 87; GDP, 248; Israel,
 172; during Restoration, 92; post-
 WWII, 92
Frigard, Siri, 285
Fuller, Lon, 190, 213, 222

Genocide: Armenian, 171; Bosnian,
 336, 338, 346–47, 354–55n26,
 355n40, 357n56, 358n65, 358–59n69;
 compensation, 10, 171; International
 Criminal Tribunals, 3; irreparability,
 13–14, 136, 144, 167; prosecutions,
 270, 320; SPSC, 263, 266
Germany, 13, 86, 92–93, 147n2, 155–
 57, 161, 202; West Germany, 167,
 170–175
Guatemala, 36

Habermas, Jürgen, 72n45,
Hart, HLA, 204
Hobbes: authoritarianism, 200, 208;
 civic religion, 200, 220; Hobbist interpretation, 16, 185–86, 202, 218,
 221–27; international relations,
 187–92, 210, 220; legal theory, 193–
 97, 201; Machiavelli, 203; Malcolm,
 Noel, 187–92. 200, 203–236, 209–10;
 political education, 190; promising, 16, 188, 193–94, 221–23, 228;
 South Africa, 194–97, 220, 223–30;

sovereignty and law, 204–47, 216n81,
 216n82; sovereignty by institution
 (SBI), 198, 209; transitional justice
 in Leviathan, 15–16, 180–230; violence, 89
Holocaust: apology, 14, 86; compensation, 144, 147n2, 168, 177; Israel and
 West Germany, 172, 174; 177–79,
 321; trials, 169, 321
Human Rights violations: East Timor,
 25, 262, 276, 293, 299–300, 304;
 Chile, 82–83; confessions, 344; liberal democracy, 23; prosecutorial
 deterrent, 93–94; punishment, 17,
 22–24, 34-35, 70n28, 76–77n85, 353;
 South Africa, 201; Yugoslavia, 27,
 317, 320, 325, 329
Hungary, 93

Identity: group, 140, 143, 157, 336,
 356n42; perpetrator, 82–83, 94;
 political, 46
Indonesia. *See* East Timor
International Criminal Court (ICC),
 4, 320; Colombia, 95n7; retributive
 justice, 238, 252n25; Rome Statute,
 278; Uganda, 7. *See also* International
 Criminal Tribunals
International Court of Justice, 131
International Criminal Tribunals, 3,
 4; ICTR (Rwanda), 313n79; ICTY
 (Yugoslavia), 3, 4; ICTY prosecutorial
 strategy, 27, 317–44, 349; mechanism
 of transitional justice 68n17; suitabil-
 ity in East Timor, 303
Indigenous peoples, 10; colonization
 and oppression, 111–12, 120–21,
 126n32; in liberal democracy, 23
International law, 108, 353n16; in East
 Timor, 278; Nuremberg trials, 118,
 321; tribunals, 120;
Iraq, 8; 109–112; torture, 168
Israel: Germany and reparations, 157,
 167, 171–77, 214; Palestine, 85,
 214n45
Ivory Coast, 1